P9-DHB-613

NEW STRATEGIES FOR SOCIAL EDUCATION

Bruce R. Joyce TEACHERS COLLEGE, COLUMBIA UNIVERSITY

NEW STRATEGIES FOR SOCIAL EDUCATION

93672

 SCIENCE RESEARCH ASSOCIATES, INC.
Chicago, Palo Alto, Toronto, Henley-on-Thames, Sydney
A Subsidiary of IBM

© 1972, Science Research Associates, Inc. All rights reserved. Printed in the United States of America.

Library of Congress Catalog Card Number: 73–172886

Some of this material has been adapted from Bruce R. Joyce, *Strategies for Elementary Social Science Education*, © 1965, Science Research Associates, Inc.

We wish to acknowledge the following for permission to reprint or adapt material.

INTRODUCTION

EXPERIENCE AND EDUCATION. Copyright 1928 by Kappa Delta Pi; Copyright Renewed 1965 by Mrs. John Dewey. Used by permission of Kappa Delta Pi, An Honor Society in Education, owners of the copyright.

A Charter for the Social Sciences, by Charles A. Beard. Courtesy of Charles Scribner's Sons.

Automation, Cybernetics, and Society, by F. H. George. Used by permission of Leonard Hill Books, International Textbook Company, Ltd.

"Citizenship and Schools for the American Future," by Franklin Patterson in *Citizenship and a Free Society*. Courtesy of the National Council for the Social Studies, National Education Association.

"The Challenge to the Social Studies," by Jean D. Grambs, in *Citizenship and a Free Society*. Courtesy of the National Council for the Social Studies, National Education Association.

. "Preface to 'Excellence and Leadership in a Democracy,'" by Stephen R. Graubard. Reprinted by permission from DAEDALUS, Journal of The American Academy of Arts and Sciences, Boston, Massachusetts, Volume 90 Number 4.

"Primary Day? What Primary? Excuses Keep Many from the Polls," by Fred Powledge. © 1963/1964 by the New York Times Co. Reprinted by permission.

"Design for a Social Studies Program," by Paul R. Hanna. Copyright 1965, National Association of Elementary School Principals, N.E.A. All rights reserved.

The Social Studies and the Social Sciences, by Bernard Berelson and others. Courtesy of Harcourt Brace Jovanovich, Inc.

"Sociology," by Gresham M. Sykes, in *The Social Studies and the Social Sciences*. Courtesy of Harcourt Brace Jovanovich, Inc.

The Concept of Culture: Teachers Guide, Grade Four. Courtesy of the Anthropology Curriculum Project, University of Georgia.

John U. Michaelis, SOCIAL STUDIES FOR CHILDREN IN A DEMOCRACY, 2nd ed., © 1956. Reprinted by permission of Prentice-Hall, Inc., Englewood Cliffs, New Jersey.

International Dimensions in the Social Studies, edited by James M. Becker and Howard D. Mehlinger. Courtesy of the National Council for the Social Studies, National Education Association.

Summerhill, by A. S. Neill. Courtesy of Hart Publishing Company.

COMING OF AGE IN AMERICA: GROWTH AND ACQUIES-CENCE, by Edgar Z. Friedenberg. Copyright 1965. Courtesy of Random House, Inc.

Reprinted with the permission of the publishers from Arthur T. Jersild's *In Search of Self* (New York: Teachers College Press), copyright 1952.

E. Paul Torrance, REWARDING CREATIVE BEHAVIOR: Experiments in Classroom Creativity, © 1965. By permission of Prentice-Hall, Inc., Englewood Cliffs, New Jersey.

Fig. 1. From Paul R. Hanna, "Design for a Social Studies Program," *Focus on the Social Studies*, p. 34. Copyright 1965, National Association of Elementary School Principals, N.E.A. All rights reserved.

CHAPTER 1

The Aims of Education and Other Essays, by Alfred North Whitehead. Copyright 1929 by The Macmillan Company. Copyright renewed 1957 by Evelyn Whitehead. Courtesy of Macmillan Company and Ernest Benn Ltd.

The Nature of the Social Sciences, by Charles A. Beard. Courtesy of Charles Scribner's Sons.

The Proper Study of Mankind, by Stuart Chase. Courtesy of Harper & Row, Publishers, Incorporated.

Essays in Experimental Logic, by John Dewey. Copyright 1916 by The University of Chicago. All Rights Reserved. Used by permission of The University of Chicago Press.

The Teaching of Science, by Joseph J. Schwab. Courtesy of Harvard University Press.

"Social Sciencing: New Concept in Social Studies," by Bruce R. Joyce. Reprinted from INSTRUCTOR, © October 1968, The Instructor Publications, Inc., Dansville, N.Y. 14437.

CHAPTER 2

"A Question About Questions," by Malcolm C. Collier. Courtesy of the National Council for the Social Studies, National Education Association.

From *Instructors' Guide for* SCIENCE AND SOCIETY by Sociological Resources for the Social Studies (Boston: Allyn and Bacon, Inc., 1971). Reprinted by permission.

"Sociology," by Caroline B. Rose. Courtesy of Minnesota Project Social Studies, University of Minnesota.

CHAPTER 3

The World of Man, by John J. Honigmann. Courtesy of Harper & Row, Publishers, Incorporated.

The Study of Culture at a Distance, edited by Margaret Mead and Rhoda Metraux. Copyright 1953 by The University of Chicago. All rights reserved. Used by permission of The University of Chicago Press.

V

The Concept of Culture: Teachers Guide, Grade Two; *Pupils Guide*, Grade Two. Courtesy of the Anthropology Curriculum Project, University of Georgia.

"The Many Meanings of History," by Robert F. Berkhofer, Jr. Courtesy of the Project Social Studies Curriculum Center, University of Minnesota.

The Nature and the Study of History, by Henry Steele Commager. Courtesy of Charles E. Merrill Publishing Company.

"United States History," by Bernard A. Weisberger, in Erling M. Hunt and others, *High School Social Studies Perspectives*. Courtesy of Houghton Mifflin Company.

What Happened at Lexington Green? An Inquiry into the Nature and Methods of History, by Peter S. Bennett. Courtesy of Addison-Wesley Publishing Company.

from *Our American Republic, New Edition*, by Arthur S. Link and David S. Muzzey, © Copyright, 1966, 1963, by Ginn and Company.

From THE UNITED STATES: STORY OF A FREE PEOPLE by Samuel Steinberg. © Copyright 1954, 1958, 1963 by Allyn and Bacon, Inc. Reprinted by permission of Allyn and Bacon, Inc.

Teacher's Guide to the Sixth Grade Course on United States History: From Community to Society. Courtesy of the Project Social Studies Curriculum Center, University of Minnesota.

"Friendly and Unfriendly Behavior." From SOCIAL SCIENCE LABORATORY UNITS, PROJECT BOOK 3. © 1969, Science Research Associates, Inc. Used by permission of publisher.

"Anthropology, Sociology, and Social Psychology," by Meyer F. Nimkoff, in Erling M. Hunt and others, *High School Social Studies Perspectives*. Courtesy of Houghton Mifflin Company.

CHAPTER 4

The Study of Politics: The Present State of American Political Science, by Charles S. Hyneman. Courtesy of University of Illinois Press.

"Political Science," by Evron M. Kirkpatrick and Jeane J. Kirkpatrick, in Erling M. Hunt and others, *High School Social Studies Perspectives*. Courtesy of Houghton Mifflin Company.

An Introduction to the Social Sciences with Special Reference to Their Methods, by Maurice Duverger. Courtesy of Frederick A. Praeger, Inc., and George Allen & Unwin Ltd.

"American Political Behavior: A New Approach to Civic Education in Secondary Schools," by John Patrick. Courtesy of the High School Curriculum Center in Government, University of Indiana.

American Political Behavior, by Howard D. Mehlinger and John Patrick. Courtesy of the High School Curriculum Center in Government, University of Indiana.

"A Systems Approach to Political Life," by David Easton. Courtesy of Social Science Education Consortium.

Economics, by Bruce W. Knight and Lawrence G. Hines. © 1952. Courtesy of Random House, Inc.

"The Organic Curriculum: A New Experiment in Economic Education," by Lawrence Senesh, in *The Councilor*. Courtesy of the Illinois Council for the Social Studies.

Reprinted by permission from Economic Man. Elementary Economics Project, William D. Rader, Director. Industrial Relations Center, University of Chicago. Copyright Benefic Press, 1971.

"Geography," by George B. Cressey, in Erling M. Hunt and others, *High School Social Studies Perspectives*. Courtesy of Houghton Mifflin.

"Modern Viewpoints in Geography," by Jan O. M. Broek, in *Geography: Its Scope and Sequence*. Courtesy of Charles E. Merrill Publishing Company.

Fig. 2. Reprinted, by permission, from David Easton, "A Systems Approach to Political Life," Social Science Education Consortium, publication No. 104 (970 Aurora, Boulder, Colo. 80302, n.d.) p. 6.

Fig. 3. From *Economic Man*, p. 40. Used by permission of William D. Rader, Director of the Elementary Economics Project. Industrial Relations Center, University of Chicago. Copyright 1971, Benefic Press.

Fig. 4. From *Economic Man*, p. 79. Used by permission of William D. Rader, Director of the Elementary Economics Project. Industrial Relations Center, University of Chicago. Copyright 1971, Benefic Press.

Fig. 5. Reprinted, by permission, from John E. Steinbrink, "Comparative Rural Landscapes," Geography Curriculum Project. Athens: Univ. of Georgia, 1970. p. M3.

CHAPTER 5

Man: A Course of Study. Talks to Teachers, Teachers Guide, and "Herring Gulls." By special permission of the Social Studies Curriculum Program of Education Development Center.

"The Role of Social Studies in Elementary Education," by Ralph C. Preston, in *Social Studies in the Elementary School*. Courtesy of the National Society for the Study of Education.

The Process of Education, by Jerome S. Bruner. Courtesy of Harvard University Press.

"Current Social Trends and Their Implications for the Social Studies Program," by Stanley E. Diamond, in *Social Studies in the Elementary School*. Courtesy of the National Society for the Study of Education.

Teaching Strategies and Cognitive Functioning in Elementary School Children, by Hilda Taba. Courtesy of San Francisco State College Cooperative Research Project.

Teachers Handbook for Elementary Social Studies, by Hilda Taba. Copyright © 1969 by Addison-Wesley Publishing Company, Inc. All Rights Reserved.

Fig. 6. Reprinted from Hilda Taba, *Teachers Handbook for Elementary*

Social Studies, p. 92. Copyright © 1969 by Addison-Wesley Publishing Company, Inc. All Rights Reserved.

CHAPTER 6

Education and the Human Quest, by Herbert A. Thelen. Courtesy of Harper & Row, Publishers, Incorporated.
"Food for India: A Democratic Process Project." By permission of Miss Dolores Greco.

CHAPTER 7

The Intergroup Relations Curriculum: A Program for Elementary School Education, by John S. Gibson. Courtesy of the Lincoln-Filene Center for Citizenship and Public Affairs, Tufts University.
Fannie R. Shaftel and George Shaftel, ROLE-PLAYING FOR SOCIAL VALUES: Decision-Making in the Social Studies, © 1967. Reprinted by permission of Prentice-Hall, Inc., Englewood Cliffs, New Jersey.
Fig. 7. Reprinted, by permission, from John S. Gibson, *The Intergroup Relations Curriculum: A Program for Elementary School Education*, vol. 2, Lincoln-Filene Center for Citizenship and Public Affairs, Tufts Univ. (Medford, Mass. 1969), p. 6.

CHAPTER 8

Barbara Ward. *Spaceship Earth.* New York: Columbia University Press, 1966, p. 14.
"International Education for Spaceship Earth." Courtesy of the Foreign Policy Association.
"Introducing Children to the World," by Leonard S. Kenworthy. Courtesy of Harper & Row, Publishers, Incorporated.
"The Golden Stag," from THE GOLDEN STAG AND OTHER FOLK TALES FROM INDIA. Copyright © 1962 by Isabel Wyatt. Reprinted by permission of David McKay Company, Inc., and Margaret Christie, representative and author's agent.
From the book THE LAND AND PEOPLE OF PORTUGAL by Raymond A. Wohlrabe and Werner Krusch. Revised Edition 1963. Copyright, ©, 1960 by Raymond A. Wohlrabe and Werner E. Krusch. Reprinted by permission of J. B. Lippincott Company.

CHAPTER 9

CHILDHOOD AND SOCIETY, by Erik H. Erikson. Courtesy of W. W. Norton & Company.
American Life: Dream and Reality, by W. Lloyd Warner. Copyright 1953 by The University of Chicago. All rights reserved. Used by permission of The University of Chicago Press.

"Moral Education," by Larry Kohlberg, in *School Review*. Copyright 1966 by the University of Chicago. Used by permission of The University of Chicago Press.

CHAPTER 10

Planning and Organizing for Teaching and *Deciding What to Teach*, Project on the Instructional Program of the Public Schools. Courtesy of the National Education Association.

"Generalizations from the Social Sciences," by Paul R. Hanna and John R. Lee, in *Social Studies in Elementary Schools*. Courtesy of the National Council for the Social Studies, National Education Association.

Elementary Social Studies Curriculum: Scope and Sequence. Courtesy of Montgomery County Public Schools, Maryland.

Social Studies for Elementary School Children. Courtesy of St. Paul Public Schools.

Teaching Social Studies in the Elementary School, by Ralph C. Preston. Courtesy of Holt, Rinehart & Winston, Inc.

Intelligence in the Modern World, by John Dewey. Used by permission of Joseph Ratner.

THE PUPIL'S THINKING, by E. A. Peel. Courtesy of B.P.C. Publishing, Ltd.

"Teaching For Depth," by Ralph C. Preston, in *Childhood Education*. Courtesy of the Association for Childhood Education International.

Arthur T. Jersild, CHILD PSYCHOLOGY, 4th ed., © 1954, Prentice-Hall, Inc., Englewood Cliffs, New Jersey.

"Adding Depth to Elementary School Social Studies," by Melvin Arnoff in *Social Education*. Courtesy of the National Council for the Social Studies, National Education Association.

"Concepts, Generalizations, and Theories," by Edith West. Courtesy of Minnesota Project Social Studies, University of Minnesota.

Fig. 8. Reprinted, by permission, from Edith West, "Concepts, Generalizations, and Theories," Background Paper no. 3, Minnesota Project Social Studies (Minneapolis: Univ. of Minnesota, n.d.), p. 8.

Fig. 9. Reprinted, by permission, from Edith West, "Concepts, Generalizations, and Theories," Background Paper no. 3, Minnesota Project Social Studies (Minneapolis: Univ. of Minnesota, n.d.), p. 10.

CHAPTER 12

"The Social Science Disciplines," by Edith West. Courtesy of the Social Studies Curriculum Center, University of Minnesota.

Social Sciences Education Framework for California Public Schools. Courtesy of the Statewide Social Sciences Study Committee.

Fig. 10. Reprinted from *Social Sciences Education Framework for California Public Schools* (Sacramento, 1968), p. 6. Courtesy of the Statewide Social Sciences Study Committee.

CHAPTER 13

From The Introduction to SOCIAL STUDIES IN THE UNITED STATES by C. Benjamin Cox and Byron G. Massialas, © 1967 by Harcourt Brace Jovanovich, Inc., and reprinted with their permission.

Paul R. Hanna and Genevieve Anderson Hoyt, *Guidebook to Accompany At School* (Chicago: Scott, Foresman, 1963).

From LEARNING ABOUT OUR COUNTRY by Kenneth D. Wann, Jane D. Vreeland, and Marguerite A. Conklin. © Copyright 1963, 1967 by Allyn and Bacon, Inc. Reprinted by permission of Allyn and Bacon, Inc.

Children's Literature in the Elementary School, by Charlotte Huck and Doris Young. Courtesy of Holt, Rinehart & Winston, Inc.

May Arbuthnot, CHILDREN AND BOOKS (Chicago: Scott, Foresman, 1957), p. 559. Courtesy of Scott, Foresman.

From the book MADE IN THE MIDDLE AGES by Christine Price. Copyright © 1961 by Christine Price. Published by E. P. Dutton & Co., Inc., and reprinted with their permission.

From the book MADE IN THE RENAISSANCE by Christine Price. Copyright © 1963 by Christine Price. Published by E. P. Dutton & Co., Inc., and reprinted with their permission.

Methods of Instruction in the Social Studies, by Ernest Horn, in *Report of the Commission on the Social Studies*. Courtesy of Charles Scribner's Sons.

Jackdaw No. 7, SHAFTESBURY AND THE WORKING CHILDREN, compiled by John Langdon-Davies. Jonathan Cape Limited, London. Distributed in the United States by Viking Press, Grossman Publishers.

Teachers Guide to H.P.I. Filmstrips. Courtesy of Hudson Photographic Industries.

Ships and Navigation, by Tompsie Baxter and Bess M. Young. Courtesy of Teachers College, Columbia University.

Fig. 11. From *Voting in Mississippi*, a report of the U.S. Commission on Civil Rights (Washington, 1964), p. 11.

CHAPTER 14

Geography in the Teaching of the Social Studies: Concepts and Skills, by Paul R. Hanna and others. Courtesy of Houghton Mifflin Company.

PHOTOGRAPHS

cover   child–Based on a photograph by George B. Fry III.

Photo Essay: Kent State University, May 1970
   city limits sign; map of campus–Photographs from Wide World Photos. student lying on a hill; National Guardsman in profile; National Guardsmen behind rope fence; National Guardsmen on a hill–Photographs by Terry Knowles. students fleeing tear gas–Photograph from United Press International. National Guardsmen throwing tear gas–

Photograph from Wide World Photos. slain student on pavement–Photograph from United Press International. wounded student being helped; stretcher being brought; Attorney General receives F.B.I. report; preparation for Kent State Grand Jury investigation; coffin demonstrators; remember Kent–Photographs from Wide World Photos.

p. 30   Thomas Jefferson, painting by Thomas Sully–Courtesy of the Library of Congress. Margaret Mead–Photograph from United Press International. Mao–Photograph from Charles Phelps Cushing. Child's head–SRA photo.

pp. 42, 43, 47, 48, 50   Courtesy of the Smithsonian Institution National Anthropological Archives, neg. nos. 1057, 1084, 1054, 1080, 1082, 1078.

p. 69   two classroom scenes–Used by permission of George B. Fry III. boy doing homework–SRA photo.

p. 84   Eskimo family in boat–Courtesy of the State of Alaska Department of Economic Development. Indian women hauling water–Courtesy of the Bureau of Indian Affairs, Department of the Interior. teacher and student–Used by permission of George B. Fry III.

p. 91   Slave Sale, Charleston, South Carolina, 1856–Photograph from Charles Phelps Cushing. Lincoln lithograph (The Outbreak of the Rebellion in the United States, 1861); Lincoln and Hamlin campaign poster; preparing cotton on a plantation, South Carolina, 1862; Inauguration of Jefferson Davis, Montgomery, Alabama, 1861–Courtesy of the Library of Congress.

p. 98   From SOCIAL SCIENCE LABORATORY UNITS, PROJECT BOOK 3. © 1969, Science Research Associates, Inc. Used by permission of publisher.

p. 111   Photographs from United Press International.

p. 115   cartoons by Gray Smith, *San Francisco Chronicle*, April 25, 1971 (welfare system) and May 11, 1971 (German mark). © Chronicle Publishing Co. 1971.

p. 123   oily bird–Used by permission of Judy Horst. city trash cans–Photograph by Gretchen Hargis. girl playing hopscotch–Used by permission of Marion Bernstein.

p. 136   Cherry Blossom Festival–Courtesy of San Francisco Convention and Visitors Bureau. apartments–SRA photo. Congress in session–Photograph from United Press International. orchestra–Used by permission of Robert A. Isaacs.

p. 141   Used by permission of George B. Fry III.

p. 145   Photographs by the author.

p. 146   students; street scene–SRA photos. Vietnam scene–U.S. Army Photograph.

p. 154   Indian classroom–SRA photo. American classroom; American child–Used by permission of George B. Fry III. Indian girl–Photograph from United Press International.

p. 173   house in Appalachia–Courtesy of Office of Economic Opportunity. Copse Hill, owner occupied houses–Used by permission of

xi

Harlow Development Corporation, Photograph by John McCann. Appalachian family–Photograph by Daniel J. Ransohoff, Courtesy of *Appalachia* (February 1971). dinner scene–Used by permission of George B. Fry III.

p. 177   Photographs by Barbara Ravizza.

p. 180   public market, Fort Lamy, Chad, Africa–Courtesy of the American Museum of Natural History. Senegalese girls with traditional coiffures– Courtesy of the United Nations. African woman carrying basket on head–Otto Lang/Photophile. black couple–Used by permission of George B. Fry III. Southwest Washington before redevelopment– Courtesy of the D.C. Redevelopment Land Agency. residents of Sangmelima help neighbor build new home–Courtesy of the United Nations.

p. 191   American city scene–Photograph: Joy Locke. French city– Photograph by the author. American classroom–Used by permission of George B. Fry III. French classroom–Photograph from United Press International.

p. 206   SRA photo.

p. 210   black parents; city wall–Photography: Joy Locke. group of children; black girl reading; black girl dancing–Used by permission of Robert A. Isaacs.

p. 213   girl fighting–Used by permission of George B. Fry III. girl raising her hand–SRA photo. young woman–Photography: Deborah Jackson.

p. 238   Used by permission of George B. Fry III.

p. 271   children using map; boy and librarian–SRA photos. boy reading– Used by permission of George B. Fry III.

p. 276   young family–Photography: Joy Locke. Capitol building– Photo by JMR, National Park Service, Department of the Interior. children at U.N. International School–Courtesy of the United Nations.

p. 280   nineteenth century family–Courtesy of the Library of Congress. young contemporary family; boy wearing glasses–Photography: Joy Locke.

p. 302   Used by permission of George B. Fry III.

p. 344   Robert Mosher/Photophile.

p. 351   boy riding bicycle–Photography: Joy Locke. traffic congestion– Used by permission of George B. Fry III. buses and pedestrians– SRA photo. boy–Photography: Joy Locke.

p. 357   Used by permission of George B. Fry III.

p. 361   child watching TV–Photograph by Barbara Ravizza. Vietnam scene–U.S. Army Photograph.

p. 379   Actionmap–Courtesy of Denoyer-Geppert Company.

p. 410   sketch–concept sketch by Lawrence Halprin & Associates. boy playing violin; political rally; and interracial class–Used by permission of Marion Bernstein. telephone poles–Photography: Joy Locke. aerial view of city–Steve McCarroll/Photophile.

*To my doctoral students at
Teachers College, Columbia University,
for pushing my capacity for thought,
affection, and social commitment.*

CONTENTS

xvi

PREFACE

The social studies have been caught in a trough of indecision and neglect. Schools and parents have emphasized the three R's in the belief that children can survive in a technical society only if they get good grades, master the basic skills, and pursue their education at least through college. In this rush for the efficient transmission of skills, the social studies, along with the humanities and the natural sciences, have been eclipsed. Procedures to increase "accountability," (including several originally developed by the Defense Department to help in the planning and construction of missile systems) are being applied to education.

No doubt schools are inefficient and basic skills must be taught. The overwhelming need in our society, however, is for social, scientific, humanistic education. Only such an education can heal our alienated society, provide the values and moral judgment necessary for a meaningful life, and help children develop a social consciousness that will lead them to create a better society.

We are fortunate that while the social studies in most schools have been sleeping, some schools and some curriculum developers have been preparing new approaches: these approaches can provide the basis for the vitally needed resurgence of social education. Some of them focus on the social sciences and ways of teaching social science concepts and methods. Some focus on democratic and international citizenship, on interpersonal and interracial relations, and on strategies for developing social values and skills. Others concentrate on the child's need to find personal meaning and to make his world comprehensible. The result is that teachers and school faculties can choose from a wealth of alternative strategies and generate a social education relevant to their children and to the time in which they live.

The purpose of this book is to introduce pre-service teachers as well as in-service teachers and curriculum developers to the many alternatives in the social studies. Suggestions are made concerning ways of choosing from among these alternatives to suit individual purposes. I have tried to do this vividly and concretely so that a beginning teacher can use the book as a practical guide to social studies teaching. The modules on teaching skills and strategies, filmstrips, and audio tapes contain instructional programs through which a basic set of teaching strategies for the social studies can be learned.

We have taken these pains with this program of materials because a new social studies is beginning. Among curriculum planners and in classrooms it is coming to life. Teachers of the new social studies must be able to take ideas from the social sciences and from social philosophy and to implement them in creating a vital environment for children to grow in.

XX

Photo Essay
KENT STATE UNIVERSITY
MAY 1970

Kent State was a national tragedy. It was not,
however, a unique tragedy.
*Report of the President's Commission
on Campus Unrest*

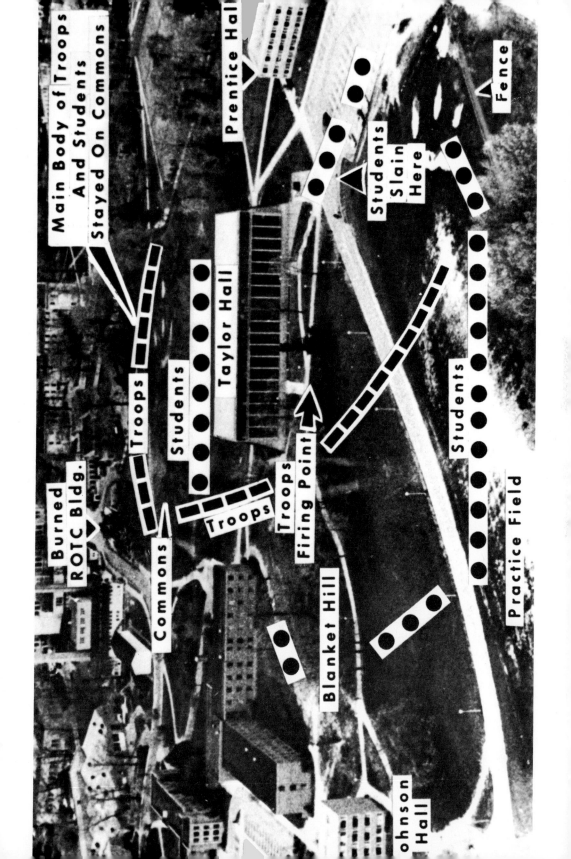

We find that the rally on the Commons on Saturday, May 2, 1970, which resulted in the burning of the R.O.T.C. building, constituted a riot. . . . Arson is arson, whether committed on a college campus or elsewhere. *Special Grand Jury Report*

The conduct of many students and nonstudent protestors at Kent State on the first four days of May 1970 was plainly intolerable. . . . Violence by students on or off the campus can never be justified by any grievance, philosophy, or political idea. *Report of the President's Commission on Campus Unrest*

We find that all the persons assembled were ordered to disperse on numerous occasions, but failed to do so. *Special Grand Jury Report*

Even if the Guard had authority to prohibit a peaceful gathering—a question that is at least debatable—the decision to disperse the noon rally was a serious error. The timing and manner of the dispersal were disastrous. *Report of the President's Commission on Campus Unrest*

Tear gas was admittedly ineffective because of wind direction and velocity. . . . *Special Grand Jury Report*

For students deeply opposed to the war, the Guard was a living symbol of the military system they opposed. For other students, the Guard was an outsider on their campus, prohibiting all their rallies, even peaceful ones, ordering them about, and tear gassing them when they refused to obey. *Report of the President's Commission on Campus Unrest*

It should be made clear that we do not condone all of the activities of the National Guard on the Kent State University campus on May 4, 1970. *Special Grand Jury Report*

The actions of some students were violent and criminal and those of some others were dangerous, reckless, and irresponsible. The indiscriminate firing of rifles into a crowd of students and the deaths that followed were unnecessary, unwarranted, and inexcusable. *Report of the President's Commission on Campus Unrest*

We have carefully examined all such matters as have legitimately come to our notice and within our charge. . . . *Special Grand Jury Report*

There can be no sanctuary or immunity from prosecution on the campus. Criminal acts by students must be treated as such wherever they occur and whatever their purpose. *Report of the President's Commission on Campus Unrest*

The members of this Special Grand Jury find that all the conditions that led to the May tragedy still exist. *Special Grand Jury Report*

We must learn from the particular horror of Kent State and insure that it is never repeated. *Report of the President's Commission on Campus Unrest*

Postscript: The report prepared by the Special Grand Jury has since been ordered by a federal judge to be physically expunged and destroyed on the ground that the jury had overstepped its legal limits, thus endangering the defendants' rights to a fair trial.

THE THREE DIMENSIONS OF THE SOCIAL STUDIES

I

A social studies curriculum and method of instruction has the opportunity to influence three different aspects of education.

Intellectual education. To identify and solve social problems, a person needs to know how to use the analytic ideas and problem-solving tools developed by scholars in the social sciences.

Social education. The content and procedures involved in the social studies can prepare a child to participate effectively in his society.

Personal education. Through the exploration of culture, society, and the individual, a child can come to comprehend his experience and find meaning to it.

Although American public schools have had great difficulty reconciling and fulfilling their function in these three areas, these aspects of education are compatible with each other and with activities designed to teach the social studies. These general aspects of education can thus be treated as dimensions of the social studies in particular. They serve as reference points by which to estimate the scope of the social studies. An academic

introduction

Dimensions of the social studies

area with such potential for bringing about educational growth throughout a person's schooling demands a well-formulated teaching strategy. The purpose of this book is to present such a strategy.

Intellectual Education: Introducing the Child to the Social Sciences

The purpose of the intellectual dimension of the social studies is to introduce children to the modes of thinking of the social scientist. Although the methods of the social sciences prepare the child for citizenship and help him to comprehend his world, the social sciences must also be taught in their own right. A social studies curriculum concerned only with citizenship or with the current life experience of the child cannot fulfill the intellectual character of the school.

> Experiences in order to be educative must lead out into an expanding world of subject matter, a subject matter of facts or information or ideas. This condition is satisfied only as the educator views teaching and learning as a continuous process of reconstruction of experience.[1]

Adequate cultivation of the intellect means involvement with the best knowledge available, with the minds of wise men and inventive scholars. One of the central purposes of the public school, as José Ortega y Gasset phrased it for the university, is to enable men to live at the level of the best ideas of their time.[2] Insofar as we can find the best ideas about the social world in the social sciences, we need to expose children to them.

The social sciences have developed effective methods with which to analyze interpersonal relations, community life, and society at the national and international levels. As the child matures, he can learn these methods in more and more sophisticated forms and use them to analyze these three important areas of social life.[3]

A teacher needs to understand these three areas of the social studies so that in his teaching there will be no conflict between them. In the past, many people have felt that helping the child understand his life and solve his problems conflicted with teaching him content from the subject disciplines. These goals, however, need not conflict. The tactics of the social sciences are taught to the child precisely because they are the best tools we have found for helping him face social problems and comprehend his life.

Many social scientists believe that the social sciences should be taught in a way that preserves the integrity of each. This belief is sometimes taken to mean that there have to be separate courses for each of the disciplines. The social sciences have much content in common, however. A curriculum can be made to emphasize the unique concepts of each without using separate courses. It is not possible to teach all the findings of all the social sciences, or even a significant part of them. Yet it is possible to teach their central ideas in such a way that they will be useful to the child in dealing with social as well as personal problems.

3

Social Education:
Preparing the Child for Social Responsibility

The purpose of the social dimension of the social studies is to prepare citizens who can perpetuate and improve their society. Charles A. Beard summed up the requirements of citizenship education in one of the seventeen volumes of the American Historical Association's Commission on Social Studies. He said that the supreme purpose is

> the creation of rich, many-sided personalities, equipped with practical knowledge and inspired by ideals so that they can make their way and fulfill their mission in a changing society which is part of a world complex. . . . They are firm of will, for without will nothing great will be accomplished. They are imbued with the highest aspirations of the human race, for without aspiration there is not great motive power for action.[4]

The American public has charged its schools with the development of citizens who know the heritage of their society and are equipped to participate fully in political and social life. Yet, as Beard has pointed out, the social world is shifting and changing. Long-lasting dogmas about what the citizen should know cannot be formulated.

> The primary information which social science must supply through the schools to individuals is information concerning the conditioning elements, forces, and ideas of the modern world in which life must be lived. Any representation of them is bound to be partial and out of perspective—such is the frailty of the human mind—but it must be attempted in . . . every possible apparatus for conveying information vividly and realistically to the immature mind.[5]

The citizen needs to acquire informal skills and information not only to adapt to his rapidly changing world but also to help shape his future society. F. H. George has pointed out:

> We are at the beginning of the biggest social revolution that the world has ever seen, far greater in size and implication than the industrial revolution, and this time we cannot afford to be ignorant of the facts. . . . We are building, or are about to build, machines that will change the face of our civilization and unless we are ready to change ourselves at the same time and see the reasons for the changes, we

4

may be without a future in which to change at all. . . . The tendency towards inertia, or even active resistance, when confronted with change, is deeprooted in the biological make-up of man. Change implies new stimuli to which we may not know how to react, and this is a threat to our feeling of security, a feeling which thrives on the familiar. This basic need for security, through the familiar, is especially deeply ingrained in a society that has been successful to any extent. This applies to Britain and other countries whose very successful background has encouraged a degree of conservatism that makes it difficult to accept even the smallest modification. We tend to live, like an aged matinee idol, on our past glories.[6]

Citizenship education must seek to develop people who can "formulate, propose, advocate, dare and direct."[7] It must also, however, seek to provide stability in society. If citizens fail to appreciate freedom, justice, and equality, then the struggle for the realization of these ideals falters. The recent gains of the American Negro are certainly a reflection not only of education for change but also of education to appreciate and deepen the meanings of freedom and equality.

The faster the world changes, the more its social institutions will be shaken as they adapt or fail to adapt. In the nineteenth century, enculturation of the young was accomplished by means of social pressures outside the school. Twentieth-century man may find that education is the main source of his ability to see values and purposes in the unfamiliar situations of his social life. Perhaps the school will become the chief agent of social solidarity.

American society has made it difficult, however, for the school to meet this challenge. Many areas of culture are at least partially tabooed from examination in schools. The development of areas relatively closed to school debate is symptomatic of a successful society trying to preserve the patterns that have served it well. These areas may be described as follows:

1. Economics. While open to professional economists and many laymen, this field is so affected by taboos, confusion, and emotion that schools tend to avoid it as a subject for rational study.
2. Race and minority-group relations. In recent years this field has become more open to reflective inquiry in schools, but in some places fears, tensions, and confusions continue to make it a closed area.
3. Social class. Here is a "truly closed area," in the writer's judgment, "neatly ignored as a result of the widespread belief, 'There are no social classes in America.' "

4. Sex, courtship, marriage. This area is more open to inquiry than it was a few years ago, but critical analysis of contradictions and problems is not usually encouraged.
5. Religion and morality. Morality is somewhat more open to reflective inquiry than are religious beliefs, but both tend to form a closed area as far as schools are concerned.
6. Nationalism and patriotism. This area is one in which it is difficult to question traditional beliefs, even if they are inconsistent with real behavior or the requirements of national survival.[8]

Often communities whose schools are undergoing racial integration will resist discussion of race in their classrooms. Some schools whose students are rebelling will try to suppress debate. These are situations in which citizenship education for a changing society comes up against mechanisms for maintaining the status quo. If effective education for citizenship is to take place, "teachers, administrators, and the public at large will have to accept the fact that the social studies are one of the major places in the school curriculum where unpleasant questions are asked and perhaps even unpleasant answers are to be found. . . . The taboo areas of social inquiry are exactly those areas into which the social studies, from the elementary grades through the graduate school, must penetrate."[9]

How can we help future citizens develop the commitment and insight that will help them preserve and improve their culture? First, we can operate school and classroom so that the child experiences the kinds of human interaction and problems that he will face. We can involve him in citizenship activities through which he can learn the commitment to social process and the skills that will make him effective. Second, we can expose him to discussion of the serious social movements and problems shaping the world so that he will learn to cope with a changing world. Third, we can provide him with the tactics that social scientists use to approach social problems. These tools will enhance his effectiveness as a citizen as much as they will enhance his personal quest for meaning. Fourth, we can help him explore his heritage and the heritage of other peoples. We can help him examine the values he is inheriting and learn their significance.

The enormous social ferment of the contemporary world presents to the social studies a vital opportunity and a serious challenge. Student activism and participation in school government give citizenship education more immediacy than was the case even a few years ago. As individuals and citizens, students need social education. The social dimension of the social studies answers this need.

Personal Education:
Helping the Child to Comprehend His Life

Every human being is shaped by the culture that surrounds him. Before he is old enough to resist, his social world moves in on him, teaches him, forms him. Unless he learns to examine his society and to see how it shapes him, he will very likely be swallowed up by it. To resist cultural determinism and help make a better society, he must know how to analyze the society and the ways it works upon him. "To the extent that we are able, by whatever device we choose, to use our critical faculties to interpret existing ideas and institutions, to that extent are we saved from falling into an idolatrous pose before them."[10]

The purpose of the personal dimension of the social studies is to help the child sort out the confusion of the social world and thus find meaning for his life. Through this kind of education, he comes to understand the causes of behavior, including his own, and develops tactics for inquiring into social problems; he learns to analyze social interaction and ask questions about it, to seek out information and use it to explain and improve interaction. He also becomes aware of the values he is absorbing and develops rational means of modifying and extending his values, especially when they conflict with those of other people.

The ideas that will help the child comprehend his social world come from the social sciences.

> Scientific method is the only authentic means at our command for getting at the significance of our everyday experiences of the world in which we live. . . . Scientific method provides a working pattern of the way in which and the conditions under which experiences are used to lead ever onward and outward.[11]

The tools of economics can help the child understand his economic life. The tactics of the historian and the anthropologist can help him comprehend his heritage. And so on. In studying the social sciences, he opens himself and his values to inquiry and scrutiny. The personal dimension focuses on the quest for personal meaning and effectiveness.

The following passage is a reporter's description of an election day in New York City. Imagine what difference it might make if the people described were to look at themselves as the political scientist or the sociologist or the anthropologist might look at them.

Primary Day? What Primary?
Excuses Keep Many From Polls

There were all sorts of good reasons for voting in yesterday's primary elections, but the majority of registered New Yorkers found better reasons not to.

The weather was almost idyllic, the voting precincts numerous, and the choices varied. The polls were open from 3 p.m. until 10 p.m., so most working people could vote. But, for one reason or another, the majority preferred to sit on front steps in the sunshine, take the children to the park, eat pizza beneath sidewalk awnings, or sit at home and watch television.

The 19th Congressional District was a microcosm of the city yesterday. In the 19th, a crescent-shaped territory that runs south from West 86th Street around the tip of Manhattan and up through the Lower East Side to East 20th Street, Leonard Farbstein, the incumbent, and William F. Haddad, the challenger, had been battling for two months.

But a walking tour of the district yesterday revealed little interest in this Democratic campaign or the primary. It also showed that some of those who didn't vote felt guilty about it.

"I voted already," said a middle-aged woman on upper Broadway yesterday morning, several hours before the polls opened. She spoke with all the dignity and pride of someone who really had voted.

"I don't live in this district," said a butcher, apologetically, as he carved a side of beef. "So I can't vote. I live in the Bronx, you see." He had forgotten that there was a primary in the Bronx, too.

Several persons who said they were registered voters made comments that indicated they did not know the difference between a primary and a general election.

One man expressed surprise when asked about the voting. "I thought that was all next November," he said.

South of Bleecker Street, where the 19th takes a turn around the base of Greenwich Village, a large woman with bushy eyebrows sat on a folding chair on the sidewalk outside her apartment.

"They won't help us, so why should we help them?" she said of the politicians.

A grizzled man sat on the steps nearby. He cursed his employer for not allowing him time off from work to vote. His working hours, he said, corresponded with those of the polls. He was asked for whom he would vote if he could vote.

"I don't know," he said. "Who's running?"

In Chelsea, a handsome woman with long, black hair explained why she would not vote. "I am a Puerto Rican," she said, "and therefore I cannot vote."

On the Bowery, which is also part of the district, Tommy McCarthy and Frank Joyce lounged in the shadows of a brick building. The two men said they had failed to remember somehow that this was Primary Day.

But Mr. McCarthy said that if a stranger would just tell him who was running—"Who's the G.I. Joe candidate this time, I always vote for the G.I. Joe candidate"—he would immediately perform his civic duty.

"Well," said the stranger, "in your district the men who are running are Haddad and Farbstein."

"Haddadfarbstein," Mr. McCarthy said. "O.K., I'll vote for him."[12]

If a person cannot understand his social life and relate to it effectively, if social life is too confusing and chaotic, or if a person does not develop social values that anchor his identity, then life becomes frightening and meaningless.

9

Goals and Methods of the Social Studies, 1920–1960

Currently there is much diversity in social studies curricula, but for forty years social studies curriculum patterns were relatively homogeneous across the nation. As in most curriculum areas, there was some disparity between what was recommended by theoreticians and what was actually done in the schools; but with respect to the placement of content through the school years, theory was largely put into practice. Theoretically, the chief purpose of the social studies was to prepare citizens for participation in United States democracy. Programs were constructed to accomplish this purpose through both content and methods.

The best preparation for democracy, it was argued, was to practice it. The basic teaching method was to organize classes into problem-solving, democratic groups. Courses from the primary grades through high school were to be organized around social problems. The teacher was to help the students define and attack problems, teaching them democratic procedures simultaneously with content.[13] Nowhere was the separation between theory and practice more prominent than in this area. The democratic method flourished in a few schools and classrooms, but in the majority, structured, teacher-directed teaching prevailed.[14]

In both elementary and secondary schools, the patterns of content were designed to introduce students to Western society and the social needs of man. In the elementary school, a pattern called the "expanding horizons" approach dominated. It assumed that children are best able to understand content within their own experience and that the social studies should expand the child's horizons to his nation and the world. Paul Hanna, one of the leading spokesmen for this point of view, has described the sequence as follows:

1. Family Community
2. School Community
3. Neighborhood Community
4. Local, County, and Metropolitan Communities
5. State Community
6. Region-of-States Community
7. U.S. National Community
8. Inter-American Community
9. Atlantic Community
10. Pacific Community
11. The World Community[15]

During elementary school the child would successively study these communities in terms of several basic human activities. These activities are depicted in figure 1. Each activity takes place in each community, but in a different way.

Under this plan social studies curricula and textbooks were developed showing the social sciences as sets of concepts that illuminate various human activities at each level of community. For example, "Light from *political science* shows us how the national efforts of both government and private sectors solve the problems of organizing and governing and helps us to understand the rationale behind the diverse solutions."[16] The use of the social sciences was controlled by the nature of the community and the basic activity being studied. When studying government at the state level, for example, students turned to political science.

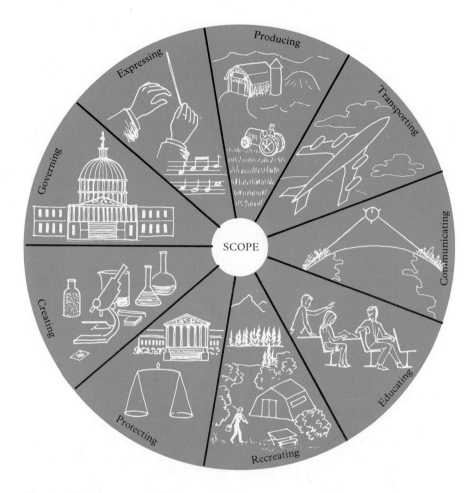

Fig. 1. Basic human activities

The social sciences were taught only as they related to the areas being studied, not as separate disciplines.

In junior high, American history dominated the social studies, although regional geography usually was offered as well. In senior high, world history and American government predominated. The world history course usually centered on the politics of the Western world, while the government course emphasized constitutional provisions for governing agencies.

A course on problems of democracy was offered in over three-fourths of the nation's high schools. This course was initiated after 1917 as a reaction against formalized content and to provide an experience based on democratic, problem-solving activity. As originally conceived, each problems-of-democracy class would identify and study significant social problems, even to the extent of planning and taking social action. This course was criticized on the ground that its content was not drawn directly from one of the disciplines and also that, for the most part, it did not live up to its intended promise. However, in a "contemporary social issues" version, it is undergoing a revival due to the present-day concern with social problems.

One of the two philosophies competing for control of the internal organization of courses and the selection of instructional materials sought to center teaching on problem-solving, democratic processes. This philosophy advocated variations on problem-centered units of instruction. Whether in the primary grades or in high school, the students would seek to understand puzzling aspects of social behavior. In the first or second grade, they might try to find out how their town feeds itself, or where toys come from, or how members of families around the world behave toward one another. In the fifth or sixth grade, they might try to understand how their government has developed, or how and why wars have occurred between nations. In high school, problems such as poverty, conservation, and urbanization might demand their attention.

The other philosophy manifested itself as a desire to organize instruction logically, so that students would master predictable bodies of knowledge. In the primary grades, this philosophy resulted in a series of preorganized units, such as the Mexican Family, the Japanese Family, Life in the Swiss Alps, the Lapland Family, and so on. By grade five, history was treated chronologically and geography regionally. The more or less logical arrangements of history, economic geography, and government dominated instruction from the middle grades through high school.

These two philosophies required very different materials for children. The problem-centered approach called for open-ended resources that teachers and children could use to suit their purposes. People and places in the community were needed, as well as pen pals and the Department of the Interior.[17] The logical-coverage philosophy, however, lent itself to the development of the familiar social studies textbook. The text, with supplementary readings and audio-visual aids, became the mainstay in most classrooms, at least above the primary level.

Emerging Approaches to the Social Studies

Until recently, most social studies instruction followed these patterns. As the number of approaches to the social studies increases, however, identifying patterns is more complex. There are many important areas of social concern where neither new nor old patterns are functioning well. Today the challenge to the teacher is not only to learn and strengthen existing patterns, but to initiate new forms of social education.

During the last few years many new social studies programs have been developed, some for elementary school, some for secondary school, some for both. The diversity of these approaches stems partly from emphasis on one or more of the dimensions of the social studies, each of which involves distinct goals and teaching strategies. These dimensions necessarily affect the student in different ways. We can, for example, attempt to teach him academic skills and ways of dealing intellectually with complexity. Or we can attempt to change his interaction with his fellowman. Or we can attempt to improve his abilities as an individual.

THE INTELLECTUAL DIMENSION

Berelson poses the question, "Should the social studies curriculum aim to produce good citizens or knowledgeable students of the major fields of learning?" and answers it:

> My own impression is that this is a largely spurious issue that will go away if it is put into a different semantic frame. As a starter, suppose we were to say that we—all of us involved—want to give high school students the best introduction we can within the limits of practicality to the best available knowledge in the social science disciplines as a *means to the end* of producing responsible citizens.[18]

Although Berelson is at pains to reduce any conflicts between citizenship and social science education, the contents of the book he edited impelled him to include the above statements in the preface. In this book source papers on the social science disciplines and on world area studies are presented as academic guidelines for the redevelopment of social studies curricula. The tone of many of the articles suggests an extremely academic emphasis: the social sciences are to be taught as such. It is assumed that the student, armed with concepts and modes of inquiry from the disciplines, can make his own transfer to social problems. Sykes's words illustrate this point as he writes about the relation between sociology and the social sciences.

> The difficulty is that many teachers of sociology in colleges and universities doubt at the present time that their discipline is adequately represented in the high school regardless of whether it is called social studies or something else—and regardless of whether the work in the high school is a preparation for more advanced training or the end of academic schooling.[19]

Sykes argues that nothing but confusion can result from equating the objective study of society with the means for securing the good life. A knowledge of society may prove useful to the student, but not necessarily. Furthermore, excessive concern with the usefulness of a discipline may distort its content. Sykes's view is that the purpose of the intellectual dimension of the social studies is independent of the social and personal dimensions and can be justified on its own terms.

While I think most social scientists would tend to agree with Berelson rather than with Sykes, the use of the intellectual dimension of the social studies as the means for citizenship education affects the student differently than would a program that focuses on personal characteristics or on processes of social behavior.

One approach that emphasizes a particular discipline is the Georgia Anthropology Curriculum Project. This project has been carried on under the direction of Marion Rice at the University of Georgia and has generated materials for introducing students in grades one through seven to the organizing concepts of anthropology. The rationale of the project is based on several premises:

1. Any field of knowledge, such as anthropology, consists of a system of symbols, or word labels, which are used to express ideas and describe relationships. An understanding or mastery of any field of knowledge begins with an understanding of the symbol system, the meaning of which expands and develops as the knowledge of the discipline is extended.
2. Symbol systems are usually organized for transmission of a core of congruent ideas, usually referred to as subject matter, discipline, or field. For almost thirty years the social studies movement has

contended that a subject approach to the transmission of social studies is inappropriate for the elementary grades. It is thought [by the authors of this curriculum project] that any type of organization of material, irrespective of its method, is designed to transmit knowledge, and that there is nothing incompatible, except preference and tradition, with a subject presentation of a social science in the elementary grades.

3. Anthropological material is frequently used in the public school, but, in the absence of emphasis on anthropological concepts and terminology, the contribution that anthropology has to make to an understanding of man and of different cultures is frequently obscured. The material [Georgia Project] deliberately introduces anthropological terminology which may at first be somewhat difficult for the student. As his familiarity with these terms increases, however, it is expected that they will help him to organize and interpret in a more meaningful manner the world in which he lives.[20]

This general rationale can be specifically implemented in the objectives for the fourth-grade unit:

1. To gain some insight into the way an anthropologist studies people.
2. To obtain a general idea of the *concept of culture.*
3. To learn that culture is universal. Culture is universal and people everywhere have the same basic problems of survival and getting along with people. However, each group of people or culture develops its own solution to these problems and these solutions may vary greatly in detail. (Cultural universals and cultural variation)
4. To understand how people learn the traits of their culture. (Enculturation)
5. To acquire an idea of how cultures change and grow. Cultures may continue for a long period of time but change does take place. (Cultural dynamics)[21]

Although not eschewing the development of citizenship behavior, this project emphasizes the teaching of the structure of anthropology. The above quotations indicate that the creators of the project recognize the controversy over the appropriateness of an intellectual approach for elementary school children, but they clearly believe that it is appropriate.

There are many approaches to the intellectual dimension of the social studies. Entire curricula are built around one or two disciplines, as is the University of Georgia Anthropology Curriculum

Project. Other approaches, such as the University of Minnesota Social Studies Project, blend several disciplines along with objectives from the personal and social dimensions.[22] Some approaches emphasize the system of ideas from a discipline, its intellectual structure. One example is the economics curriculum developed at the University of Chicago. Others emphasize the modes of inquiry of the discipline, the ideas and research methods used by scholars to add to and revise knowledge in the field. An example of this is the Michigan Social Science Curriculum, which is designed to teach children how to use the research methods of social psychology to study interpersonal life, including their own. Another way of treating the disciplines is to emphasize the philosophical questions involved in man's study of man. *Man: A Course of Study*, a program for children at the fifth-grade level, uses this approach, as does the Amherst History Project. All these approaches can be distinguished from each other in terms of the number of disciplines involved, the aspect of the disciplines (structure or modes of inquiry), and their relation to the other dimensions and to philosophy.

THE SOCIAL DIMENSION

As might be expected, the social studies programs in the United States emphasize the social dimension. After all, the social studies were created as a reaction against formalized study unrelated to the needs of society and the problems of regenerating the society. The most widely used textbook on elementary social studies begins with the following statements:

> The schools of America are dedicated to the preservation and extension of democratic ideals and to the development of the highest type of democratic citizenship on the part of each child. The discharge of this responsibility requires an education program that will develop each child's potentialities to the fullest and at the same time bring growth in the competencies essential to democratic living.[23]

Michaelis has provided a concise statement of purpose for the social dimension:

> The teacher must be aware of the kind of behavior which is consistent with democratic values. Little would be gained unless the behavior that the children develop is democratic in nature. . . . Implicit in the

foregoing statement of democratic values are the following categories of behavior: responsibility, concern for others, open-mindedness, creativeness, and cooperation. Each unit of work that is planned should make a contribution to the development of the foregoing categories of behavior.[24]

Michaelis has also described the democratic values, which are the core of the democratic process: "government by the group; human well-being, happiness and good will toward others; faith in the ability of men to govern themselves wisely; consent of the governed; self-direction and self-control in accordance with group welfare; freedom of inquiry with free play of intelligence about our problems; majority decision with minority protection; equal justice and equal opportunity; individual freedom and responsibility."[25] Most textbooks and most school district curriculum guides have emphasized the virtues of American democracy. Many people, however, feel that students should be taught to consider the reforms necessary to achieve these democratic values.

While in no way undermining the function of American education to promote democratic citizenship, Becker and Mehlinger point out that the trend toward an international society requires an education conceptually different from what has been carried on before.

What would formerly have been judged to be a national problem is now believed to be an international concern. The alarm felt in the United States over the population explosion in India, China, and the nations of Latin America results not only from an interest in the welfare of the people in those nations. In part, this concern stems from the recognition that the contemporary world cannot remain peaceful if people in significant portions of the globe are left to suffer and die from hunger and disease. Similarly, problems of managing and preserving the natural environment are global, not just local in scope. Ultimately, everyone is threatened by polluted air, impure water, and dwindling natural resources. These hazards are now reaching the point where national solutions no longer suffice. Man's health and perhaps even his survival depend upon the ability of nations to take collective measures against the pollution and destruction of the environment.[26]

A social studies program with an international orientation is likely to be different from one that emphasizes the democratic process but not international understanding.

A third approach within the social dimension emphasizes interpersonal attitudes and skills. Recently many educators, Shaftel among them, have urged that the social studies teach people how to find greater fulfillment in interpersonal relations. Joyce and Weinberg have proposed a method for doing this: Teach students an analytic framework they can apply to interpersonal relations and use to improve their ability to work with other people. Another intellectual approach has been proposed by Oliver and Shaver, who suggest that the problems of public conflict and political controversy be the focus of general education and social studies. They argue that in the process of dialogue society can clarify value alternatives and reach agreement on ways of implementing certain value positions.[27] This approach implies that since there is no single, certain solution to social problems, the teacher is obliged to tolerate a variety of ideals, values, or creeds among his students. Furthermore, although the teacher may find a personal solution to ideological conflict, he must condone the constant discourse and even conflict between various groups within society as they are represented in the classroom. The good society is not to be construed as one in which people behave uniformly. Rather it is one in which individuals in groups have wide latitude for developing their own standards and tastes. Progress consists of longer and longer periods of nonviolent conflict between groups of free men who have chosen a variety of modes of conduct exemplifying the good life.[28]

A social dimension–oriented curriculum may emphasize one of these aspects or treat each equally.

THE PERSONAL DIMENSION

A person is capable of responding to his environment in many ways. He can use his intelligence to solve problems, analyze and synthesize information, or build new ideas. He can create by doing new and interesting things. He can feel open and grow through facing complexity. He can feel independent enough to respond fearlessly and on his own terms. He can feel warmth and affection toward others.

It is possible for education to try to develop one or more of these capacities. A program may emphasize creativity, for example, and teach students to make a creative, esthetic response to life. Or it may attempt to increase intelligence and rationality. Or it may focus on personality development. A social studies program with this last goal will try to challenge the individual, to free him, to teach him how to teach himself.

Aspects of the social dimension

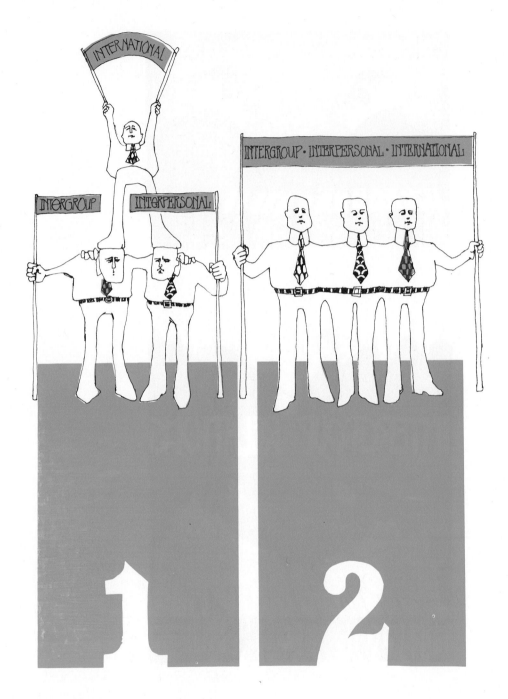

Possible social dimension-oriented curricula

In the words of A. S. Neill, "I hold that the aim of life is to find happiness, which means to find interest. Education should be a preparation of life. Our culture has not been very successful. Our education, politics, and economics lead to war, etc. . . ."[29] To Neill the primary aim of education is to help the student respond to life in his own way and to seek self-fulfillment fearlessly. In some ways Neill's school is a social studies program in itself—a way of life that encourages students to work in their own way and to solve their own problems. Education at Summerhill is devoted to the personal dimension, and the social and intellectual dimensions are not permitted to intrude on the development of the individual.

Edgar Z. Friedenberg emphasizes the personal dimension in a somewhat different way than does Neill. Friedenberg is greatly concerned with the consistency of society, but he is more concerned with some of its effects.

> Being different, notoriously, does not get you to the top. If individuals must believe they are on their way there in order to preserve their self-esteem, they will be under constant pressure, initially from anxious adults and later from their own aspirations, to repudiate the divergent elements of their character in order to make it under the terms common to mass culture. They choose the path most traveled by, and that makes the difference. . . . To anyone who is concerned about what his life means, this pressure is repugnant.[30]

To Friedenberg, the great question in education is how to help young people comprehend the culture and use and improve it without having their individuality submerged. Friedenberg feels that the social education of the schools should be designed to free the student from the enormous pressure inherent in a technological society with possibilities for upward mobility. The school today, however, is dominated by this technological reality and accentuates this pressure to conform. Although Friedenberg looks at education from a sociological perspective, he emphasizes the goals of the school with regard to the individual.

Rogers, Combs, and Jersild are among the psychologists who have urged that the school pay greater attention to the developing personality of the individual.[31] They tend to see the activities of the school in terms of their effect on the organization of personality. "Nearly everything in the curriculum is charged with psychological meaning when viewed from the standpoint of what it might do to help learners find themselves, realize their potentialities, use their resources in productive ways, and enter into relationships which have a bearing on their ideas and attitudes toward themselves."[32] These theorists recommend that the school environment be shaped to help the student develop his internal organization and relate to his environment without fear. They do not see this emphasis as antithetical to the needs of society. They reason that if the school develops individuals fully, a good society will result.

Many educators, among them E. Paul Torrance, have emphasized the development of creative thinking capacity.

> Perhaps nothing could contribute more to the general welfare of our nation and the satisfactions and mental health of its people than a general raising of the level of creative behavior. There is little doubt but that the prolonged and severe stifling of creative thinking cuts at the very roots of satisfaction in living. This must inevitably create overwhelming tension and breakdown.[33]

Torrance and like-minded educators believe that the educational environment should reward creative thinking and help develop it.

> Creativity needs to be energized and guided almost from birth. If it is stifled early, apparently it will only become imitative if it survives at all. The vigorous creative imaginations which survive early stifling and opposition may become dangerous to society and civilization if they learn only to act vigorously without guidance.[34]

The implication is that society must encourage individual development for its own protection as well as for the benefit of the individual.

There are many other approaches to the personal dimension. Even these few illustrate the possibility of building educational programs that emphasize personal development. The social education of the child can be shaped as it is at Summerhill, where individuals are the center. Or the social studies can be organized to help young people see and understand the pressures for conformity and the ways in which they submit to those pressures. The social studies could be shaped to help them cope with conformity and develop social attitudes that do not conflict with their own development. Or, as Jersild suggests, the social studies could be devoted to helping the individual grow through interaction with his environment. Or, as Torrance suggests, social studies could emphasize productive thinking about society, helping young people to generate creative solutions to social problems. Emphasis on the personal, however, need not eschew the intellectual or social.

Classifying Social Studies Approaches within the Three Dimensions

It is not possible to describe in detail all the social studies approaches presently emerging. The following list provides a classification of many of the approaches and sources so that the reader can relate these approaches according to their emphasis on the various dimensions. Very few of these approaches belong solely to one dimension or emphasize one dimension alone. Many authors of approaches that emphasize one dimension feel that their approach affects the other dimensions also.

The approaches mentioned below are taken from curriculum-development activities, the writings of theorists, or research activity. In addition to those in the bibliography, a list of ongoing projects is provided.

23

THE INTELLECTUAL DIMENSION

1. The Georgia Anthropology Project (pp. 14–15, 85–87) focuses on the study of anthropology and its application to American life.
2. The Elkhart Economics Project is built around the basic concepts of economics.
3. The Carnegie History Project, Edwin Fenton, director, emphasizes the methodology of historians as an inductive entry to the study of American society.
4. The High School Geography Project is developing materials for tenth-grade geography courses emphasizing the structure and approaches used by geographers.
5. *Sociological Resources for the Social Studies* (pp. 73–74) is an extensive project based on sociology as a discipline.
6. The Michigan Social Science Project uses the strategies of social psychology and attempts to teach them to elementary school children.

7. The Asian Studies Project of Berkeley (p. 204), John Michaelis, director, uses area studies techniques in teaching students about Asia.

8. Mark Krug's *History in the Social Sciences* (p. 88) emphasizes teaching history as a discipline and contrasts this with other approaches to the discipline.

9. The Minnesota Social Studies Project (pp. 285–89), Edith West, director, uses objectives from the social sciences and from civics education and combines these in interesting ways, uniting social issues and social science concepts.

10. The High School Curriculum Center in Government (pp. 108–12), Howard Mehlinger, director, is developing courses in American political behavior for the ninth grade and comparative political systems for the twelfth grade. Both political science concepts and techniques of inquiry are emphasized.

THE SOCIAL DIMENSION

1. The Harvard Social Studies project, Donald Oliver, director, emphasizes an intellectual framework for analyzing public issues.

2. The Foreign Policy Association has generated several programs (pp. 187–89) that emphasize the social dimension, particularly with respect to international relations.

3. The Glens Falls Project of the National Council for the Social Studies in the Glens Falls (New York) Public School System emphasizes international relations.

4. Leonard Kenworthy (pp. 313–14) advocates intercultural study from the primary years on. (See *Introducing Children to the World* and *Social Studies for the Seventies.*)

5. Training-group approaches are described in *T-Group Theory and Laboratory Method,* by Benne, Gibb, and Bradford. These emphasize a variety of ways of helping people cope with interpersonal problems and develop greater interpersonal capacity. Schutz and Leonard (see 3 under "The Personal Dimension") also emphasize encounter-group approaches to increasing interpersonal awareness and capacity.

6. Dale L. Brubaker's *Social Studies in a Mass Society* emphasizes the problems of mass society.

7. The Chicago Anthropology Project, while based on the discipline of anthropology, emphasizes problems of freedom and authority in American culture and similar major issues in-

volved in understanding society. They do not employ a sequenced approach to the discipline so much as a social issues approach.

8. Mario Fantini and Gerald Weinstein, *Toward a Contact Curriculum* (New York: Ford Foundation, 1967) emphasizes basic social concerns as the point of entry.

9. The Lincoln-Filene Center for Citizenship and Public Affairs (pp. 167–75) has developed a number of diverse approaches to civics education. Current work emphasizes approaches to the study of race and culture in American life.

10. Improvement of ethnic and racial relations is the purpose of many curricula. Jean Grambs has developed a comprehensive guide to contemporary approaches and relevant literature.

THE PERSONAL DIMENSION

1. In the preventive psychiatry research at the University of Iowa (Ralph Ojemann, director), materials have been prepared to help children analyze and improve their development.

2. Approaches to role-playing (pp. 176–79) developed by Fanny and George Shaftel, Stanford University, emphasize growth in empathy, role-taking ability, and interpersonal capacity.

3. The writings of William Schutz (pp. 419, 420) and George B. Leonard emphasize the development of greater awareness and the expansion of emotional possibilities through sensitivity training.

4. David Hunt (pp. 220–24) has identified sets of teaching strategies that can be used to bring about personality growth, especially open-minded flexibility and greater ability to relate to others and deal with values.

25

The above list is partial. It scarcely indicates all the approaches emerging in school districts throughout the United States. In the area of black studies alone, there are projects on academic study using historians' techniques, social development through Black Power, and personal identity through study of the heritage. Schools and teachers need to become aware of the alternative approaches and to sort out the ones most useful in their own approach to the social studies.

It should be apparent that no one school or teacher can carry on curriculum efforts representing all the possibilities within the three dimensions. A middle school course represents only about

120 hours of instruction in one year. It can scarcely focus on two or three possibilities in each dimension and do any of them justice. Consequently, schools and teachers must choose their objectives. A carefully planned program cannot achieve more than a few closely integrated goals. Goals representing two or even three dimensions can be combined, as in a course with a sociological (academic) approach to racial (social) problems through which students clarify personal values and come to understand their biases.

Not only are there many possible goals, but the differences between them are often educationally significant. A curriculum designed to help children understand and cope with identity crises has a very different focus from one designed to help students comprehend and solve urban problems. The social studies teacher should not adopt one approach or curriculum project simply because it is produced locally or is well publicized. The different goals represent real potential differences in the lives of children and in service to society.

CHOICES TO MAKE

WITHIN THE INTELLECTUAL DIMENSION	WITHIN THE SOCIAL DIMENSION	WITHIN THE PERSONAL DIMENSION
Anthropology	Racial attitudes	Creativity
Sociology	Internationalism	Sensitivity
History	Interpersonal	Personality
Political science	behavior	Mental health
Social psychology	Urban affairs	Open-mindedness
Economics	National heritage	
Geography	and citizenship	

In this book we will explore each of the three dimensions, attempting to clarify goals and the means for carrying them out both in curriculum design and in teaching activities.

INQUIRIES

To Help the Reader Unify and Apply the Material in the Chapter

1. Obtain a current social studies curriculum guide. Analyze the provisions made for helping children grow in the intellectual, social, and personal dimensions. Develop recommendations for improving the provisions made in the curriculum guide to help children grow in the three dimensions.
2. From a social studies textbook series, select a book for the elementary years. Analyze the provisions it makes for helping children grow in the intellectual, social, and personal dimensions. If several class members were each to select and analyze a book from a different series, their analyses would probably constitute a useful survey.
3. Identify a contemporary social issue that you believe would interest elementary school children. Develop a plan for exploring it with children so that the intellectual, social, and personal dimensions come alive for them.

NOTES

1. John Dewey, *Experience and Education* (New York: Collier, 1963), p. 87.
2. José Ortega y Gasset, *The Mission of the University* (Princeton, N.J.: Princeton Univ. Press, 1944).
3. See Jerome S. Bruner, *The Process of Education* (Cambridge, Mass.: Harvard Univ. Press, 1960).
4. Charles A. Beard, *A Charter for the Social Sciences* (New York: Scribner, 1932), pp. 96–97.
5. Ibid., pp. 98–99.
6. F. H. George, *Automation, Cybernetics, and Society* (New York: Philosophical Library, 1959), pp. 11–13.
7. Beard, *Charter*, p. 100.
8. The original categorization was made by Maurice P. Hunt and Lawrence E. Metcalf, *High School Social Studies: Problems in Reflective Thinking and Social Understanding* (New York: Harper, 1955). This paraphrase comes from Franklin Patterson, "Citizenship and Schools for the American Future," in *Citizenship and a Free Society,* 30th Yearbook of the National Council for the Social Studies (Washington: National Education Assn., 1960), p. 12.

9. Jean D. Grambs, "The Challenge to the Social Studies," in *Citizenship and a Free Society*, 30th Yearbook of the National Council for the Social Studies (Washington: National Education Assn., 1960), pp. 281–82.

10. Stephen R. Graubard, "Preface to 'Excellence and Leadership in a Democracy,'" *Daedalus* 90 (Fall 1961), p. 626.

11. Dewey, *Experience and Education*, p. 88.

12. Fred Powledge, "Primary Day? What Primary? Excuses Keep Many From Polls," *New York Times*, June 3, 1964.

13. See John U. Michaelis, *Social Studies for Children in a Democracy* (Englewood Cliffs, N.J.: Prentice-Hall, 1956).

14. James Hoetker and William P. Ahlbrand, Jr., "The Persistence of the Recitation," *American Education Research Journal* 6 (March 1969), pp. 145–68. This article provides an excellent summary of research findings on teaching methods.

15. Paul R. Hanna, "Design for a Social Studies Program," *Focus on the Social Studies* (Washington: National Education Assn., Department of Elementary School Principals, 1965), p. 39.

16. Ibid., p. 43.

17. See, for example, the units developed in the Horace Mann–Lincoln School, such as: Tompsie Baxter and Bess M. Young, *Ships and Navigation* (New York: Teachers College, Columbia Univ., 1933).

18. Bernard Berelson and others, *The Social Studies and the Social Sciences*, American Council of Learned Societies and the National Council for the Social Studies (New York: Harcourt, Brace & World, 1962), pp. 6–7.

19. Gresham M. Sykes, "Sociology," in *The Social Studies and the Social Sciences*, American Council of Learned Societies and the National Council for the Social Studies (New York: Harcourt, Brace & World, 1962), p. 157.

20. Anthropology Curriculum Project, *The Concept of Culture: Teachers Guide, Grade Four* (Athens: Univ. of Georgia, 1965), pp. 1–2.

21. Ibid., p. 1.

22. Edith West, *Preparation and Evaluation of Social Studies Curriculum Guides and Materials for Grades K–14* (Washington: U.S. Office of Education, 1969).

23. Michaelis, *Social Studies for Children in a Democracy*, p. 1.

24. Ibid., p. 18.

25. Ibid., pp. 13–18.

26. James M. Becker and Howard D. Mehlinger, eds., *International Dimensions in the Social Studies*, 38th Yearbook of the National Council for the Social Studies (Washington: National Education Assn., 1968), p. 9.

27. Donald W. Oliver and James P. Shaver, *Teaching Public Issues in the High School* (Boston: Houghton Mifflin, 1966).

28. Ibid., p. 13.

29. A. S. Neill, *Summerhill* (New York: Hart Publishing, 1960), p. 24.

28

30. Edgar Z. Friedenberg, *Coming of Age in America: Growth and Acquiescence* (New York: Random House, 1965), p. 12.

31. Carl Rogers, *Client-Centered Therapy* (Boston: Houghton Mifflin, 1965); Arthur W. Combs, *The Professional Education of Teachers* (Boston: Allyn & Bacon, 1965); Arthur T. Jersild, *In Search of Self* (New York: Teachers College, Columbia Univ., 1952).

32. Jersild, *In Search of Self*, p. 103.

33. E. Paul Torrance, *Rewarding Creative Behavior* (Englewood Cliffs, N.J.: Prentice-Hall, 1965), p. 11.

34. Ibid., p. 12.

29

part 1

THE INTELLECTUAL DIMENSION

THE
SPIRIT
OF THE
SOCIAL
SCIENCES

Scholarly information has increased so greatly that even a specialist cannot master the knowledge in his field. We need a method for sorting out the truly important material and organizing it in such a way that the relatively few things we are able to teach have maximum educational effect.

For many years educators have pondered how the central ideas in each scholarly field might be identified and translated so that even a child can learn up-to-date ideas and ways of thinking. A half century ago John Dewey suggested that the main ideas of each subject discipline be organized and taught. He argued that the scholar and the educator, working together, might find a means whereby a learner could be led to construct advanced ideas out of his own experience, at first simply and then in more complex forms.[1] Some years later Charles Hubbard Judd similarly stated that the specialist should select the significant "lines of thought," which the teacher should organize in a way suitable for presentation to "immature minds."[2] Alfred North Whitehead phrased the suggestion in a slightly different fashion when he proposed that a few especially illuminating ideas be identified and then introduced early and reiterated until the learner could use them with ease:

> Let the main ideas which are introduced into a child's education be few and important, and let them be thrown into every combination possible. The child should make them his own, and should understand their application here and now in the circumstances of his actual life. From the very beginning of his education, the child should experience the joy of discovery. The discovery which he has to make is that general ideas give an understanding of that stream of events which pours through his life, which is his life.[3]

What is the nature of these main ideas? Charles A. Beard defined their essential character as follows:

> The social sciences are primarily concerned with those manifestations of human activity and those activities occurring within society which involve social *consequences* and *relations*—called for convenience political, economic, and cultural—and with the *interrelationships* which accompany the functioning of society as a whole in its world setting.[4]

About ten years ago in a report on a conference of scholars, Jerome Bruner restated and popularized this approach.[5] According to Bruner, scholarly endeavor leads to a series of major ideas explaining the findings within a subject area. The scholar collects facts, which he explains and organizes according to the relations he sees between them. When established as working principles, these relations may be called organizing concepts.[6]

Anthropology provides an example of the development of a major organizing concept. Early in anthropological research it was established that each human society has developed distinctive modes of behavior, or norms. This concept was recognized even by the ancient Greeks. The idea that culture conditions the psychological makeup of individuals, however, was not formulated until the 1930s, when Ruth Benedict found that the Southwest Pueblos thought in ways strikingly different from those of surrounding peoples, even though their physical environment was similar. She reasoned that the difference was the result of a unique "psychological set," or orientation toward reality, evolving within a society. Culture, she concluded, affects the very ways in which minds work. This discovery made the facts of anthropology more understandable, and prompted a search for more information and relations of the same sort in other cultures.[7]

Another example of the evolution of an organizing concept may be seen in the socioeconomic experiments conducted in 1927 at a Western Electric plant in Hawthorne, Illinois. For generations, business managers (and even economists) had assumed that labor was a commodity to be bought and sold, and that therefore higher wages or longer hours increased total output. If a factory worker's wages were increased, he would work faster and process more items; if his workday were lengthened, he would have time to produce more. The Hawthorne experiments scotched these assumptions. For almost a year, a group of girls assembling telephone relays at the plant were subjects in experiments testing their reaction to changes in hours, wages, and rest periods. It was found that throughout the experiment, the girls' output of relays increased regardless of whether their pay and working conditions were made better or worse. The scientists conducting the research finally discovered that the experiment itself had introduced a new incentive. "By putting them in a little friendly society of their own, by consulting them often, the scientists had caused a psychological change in these young women and given them a new sense of their status and value. The girls were no longer cogs in an impersonal, pecuniary machine; they were helping in a small way to direct the machine. So their output went up no matter how conditions were changed under them."[8]

Two organizing concepts, with social as well as economic implications, resulted from these experiments. First, workers (perhaps all men) can be highly motivated if their interest is engaged and they realize that both they and their work are important. Second, a group of workers (or any similar group of allied persons) constitutes a microsociety, within which will grow all the customary societal teams, bands, and personal alliances; these must be considered and, if possible, utilized.[9]

Bruner has provided a series of hypotheses concerning the application of organizing concepts to education:

1. In the scholarly disciplines, the major organizing concepts are essentially very simple.
2. These concepts can be developed in a form that even young children can discover (in childish terms, at first, and gradually in more sophisticated forms).
3. Organizing concepts can be utilized as focal themes in curricula, to be reiterated and rediscovered in more complex and adequate terms as one advances through the grades.

4. The child who is taught so that he discovers the organizing concepts in disciplines will benefit for the following reasons:
   a) Organizing concepts facilitate memory. Learning how things are related makes it easier to remember facts.
   b) Organizing concepts provide intellectual power by ensuring greater comprehension of the area concerned.
   c) Organizing concepts facilitate transfer of learning to new situations and problems.
   d) Organizing concepts are the language of the scholar. By learning these concepts the learner is brought closer to the leading edge of the discipline. He learns to think with the most advanced minds in the field.[10]

These hypotheses are so tantalizing that one might ask why we do not immediately proceed to test them. One problem is that the social sciences include a variety of disciplines. Unlike the preparation of a math curriculum, which usually requires the teamwork of only mathematicians and educators, the preparation of a social studies curriculum requires the joint efforts of political scientists, economists, historians, and other social scientists. The ideas from each discipline must be mixed together.

Another problem is that the social sciences have yet to organize a system of concepts as thoroughly as have the natural sciences. The older social sciences lack a tradition of quantitative methods; usually their primary concepts are not expressed with the mathematical logic that has helped sort out the content of the natural sciences. In many of the older disciplines, especially history and political science, behaviorists who think in terms of systems and quantitative tools have been criticized for using positivistic tools.[11] Although the new social sciences, such as social psychology, are accustomed to using quantitative approaches, they are vexed by their newness. Their content is developing so fast that their taxonomies, terms, and methods are less distinct than those of the older disciplines.

A third problem is that the social world is elusive. It submits to observation, analysis, and experimentation less readily than does the physical world. For example, social psychology must define *attitude* in several ways, because attitudes manifest themselves variously and differ enormously according to conditions. Uncertainty in the social sciences is reflected in the statistical levels of confidence they use compared with those used in the natural sciences. The psychologist will accept a proposition at the level of a 5 percent probability of error. Imagine a physicist who reported that we could accept his observation that day is brighter than night, with the probability that he would be correct nineteen out of twenty times!

Only through a long-term effort by both social scientists and educators can the organizing concepts of the social sciences be defined for use by teachers. The educators involved in such work must not only be acquainted with behavioral sciences, but also be able to translate concepts into operational constructs appropriate for children. (Operational constructs are ideas that are used to analyze social life, but they are continually revised to fit new information and new insights; the child needs constructs that are written within his range of competence so that he can modify them.) During the last ten years, a variety of theories, experiments, and materials of instruction have been developed. This work is still experimental, however, and the bulk of the inquiry has yet to take shape.

Organizing Concepts as Modes of Inquiry

The work of defining organizing concepts for the social sciences is likely to be based on certain assumptions about the kind of knowledge that should be taught. Already in the seventeenth century a Czech educator named Comenius (1592–1670) tried to judge content by its social utility.[12] He viewed education as the process by which a child approaches and solves problems and acquires certain ideas about the world. His English contemporary John Locke (1632–1704) saw childhood as the time when the child acquires the essential knowledge that prepares him to be a rational thinker. He believed that the ideas of past thinkers should be mastered by the child in preparation for the time when he, too, would be able to be an independent thinker. This view of subject matter, or some version of it, prevailed to the end of the nineteenth century. Once something had been "found out," it took its place as a fact to be learned.

The pragmatists struck hard at the notion that knowledge is fixed. They differentiated between physical reality and human conceptions of it. Because our conceptions of reality are imperfect, subject matter is imperfect. It is a product of the mind rather than an accurate representation of external reality. John Dewey, a pragmatist, said:

> All knowledge, as issuing from reflection, is experimental in the literal physical sense of experimental. . . . It involves the explorations by which relevant data are procured and the physical analyses by which they are refined and made precise; it comprises the readings by which information is got hold of, the words which are experimented with, and the calculations by which the significance of entertained conceptions or hypotheses is elaborated.[13]

The pragmatists turned scholarly ideas into hypotheses. A conclusion is not a concept that will last forever, but a hypothesis that merits further experimentation. This view of knowledge emphasizes that knowledge is constructed, not given externally.

Although this constructionist view accords with what is happening in every scholarly discipline, textbooks and instructional methods have largely concentrated on identifying verbal conclusions that can be taught to children. A social studies text for elementary school, for example, contains statements of conclusions to be learned. ("The greatest corn-growing region of our country is the north central states. It is called the corn belt." "In most of the Latin American nations the greatest problems are poverty and lack of education." "The Christian Church gave Europe a kind of unity in feudal times.") Most of these books, however, cover too many topics too quickly to permit the presentation of data from which the conclusions were deduced. Knowledge, then—at least the conception of knowledge that we frequently teach children— becomes a system of pronouncements. When we ask children to learn statements as if those statements represented fixed and unchanging ideas, we are teaching them a conception of the nature of knowledge that is obsolete.

Organizing Concepts and Certainty

What is an organizing concept? In explaining his term *structure*, Bruner says that it is "the way things are related." This definition

Constructionist view
of knowledge

may be interpreted to mean that an organizing concept formulates the way we *think* things are related. Bruner gives the example of an inchworm crawling up graph paper held at various inclinations. The inchworm varies its path across the graph paper so that its angle of climb does not exceed a certain proportion. We have discovered a relation between slope and climb.

How does the identification of that relation help us select content for the child to learn? This will become apparent as we examine another living organism to see whether it moves in patterns similar to those of the inchworm. If we look at the movements of a sunflower plant, for example, we find that it reacts to directions and intensity of illumination, turning its blossom to face the light source. We could examine further examples, but perhaps these will be sufficient to show that we have discovered a principle called tropism, an innate tendency to react to a stimulus in a definite way. The tropistic relation between organisms and stimuli can be considered an organizing concept in those sciences that study the physical behavior of living things. A person who discovers the idea of tropism is prepared to investigate similar behavior in other organisms.

Bruner suggests that if we can identify the major concepts in a discipline we will have identified the organization of that discipline. By teaching, or at least introducing, organizing concepts to a child, we help him organize the things he learns in a way similar to the way a scholar organizes the information in his discipline. By teaching organizing concepts we avoid teaching fragmented bits of knowledge from a field. The child is thus more likely to comprehend an area of knowledge as well as remember what he has learned. His learning will be much closer to front-line scholarly thinking. Furthermore, a program of instruction that is centered around organizing concepts will encourage the child to discover relations and hence prepare him to be an independent thinker. Bruner rather carefully stresses that the concepts developed by a child for his own use need not be in the sophisticated form a scholar would use. A child should discover organizing concepts in a form he can handle, and then rediscover more and more complex and adequate forms as he advances through the curriculum. The practice of revising concepts will keep him from believing that present knowledge will last for all time.

Joseph Schwab has approached the idea of organizing concepts in a manner similar to Bruner's. Schwab emphasizes the changing

39

views of subject matter that recent scientific discoveries have forced upon us:

> Forty years ago, it was possible for many scientists and most educators to nurse the illusion that science was a matter of patiently seeking the facts of nature and accurately reporting them. The conclusions of science were supposed to be nothing more than the summaries of these facts. . . . By the mid-twenties, the revolution in physics had gone so far that we were faced with the fact that some of the oldest and least questioned of our ideas could no longer be treated as literally true—or literally false. . . . Our old assertions about these matters were changed because physicists agreed to treat them in a new way— neither as self-evident truths nor as matters for immediate empirical verification. They were to be treated, instead, as *principles of enquiry*, conceptual structures which could be revised when necessary in directions dictated by large complexes of theory, diverse bodies of data, and numerous criteria of progress in sciences.[14]

The tentative nature of organizing concepts should be revealed to children as they pursue their inquiries. Imagine, for example, that second-graders are studying an Eskimo family. They find that various family members perform various functions. They learn that when a person does certain things regularly his cluster of behaviors can be referred to as a *role* (one of the organizing concepts shared by sociology and anthropology). Having got a notion of what roles are, they then study a Navaho family and soon begin to conclude that the sexes in families have distinct roles—the men do certain things and the women certain other things. In studying the American family, they find that sex roles of American men and women are becoming less and less distinct. Males are doing housework, females are earning money, both paint the house and drive the car, and so on.

In the first place, the children learned the idea of role as it pertained to the Eskimo. Then, studying the Navaho, they concentrated on ideas about sex roles. Finally, they had to revise their conclusions about sex roles to see that roles are not always clear or well defined. These second-graders, engaging in sociological exploration, had to develop, test, and revise ideas just as the social scientist does.

In sum, organizing concepts function within the social sciences in several ways. They show how things are related in any given sphere of inquiry. They provide a basis for organizing knowledge in a field. They guide the search for further knowledge.

40

Functions of organizing concepts

Using Organizing Concepts in Education

How can these concepts function in education? We want the organizing concepts we present to become, insofar as possible, part of the learner's intellectual equipment that he uses to attack new problems. To achieve this ultimate goal, they should serve one or more of the following functions:

1. They should illuminate a child's study of topics, such as American history, that he will meet throughout life. Such concepts will get exercise and thus become second nature to the child.
2. They should be applicable to the social and personal problems dealt with in the curriculum. The study of economic relations in his own community, for example, should produce some organizing concepts that the child can apply to the study of economic relations in other nations or in other periods of American history.

Just as organizing concepts provide the scholar with methods for acquiring knowledge, so should these organizing concepts provide the child with a systematic method of attack on areas where he seeks new knowledge. When the child learns how rainfall and land use are related in the United States, he may consider that relation in examining land use or climate in other nations. As he learns how political beliefs and economic interests were related in Revolutionary times, he may inquire whether the same relation holds true today. If organizing concepts are to be useful educationally, it will be because we have found a method for helping children to learn them and to employ them in pursuing research of their own.

An Example of a Child Practicing Social Science

Let us look at an example of a child in a school laboratory specially designed to help children explore cultures by using anthropological concepts. What is described here takes place at the Broad River School in Norwalk, Connecticut. The description focuses on the inquiry of a fourth-grade student named Charles. His teacher is Mrs. Josephine Green. From a large bank of data Charles retrieves information about an Indian pueblo community. Mrs. Green helps him teach himself social science concepts that can improve and extend his inquiry. Yet, throughout his work, Charles formulates his own questions, withdraws material from the banks of data, and organizes his own findings.

In the following presentation, side notes help identify social science methods presented to the student as he pursues his inquiry.[15]

Nine-year-old Charles takes his seat in a small room. It is fairly dark, but its walls are covered with drawings of ceremonial articles from a certain New Mexico pueblo. There are pictures of the town from the 1880s to the present.

Charles has a tape recorder and a slide projector. His teacher has shown him how to operate the tape recorder and given him a tape. He threads it and begins to listen.

"Welcome to La Stella," the voice on the tape begins. "La Stella is a small town in New Mexico. While it is not very large, it is very important to the people who try to understand human beings. For La Stella has been where it is for a long time. Many people have studied it and tried to understand it for almost four hundred years.

"You are now *in* La Stella. Oh, you are not really there, of course. But in this room there are over four thousand pictures and written pages and maps and charts that can tell you something about La Stella. And every picture and every written page has a tape recording that goes with it. You can get information about La Stella by listening as well as by watching and reading.

"In this room you can visit La Stella and learn about it by looking at pictures, reading, and listening to tapes. Whenever you have a question about La Stella, write it on a card and give it to your teacher. He will give you a number. You look up that number in the storage center across the room, and you can get the slides and tapes you need in order to try to answer your question. Then you can make a record of what you learn on your card.

Note that Charles's orientation was not teacher-directed (which often means teacher-dominated). Charles embarked on his study alone.

43

Even though Charles is proceeding on his own, he is conscious of support. His teacher is there on a standby basis. It is his project, but she is with him all the way.

From the beginning, Charles's experiences are with several media. He will continue throughout to use many different sources, both visual and auditory.

44

Charles sees the importance of classifying and arranging information for easy access. Gradually he'll learn to use more sophisticated systems of information retrieval.

"Before you begin, let's take a little trip to La Stella to give you some idea what it is like there. Turn on your slide projector and show yourself the first slide in the box in front of you. It's the one marked 'Orientation to La Stella.' In this slide you see a mountain. Now look at your map of La Stella. Do you see the number 1? If you were in La Stella, and you were to stand at the 1 and look toward the south, you would see this mountain.

"Now show yourself the next slide. In *this* picture you can see—"

The voice goes on, leading Charles through a guided tour of the pueblo and showing him how to obtain the tapes and slides that contain pictures or written descriptions of the various aspects of the pueblo.

After the "tour," Charles is given another tape and a group of slides. They start him off on one of several tasks or assignments designed to help him explore pueblo culture. This is also teaching him to try the methods used by social scientists as he explores. The first job given by the tape is: "Learn all you can about La Stella until you think you are ready to teach someone else about it."

"Do they play baseball in La Stella?" is the first question Charles wonders about. He is given the number for "Sports and Recreation" by his teacher. Using this number, he retrieves twenty 35 mm slides and shows them to himself. He discovers that baseball (among several other athletic games) *is* played in La Stella. On his 3-by-5 file card where he had written his question he now writes his answer, "Yes, they play baseball and other things." In a very natural way he has used a recording technique that any social scientist would use.

He asks another question. "What kind of animals do they have in La Stella?" This time Mrs. Green gives him two numbers, and he retrieves two batches of slides, one for "Domesticated animals" and one for "Fauna." He finds out about domesticated cattle and horses, and begins to absorb information about desert animals of several kinds.

The animals are so different from the ones he knows that he is prompted to ask: "What is the land like?" and "What is the weather like?" Again he gets numbers that refer him to quantities of slides, some with pictures, some with graphs, and some with written passages on them. It takes him a long time to progress through this batch of slides, for he has trouble extracting meaning from some of the charts. He asks for tapes and with the help of the taped commentary he is able to use the charts more comfortably.

When he has trouble interpreting the charts, Charles gets an assist from the tapes. This allows for individual differences; another child might not have needed them.

These activities take two or three days. At the end of each session Charles returns to the normal activities of his class.

Several days later Charles is still asking questions: "How do they get water?" "What are their houses like?" "How do people make a living?"

Now his interest takes a new turn and he writes on a card: "What is their religion?" With the information he gets from the last question, Charles begins to grasp the fact that the pueblo reveals a very complex pattern of interaction among several cultures. He would not articulate it that way, of course. But more than likely he is thinking something like this: "Hey, they have their own religion and they are Catholics, too. The Spanish tried to make them stop their own religion, but they wouldn't do it, even when the soldiers killed some of them. Now lots of them work in the towns near there, where the people are just like us. That is, they're not Indians. But there is trouble between our people and the people from La Stella. I wonder if they have their own country." (Charles is thinking of *nationality* but he isn't saying that yet.)

Interaction between cultures is a fundamental part of the social studies. Children need to recognize these patterns and identify ways in which such interaction takes place.

45

On a new card he asks, "What country are the people of La Stella from?"

He discovers that they are United States citizens, but they were once colonials of Mexico, and before that Spain. Before that, they governed themselves.

"Who makes their laws?" In return for this question he finds information about the internal political organization of the pueblo (tribal) and its relation to the United States government and the government of New Mexico. He also sees that some members of the La Stella tribe have political and religious duties that overlap or are entwined. Now he remembers his earlier question about religion. Triggered by the information he received, he

Can you see that Charles is really having an interdisciplinary experience? He has studied ideas from both political science and ethnology

in pursuing the early government of La Stella.

asks, "What are their religious stories like?" As a result of asking this, Charles receives a group of old myths, rewritten from notes made by anthropologists who first visited La Stella around 1880. He finds them intriguing.

The myths are very rich. To a sophisticated reader they would tell much about the feelings and thoughts of the people of La Stella. To Charles, however, they are beautiful and strange stories. He likes them, but he does not know what to make of them. He discusses them with Mrs. Green. He has some questions but Mrs. Green avoids direct answers. Charles and Mrs. Green "think out" the questions together.

One morning when Charles arrives at school he tells Mrs. Green that he is ready to teach another youngster about La Stella. She gives him a reel of magnetic tape, and he makes the following statement, transcribed here just as Charles dictated it:

Charles is going to be a teacher!—a tremendous motivation for him to record what he knows—the exact opposite of being assigned to write a report to show what he learned.

46

Charles isn't thinking in paragraphs. Neither are his thoughts very well organized as yet. But he goes readily from one idea to another with simple if unthought-out logic. This is typical of a researcher in his early stages.

"La Stella. In the town of La Stella, which is in the United States, there are many people. These people are Indians. They have founded the town many many years ago. The families of La Stella are supported by usually the father. The most important income to the family is that what comes from the making of pottery. This pottery is used for many things in the home. Sometimes it's just decoration, sometimes it is used for things like carrying water, and holding corn and corn meal, and many other things. They also are farmers in La Stella. The men take care of the farms and when a boy gets old enough he is able to help the parent. On the farm there are grown wheat and corn and other things. This corn can be used as to making bread, and so can the wheat, and it can be sold to people from out of town for use. The education of the children of La Stella starts at the age of five—as the normal school here does. They go through until sixth grade, and if they want any more education they have to go out of town to boarding schools. People have been leaving La Stella because the Indian ways are harder and old-fashioned, and they have found out by leaving the town to go to school and for other things. The Indians do not believe in following the white man's ways. They do not like our ways because they have not been used by the ancestors of their town. The Indians do not like our ways but they participate in many of the things we do, such as playing baseball and other—um—events such as this. They also wear our kinds of clothes except for sometimes they wear headdress and beads and moccasins. In La Stella the weather is very humid. Due to the heat, sometimes they have many droughts. In the winter it is cold and sometimes—it ain't very often [tape not clear here]—they have snow, but in the spring they have warm weather, and it's very dry. In the summer they have rain, which is usually a lot of rain, but they still have to use irrigation instead of—um—this rain-water—um—just depending on the rains that come. They have to irrigate. The town itself is very small. The houses themselves are made of adobe, which is clay. And on the inside the floor is either made of wood or adobe, and in the middle of the house, which is very curious, they have a large pole. And on the pole they hang many things such as coats, and they hang—instead of having cradles they hang their children from the ceiling in like a basket. The pole is also used to help the ceiling hold up. On the ceiling instead of having it like painted they have like tar paper going across the ceiling. The normal home has a herd of horses to itself. It's not exactly a herd, but it's a group of horses that is owned by the family. The children play in many games, in events—such as races and special relay games—and the children also play some doing the thing we play, such as hopscotch and jump rope, and even baseball. But baseball is mostly played on good events like saints' days. If someone should get sick in La Stella, they would have as much care as they would here. There are no facilities that they have that we don't have and we don't have anything that they don't. It is a very odd town because of the old ways and the houses and everything, but it is still part of the United States and the people have the right to vote and everything that we have a right to. And as I said there are no facilities such as—um—um—household appliances mostly. Some houses have them, but very few do. La Stella is a very interesting place because of the way that they live that is so different from us. Another source of income is

Charles rather naturally focuses on cultural comparison, interpreting La Stella in terms of his own life.

Charles speaks in specifics rather than vague generalities. From his description the reader can easily picture the inside of the pueblo house.

47

Unconsciously Charles is delineating the economic structure of La Stella.

Children are usually able to apply generalizations before they are ready to make them their own. Practice in the one leads to the other.

selling pottery itself and making drums. Drums are made from animal hides and gourds. The drums are very colorful and they also bring a lot of money from tourists. Tourists come just to see how the people live and festivals in La Stella. They have many events such as I have mentioned as the sports. And they also have dances. In these dances they wear special costumes, such as very colorful hats and feathers and very religious clothing as to their faith used to be. The normal clothing is still like ours, but they still wear the clothes that they used to wear long ago—"

Charles plays back his tape several times. He likes what he hears. He decides it would give the listener a good picture of La Stella.

So far, in his excursions to the laboratory, Charles has been an interested inquirer. He has learned many facts about La Stella. However, his search is raw and unsophisticated. He simply raises questions as they come to mind. He knows no systematic way to inquire into a society, whether his own or another.

Mrs. Green, fortunately, has many available ways of helping Charles to learn to study a society as a social scientist would. She can give him practice applying social science generalizations. She can give him material designed to teach him the methods of archaeology, anthropology, geography, sociology, economics, or social psychology. She has materials designed to teach him how the social scientist formulates questions, collects and organizes data, and builds theories. She also has devised tasks or assignments designed to confront Charles with the kinds of problems that social scientists study.

If Charles is to proceed as a social scientist, he can carry on activities by himself part of the time. But in other situations he will become one of a group that is using the methods of social scientists to solve problems.

Mrs. Green has studied Charles's pattern of questions and his description of the pueblo. She decides that he should begin to work with structured tasks that will help him to substantiate generalizations such as the ones that social scientists use for drawing conclusions. She attaches him to a group of three other children who have also been studying La Stella. She introduces them to Prestonport, the New England community that is also in the data bank. Having had the research experience with La Stella, the children pursue their questions about Prestonport in a somewhat more orderly fashion (but not entirely so by adult standards). Almost automatically they begin to make comparisons between La Stella and Prestonport.

Daily, they come to the laboratory and try to apply social science generalizations to the two societies. In one meeting, the group listens to a tape that organizes their tasks and then presents the generalizations. Excerpts from the tape, plus five of the generalizations, follow:

Prestonport and La Stella are towns whose people belong to different societies. La Stella is an Indian society which has been influenced by the Spanish and by European society. Prestonport is an example of the North American version of a Western society.

Social scientists who have studied different societies have come to believe certain things about human societies. For example, they believe that all societies have religion, families, sports, and certain other things.

We want to listen to several statements that social scientists make about societies and see if you can find out whether those statements are true with respect to La Stella and Prestonport. For example, if we gave you the statement, "All societies have religion," you might ask to see the information we have about religion in La Stella and Prestonport. You will find that both have religions—in fact, each has more than one form of religion.

Statement 1: All societies divide people by age and give people of different ages different things to do. Children, for example, do different things from old people.

Find out if this is true in La Stella. You may ask any questions you wish about La Stella. Your teacher will give you numbers in response to your questions so you will know where to look to find information to help you

Flexible grouping is a characteristic of the new social studies. Similar interests, problems, or abilities are all bases for grouping.

La Stella and Prestonport are about the same size. It is easier to compare two cultures if they have a similar degree of complexity—in other words some basis for comparison.

Note the tone of what is said on the tape. It talks to Charles with clarity but never with condescension.

49

How often do you present generalizations to your class for discussion and testing? Note that these generalizations have varying degrees of authenticity.

decide whether the statement applies. Discuss your ideas with each other. When you have decided what you think, please call your teacher. [The same procedure is suggested after each statement.]

Statement 2: Most adults (grown-ups) in all societies are married. Find out if this is true in La Stella and Prestonport.

Statement 3: In all societies, the father is more likely to have authority (be the boss) than is the mother. In other words, the leader of the family is likely to be the father. Is this true in La Stella and Prestonport?

Statement 4: The closer you get to the center of a modern town, the less money the people who live there are likely to have. Is this true in Prestonport?

Statement 5: If a society depends on industry (factories or places that make things) families under one roof are likely to be smaller (just father, mother, and children) than when a society depends on herding and farming. (Then families under one roof often include uncles, aunts, grandfather, grandmother, and so on.) Is this true for La Stella and Prestonport?

The children cannot research all the concepts. If they could, it would indicate that the exercise was geared below the proper level. The strategy lets them select concepts and emphasize one or two that especially interest them.

The laboratory uses materials from many social studies projects to introduce students

The children retrieve data from the storage centers and debate their answers to the questions. In all, they try to validate ten generalizations. In a sense they are having a practice exercise. Its purpose is to familiarize them with the types of concepts that social scientists use to guide their study of society. Mrs. Green then asks them to see if they can find out whether the statements are true for their own town. They return in a week with solutions to seven concepts, but have been unable to find information about the other three.

Quite a few weeks have gone by. Charles is now working with two friends. Mrs. Green decides they should learn how to analyze tangible aspects of cultures. The first step involves their working through two of the units from the University of Chicago Economics Program, which was developed for use in grades four to six. The units she selects are designed to introduce the children to concepts that are used to analyze trade and the use of capital investment. With occasional help from Mrs. Green, Charles and his two friends proceed with the economics units and keep a careful list of the economics concepts.

Next, Mrs. Green presents them with another tape, labeled "Orientation—The New Business Task." They find they are being asked to study La Stella and Prestonport once more. This time their job is to make recommendations about the kinds of businesses likely to thrive in the two towns.

Once again they begin to ask questions and to retrieve information about La Stella and Prestonport. At first their questions are awkward and unordered; again they have no strategies. But during their second hour Charles has an "aha" experience. "Hey," he says, "how about some of those ideas we just learned? Didn't some of them have something to do with starting a business?" They discuss this, and eventually decide to try to identify products for which there would be a special demand within either town. They concentrated on products which La Stella and Prestonport are in an especially good position to create.

Using the question and number method, they retrieve information on house furnishings, diet, and transportation and find that nearly all of these are well satisfied by businesses that already exist in Prestonport. But such businesses are not found in La Stella, where nearly all furnishings and foodstuffs are purchased in stores outside the pueblo. And so their search goes on. All together they explore the possibility of more than thirty businesses before arriving at a list of five which they feel they can defend.

When they discuss their list with Mrs. Green, she has some suggestions to make, but she does not ask them to continue this task. Before she can suggest what they should do next, one of the boys says, "Don't tell us, we've guessed. Now you want us to find some good businesses for our own town."

During the next two weeks, the boys study their own home community. They develop a list of possible businesses and Mrs. Green decides that they are ready to deal with more difficult concepts that pertain to the

to social studies ideas. The Chicago Economics Program (pp. 119–22) teaches students sets of ideas from economics.

A sign of Charles's growth is his ability to list and record concepts. He would not have recognized these concepts when he first started.

While Charles still lacks strategies at the beginning of a new project, he now is able to establish them more quickly.

51

Charles and his friends are beginning to relate and apply to their own community the organizing concepts they have learned while studying other cultures.

whole of a culture. To prepare them, she introduces a set of self-instructional units which were developed by the University of Georgia Anthropology Project. These units are designed to teach children how to analyze cultures using the cultural universals—a set of concepts that can be applied to the study of any culture.

Weeks later, when they are asking for another problem to solve, Mrs. Green gives them their last assignment: "One way that cultures change is by borrowing and trading with other cultures. See if you can find out how La Stella has changed over the years by borrowing things and ways of doing things originally developed by other people. You may find that life in La Stella has changed in some ways, but not in others. If you think of the cultural universals, they may help you find places where La Stella has both changed and stayed the same."

This activity stresses that borrowing from other cultures is one of the primary methods of cultural change —a basic generalization children should be exposed to over and over again.

Once again the boys begin to retrieve information about La Stella. They work for nearly two weeks, spending about an hour a day in the laboratory. When they have finished, they make a tape recording. It is their end-of-the-year project and they remake the recording several times before they are satisfied to have Mrs. Green listen to it. The transcript follows:

La Stella is a small Indian village in New Mexico. It is called a *pueblo*, which is the Spanish name for *town*. When the Spanish first saw La Stella hundreds of years ago, that was the name they gave it.

Compare this report with Charles's original tape. Now he is "thinking in paragraphs." He identifies causative factors and shows their results.

The Spanish gave La Stella Pueblo many things besides its name. The Indians didn't have any horses or cattle until the Spanish came. They had fire, but the Spanish taught them how to build stoves out of adobe. They had their own religion, with their own gods, but the Spanish taught them the religion of Christianity. Up till then they had used the water from the river to flood their fields. The Spanish had the idea of making ditches.

The Pueblo Indians didn't always like what the Spanish brought them. They really didn't like to be Christians. But the Spanish soldiers were strong and sometimes mean. The Indians pretended to be Christians, and kept their old religion, too.

In that time, the Spanish and Indians were living close together. They borrowed and stole from one another. The Spanish took jewelry when they could, and Indian blankets. They liked the Indian adobe for houses, and when they built their town, Santa Fe, they used adobe bricks for houses. We don't know how the Indians plowed their fields before the Spanish came, but afterward they used horses and Spanish plows; and they learned to talk Spanish. So they borrowed, too.

When New Mexico became part of our country, La Stella Pueblo seemed like a Mexican town. The people spoke Spanish and wore some Mexican clothes. Their ovens were Spanish and their plows. They even had carts with big wooden wheels like the kind they have in Spain! But they weren't Spanish or Mexican—they were Indians.

Now the people who live in La Stella seem like other Americans. They dress like us, have schools like ours, and they all speak English (except the very old people, who don't). They have television and new machinery for their farms. Some of the young men from La Stella are fighting in Vietnam. The fathers are working in the American towns. They want to be more American. They remember their old ways and their old religion, but they want to be more like Americans now.

This is about what the people of La Stella have borrowed from their neighbors.

Although he is not stating specific social science concepts, he has grasped the basic elements of the economic system and is aware of the process of cultural change and exchange. He sees the culture more as a whole than just in fragments. He is beginning to internalize organizing concepts and use them as he thinks.

You can sense the growth that has taken place because of the children's experience. The content shows perception and illustrates concepts developed throughout the study. Charles is more objective in his choice and treatment of ideas.

The Broad River Laboratory

The backbone of the Broad River School laboratory is a set of data banks for children. Each data bank is a random-access data-storage and retrieval system on a particular culture, such as the pueblo called La Stella and the small New England town of Prestonport. Other storage systems on small towns around the world are being added, each representing a particular cultural pattern.

To make the data bank, a research team started with the index system used to store anthropological data.[16] The major categories (seventy-nine) together with the subcategories (up to ten for each major category) provide a complete spectrum for any known culture. Working with original sources, the team obtained information about each of the towns. For the pueblo, these sources included results of archaeological explorations, pictures and field notes of anthropologists between 1850 and 1900, government records, and work by contemporary anthropologists.

In addition, a research team traveled to each town, took hundreds of pictures, interviewed citizens, and collected much information from state and federal government sources. The team then rewrote information, put pictures together with written passages, and created charts and graphs, in an attempt to fill all possible categories with information packages so that, with the aid of tapes, an average second-grader could have access to it.

The laboratory uses a couple of methods to encourage the children to think for themselves: all items emphasize facts rather than interpretations; tape-film-map orientation units allow the children to be maximally free of the teacher. In this situation the teacher serves mainly in two ways. First, she translates questions into index numbers, a procedure the child is not ready to attempt. Second, she selects tasks or assignments that gradually increase the child's ability to apply the tactics of the social sciences to the study of human culture. She also has at hand some self-instructional units and tasks.

Applying the Laboratory Techniques

Charles, his friends, and Mrs. Green are part of an experiment in ways of teaching children to "try on" the concepts and methods of the social sciences. Its ultimate goal is to teach children to analyze their social life and that of other cultures with the tools of the social scientist. But some of what they are doing can happen in any classroom. Many of the materials, in fact, are the products of curriculum projects and are available to schools at a nominal cost.

The basic teaching strategy used in this example involves two simple steps: identifying the concepts and methods of the social sciences and applying them to new content. Preferably, also, the concepts and methods should be applied to the child's own life and community. Using this strategy, a teacher or a group of teachers could produce their own data bank.

Some teachers may prefer, at first, to rely on existing instructional materials to introduce the ideas that are drawn from the social sciences. However, it is much more vital to help children to collect and analyze data and to give them opportunities to explain and evaluate human situations in their own spontaneous fashion. In this way present social studies programs can be transformed. They may lose some of the formal quality of science, but they will become a vital part of the child's experience. The raw data of a child's social life are always available for him to study. He can learn to organize and comprehend his experience by using the methods of the social scientist.

The work of Mrs. Green and her associates expresses the constructionist spirit of the social sciences. This spirit turns the study of society into a leisurely, emergent process, in which students use social science modes of inquiry to formulate concepts from data. In keeping with the social scientist's viewpoint, knowledge becomes a network of tentative concepts. As the social scientist acquires new data, he may put them into previously established categories or he may alter the categories or make new ones. Such revisions are part of the process whereby an organizing concept in the social sciences is formulated.

Steps in the Development of a Concept in Social Science

Step 1 The social scientist observes social behavior.

Step 2 He formulates a concept to explain the observed behavior.

Step 3 He collects some samples of behavior under controlled conditions.

Step 4 He checks his concept (step 2) against observations of the behavior under controlled conditions.

Step 5 He checks his concept against other concepts dealing with the same kind of behavior.

Step 6 He revises his concept and the concepts in step 5, and he plans further investigation.

These steps need not occur in the order just given. Organizing concepts are always being checked and revised. At the same time, existing concepts enable us to explore areas of life.

Let us suppose that a fifth-grade class is embarking on a study designed to help them discover and revise one of the central concepts of human geography: Culture and environment interact to affect patterns of human life. This interaction is the source of subject matter in geography. The class begins with the study of Bedouin groups in the Sahara around 1900. They find the following information:

The Bedouins wore white clothing to reflect the heat.

They used camels for transport because the camel is an effective carrier in the desert.

Their tents were constructed to shield out the sun and the cold night wind but to admit the daytime breeze.

Trails and settlements closely followed the incidence of surface water.

Their literature tended to be oral rather than written.

One of their main sources of fuel was camel dung, because trees are scarce in the desert and precious for shade and food.

The cloth for their tents was made of spun camel hair.

They were Moslems, followers of Mohammed, and were allowed to take more than one wife.

When guests came, the Bedouin felt honored and prepared a feast. The more guests there were, the more honored he felt.

The wives lived together in the harem side of the tent. They sewed, cooked, wove, and cared for the children.

The men herded sheep and camels and grew tobacco. They traded the wool of sheep and camels for money, which they used to buy rice, coffee, pottery, and utensils. Market towns and grazing lands were located near sources of water.

Any of this information and much more can be found in encyclopedias, geographies, and trade books like Sonia and Tim Gidal's *Sons of the Desert* (New York: Pantheon, 1964). Encouraged by fiction, Bible stories, and folklore, the children begin to form ideas about life in the desert:

"Grazing herds, moving from place to place, are the source of food, cloth, fuel, goods to trade."

"Desert people are Moslems."

"They use camels for transportation."

"They wear flowing white robes to keep off the heat."

"The desert is too dry to grow crops. They have to buy rice and tobacco unless they live by a river, like the Nile."

"The sheik, or clan leader, makes the rules."

The children are encouraged to form these ideas and to support them with facts. Then they are given information about other desert dwellers. They read about Israel, and find out the following:

Not far from Beersheba, one of the main Bedouin trading villages in the Negev, huge modern air-conditioned apartment houses rise from the desert.

A copper refinery operates in the Negev.

Dead Sea salts are dug and used for fertilizer and glass.

Canals, pipes, and pumps are used for irrigation, bringing forth fruit trees and vegetables.

The religion is mostly Jewish, but Druses, Moslems, Greek Catholics, Greek Orthodox, Roman Catholics, Maronites, Circassians, Protestants, Armenian-Gregorians, and Copts are also found.

Fuel includes natural gases, obtained chiefly from a deposit in the Negev.

Some families are banded together in kibbutzim, in which children are raised in common. Others are gathered in extended-family groups. Others form conjugal units that keep to themselves.

The people are individualistic and the government republican. Even sheiks are subject to the common law.

Both men and women in Israel receive military training; and most jobs, including high government positions, are open to both sexes.

All this information and much more can be found in *Israel*, by Robert St. John and the editors of *Life* (New York: Time Inc., 1962); in encyclopedias; in the Gidals' *My Village in Israel* (New York: Pantheon, 1959); and in other trade books and films. Now the fifth-graders take another look at the ideas they have formed about life in the desert. Every idea has to be modified, for in this second desert group, life is quite different.

"Maybe it's got something to do with the history of your people. Maybe history shows how you're going to live."

"The Bedouins seem to live as they did a long time ago. In Israel almost everybody but the Bedouins seems very modern."

57

The children are beginning to realize that environment is not the sole determinant of human life. They are ready, perhaps, to study how culture is passed down and evolves. Perhaps now they can compare a Virginia plantation of colonial times with a modern cotton or tobacco farm to see how things have and have not changed. Or, possibly, they can study the Navaho, the ways and things he has borrowed from others, to determine how culture is transmitted from people to people.

These fifth-graders cannot yet define *culture*. They still lack the depth knowledge of another culture—knowledge they will need in order to see how culture forms and operates. They have, however, made concepts, found them wanting, and revised them. They are beginning to develop the habits of analysis and self-doubt that characterize the social sciences. When they study a jungle people, they will not be so likely to say "This is how people live in the jungle." More likely, they will say "This is how *one* jungle people lives. Let's see how some others manage it."

Two Teaching Principles

A principle of teaching that recognizes the changing nature of ideas can now be stated: *Social ideas should be taught as tentative, changing concepts, constantly to be verified as new evidence is acquired.* By exploring concepts in this way, the child can prepare himself for lifelong revision of ideas that will enable him to adapt to a changing world.

A second principle of teaching is that *the perspectives of all the social sciences should be made available to the child.* Each social scientist views the world of human interaction from a slightly different perspective. For example, in studying a desert people, the sociologist might focus on the family or the structure of groups; the political scientist might study their electoral processes or their power relationships with one another and with their leaders; the economist might examine their roles in production or the ways in which they are consumers; the anthropologist might be interested in the ways they transmit culture to their children. It is important that a child see life from all these perspectives and learn to use them to comprehend his own life and that of others.

Perspectives on man

The Beginnings of a Strategy for
Teaching the Social Studies

A teaching strategy should be based on the following:

1. The learner should be led to examine his own life and the societal life of others, the raw data of the social studies. In this way, the intellectual dimension of the social studies complements the personal dimension (which has as its goal to help the child comprehend his own life and find meaning in it) and the social dimension (which tries to help him understand his society and prepare him to make active contributions to it).

2. This examination should gradually reveal to him the organizing concepts that social scientists use to analyze human life.

3. The child should be led to apply these tools to his study of social life. For example, as he arrives at a generalization about family life in his community, he should test the concepts when he studies other communities. Conversely, as he learns about family life in a foreign community, he should apply what he learns to the study of nearby families.

4. The child should learn to make revisions as he finds more data. In fact, information should be presented to the child in a sequence that requires him to revise general concepts. Knowledge of society is, after all, tentative and shifting. Social life is also constantly changing and therefore requires flexible ways of dealing with problems.

INQUIRIES

1. The concept of "race" is important in anthropology and relevant to the study of contemporary society. Using scholarly references, develop a definition of this concept. Then work out a way of helping children use this concept to explore contemporary society.

2. Select a concept you believe would help children comprehend their neighborhood. Define the concept and develop an approach that helps children use the concept to study their neighborhood.

3. Develop an approach that will help children come to understand the emergent character of their own knowledge and that of scholars. Compare your approach with those of others in your group. (You might, for example, identify a stereotyped or erroneous idea the children have and

find sources of data for them to test their idea against. Discuss the process of changing an idea.)

NOTES

1. John Dewey, *Democracy and Education* (New York: Macmillan, 1916).

2. Charles Hubbard Judd, *Education and Social Progress* (New York: Harcourt, Brace & World, 1934), p. 263.

3. Alfred North Whitehead, *The Aims of Education and Other Essays* (New York: Macmillan, 1929), p. 3.

4. Charles A. Beard, *The Nature of the Social Sciences* (New York: Scribner, 1934), p. 11.

5. Jerome S. Bruner, *The Process of Education* (Cambridge, Mass.: Harvard Univ. Press, 1960).

6. In this book the term *organizing concept* is used in a sense identical to that of Bruner's *structure.* Joseph Schwab uses *structure* interchangeably with *principle of enquiry* (see pp. 39–40); and John Honigmann, using a somewhat different approach, has relied on the word *concept* (see pp. 79–81). We have chosen the term *organizing concept* in order to avoid the misconception that these ideas, which explore and define consequences and relations, are static or purely formal in nature; they are, instead, to be used daily in encountering and organizing reality.

7. Milton Singer, "A Survey of Culture and Personality Theory and Research," in *Studying Personality Cross-Culturally,* ed. Bert Kaplan (New York: Harper & Row, 1961), p. 23.

8. Stuart Chase, *The Proper Study of Mankind* (New York: Harper, 1956), pp. 160–63.

9. Ibid.

10. Bruner, *The Process of Education.*

11. For a defense of traditional methods in history and history teaching, see Mark M. Krug, *History and the Social Sciences* (Toronto: Blaisdell, 1967). For a radically new approach to thinking in political science, see David Easton, "A Systems Approach to Political Life," Social Science Education Consortium, publication no. 104 (Boulder: Univ. of Colorado, n.d.). See also pp. 112–13 and 114 of this book.

12. John Amos Comenius, *Selections* (Lausanne, Switzerland: UNESCO, 1957).

13. John Dewey, *Essays in Experimental Logic* (Chicago: Univ. of Chicago Press, 1916).

14. Joseph J. Schwab, *The Teaching of Science* (Cambridge, Mass.: Harvard Univ. Press, 1962). The text printed here is from a speech, with minor changes in wording, given in Washington, D.C., in 1961.

15. The following account originally appeared in Bruce R. Joyce, "Social Sciencing: New Concept in Social Studies," *The Instructor Magazine* (October 1968), pp. 85–92.

16. For a more detailed account of the procedures used in making the data bank, see chapter 13, pp. 319–26.

TRANSLATING SOCIAL SCIENCE KNOWLEDGE INTO FORMS CHILDREN CAN LEARN

Scholarly knowledge is not created in the language of the child or for his particular use. The geographer invents concepts that he and other geographers can use to explain phenomena. When he speaks of a *savanna climate* or a *peninsula*, he is using a term because it has a precise meaning for him, not because children will learn it quickly. When the economist speaks of *balance of trade*, he refers to a useful concept, not necessarily an easy one to teach.

One of the most difficult tasks facing the educator is to translate scholarly concepts and methods into forms that can be readily taught to children. The process whereby scholarly ideas can be made accessible to children involves analyzing the social sciences and organizing them for teaching.

Perspectives on the Social Sciences

What organizing concepts and modes of inquiry from the social sciences should be taught? What disciplines should be empha-

chapter 2

sized? What kinds of content should be examined? To answer these questions, we must understand how much unity there is among the various disciplines and how important their differences are.

Much has been written on the nature of social science: Ernest Nagel's *The Structure of Science*, Abraham Kaplan's *The Conduct of Inquiry*, Saventh's *American History and the Social Sciences*, and Cahnman and Boscoff's *Sociology and History*, among others. Better known to educators, perhaps, is *Realms of Meaning* by Philip Phenix, in which the author asks: Should we package knowledge in the ways we produce it, or should we group content and modes of inquiry in terms of what they will mean to the student?[1] Hence he has grouped elements of language and mathematics as "symbiotics," and elements of the sciences and social sciences as "empirics."

Many other works could be mentioned, from Beard's initial effort in the early thirties to the efforts by Hyneman and others in the last decade. Even introductory college texts on the social sciences are beginning to show an awareness of the basic premises and concepts of the various fields, as, for example, Honigmann's excellent analysis of the nature of anthropological research. Nearly all the contemporary social studies projects include some statement on the nature of the field. Some of them reflect interest in the social sciences as a whole, while others are written as if one discipline were the whole.

For years, competent educators have also been worrying the the problem. I am amazed at the lack of attention given the monumental series of studies by Hanna and his students. Although some of their work was done from a point of view different from that predominant today, it is honest work and offers much to the scholar. Theoreticians, developers of social studies projects, and groups of social scientists have much to build on, if a cumulative dialogue can be started and maintained.

Although I am reluctant to add yet another scheme to the growing list of ways of analyzing the structures of the disciplines, my own work has led me to use a fairly simple system. I generally distinguish four aspects of the social sciences.

1. The view of knowledge held by scholars in the field. This metatheoretical aspect refers to the way the scholar thinks about his field. Is he a constructionist (one who states ideas in hypothetical terms and expects to revise them)? Are deductive theories permissible? Can one attempt grand theory (theory that tries to

explain large ideas, such as history or society, and does not suggest that situations are relatively unique)?

In general, all social sciences share the view that knowledge is a tentative set of hypotheses constantly revised, regrouped, and reformulated as new knowledge and structures appear. To use Collier's words: "These hypotheses must be reformulated because the observers grow in ability to see, to analyze, and to hypothesize. That is what the social sciences have in common—a series of dynamic, self-developing ways of looking at man and his activities."[2] When curriculum committees ask me where to start looking for fundamentals to teach, I refer them to the constant revision of knowledge as the fundamental characteristic of scholarly inquiry.

2. The frame of reference of the discipline. The frame of reference for each of the social sciences causes some features to stand out and others to recede. All social scientists try to describe and explain human behavior, but not all evaluate aspects of society in the same way. For example, the economist studies the process whereby persons use resources to meet their needs; the anthropologist sees the same process, but to him it is one aspect of culture. It is important to identify the specific domain studied by a particular kind of social scientist.

Another important aspect of the scholar's frame of reference is the system of organizing concepts in the field, what Bruner calls the structure of the discipline. These concepts serve to describe relationships among data and to direct inquiry. For example, the economist organizes much information under the concept of division of labor; in studying a new economic unit, he may look for, among other things, ways in which labor is divided. These concepts delineate the ways in which information is stored. They provide guidelines for research, for they tell the scholar where to look as he begins a new study. The bulk of any field consists of its organizing concepts and their supporting data.

3. The mode of inquiry. This aspect of the disciplines may be referred to as the "scientific method." It defines what data will be accepted and how that data will be measured, quantified, and manipulated to prove hypotheses. The mode, or methodology, of inquiry describes the scientist at work collecting and manipulating data. His frame of reference determines what he considers important and what questions he asks or does not ask. Making observations, inferring cause and effect, reducing data and testing hypotheses, however, are reasonably similar processes throughout the social sciences.

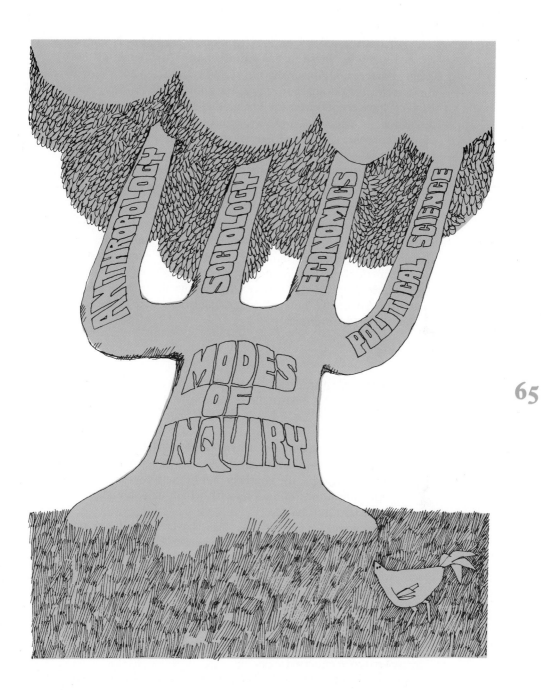

Modes of inquiry as the basis for a social studies curriculum

4. A language system. Each of the social sciences has developed its own symbols. Progress toward a common mathematical language, however, is slower than in the physical sciences. Many of the current curriculum projects (such as the Georgia Anthropology Project) have emphasized the teaching of the symbol system of a discipline. In the past, however, educators have usually let the children provide their own linguistic handles for the concepts they form. Be that as it may, each discipline does have a rather complicated language system with many terms that are unique to it.

Reexamination of these aspects of each discipline may reveal that on some levels (their view of knowledge and research methodology) they have much in common, in some areas (their frame of reference) they have some differences and some similarities, and in others (language) they are far apart. A social studies curriculum can emphasize modes of inquiry common to several disciplines, or it can emphasize certain aspects of one discipline. Similarly, the work of curriculum builders in the social studies varies in emphasis.

Translating Organizing Concepts of Sociology—An Example

66

Sociology provides several organizing concepts that the child can derive if he is encouraged to draw on his own experience. Having learned these concepts, the child can apply them to many family, school, and community situations with which he is familiar, and thus gain insight into his life.

Four sociological concepts have been selected for illustration. These concepts were tested in the classroom by Carl Weinberg and the author; the questions and responses in the following pages were actually recorded in third- and fifth-grade classes. These four organizing concepts, even though designed by sociologists to analyze and describe human groups in a sophisticated fashion, can be understood in elementary terms by the child.

Norm. A rule that prescribes certain types of action and forbids other types of action.

Sanction. A penalty for unacceptable behavior or a reward for conforming to standards. Sanctions operate in groups to cause group members to conform to norms.

Modes of inquiry of one discipline as the basis for a social studies curriculum

Value. An object of preference by a social group. Frequently values are cited as the reason for norms. A group that values cleanliness may apply sanctions to persons who do not observe the normative behavior of "keeping clean."

Role. A behavior pattern that is assigned to certain individuals, such as a decision-making pattern, an economic pattern, and the like. Wherever differentiation of behavior is found, roles appear. Values are attached to roles, and roles are circumscribed by norms. Sanctions may be used to enforce role-linked behavior.

These four organizing concepts need not be taught directly; the teacher does not, for example, have to define *norm* abstractly and then list the ways in which norms manifest themselves in everyday life. Rather the manifestations, or "observed forms," of these concepts can be explored first, so that the children come to formulate the concepts just as the social scientist has developed them from his observations. Organizing concepts should be constructed by the child out of his own experience, with the guidance of the teacher. So learned, concepts can be viewed as working ideas that unfold with experience and analysis.

After selecting the organizing concepts to be sought (in this case norms, sanctions, values, and roles), the teacher finds familiar forms in which the concepts can be observed by the child. The social groups with which the child is most familiar are his community, his family, his school, and his peer group. How do norms, sanctions, values, and roles operate in these groups? The following lists contain some forms of the concept "norm" that may be observed by children. A teacher may want to use these lists in asking questions and directing the inquiry of his pupils.

In their community

We greet our neighbors.
We cut our lawns.
We shovel our walks when it snows.
We don't make noise outside late at night.
We pay our bills.
We go to work or school in the morning.
We dress up for church.
We register to vote.
We do not tell others how to vote.
We help our neighbors when they ask us.
We do not throw food on people's lawns.
We walk on sidewalks and not on people's lawns or flower beds.

68

In their school

We read.
We pay attention.
We wear clean clothes to school.
We do our homework.
We do our work in class.
We do not talk without permission.
We do not cheat on exams.
We do not talk back to the teacher.
We come to class on time.
We do not curse in class.
We do not push in line.
We help the teacher.
The teacher treats us fairly.
The teacher does not give us more work than we can do.

With their family

We ask our parents' permission to go out at night or after
school.
We clean our room.
We do chores that our parents ask us to do.
We love our parents and our parents love us.
Our parents feed, clothe, and take care of us.
We come home when our parents expect us.
We do not hurt our younger brothers and sisters.

In their peer group

We do not push or bully.
We play fair in games.
We do not quit.
We help our classmates with homework.
We lend money when someone who has none asks us.
We accept the vote of the group.
We defend boys in our group against outsiders.
We join in games.
We play safely.

After listing a variety of these simple statements (they can be
made more sophisticated for older children), the teacher formulates questions to help the children discover and identify observable forms of the concept "norm." Children should not be
asked to identify norms abstractly before they know what norms
are concretely. Having thought about data that they have observed,
they will begin to arrive at some approximation of what the scholar
means when he uses the term *norm*. The following is a list of
questions the teacher might ask students to stimulate inquiry
about norms.

In their community

What are some things that people on our street do all the time?
How do people living on our block behave?
What are some things we never do on the street or in public
that we do in our house?
What are some rules that can help us get along with people
in our neighborhood? What do our neighbors expect of us
and what do we expect of them?

In their school

> What are some things that our teachers and principal expect us to do and would not like if we didn't do?
>
> What are some things the teacher does that we would not like if she didn't do?

In their family

> When we are at home, what are some things our parents expect us to do and would not like if we didn't do?
>
> What are some things we expect our parents to do and would not like if they didn't do?

In their peer group

> What are some things we expect our friends to do that we would not like if they didn't do? On the playground? In class? In games?

By asking children guiding questions such as these, a teacher can stimulate them to examine examples of the concepts. Carl Weinberg and the author found, for example, that third-grade and fifth-grade children found examples of norms when asked: "What are some things that you expect each other to do all the time and you believe others expect of you?" The children mentioned many examples of classroom behavior that were expected: "You expect them to be quiet in class and do their work." They also mentioned examples of playground behavior: "Well, when you're playing, you expect them not to knock it [the ball] out of people's hands and not to come over and catch it if they're not in the game." They found examples of norms in the home as well as at school. They found expectations that were shared by adults and expectations that were shared only by children.

They were also able to identify evidence of norms. Particularly interesting was the evidence they found of sanctions applied to individuals who failed to observe the norms. For example, the following question was asked:

> "What are things we do to show others that we are not happy with what they do? For example, if somebody is not playing fair or breaking up our game, how could we show him that we don't like it?"

71

Here are a few of the children's answers:

"You could holler at him."
"You could just move away and not play with him."
"You could tell him that you'll never let him play in any of your games ever again."

The children were also able to identify sanctions that might be applied at home for a violation of norms or for obedience to norms.

"They could send you to bed."
"They could take away your allowance."
"They could tell you that they were very angry."
"They can say they're proud of you and show that they like it."
"They can give you compliments."
"When you do something for somebody, just expect a thank-you."

In these ways a teacher who has identified organizing concepts from the social sciences and concrete examples of these concepts can lead the children to discover these concepts on a level they can understand.

72

Using the Organizing Concepts of Sociology as Tools of Inquiry

After helping the children to find observable forms of norms, sanctions, values, and roles, the teacher can encourage them to apply the guiding questions to analyses of other social behavior. Not only must children, like social scientists, learn to create organizing concepts; they must also learn to use them as tools of inquiry, as means of examining life and classifying information. If the child studies the English family, the Japanese family, the Indian family, and his own family, using the guiding questions, he will be ready to compare these families in terms of norms, sanctions, values, and roles—the very concepts used by the sociologist to analyze the family and other social groups. When the child studies other people in depth, he should have the guiding questions ready. When he studies current events, he can ask, for example, "What is it that these people believe is important?" The sociologist would say, "What are their *values*?" Even though the child may not use the proper terms, he will develop these organizing concepts. When he has learned the concepts, however, learning the terms for them is easy. Whenever possible, he should learn the proper terms because they are linguistic handles that will help him think more effectively. A single term for a concept is much easier to use than a long, awkward statement, and we do the child no favor when we fail to give him a precise language.

To help the child think clearly, we need materials that offer raw data rather than conclusions. *Sociological Resources for the Social Studies*, a project sponsored by the American Sociological Association and funded by the National Science Foundation, provides data for students to work with and analyze. In order to teach the organizing concepts of sociology as modes of inquiry, the program uses three kinds of instructional materials: a series entitled *Episodes in Social Inquiry*, a sociology course entitled *Inquiries in Sociology*, and seven paperback books of readings about broad sociological topics.

> The episodes and sociology course are based on the assumption that learning occurs most effectively when students themselves actively participate in the gathering and analyzing of data to reach meaningful conclusions. Imagination and creativity are developed concurrently through this scientific process of original inquiry.
>
> An *episode* may be defined as *a set of instructional materials designed to provide a brief but dramatic and enlightening firsthand encounter with social data*. It neither reviews the literature in a field nor provides a textbook summary. We do not want the student to accept what he is told simply because sociologists have discovered something and said it is true. So far as possible, we want him to be convinced by evidence and reasoning and to come to appreciate the usefulness of sociological concepts and procedures as he gains knowledge through their use. Direct contact with data, learning through one's own experience, careful scrutiny of evidence, exposure to scientific methods of inquiry, and relative brevity therefore characterize the episodes.[3]

73

One episode, for example, leads students to explore the sociology of religion. In the introductory activity, the students map the distribution of church members in their community according to neighborhood and compare the data with the distribution in Chicago. They then explore questions about the reasons for these patterns, thus discovering relationships between religious and other aspects of behavior. They proceed to collect data or organize data provided them concerning intermarriage between religious groups, religion and occupational type and income level, and so on. In these ways, the episodes help the students to learn the kinds of questions sociologists ask, the methodologies they use, and the constructs they have developed about American religious behavior.

This empirical approach implies that knowledge is constructed. In learning how concepts are formed, the student comes to see that reality is not identical with knowledge, that knowledge is imperfect, and that perspective has much to do with the ways experience is interpreted.

Caroline Rose has developed a clear statement of the constructionist position:

> Behind the sociology presented here is a theory of science—an epistemology—sometimes called operationalism, sometimes instrumentalism, and sometimes pragmatism. If one does not understand this theory, one can neither teach nor learn this version of sociology.
>
> Instrumentalism regards science as an instrument or tool for understanding the real or natural world, which is assumed to exist, and which consists of a great mass of *facts* related to each other in some way, including the material of dreams, private thoughts, abstract ideals, and values. A *fact* or a series of related facts has no *meaning* until some human being gives it a *meaning*. A *meaning* is roughly the same thing as a dictionary definition. It arises in communication when someone tries to explain "what he means" to himself or somebody else. A meaning may range in length and complexity from a synonym to a big fat book. It follows that a *fact may have a very large number of different meanings* depending on how it is explained. It also follows that in the strict sense, induction is not possible in this system, since facts always acquire their meaning by the application of a concept.[4]

As she develops an outline of concepts critical in sociology, she stresses the philosophical implications of the instrumentalist position. What emerges is a position that the social sciences provide the following kinds of material for the social studies: (1) the philosophical conceptions of knowing that can be taught to children; (2) the perspective of the particular social science and social scientists (each perspective provides a framework for the development of meaning); (3) the framework of organizing concepts that develops and changes within the perspectives and conceptions of knowing; (4) the methods of inquiry that guide the making and interpreting of data relative to (1), (2), and (3) above.

INQUIRIES

1. The sociologist uses the concept *norm* to explore many types of social groups. Develop a history of the concept, identify its contemporary definitions, and organize a way it can help children comprehend their own social behavior.

2. Take the positive stance and then the negative stance toward the following propositions:

    The system of concepts from sociology should be taught to children so that they will have a tool for analyzing social life.

    The child should study his own social life and develop his own concepts for understanding it.

    If possible, hold debates on these questions.

3. The following narrative describes life in a medieval English town. How can children apply the sociological perspective as they examine this narrative? (You might, for example, use the concepts—norms, values, roles, sanctions—we have been discussing or concepts such as *status* or *institution* from some other aspect of the discipline.)

Sunday Morning in a Medieval Village

Chilled by the early morning dampness, Robert stamped his bare feet to keep warm. From the River Teme, which wound around Ludlow, mist rose and kept Robert from seeing clearly the church only a few hundred feet away. But he knew well what it looked like and could almost make out the two gray stone towers in front and the tall tower where the arms of the church crossed.

Robert's father came hurrying from the cottage and down the path through the vegetable garden. Robert fell in step with him, and they both walked quickly toward the fields beyond the church. Robert's hopper* bounced at his side, and each of his steps ended in a small spray of sand as he dug his feet into the unpaved street. They walked by the village green in front of the church. Like his father, Robert moved his hand from his forehead across his chest to make the sign of the cross.

Suddenly they heard someone call to them: "John, Robert, wait for me." Their marrow† came running up to them. Robert saw that he and his father had become part of a procession of men and boys going out to the fields.

75

---

*A box that is held on a strap and contains seeds to be sown.

†The man who worked the adjoining strip of land. Farmers of such strips usually helped each other plow, sow, and reap.

All morning their marrow worked with them on their strip of land, scattering seeds. Robert followed him, trying to copy his smooth rhythmic motions: raise right foot to step forward, throw seeds in left hand, raise left foot to step forward, throw seeds in right hand. The marrow looked always at the red soil they had just the day before spread with manured straw and plowed. After a while Robert began to feel dizzy. The even motions of the marrow's feet and hands, the warm sun, his own exertions, and his empty stomach unsteadied him. It had been about two hours, he guessed, since his morning meal of bread and ale. Robert judged from the slant and warmth of the sun's rays that it must be time to go and dress for church. Today was Sunday and they must leave the fields early.

"Father," Robert called, "should we not be going? The others are already leaving."

His father looked up as if startled. He saw that many of the other serfs were walking along the path by the strips. Quickly he came, stopping only to straighten one of the pegs that marked off his strip from the marrow's. Although he and his marrow trusted each other, it was proper to adjust the pegs only when both of them were there.

When Robert and his father arrived home, they found that Robert's mother and sister had weeded the vegetable garden and milked the cow. Two cups of fresh milk were waiting for them on the table. Robert gulped his down and hurried to wash and change. In the chest where the Sunday clothes were kept Robert saw the dress that his sister Johanna used to wear on Sundays. Robert remembered almost nothing about the two babies that had died in birth three or four years ago. But Johanna had been a year older than him, and they had shared the same mat for two years before she became sick and died. Robert touched the hem of his sister's dress and then began to dress.

When they had all washed and dressed, they hurried to the church. Robert's father stopped at the sundial to talk with some men while Robert went on into the church, made the sign of the cross, and walked down the wide center aisle. Part way down he turned to the side and stood with a few men. His mother and sister turned to the other side and stood among the crowd of women there.

In the front of the church Sir William, dressed in long robes, bent over a high table and mumbled strange words. His voice rose and fell in a familiar pattern, mixed with the voices of the men who had come in from the green and stood in the back of the church. Sir William had gone to school at Shrewsbury twenty-seven miles away and learned many prayers. But he had to come back when his father died and the lord took the best cow William's mother had and the church claimed the second best.* Five years later the old village priest died, and William

---

*It was understood that the serf held everything on loan from the lord. When the serf died, his family honored this loan by giving up their best.

THE INTELLECTUAL DIMENSION

became Sir William, since there was no one else to say mass* for the villagers.

As Sir William turned toward the people, they moved to sit or kneel on the rushes that covered the church floor. It was time for the sermon. Sir William had not always included a sermon in the mass. But when the Bishop of Shrewsbury passed through, he had advised Sir William to take a stronger hand in guiding the villagers.

"I have already spoken to you about pride, anger, and sloth—three of the seven deadly sins. Today let us consider greed. In a certain village there was a man who went into the lord's woods and stole rabbits and killed deer." Sir William paused. "Some people in this village take wood from the lord's forest to build fires for cooking."

The priest's voice did not sound hard, and Robert wondered whether he said these things only because he knew he should. Sir William had been hungry sometimes, too, Robert knew. Suddenly Sir William's voice became stern and his eyes cold.

"He who steals from the lord's orchard so that he will have apples and pears during the winter shows that he has no faith in the goodness and mercy of God. He should trust that God will provide for him."

Robert felt confused. He remembered winters in Ludlow—how long and cold they were. He thought of the empty branches of their pear tree and the hard, frosty ground of the cabbage and onion garden. The winter before they had run out of bacon long before the spring came. Robert remembered also the stone carvings on the portals of the church: the damned were shown as suffering and the faithful as joyous. Robert knew that a soul could be saved or damned forever even in the last moment before death. But the joys of Heaven were so hard to imagine.

"Nor is it proper to say Aves over a beehive to keep evil spirits out. A prayer should be said over the ale made from the honey but not over the hive."

Robert felt confused again. He and his father always spoke an Ave over the hive before taking the honey out.

Sir William turned back to the altar, mumbled solemnly, and rang a little bell. No one in the church understood the words, but they knew that this was the most important moment in the mass: the bread and wine on the table became the body and blood of Christ. The service did not end with the Eucharist, but Robert heard some of the men leave the church and knew that they would spend the rest of the morning at the ale house across the green, talking and drinking. Robert stayed to the end, then left with his mother and sister.

---

*The Catholic Church service in which the death of Jesus Christ and his reunion with his Father in Heaven are acted out.

NOTES

1. Philip H. Phenix, *Realms of Meaning* (New York: McGraw-Hill, 1964).

2. Malcolm C. Collier, "A Question about Questions," *Social Education* 29 (December 1965), p. 555.

3. Instructors' Guide for *Science and Society*, Sociological Resources for the Social Studies (Boston: Allyn & Bacon, 1971), p. 1.

4. Caroline B. Rose, "Sociology," Background Paper no. 6 (Minnesota Project Social Studies, Univ. of Minnesota, n.d.), p. 1.

78

APPROACHES
TO CONTENT IN
ANTHROPOLOGY,
HISTORY,
AND SOCIAL
PSYCHOLOGY

In chapter 1 we defined organizing concepts according to their function: to indicate relations between facts, to organize knowledge within a discipline, and to guide research. In chapter 2 we used a few concepts from sociology—norms, sanctions, values, and roles. Now we can analyze organizing concepts further, breaking them down into three general types: observed concepts, inferred concepts, and ideal-type concepts.[1] All these concepts are used by social scientists to filter information and organize it.

Observed Concepts, Inferred Concepts,
and Ideal-type Concepts

Throughout life a person has innumerable experiences. He meets people, sees objects, participates in events. Memories of these experiences do not simply pile up in his mind like grains of sand. The mind sorts them into categories, sees relations between them, and gradually forms a system for organizing new experiences. Anyone past infancy is predisposed to organize new information

chapter 3

in accord with this gradually emerging network of categories. When organizing concepts are taught to the child, the processing methods he is developing come to resemble, at least partially, the analytical thinking of the scholar.

An observed concept is formed by noting similarities, differences, or relations between things apprehended by the senses—verbal statements, physical actions, objects. In studying various cultures, an anthropologist may note the similarities and differences in the objects used for child care, thus forming concepts about those objects. Or he may note that in some cultures the conjugal unit is basic, whereas in others the extended family is. Each similarity and difference, each relation between factors, is described by a new category or concept. Usually concepts are named so that they can be referred to easily. Thus families that revolve around the mother are called matriarchies, while those in which the father is central are called patriarchies. These concepts describe forms of family organization that have been found by observing family relationships. If a child is to form such a concept, he has to be able to see similarities and differences in objects that he has perceived or that have been described to him so completely that he sees them as real.

An inferred concept "points to unseen events which can only be inferred from some more immediately observed phenomena."[2] The observed concept of "matriarchy" could be formed through observation of family relationships. The concept "god-fearing" cannot be formed on the basis of direct observation: we cannot observe fear directly, nor can we see a belief in a deity. If people engage in worship and tell us that they do certain things because they fear a god, and if we note that their religion places strictures on behavior, then we can infer that they are god-fearing. When we form concepts such as "atheist," "believer," "fear," and "anxiety," we are inferring that certain actions we perceive are caused by unseen, hidden characteristics. While observed concepts are made about things that are seen, inferred concepts are made about things that are inferred from seen things. When helping children to form inferred concepts, we need to lead them to information from which they can infer unseen things and then note similarities or differences between them. For example, the child cannot see values directly, but by observing actions he may be able to infer what is important to people.

A third kind of concept refers to very general classes called ideal types. These concepts are made by observing similarities and differences in relations, but they refer to such complex or large-scale, perfect phenomena that they have no representative in reality. For example, we speak of Cannes, Nice, Brighton, and Atlantic City as resorts, although that is not all they are. There is no place that is purely a "resort city." But the concept is still useful, for with it we can describe some of the common functions of these places, refer to them in conversation, and manipulate them as an idea.

Ideal-type concepts enable us to classify large masses of information. We classify nation-states, for example, into *technologically developed* and *technologically underdeveloped*. We refer to *socialism, nationalism,* and *free enterprise* to describe large-scale events, social movements, and trends that have something in common but may be only loosely related. To help the child form ideal-type concepts requires that he be led to examples of the concepts and that he be able to see their common characteristics. To form a concept like "democracy," for example, the child needs to study several nation-states in enough detail to be able to identify democratic and nondemocratic characteristics in those nations and thus see what characterizes democracy.

These distinctions between types of concepts used by the social scientist can be useful in teaching concepts to elementary school children. In many cases young children can be taught to identify observed concepts. Even the youngest can note similarities, differences, and relations between objects he perceives directly. Inferred concepts, however, require an extra step, since they depend on postulating unseen forces or things and then noting similarities, differences, and relations between these unseen entities. Ideal-type concepts are not especially difficult when they refer to small units or groups of things, but are very difficult when they refer to large events, processes, or trends. It takes a long time to acquire knowledge of such large entities as wars, nations, and social movements. Several years of study about nations are necessary before one has sufficient data about them to be able to handle concepts such as "democracy" and "communism" effectively.

Anthropology and Cultural Comparison

The anthropologist studies basically three kinds of phenomena: the activities of a people, the ideas they share, and the things they produce. Some anthropologists emphasize one kind of phenomenon. Some, for instance, specialize in the structure of languages, while others combine the study of language with the study of mental processes. Whatever their specialty, anthropologists seek to contribute to the total picture of a culture.

Some anthropologists believe that each culture is the unique product of forces operating at a particular time and place, while others believe that cultures develop according to certain general laws. Regardless of their conception of the scope of the field, most would agree that the anthropological method consists mainly of comparison.

> All cultural analysis is comparative. It is assumed that without comparison culture would be imperceptible to the individual who would not be able to distinguish between cultural behavior and biologically given, unlearned behavior.[3]

On the one hand, anthropologists may study a single culture through time, comparing various stages of its cultural evolution. Lange's study of the New Mexican pueblo Cochiti is an example of a study tracing a culture from prehistory to the present.[4] On the other hand, anthropologists may compare several cultures that are more or less contemporary with each other. An example of this is *Patterns of Culture* (Boston: Houghton Mifflin, 1934) by Ruth Benedict.

The behaviors that we see around us as we grow up seem natural, biologically true to the species. Different behaviors seem abnormal, foreign to the species. When we compare our culture with another, however, we often see that what seems strange within our group is normal in another. Hence, we begin to identify characteristics that are socially acquired and processes whereby we become what we are. These characteristics are part of culture.

To help a child imitate the anthropologist, we must be sure he has access to enough information about a human community to begin to see the totality of its culture. We need to lead him to make comparisons between different cultures, so that he can begin to understand the organizing concepts of anthropology. For instance, studying families of several lands will enable him to see not only how families function in a culture, but also how forms of family life differ in various societies. Similarly, as he sees religions in several cultures, he can begin to identify what religion is, from the anthropologist's viewpoint, and what it does. If we are determined to help the child develop an awareness of the extent to which behavior, including his own, is socially inherited, we should arrange the curriculum so that the child continually makes comparisons between cultures. He can compare literature, political behavior, and so forth, noting always how social inheritance influences the patterns of the present generation.

The following description of nine- and ten-year-old children comparing families representing several cultures provides an example of a teaching strategy that uses inferred concepts as a focus. The central concept was identified from sociology, but the comparative approach is more typical of anthropology. The illustration is taken from a research study by the author and his wife.[5]

On five successive days, two classes were shown short films, each depicting a family from a different country or culture—Spanish, Eskimo, Navaho, Italian, and French—going about its daily activities. The teaching strategy was devised to help the children compare different cultural families on the basis of values. They were asked to identify in each film evidence of what was important to the family in question. Because values are an inferred concept, it was necessary to teach the children to recognize good evidence of what is important to people.

As each child ventured a hypothesis about something he believed was important to one of the families, he was asked, "What evidence makes you think so?" Then he was led to suggest all the evidence he could pertaining to that hypothesized value and to debate the merits of the evidence. In this way the children were guided to raise hypotheses about the values of the families depicted in the films, to describe and debate the evidence from which the values were inferred, to cull the films for conflicting evidence, and to compare the lists of hypothesized values for each family.

At first the children made inferences based on evidence of the physical needs of the people: "The cow was important because she gave them milk;" "The horse was important because he pulled the cart." They had difficulty balancing their inferences against conflicting ones and seemed reluctant to challenge the judgment of others. Gradually, however, the children learned to make inferences on bases unrelated to physical needs and were able to cite other kinds of evidence:

"When they went to the trading store, the man gave the little girl some candy."

"They wouldn't take the wood that the others had taken

83

out of the water and piled on the shore."

"The little girl went to the house of the sick girl so she could give her some water."

"The little girls helped the baby without being asked."

From evidence of this kind, the children made inferences about what was important to each family. Slowly they developed classifications: "things important for food and shelter," "things important because they are fun," "things that show how people feel about each other." In comparing the families on the basis of these inferred values, the children were acting as anthropologists do when they make cultural comparisons using inferred concepts.

THE INTELLECTUAL DIMENSION

Another Approach to Anthropology

The Anthropology Curriculum Project at the University of Georgia (see also pp. 14–15) developed a sequential curriculum in anthropology for elementary school (grades one through seven, in a graded organization). The project includes teachers' guides and background materials, pupil guides, pupil texts, information sources for pupils, workbooks, and programed materials. Much of the curriculum has been structured around cultural imperatives, or facets of culture (religion, housing, food procurement) that occur in varying forms, thus permitting children to explore simultaneously the similarities and differences between cultures. Anthropological concepts are introduced in the early grades and elaborated throughout the curriculum. They are taught in such a way that the methods by which they were arrived at become apparent: the student sees how the ideas he is being taught were first generated and are constantly being tested. This approach can be seen in the introduction in the *Teachers Guide* to the grade-two unit on archeological methods.

> The objective of this unit is to provide a background for the understanding of the development of man and his culture. The following fundamental principles should be emphasized:
>
> 1. Archeologists use definite and orderly methods in studying the past. These are: (*a*) archeological sites are located and classified; (*b*) archeological sites are carefully excavated using the proper tools and techniques; (*c*) archeological sites are dated using either relative or absolute dating methods; (*d*) the results of an archeological excavation are interpreted and published.
> 2. Archeological excavation can recover only a part of the past.
> 3. The entrance and development of man in the New World followed a certain sequence. This was: (*a*) man entered the New World as *Homo sapiens*, at least 10,000 years ago, following or hunting for large game animals by way of the Bering Strait; (*b*) American Indians developed various stages of culture; (*c*) these stages of culture were not in the order of a developmental sequence except in Nuclear America.[6]

The first page of the pupil guide for the same second-grade unit also shows an emphasis on anthropology as a linguistic system. The children are to learn not only the ideas that are basic to anthropology but also the linguistic map of the discipline. They can then use these to inquire into cultural life.

A. Introduction

The material on archeological methods will show you how an archeologist studies about prehistoric people. The chapter will tell you about the tools an archeologist uses. It will tell you about the methods he uses. Learn the meaning of the words in the vocabulary. The vocabulary contains many archeological words. You should learn these words so that you can understand the work of an archeologist.

B. Archeology words I must use:

absolute dating	interpret
archeologist	laboratory
archeology	organic material
artifacts	preservation
burial site	preserve
calendrical dating	publication
carbon 14 dating	quadrant
cemetery	relative dating
ceremonies	restoration
dendrochronology	site
excavate	stela
excavation	strata
glyph	stratigraphy
habitation	survey
inhabit	trenching
inorganic	vertical

C. Key ideas I am to look for and learn about:
   1. What is an archeologist?
   2. What is archeology?
   3. How do archeologists study about cultures of long ago?
   4. How much can an archeologist find out about cultures of the past?[7]

This excerpt shows that the project uses a direct teaching method, generally referred to as expository. It assumes that the most effective means to provide the student with a system of ideas is to present them to him and to show him, by example and by directing his practice, how to apply them to the study of life. Expository teaching strategies are probably the most common. They have dominated the instructional materials field for many years. Nearly all textbooks and most classroom instruction represent straight exposition of subject matter. The strategy involves identifying the material to be taught, organizing it, and then developing some way to present it to the student.

A teacher may also want to use an inductive or questioning approach to help children understand other cultures. The following questions are suggested in the *Teachers Guide* to the fourth-grade unit.

Teacher question: "What are some cultural universals?"
Anticipated pupil response: "Food, clothing, and shelter."
Teacher question: "What are some of the similarities and differences among these universals?"
Anticipated pupil response: "All men must have food to survive."
Teacher question: "Do all men eat the same types of food?"
Anticipated pupil response: "No."
Teacher question: "Can you name some different types of foods eaten by men in different cultures?"

(The teacher would lead the children into a discussion of this point until it is adequately made.)

Teacher question: "Do all men have the same types of shelter?"
Anticipated pupil response: "No."

(Again, the teacher would lead the children into a discussion of this point until it is adequately made.)

Teacher question: "Do all men wear clothing for the same purpose?"
Anticipated pupil response: "No."
Teacher question: "Can you tell me why different cultures wear different types of clothes for different purposes?"

(Again, the teacher, using the question and answer process, would establish with the children the fact that one's culture determines the purpose of wearing clothes and that geographic factors *may* also contribute to the types of clothing worn.)[8]

The authors of the Georgia Anthropology Project suggest that such questions be used for other universals such as work, tools, communication, and transportation. They also suggest that the teacher use a poster board and felt pen to list universals, similarities, and differences that have been suggested by the pupils. This poster can then be studied and revised as necessary.

The strategy of the project is simple and straightforward. The materials are to be gone over until the student has mastered them; then exercises and discussion are to be used to get the student to apply what he has learned. The project uses a number of interesting direct strategies including programed instruction and a system called "advance organizers." We will look at the latter when we consider the application of theories and principles from psychology to the teaching of the social studies.

History and Culture

What is truth? This question is critical to any perspective on history. The major task of the historian is to identify and describe as precisely as he can the events of the past. But because the historian usually has only limited sources, and because the temper of his times influences his approach to these sources, much of the historian's job is interpretive. Some historians emphasize economic factors; others investigate man's desire for freedom and his struggle against tyranny. Some believe that each historical era is unique; others, like Arnold Toynbee, look for cycles of events or for a sequential unfolding of man's destiny.

There is some controversy about distinctions between history and the social sciences. Krug, for example, builds an extensive case for a view of history as art and literature as well as science.[9] He claims that scientific procedures help to unearth and analyze documents and other evidence about history, artistry helps create a picture of the past, and literary devices help convey the richness of past life. In Krug's view, science, art, and literature constitute the making of history.

Many historians share the view that their job is to discover and comprehend, but not by building extensive predictive theories. Berkhofer says:

> The historian becomes a consumer of social science generalization but not a producer, for his basic task is different. He utilizes social science theory in the assembling and explanation of the components of the unique configuration of events, but no social science generalizations exist to explain the configuration as such. The social sciences promote an awareness of the nature of social relationships in time and allow a systematic approach to the discovery of them but they do not fully explain the entirety of those exact relationships at a given time. . . .
> The historian must continue to explain the configuration in terms of itself, for while generalizations about human behavior can supply the necessary conditions for historical explanation, they cannot produce the sufficient explanation of the configuration. Thus historical explanation must be composed of (1) specific data about individuals,

88

cultures, and societies at a given time, (2) restricted generalizations of (1), and (3) generalizations from the social sciences to explain all human behavior—all combined to produce the historical synthesis to depict the unique configuration. Such an analysis utilizes both the participants' conception of the actions and the results as seen by the historical observer. History is then seen as a dialectic between the actors' wishes and actions and the results, both anticipated and unanticipated, of them.[10]

When asked to write about the nature of history as it should be taught, Henry Steele Commager stressed the uniqueness of individual historians and schools of historical analysis in clarifying and interpreting reality:

> History as a record consists of three states, or processes, usually so skillfully blended that they appear to be a single one. The first is the collection of what are thought to be relevant facts; but remember, what seems relevant to one person will appear irrelevant to another. The second is the organization of these facts into some coherent pattern; but remember, no two patterns are ever quite alike. The third is the interpretation of the facts and of the pattern; and certainly no two interpretations are ever quite alike. Now, all of these processes flow into each other. The practiced historian is not ordinarily conscious of these separate steps any more than a skillful baseball player is conscious of the separate steps that go into a decision to strike at a ball. It is impossible to collect the facts in the first place without some theory of relationships among them; after all, what are you looking for? It is impossible to organize them into a pattern without some theory that dictates the pattern. And it is impossible to interpret them except on the basis of the material that has been selected and the pattern that has been drawn.[11]

89

Historians and educators have long collaborated to improve the teaching of history in the public schools. Unfortunately, from the point of view of the elementary school teacher, this collaboration has suffered from two serious defects: very little of it has been aimed at the elementary school, and any history not directly in the Western tradition has been almost totally neglected. Very few teacher-education programs provide the prospective elementary school teacher with a substantial background in United States history and a balanced understanding of the recorded history of the world. For the forseeable future, elementary school teachers will have to engage in more or less constant self-education projects and joint inquiries with their students. Hence, sources like the

Harvard Guide to American History, which contains excellent bibliographies of primary source materials, become critically important.

History cannot be taught honestly by simply narrating it to children. The process of historical reconstruction must be taught as part of historical fact and interpretation. Perhaps it is not always profitable to lead young children into a detailed examination of the various interpretations of historical events. Children have difficulty just developing ideas about the chronological sequence of historical events and eras. And historical units are most appropriate for the more verbal upper-grade children. Some study of history is important, however, in the lower grades: the child should at least begin to understand his place in time with respect to the evolution of his species; he should begin to learn about those societies from which he has inherited his ideals, tools, and language; and he should become aware of the extent to which historical events have conditioned the lives of various peoples of the world.

The child's earliest experiences with history should confront him with the complexity of historical events and the difficulty of interpreting them. For example, a class might study the following passages about the Civil War, taken from a centennial publication of the U.S. government.

> Other historians, such as Charles A. Beard and Harold U. Faulkner, have argued that slavery was only the surface issue. The real cause, these men state, was "the economic forces let loose by the Industrial Revolution" then taking place in the North. . . .
>
> A third theory advanced by historians is that the threat to states rights led to war. The conflict of the 1860's was thus a "War between the States. . . ."
>
> Still other writers believe "Southern nationalism" to have been the basic cause of the war. Southerners, they assert, had so strong a desire to preserve their particular way of life that they were willing to fight.[12]

As they read history books, the children can search for evidence about the particular theory held by the authors. Nearly every history book for elementary school and nearly every biography of a Civil War figure contains opinions about the origins of the war. These opinions can be examined. In these ways a teacher can avoid giving conclusive explanations of past events. As historian Bernard Weisberger points out:

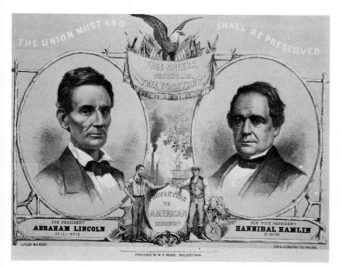

LITH BY W. H. REASE.

THE UNION MUST AND SHALL BE PRESERVED

FREE SPEECH, FREE HOMES, FREE TERRITORY

PROTECTION TO AMERICAN INDUSTRY

FOR PRESIDENT
ABRAHAM LINCOLN
OF ILLINOIS

FOR VICE PRESIDENT
HANNIBAL HAMLIN
OF MAINE

PUBLISHED BY W. H. REASE, PHILADA.

COR. 4th & CHESTNUT STS. PHILADA.

THE STARTING POINT OF THE GREAT WAR BETWEEN THE STATES.
INAUGURATION OF JEFFERSON DAVIS

The student cannot be taught *the* interpretation of our history. The honest teacher can only state that each era of the past has presented acute problems to its people, and that we can learn profitably only by rejecting dogmatism as we consider the alternatives which bygone generations weighed, examine the choices they made, and assess the results of these choices.[13]

History should be taught as the scholar studies it, with a careful attention to sources of information and with a careful development of the facts from which conclusions are drawn. For example, an upper-grade teacher might display U.S. maps showing both the navigable waterways and the areas of settlement in the years 1650, 1700, and 1750. The child, examining these data, can conclude that a distinct relation existed between population distribution and waterways. People lived near water routes. However, examining more maps from colonial times to the present, he will discover that many large population centers later developed away from water transport, and he can begin his hunt for other operative factors. When history is taught by such methods, the child has to encounter the tentative state of our conclusions about human events, and he has to participate in the process of modifying ideas as new facts come to light. He is engaged in the exciting attempt to explain—to try out ideas and see whether the data confirm them.

Many interesting questions can lead the child to historical inquiry. Why was Williamsburg abandoned as the chief city of Virginia? Why did New York become so large? What led to the founding of our town? What was the economic position of the men who wrote the Constitution? Biography enables even fairly young children to study individual lives intensively. Through the depth study of a few key individuals, children can engage in an analytical approach that is exciting as well as true to the methods of the historian.

We need more units designed to help elementary school children explore problems of interpretation. These units need to be planned and carried out carefully, both because of the complexity of the problem and because of the verbal limitations. But they can be successful with a majority of children. A simple guiding rule is to provide the children with specific data and concrete examples of events whenever possible. For example, the following information is clear and easy to reason about.

At the beginning of the Civil War, the North seemed to possess every advantage:

(1) 23 Northern states aligned against only 11 Southern states. . . .

(2) The population of the Northern states was approximately 22,000,000 people. The Southern states had only 9,105,000 people and one-third of them (3,654,000) were slaves. . . .

(3) The North had 110,000 manufacturing plants, as compared with 18,000 in the Confederate States. The North produced 97 % of all firearms in America, and it manufactured 96 % of the nation's railroad equipment.[14]

After examining the implications of these data and working out an understanding of other relevant economic and human factors, the students can proceed to an examination of the reasons why the war persisted so long.

In the presentation of its unit *What Happened on Lexington Green?* the Amherst Project Committee on the Study of History expressed the view that to comprehend history, students must understand the processes of historical reconstruction and inter-pretation. The unit leads children to study what happened at Lexington bridge in April 1775. In the first part of the unit the students examine several documents in an attempt to ascertain the facts. They use the question "Who fired the first shot?" as a focus. The following are two examples of the documents:

93

Lexington, April 23, 1775

I, Thomas Fessenden, of lawful age, testify and declare, that being in a pasture near the meeting house at said Lexington, on Wednesday, last, at about half an hour before sunrise . . . I saw three officers on horseback advance to the front of said Regulars, when one of them being within six rods of the said Militia, cried out, "Disperse, you rebels, immediately;" on which he brandished his sword over his head three times; meanwhile the second officer, who was about two rods behind him, fired a pistol pointed at said Militia, and the Regulars kept huzzaing till he had finished brandishing his sword, and when he had thus finished brandishing his sword, he pointed it down towards said Militia, and immediately on which the said Regulars fired a volley at the Militia, and then I ran off, as fast as I could, while they continued firing till I got out of their reach. I further testify, that as soon as ever the official cried "Disperse, you rebels," the said Company of Militia dispersed every way as fast as they could, and while they were dispersing the Regulars kept firing at them incessantly, and further saith not.

THOMAS FESSENDEN

The following version came from the personal diary of a young British officer, Lieutenant John Barker:

19th. At 2 o'clock we began our March by wading through a very long ford up to our Middles: after going a few miles we took 3 or 4 People who were going off to give intelligence; about 5 miles on this side of a Town called Lexington, which lay in our road, we heard there were some hundreds of People collected together intending to oppose us and stop our going on; at 5 o'clock we arrived there, and saw a number of People, I believe between 2 and 300, formed in a Common in the middle of the Town; we still continued advancing, keeping prepared against an attack tho' without intending to attack them; but on our coming near them they fired one or two shots, upon which our Men without any orders, rushed in upon them, fired and put 'em to flight; several of them were killed, we cou'd not tell how many, because they were got behind Walls and into the Woods; we had a Man of the 10th Infantry wounded, nobody else hurt. We then formed on the Common, but with some difficulty, the Men were so wild they cou'd hear no orders; we waited a considerable time there, and at length proceeded on our way to Concord. . . .[15]

As the students proceed through the conflicting evidence, they are presented with textbook statements about the day at Lexington. The purpose of this juxtaposition of various historical sources is to make the students aware of the problems of interpreting what is written about history. For example:

OUR AMERICAN REPUBLIC
by D. S. Muzzey and A. S. Link

Before the second Congress met, however, the clash of arms had come. The colonial militia had been training for several months. Bands of "minutemen" had been organized, ready to march at a minute's notice to meet any attack by the king's troops. Late in the night of April 18, 1775, Gage sent out a thousand men under Major Pitcairn to seize colonial supplies of powder at Concord, about twenty miles from Boston. But the patriots had learned of the plan. Paul Revere and William Dawes, riding by different routes, warned the countryside that the British were coming.

When Pitcairn reached Lexington, in the early dawn, he found a company of about seventy minutemen drawn up on the common to dispute his passage. He ordered the "rebels" to disperse. A shot was fired by some unknown person. It was the signal for a volley from the British, which killed eight of the minutemen.[16]

THE UNITED STATES: STORY OF A FREE PEOPLE
by Samuel Steinberg

In April 1775, General Gage, the military governor of
Massachusetts, sent out a body of troops to take possession of military
stores at Concord, a short distance from Boston. At Lexington, a
handful of "embattled farmers," who had been tipped off by
Paul Revere, barred the way. The "rebels" were ordered to disperse.
They stood their ground. The English fired a volley of shots that
killed eight patriots. It was not long before the swiftriding Paul Revere
spread the news of this new atrocity to the neighboring colonies. The
patriots of all of New England, although still a handful, were now
ready to fight the English. Even in faraway North Carolina, patriots
organized to resist them.[17]

The issues and readings become more and more complex.
Questions are asked about the nature of reality and man's problems in apprehending it and communicating his perceptions.

Not all the units in the Amherst series are as adaptable to as
wide a range of children as this one, and not all of them stress the
nature of historical inquiry as exhaustively. Each is, however, a
depth study in which the nature of inquiry receives as much
attention as the subject matter. Each unit reiterates that human
behavior cannot be discussed meaningfully apart from the
processes by which it is apprehended. The topics for the units
have been selected not simply to illustrate epistemological
questions, but for their social significance as well. For example,
depth studies have been developed on the following topics:

Korea and the Limits of Limited War

Freedom and Authority in Puritan New England

Communism in America: Liberty and Security in Conflicts

Hiroshima: A Study in Science, Politics, and the Ethics of
War

Liberty and Law: The Nature of Individual Rights

The Embargo of 1807: A Study in Policymaking

God and the Government: Problems of Church and State

Conscience and the Law: The Uses and Limits of Civil
Disobedience

We find the same kind of thinking about how to teach history
in the Minnesota Social Studies project. In the teacher's guide

95

to the sixth-grade history course, there appears the following passage:

> When we turn from the causes of the Revolution to the accomplishments we are as perplexed as before. According to recent interpreters, the colonists fought to preserve their already possessed rights, not to gain new ones. If this is so, then was the Revolution a "Revolution" in the sense that the word is usually used? To interpret the war as a "conservative revolution" as is now popular, does not mean, however, that certain things that represented a changed condition did not occur. But were these aimed-for or unaimed-for consequences of the initial urge to fight? If they were unaimed-for, then can we call them part of the Revolution in the same sense that we say the aimed-for consequences were? For example, the colonists obviously wanted written constitutions for their newly-established governments, but was the federal constitution so obviously the result of the Revolution from the viewpoint of the actor? Lastly, the Americans conceived of the Revolution as a real revolution in the history of Western Civilization. According to them, it ushered in a new kind of nation never before existing in the world. This is yet another meaning of the term American Revolution in comparative perspective.
>
> To teach fully the American Revolution, the teacher would have to cover all these many meanings of the phrase and still more. The extent to which this can be accomplished even in the high school level is doubtful, and it is clearly impossible in the sixth grade. Yet some image of this crucial period in American history must be conveyed even to a student upon this level. In order to do this, the strategy must be to select those aspects of the cluster of multiple meanings that can be understood in an elementary level without distortion and leave the remainder for comprehension at an advanced grade. Varying amounts of understanding can be achieved on all three phases of causes, hostilities, and results of the Revolution, but none will be understood completely by a sixth-grader.[18]

To teach history by mingling the study of historical process with the attempt to help children apprehend and interpret the record of a culture, a series of depth studies should be organized. As the children study the heritage, they see how the record was gathered and interpreted, and they can improve their capacity to create knowledge as well as to consume knowledge and interpretations developed by others.

Social Psychology Research Methods:
A Human Relations Curriculum

Until recently there were many experiments in human relations teaching at the elementary school level but relatively few systematic attempts to teach children how to use social science methods to probe interpersonal life. The Michigan Social Science Curriculum Project, directed by Ronald Lippitt and Robert Fox, developed a very powerful but simple approach: teach the research techniques of social psychology directly to children through human relations content, including their own behavior. The project presents social psychology as a living discipline whose concepts and method emerge through continuous inquiry into human behavior. It also demonstrates the relevance of social science to human affairs.

Their materials include seven laboratory units organized around a resource book, or text, and a series of project books. These units begin with a unit entitled "Learning to Use Social Science." In this unit the children learn how samples of behavior can be obtained; how observations can be used to make descriptions, inferences, or value judgments; how causal relationships can be found among physical phenomena as well as among human behaviors; how to deal with multiple causation and circularity in human interaction. After introducing general methods such as diagraming multiple causation, the units proceed to human relations situations, such as the following.

97

> Julia was tired of standing in line. Why doesn't the teacher open the door and let us in? she wondered. The bell rang a long time ago, and besides, it's cold outside.
>
> Julia looked at Wendy, who was standing ahead of her in line. She was talking to Dick. Why doesn't she turn around and talk to me? Julia thought.
>
> Dick and Wendy started to laugh. Julia became angry. I bet they're laughing at me, she told herself. They were probably talking about me. I'll get even with them!
>
> Finally the teacher opened the door and the line started to move. Julia gave Wendy a hard push. Wendy fell against Dick and almost knocked him down.
>
> Dick glared at Wendy. "What's the matter with you!" he exclaimed.
> "Julia pushed me," said Wendy.

"I did not," Julia said. "Caroline pushed me and I couldn't help hitting you."

"I did not!" Caroline protested. Several children had seen what happened. "Liar! Liar!" they cried, "Julia is a liar!"

The teacher came to see what was the matter. "What's going on here?" she said.

Caroline's best friend, Martha, spoke up. "Julia pushed Wendy. I saw her do it, and now she's trying to blame it on Caroline."

Julia began to cry. Nobody likes me, she thought. I don't know why, but nobody likes me.[19]

After reading this behavioral sample, the students are helped to analyze it.

THE INTELLECTUAL DIMENSION

Directions: As you read the story about Julia, you probably noticed that Julia's *feelings*, *intentions*, and *actions* formed a circular process as she interacted with the other children. Fill in the *feelings*, *intentions*, and *actions* of Julia and the other children in the appropriate circles below.[20]

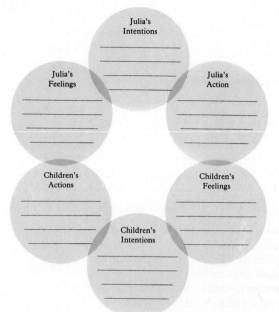

Julia's
Intentions
_____
_____

Julia's
Feelings
_____
_____

Julia's
Action
_____
_____

Children's
Actions
_____
_____

Children's
Feelings
_____
_____

Children's
Intentions
_____
_____

The children compare their analyses of this and other samples. In checking observations and inferences against one another, they come to understand problems of obtaining agreement about observations. They also learn to analyze interaction using circular analysis.

Another activity involves using observation guides to analyze the behavior of participants in situations called behavior specimens. The following guide is part of a set of activities designed to help the children identify and theorize about multiple causation.

Directions: You will observe Bob in the behavior specimen "Going Fishing." Try to put yourself in Bob's shoes. Think about how Bob feels. Think about why Bob acts the way he does. The questions below will help you make your observation report. Answer the questions when the specimen is over.

At the end of the specimen Bob goes away. This behavior is the effect. You will report some of the causes for this effect.[21]

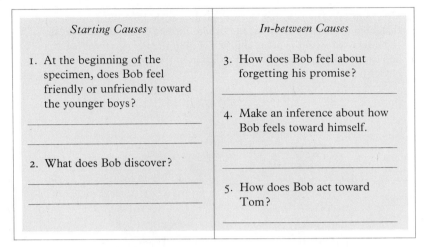

Starting Causes	In-between Causes
1. At the beginning of the specimen, does Bob feel friendly or unfriendly toward the younger boys? _____ _____	3. How does Bob feel about forgetting his promise? _____
2. What does Bob discover? _____ _____	4. Make an inference about how Bob feels toward himself. _____ _____
	5. How does Bob act toward Tom? _____

BOB

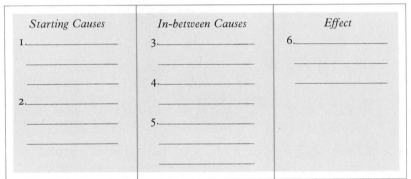

Starting Causes	In-between Causes	Effect
1._____ _____ _____ 2._____ _____ _____	3._____ _____ 4._____ _____ 5._____ _____ _____	6._____ _____ _____

A final series of activities introduces the children to experiments that have generated interesting theories about friendly and unfriendly behavior and cooperation and competition.

This type of approach focuses the children's study on human interaction, provides an academic frame of reference and techniques for delineating and carrying out inquiry, and involves the student in the study of his own behavior and that of people around him. The intention of the project is that the student take on some of the characteristics of the social scientist as he makes his way through the interpersonal world. Thus the intellectual, social, and personal dimensions are unified, although the organizing concepts of social psychology provide the scaffolding for the curriculum.

INQUIRIES

1. Imagine that you are helping upper-grade students plan a study of the family in their community. How would you help them plan their study so that some of the organizing concepts of anthropology, history, and social psychology, as suggested in this chapter, are brought to bear on it?

2. The following is a document about life in a medieval town. How might children learn to handle information like this using the organizing concepts of history or anthropology?

From a letter to Lord Montgomery from his steward* while at Ludlow.

October 19, 1095

My Dear Lord.

After spending this past month at Ludlow, I can write that all goes well. I hope that it is so also with you and your Lady.

The apples and pears are gathered and stored in the castle. This year's crop sold high at the Shrewsbury Fair. I have begun the building of a new ox-shed one hundred feet long. John Holcom, your reeve† here, knows what must be done to complete it. He has proved a loyal servant to you and a good helper to your steward. I recommend that he be reelected to serve you for another year.

The lamb's fur has been laid in for the winter as has wood for burning, brewing, and baking. Three hundred ells‡ of cloth have been bought from Shrewsbury Fair for the poor pensioners. I do not advise selling the cattle at Ludlow this year. Herefordshire has brought so many that the price is very low.

The hops have been gathered as well as the honey, and brewing of the ale has begun. I fear that I must urge you to take immediate action to halt the progress of your neighbor on the east. His peasants each day plow a few more inches into your land and thus enlarge their Lord's own.

With regard to the purchase of Lady Mortimer's property I advise you to drive a hard bargain. She is very pressed at this time and her land may go cheaply.

Two of our men were again stopped by the bailiffs§ of Temebury while crossing the bridge over the Teme. There was a fair fight and

---

*One who manages domestic concerns
†An official who made sure that feudal obligations were fulfilled
‡A former English unit of length chiefly for cloth—about 45 inches
§One who manages an estate or farm

nothing was lost on our side. One bailiff was badly hurt. I think this
will be the last time the bailiffs try to get tribute* from
your Lordship.

On the matter of your bailiff at Ludlow; many of the serfs have
complained bitterly about him to me. It is not only the usual crying
that he demands too much service on his strips. They claim that he
makes them buy ale from him at double the lawful price and that he
treats them roughly. What's more, your auditors have found him to be
either a poor record keeper or a thief. His accounts show hay,
victuals,† and cloth, marked down as offered to three travelers.
The bailiff says he extended your hospitality to them knowing that
you would have wished him to. But the auditors say there was not
authority from you either saved or recorded.

3. The following two conversations might have taken place in a little town
in southern France. Two versions of each conversation are given. One
indicates a relationship that is punitive and suspicious; the other a
relationship that is open to change and allows its participants to reach
out to one another. Which version would be more likely to occur in our
culture? How can culture influence personal relationships? Can healthy
personal relationships be strong enough to counteract cultural influences? How might children explore these conversations from the
perspective of social psychology?

M. Minot and Pierre

Version A

M. Minot: Pierre Rivet! Are you in here again? I thought I told you
to stay out of here.

Pierre: But M'sieu, Mama needs the bread for dinner. Papa is
away. When he comes home, he'll pay you.

M. Minot: Just what you said last week. And the week before. I want
to talk to your mother. Now she owes me almost a hundred
francs [about twenty dollars]. When is she going to pay
me? I can't run a business like this. No money, no bread.

Pierre: If we don't have the bread, we'll only have soup for supper.

M. Minot: That's fine with me. You tell your Papa to pay his debt to
me. And in the future no credit.

---

*An excessive tax, rental, or tariff
†Food

Version B

PIERRE: M. Minot, Mama asked me to come get some bread for supper.

M. MINOT: And did your Mama send some money along to pay for the bread?

PIERRE: Mama doesn't have any money. And Papa is away. Mama said, would it be all right if Papa paid when he got back?

M. MINOT: Let's see, Pierre. You've been buying bread and some other things here for a month without paying. The bill is almost a hundred francs. When will your Papa be home?

PIERRE: He's helping down in the stables at Marseilles. The horses are to go North next week. He'll be home then for the summer.

M. MINOT: All right, Pierre. Here is your bread. And send your Papa in to settle the bill. Anytime next week is fine.

Jacqueline and Michelle

Version A

MICHELLE: Jacqueline! Wait for me! I'm coming! We're going to be late for school!

JACQUELINE: No we're not. There's plenty of time. The bell hasn't rung yet. Anyway, I'm not supposed to talk to you.

MICHELLE: Why not? Are you mad at me?

JACQUELINE: Of course not! What for? It's Mama. She and your Mama had a fight yesterday. My Mama said that our Charles was too good for your sister. She doesn't want him to marry her. He will be a lawyer soon. He will make a lot of money and live in a big house. She thinks that he can marry anyone he likes. And Marie has always stayed here in the village. She doesn't have much schooling and she's never been anywhere. Now my Mama and your Mama are "brouillées"—not speaking.

MICHELLE: Oh, Jacqueline! That is terrible. Poor Marie! She has thought of nothing but Charles for the last five years. What is going to happen to her—and to us?

JACQUELINE: Oh, don't worry about it. Mama still thinks that the world is like it was when she was young. Charles is quiet when she talks. Then he does as he pleases.

MICHELLE: And us? Can we still be friends?

JACQUELINE: Yes—Mama will change. She has always liked Marie. And when Marie and Charles get married, we'll almost be sisters! Don't worry, Michelle.

Version B

MICHELLE: Jacqueline! The school bell is going to ring in a minute! Let's hurry.

JACQUELINE: I'm not talking to you.

MICHELLE: Why not? Are you mad at me?

JACQUELINE: Not really. But my Mama is mad at your Mama. Now we are "brouillées"—not speaking.

MICHELLE: Did they have a fight?

JACQUELINE: Don't you know *anything*? It's about Marie and Charles. All this time Charles has been away getting his education and Marie has stayed home. Now they want to get married! Marie will not make a good wife for an important man like Charles is going to be! Mama says so. And even Charles is beginning to wonder about it.

MICHELLE: That's not fair. Marie is the best cook for miles around. She'll be helping the chef at the new hotel this summer. And she can sew and keep house. Charles isn't going to be *that* important. Marie will make him a very good wife.

JACQUELINE: What do you know about it? Charles is going to be a lawyer. He will know everyone important in the city. He'll have to give parties and everything. What can Marie do to help him? Keeping house and cooking are not enough.

MICHELLE: If that's the way you feel, I'm glad we're not speaking. You and your Mama can keep your old Charles. He's not good enough for Marie, if all he thinks about is getting to be important. And you need never speak to me again, Jacqueline. Because I'll never speak to you.

NOTES

1. Although we have altered the nomenclature slightly, the three kinds of concepts discussed here were developed by anthropologist John J. Honigmann in his book *The World of Man* (New York: Harper, 1959). For what we have designated as observed, inferred, and ideal-type concepts,

Honigmann uses the terms *concept by inspection, concept by postulation,* and *ideal-type concept,* respectively.

2. Honigmann, *The World of Man,* p. 53.

3. Margaret Mead and Rhoda Metraux, eds., *The Study of Culture at a Distance* (Chicago: Univ. of Chicago Press, 1953), p. 26. Anthropologist Meyer F. Nimkoff has defined cultural behavior similarly: "Of central importance in the culture concept is the idea that such behavior is learned from the group and is not inherent or biological" ("Anthropology, Sociology, and Social Psychology," in Erling M. Hunt and others, *High School Social Studies Perspectives* [Boston: Houghton Mifflin, 1962], p. 31).

4. Charles W. Lange, *Cochiti: A New Mexico Pueblo, Past and Present* (Austin: Univ. of Texas Press, 1959).

5. Bruce R. and Elizabeth H. Joyce, "Searching for Strategies for Social Education," *Elementary School Journal* 66 (February 1966), pp. 272–83.

6. Anthropology Curriculum Project, *The Concept of Culture: Teachers Guide,* Grade Two (Athens: Univ. of Georgia, 1965), p. 1.

7. Anthropology Curriculum Project, *The Concept of Culture: Pupils Guide,* Grade Two, p. 1.

8. Anthropology Curriculum Project, *The Concept of Culture: Teachers Guide,* Grade Four, pp. 4–6.

9. Mark M. Krug, *History and the Social Sciences* (Toronto: Blaisdell, 1967).

10. Robert F. Berkhofer, Jr., "The Many Meanings of History," Project Social Studies Discipline Paper (Univ. of Minnesota, n.d.), pp. 11–12.

11. Henry Steele Commager, *The Nature and the Study of History* (Columbus, Ohio: Merrill, 1965), p. 5.

12. U.S. Civil War Centennial Commission, *The Civil War,* prepared by James I. Robertson, Jr. (Washington, 1963), p. 5.

13. Bernard A. Weisberger, "United States History," in Erling M. Hunt and others, *High School Social Studies Perspectives* (Boston: Houghton Mifflin, 1962), p. 130.

14. Centennial Commission, *The Civil War,* pp. 7–8.

15. Peter S. Bennett, *What Happened at Lexington Green? An Inquiry into the Nature and Methods of History,* Student Handbook, ed. Richard H. Brown and Van R. Halsey (Reading, Mass.: Addison-Wesley, 1970), pp. 9–10.

16. D. S. Muzzey and A. S. Link, *Our American Republic* (Boston: Ginn, 1963), p. 78.

17. Samuel Steinberg, *The United States: Story of a Free People* (Boston: Allyn & Bacon, 1963), p. 92.

18. *Teacher's Guide to the Sixth Grade Course on United States History: From Community to Society,* Project Social Studies Curriculum Center (Univ. of Minnesota, 1968), pp. 8–9.

19. "Friendly and Unfriendly Behavior," *Social Science Laboratory Units,* Project Book 3 (Chicago: Science Research Associates, 1969) p. 1.

20. Ibid., p. 2.

21. Ibid., p. 22.

105

SYSTEMS THINKING IN THE SOCIAL SCIENCES: POLITICAL SCIENCE, ECONOMICS, AND GEOGRAPHY

As the disciplines have moved into the latter half of the twentieth century, three of them have begun to use ideas heavily influenced by systems thinking in electronics, engineering, and communications. The use of computers to simulate reality and to process huge amounts of information has encouraged the application of systems thinking within political science, economics, and geography.

Political Science: Patterns of Political Behavior

Analysts have identified a variety of approaches to the study of political science.[1] The topics that political scientists examine differ markedly.

The differences in the kinds of knowledge we seek and the methods of inquiry we pursue account for the statement so often made that in spite of the common terrain for exploration, American political scientists constitute not one discipline but several disciplines.[2]

There is general agreement, however, that "the subject matter of political science is legal government, including its history, agencies, processes, structure, functions, composition, rationale, and influence."[3] Increasingly, political scientists have been analyzing political behavior, as distinct from political structure or law. Many political scientists agree that their critical concept is power as it relates to decisions about what is valued in a society and how valued things will be allocated or regulated. This focus on power may be substantiated by a large number of quotations from authors of widely different views.

> Politics means the rise towards participation in power or influence in the distribution of power between states. (Max Weber)
>
> Politics is the study of authority relations between individuals and groups and the hierarchy of power which establishes itself within all numerous and complex communities. (Raymond Aron)
>
> A brief definition of the scope of political science is the study of power, in other words with the phenomena of command which appears in a society. (George Vedel)[4]

In every social group there are those who give the orders and those who obey. The word *power* describes both the governing group and the function that the group fulfills.[5]

The political scientist observes this power from several viewpoints. He observes and catalogs the activities over which legal government exercises control. Is speech and other communication controlled? Are economic activities regulated and to what extent? The political scientist also observes how the power to make decisions is distributed. Who exercises power? Are religious leaders also political leaders? Do industrial leaders tend to have political power? Does the newspaper editor influence political decisions? Are all people entitled to vote, and do they exercise that right? Political scientists are concerned with the distribution of power in formal and informal institutions. What is the form of the government? Is there a king, president, military dictator? Are there political parties? How are they organized? Who exercises the judicial functions? What are the mechanisms for carrying out the law?

As in anthropology, the work of political scientists can be described in terms of the three levels of concepts. Observed concepts apply, for example, when the constitutional duties of legislatures in different states are compared. A typical inferred concept is that Supreme Court decisions have changed because sentiments among the American people have changed. Ideal-type concepts apply when various regimes are compared and categorized—for instance, when the terms *totalitarian* and *democratic* are used as guides to the classification of nation-states.

Further work is needed to pull together the thinking of political scientists and to identify the central concepts, but perhaps these characteristics of political science inquiry can help us determine how best to introduce young children to the political aspects of society. The teaching strategy can lead children to examine power in human groups from the viewpoint of the activities that are controlled, the ways power is distributed, and the institutions that implement power. A fourth-grade class, for example, studying the government of its local community, might interview public officials. In their conversation with the chief of police the children may find that he is not formally a member of a political party and has no official place in the lawmaking process. However, they may also find that the city council sometimes accepts the police chief's recommendations, thus giving him a part in decision making even though he has no vote in that body. The children may learn that their city charter permits the city council and the school board to assess taxes on real estate and that the council or a zoning board makes rules about the kind of building or the use of land permitted in various areas of the town. They may also find that the right to assemble is protected by the U.S. Constitution but that the number of people who can assemble under one roof is determined by the fire marshal.

At the High School Curriculum Center in Government, Indiana University, John Patrick and Howard Mehlinger have developed a high school civics program entitled *American Political Behavior*. The instructional materials use a social science perspective that might be useful for the elementary level. The program seeks to help students become better observers of American political behavior, including their own, and thus to become more politically effective. Most lessons open with the presentation of political incidents, case studies, or data about political behavior. The students are led to analyze this material and to draw conclusions. Lessons build on one another so that areas of political life are covered and student analysis becomes more sophisticated and scientific. The course consists of five major units.

Introduction to the Study of Political Behavior. In this unit students are introduced to the meaning of political behavior, to the social science approach to the study of politics, and to the process of making value judgments and policy decisions about political affairs.

Similarities and Differences in Political Behavior. In this unit students learn about the relationship of social factors to political attitudes and political behavior. Basic concepts are introduced such as role, socioeconomic status, culture, socialization, and personality. This unit includes material about the political behavior of ethnic groups.

Elections and Voting Behavior. This unit focuses on the relationship of various social and psychological factors to voting behavior. Other topics are the formal and informal rules that direct the election process in our society, the differences between the major political parties, and the consequences of voting behavior.

Political Decision-Makers. In this unit students learn about the political roles of four types of public officials in the national government: the President, congressmen, bureaucrats, and judges. The rights and duties of each role type, the recruitment of individuals to the role, and the decision-making activities of the role occupant are emphasized.

Unofficial Political Specialists. In this unit students learn about individuals who influence public policy decisions, but who do not hold formal positions in the government. Four types of unofficial political leaders are studied: the interest group leader, the news commentator, the expert-consultant, and the political party leader.[6]

The following case study, which treats the campaign strategies of the 1964 presidential candidates, appeared in the early, trial version of the course. Although not a part of the published version, it represents one kind of material in the course.

Barry Goldwater and his Republican supporters waged a hard-hitting campaign. They realized that they faced a difficult, "up-hill" campaign battle. Yet, persistent optimism and a firm faith in the "rightness" of their cause motivated the Goldwater forces to wage a spirited fight.

Goldwater based his campaign strategy upon three assumptions: First, he argued that the American people were ready to embrace "conservative" political ideas. Goldwater believed that they wanted a clear-cut alternative to the big government, welfare-program policies of the Democrats. According to Goldwater, Republican candidates had failed in the past because they tried too hard to be like the Democrats. Goldwater claimed that his policies would attract Republican support as never before. He argued that too many Republican voters were staying away from the polls on election day, because neither the Republican nor the Democratic Presidential candidates were attractive choices. Thus, Goldwater's campaign slogan became "a choice, not an echo," which reflected his belief that his candidacy would attract large numbers of "stay-at-home" Republicans to his banner. Also, Goldwater sincerely believed that the tide of public opinion was rising in favor of his "conservative" political policies and values.

The second major assumption around which Goldwater built his campaign strategy was that he could win the Presidency without appealing to the large urban areas of the North and Northeast. Rather, he hoped to combine traditional Republican strength in the West and the Middle West, rural and small town centers, with newly won support in the South. Goldwater believed that this combination of states would bring enough electoral votes to gain the Presidency. His attempts to attract support from the once solidly Democratic South was a new departure for a Republican party Presidential candidate.

Goldwater's third major assumption was that his "conservative" stand on several current issues would attract the support of the American people. He took a "hard line" against Communist nations, vowing to use military force without hesitation to check Communist expansion around the world. He stated that field commanders might have the option of using tactical nuclear weapons in the Vietnam conflict. He gave the impression that he wanted to escalate the nation's military involvement in Vietnam.

Concerning domestic issues, Goldwater suggested that major government welfare programs should be limited. He said that disadvantaged people should not look to the government for assistance. Rather, they should rely on individual initiative; they should "pull themselves up by their own bootstraps." During the New Hampshire primary, he suggested that the social security program be made voluntary. Later, he attacked proposals for medical assistance to the aged. A major theme of the Goldwater campaign was denunciation of "big government" as an enemy of individual initiative and freedom.

Concerning race relations and civil rights, Goldwater favored local control and individual efforts to achieve harmony in race relations. He opposed the Civil Rights Law of 1964, because it gave the Federal government power to force mixing of the races in places of business. He claimed that this was a denial of property rights and individual freedom. This stand attracted wide support in the Southern states.

110

Lyndon Johnson's campaign strategy contrasted greatly with Goldwater's strategy. Johnson proposed a "war on poverty" and the building of a "Great Society." The power and resources of the Federal Government would be used to extend educational and economic opportunities. Johnson's proposals were directly in line with the "New Deal" policies of the Democratic President Franklin D. Roosevelt and the "New Frontier" program of President John F. Kennedy.

Johnson charged that Goldwater was hostile to the interests of organized labor and of manual workers. He claimed that a Goldwater victory would threaten the economic security of manual workers. Johnson also pictured Goldwater as "trigger happy" and warlike, because of his hard-line approach to relations with Communist nations.[7]

In cases such as this, students are presented with samples of behavior and taught techniques that political scientists use to identify political behavior and its causes. Many of the cases involve current issues.

Such material leads the students to take positions on political life as well as to form concepts about it. To ensure dialog, an integral part of the strategy, the curriculum is usually administered to classroom groups. This group interaction leads the student to examine his social life and become involved in society.

The Indiana University curriculum materials differ from most recent social studies programs, which usually treat the structure or legal setup of formal political institutions. More attention should be given to the concepts of power and to the actual behavior of politics and government. Some political scientists are beginning to use systems analysis in order to do this.

No one way of conceptualizing any major area of human behavior will do full justice to all its variety and complexity. The conceptual orientation that I am proposing—systems analysis—stems from the fundamental decision to view political life as a system of behavior. Its major and gross unit of analysis is the political system, and this theoretical orientation will be given a specific and restricted meaning.

Systems analysis, as conceived here, is built upon the following premises and only the first two of these are shared with other modes of analysis that use the "systems" concept.

1. *System:* It is useful to view political life as a system of behavior.
2. *Environment:* A system is distinguishable from its environment and open to influence from it.
3. *Response:* Variation in the structures and processes within a system may usefully be interpreted as constructive alternative efforts by

members of a system to regulate and cope with stress flowing from environmental as well as internal sources.

4. *Feedback:* The capacity of a system to persist in the face of stress depends on the flow of information, to the decision-makers in the system, about the effects of their decisions on the environment and on the system itself. The term "information" should, in this context, be construed to include influences and pressures, as well as facts.[8]

The third and fourth premises distinguish systems analysis from other approaches to the study of political life that at least implicitly interpret it as a system of behavior. The systems analyst tries to conceptualize the political system in terms of subsystems and related systems that make up the entire environment of political behavior. The resulting map (fig. 2) can be very complex, but it is handy for the study of political behavior by the advanced scholar and novice alike.

The Providence Social Studies Curriculum Project has organized a series of units to help children explore systems of political behavior. One of their sixth-grade units, for example, is devoted to the governmental systems of Latin America. The study includes cultural and historical factors, the economic systems, the processes by which authority is legitimized, and the processes through which it operates. Probably one of the most important implications of these conceptions of political life is that they urge the student to view political science as a constructed science of concepts and research methods. Through them the student also comes to view political behavior as patterned and understandable. He sees it as a system intertwined with the other subsystems (economic, status, and so on) within a cultural system. Politics itself becomes a system for deciding what will be valued and how valued things will be dealt with. Thus teaching a behavioristic political science verges on changing the average American citizen's political behavior. He becomes more analytical and concerned with the reconstruction of society.

113

Economics: Systems Approaches to the Study of Economic Systems

Like political science, economics has been defined in various ways, and individual economists emphasize different aspects of economic processes. Nonetheless, for working purposes, many economists accept this definition: "Economics is a study of the

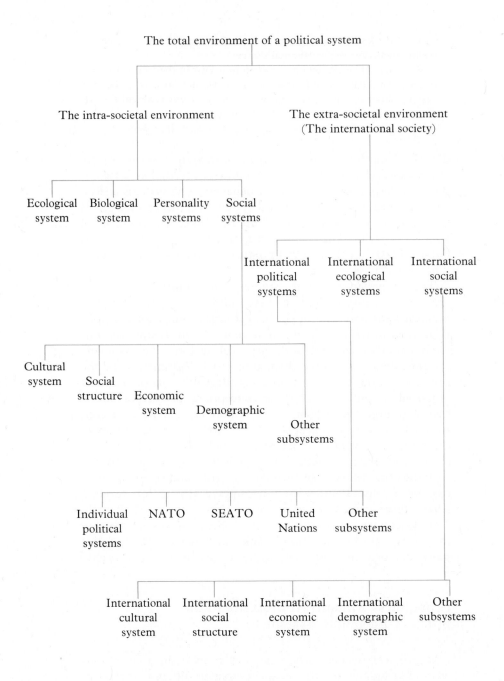

Fig. 2. Components of the total environment of a political system

problem of using the scarce means of a human society to satisfy competing ends as fully as possible."[9] Lawrence Senesh has suggested that a form of the following definition provide the frame of reference for economic education: "All people and all nations are confronted with the conflict between their unlimited wants and limited resources."[10] In his view, the center of economic study is the choice-making process involved in the production, exchange, and consumption of goods.

At times, each of these aspects can be emphasized. What is produced? How? What gives it value? What is the organization of people and resources? Who makes the decision to produce something? What relative values are assigned to various goods? How is value determined? What needs give rise to what kinds of valuation? What kinds of institutions are involved in exchange and value setting? Who gets what, and how is allocation determined? What institutions are involved in distribution?

Macroeconomics is the study of these activities on a large scale, as on a national level, and includes the role of governmental policies in actively influencing economic affairs. Macroeconomics is frequently involved with normative decisions, such as whether governments should or should not undertake to effect a balance of trade. Most questions on the macrolevel are too difficult for children, because the mass of information is too large and the relations between data too intricate. However, many of the concepts can be studied on a small scale in situations that simulate the national level of activity.

115

The concepts of economics submit to the same three-way classification that was used in anthropology and political science. Observed concepts come from the economist's observation of what goods are produced in various regions of the world, how factories, banks, and markets work, and what kinds of advertising are used to promote sales. The economist infers relations between the abundance of capital and the development of production facilities. He infers that where demand increases, prices will rise unless production keeps pace. He also classifies economic conditions into ideal-type concepts such as "free enterprise," "socialism," and "underdeveloped economy."

Senesh has conducted a series of investigations exploring economic education in the elementary school. In part of his study he has shown that economic concepts can be understood when applied to the family by young children. In the following passage from his study, each section is preceded by the statement of the concept being developed for the children.

A division of labor takes place within the family which increases the efficiency of the family.

Curriculum Interpretation: Work in the home is done more efficiently when each member of the family does what he is best fitted to do.

Student Activities: Children draw pictures or tell stories showing how the various members of the family help in the home. The children may play "A Morning at Home," with the mother preparing breakfast and putting up father's lunch, with father getting ready for work and the children getting ready for school. A second scene will show mother preparing dinner, father returning home to do repair jobs about the house, and the children running errands for the parents and feeding their pets. After the play the children discuss or draw pictures about what would happen if everyone in the family tried to cook the meals at the same time: father would be late for work, children late for school, everyone annoyed, repair jobs and errands neglected.

Within the home all members of the family are consumers, but only some are producers.

Curriculum Interpretation: In the home parents, grandparents, children, healthy and sick, young and old, use or consume durable goods, nondurable goods, and services. Only certain members of the family produce inside and outside the home.

Student Activities: The students draw pictures showing the family's consumption needs: food, clothing, shelter, electricity, automobiles, furniture, air, sunshine, water. Another drawing shows those members of the family who are consumers only: the very young and the very old. A third picture shows those members of the family who are producers at home only: mother doing house chores, a retired man working in the garden. In a fourth picture are those members of the family who are producers inside the home as well as outside the home: father working at the office and also cutting grass at home; mother working in a store, and also at home cooking meals. These drawings can be an outgrowth of a classroom discussion of what the family's needs are and how certain members of the family provide for those needs.

All producers produce goods and services in order to earn incomes. In many cases members of the family produce goods and services at home for their own use in order to save money. With every choice another opportunity is sacrificed.

Curriculum Interpretation: In most families there are bread-winners who earn incomes by working in factories, offices, stores, fields, mines, on the ocean, and in the air. Their incomes are earned as a reward for producing goods and services useful to other people. When members of the family produce goods and services at home, the money saved is the same as if earned. If the members of the family had not produced these goods and services for themselves, they would have had to hire someone else to do the job.

When one works at one job, he cannot work at another at the same time; therefore, he may not be earning as much as he could at another job.

Student Activities: Students can find out at home what their fathers do, and explain to the class the importance of the goods and services they produce. The class may prepare a mural showing the role of the father (representing the father of all the children) as a producer. Picture 1: Father leaves home for work. Picture 2: Father shown at work. Picture 3: Father returns home with income. Picture 4: Mother goes shopping. Picture 5: The goods which father produced are shown in big trucks leaving the factory for the stores. Picture 6: Many people go to the store to buy the goods which father helped to produce.

Each child may prepare a picture showing father, mother, and children at work at home, and explain to the class how much the family may save on each occasion by doing the work themselves.

Sometimes the members of the family do not save money by doing work at home. When mother is at home doing the cooking and washing, she cannot be working away from home and earning a salary. Father may have asked to stay away from his job without pay

117

to paint the house. The child may carry newspapers to earn money, but he deprives himself of time for studying and preparing himself for his future. The children may draw pictures showing how each member of the family could have other choices of work than those they are doing now.

In an agricultural economy, most of the productive activities are or were performed on the farm, satisfying the family's needs.
In an industrial market economy, the work-place has shifted to outside the home and most of the production is for the market.

Curriculum Interpretation: In pioneer days, members of the family produced most of the goods they needed and the family grew its own food, spun its own wool, made its own clothing, built its own home, and often provided education and recreation. With the development of industries, specialization of labor increased, and people began to produce for other people. Those who produced for others earned income.

Student Activities: From pioneer stories, the children may reconstruct in their own stories or in table models the relative self-sufficiency of family life. As a contrast they may prepare another story or model showing that today the home is served largely by institutions outside the home: churches, schools, factories, barber shops, restaurants, dentists' offices, meat-packing plants, supermarkets, and power plants.

Income earned by families may be spent or saved. Decisions to spend or save affect what and how much our economy will produce of each commodity.

Curriculum Interpretation: Families usually want more goods and services than they can buy with their incomes; therefore, they have to make choices. Any choice they make has an impact on the types of goods and services our industry produces.

Student Activities: Children may act out a family scene and may express all the things they want and then through discussion establish priorities. They will compromise.

If the children in their play decide to give up buying something they have bought in the past, due to change of tastes or high prices, and decide to purchase another thing, the children may draw pictures showing that the shift of demand from one good to another affects the two industries. For example, if they decide to abstain from the purchase of candy to buy ice cream, the teacher may discuss with them what will happen to the business of the candy manufacturer and the ice-cream manufacturer if lots of children should make similar decisions. The drawings could show the following sequence:

   1. Lots of children's heads and above each a cloud showing a candy bar canceled out and an ice-cream cone remaining.

THE INTELLECTUAL DIMENSION

2. Children lining up in front of an ice-cream store, and no one at the candy store next door.
3. The ice-cream factory expands and a sign is visible—"Workers Wanted." The candy factory is closed down, and a sign is visible—"Closed"—and unemployed workers are walking out.

The teacher may discuss how the children's savings may help the entire country. This can be shown through drawings. Picture 1: Johnny puts his money in the bank. Picture 2: Ice-cream manufacturer goes to bank to get a loan to build a bigger business. Picture 3: Ice-cream manufacturer with borrowed money purchases building material, hires labor, buys equipment to build a bigger ice-cream factory. Picture 4: Factory produces and sells ice cream to a large group of children lined up in front of the factory. Picture 5: Factory takes money to bank to repay loan with interest.

After discussing these pictures, the teacher may discuss what would happen if the children of this country would decide not to buy either candy or ice cream. The discussion would lead to the recognition that savings would be unused and both candy and ice-cream factories would close down. The same relationship could be developed as it applies to adults.[11]

In the same article, Senesh illustrates how these concepts can be extended beyond the family. It is interesting to note how well these sophisticated economic concepts have been developed and simplified for the lower primary grades. Indeed, the activities described above were intended for the first grade.

Like the materials prepared by Senesh, the Elementary Economics Project developed at the Industrial Relations Center of the University of Chicago attempts to make economics systems clear in terms of experiences that the student can comprehend concretely. For example, a unit on exchange is built around a hypothetical young man, appropriately named Adam Smith, who is shipwrecked on an island. Robinson Crusoe–style, he develops an economy using the tools he has saved and the natural resources of his island. He is both producer and consumer and has to make choices within both roles. After he is joined by other castaways, they make collective decisions about the division of labor and what to produce, and thus develop a more complex system.

The children are helped to analyze Adam's economic system and to conceptualize the system as an economist would. As Adam explores the island, they identify the natural resources. They identify with him his tools and intellectual resources. Then, with him, they make choices about production.

Goods That Adam Might Make	Production Times (in hours)		
	For Gathering Natural Resources	For Manufacturing	Total Production Time
Woven Basket	$\frac{1}{2}$	1	$1\frac{1}{2}$
Large Carved Bowl	$1\frac{1}{2}$	$2\frac{1}{2}$	4
Large Casting Fishnet	4	16	20
Stone Fishtrap	20	10	30
Small Raft	4	4	8
Crab-Hunting Stick	$\frac{1}{2}$	$\frac{1}{4}$	$\frac{3}{4}$
Salt-Making Beds	4	8	12
Roof over Firepit	2	$5\frac{1}{2}$	$7\frac{1}{2}$
Woven Sleeping Mat	$1\frac{1}{2}$	$4\frac{1}{2}$	6
Sleeping Shelter	2	5	7
One-Room Hut	15	30	45

Foods That Adam Might Gather	Production Notes	Gathering Time (in hours)
Bamboo Shoots	2 hours to walk round trip to NW river valley bottom; $\frac{1}{4}$ hour to cut shoots for 1 serving	$2\frac{1}{4}$
Banana Flower Buds	1 serving	$\frac{1}{4}$
Breadfruit	1 serving	$\frac{1}{4}$
Coconuts	1 serving	$\frac{1}{4}$
Limes and Oranges	4 hours to walk round trip to groves; can bring back as many as can carry but they spoil after 2 days	4
Coconut Crabs	1 serving	1
Fish: By line and hook	1 serving caught by line and hook	1
Fish: By casting net	1 serving caught by casting net	$\frac{1}{2}$
Fish: By fishtrap	1 hour to walk round trip to trap plus catch fish in trap; can bring back as many as can carry	1

Fig. 3.   Adam's production possibilities

As Adam makes his choices, the children assess his productivity and consider ways in which he could be more productive. The following is a sample exercise as it appears in the teacher's manual. The regular type shows material for the children, while the italic shows material for the teacher.

1. Compile figures on the island-wide output resulting from self-sufficient production before this activity. Use form TG 168.

During their meeting at the mountain settlement, the islanders decide they will all try sharing their output and see how it works. Today is the first day they will pool the input of all the islanders, and they plan that everyone will share the output equally. This means each islander will have more time in which to specialize because the other goods he wants will be made by someone else.

2. Review with the class their suggestions on how to prove whether or not increasing specialization will increase productivity.

Margo, Adam, and some of the others think that the islanders as a group will be more productive when they work this way. When the group is more productive, there is more output to be shared. Margo admits that each person had enough when he worked alone. But, she argues, each person will have more if they all pool their input and output.

3. Review instructions SB 76–77 and Form D.

Instructions for using Form D. You will act as foreman of production on the island today. Working alone, you must decide what every islander will do as you all pool your input and output. Today the group will try to produce more than the total amount the twelve of you produced when you were self-sufficient (Form B).

4. Provide students with the figures compiled above.

121

5. It is recommended that you review your TG for thorough guidance on the summary discussion following the exercise.

Each person plans to spend 14 hours of the day as before. This leaves each islander 10 hours apiece of possible work time. As foreman, you are to decide what each islander will do today in his 10 hours. Every student foreman will have different answers.

6. Discuss why specialization increases productivity.

Describe how specialization makes more efficient use of resources.

Someone must gather food for the two daily meals for all twelve of you, that is, enough food for 24 complete meals. In order to cook any food, someone must gather wood for a fire. To cook a complete meal for twelve people takes 2 meals' worth of firewood. That is, if you plan to cook food for both meals today, you will need 4 meals' worth of firewood. Other than necessary food and firewood, the group may produce whatever you choose. It is not necessary that everyone work all 10 hours.[12]

7. Discuss some consequences of increased specialization to the producer.

93672

As they make the analysis suggested in the teacher's guide, the children are taught how to diagram productivity.

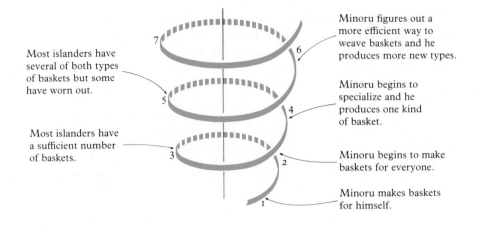

Most islanders have several of both types of baskets but some have worn out.

Minoru figures out a more efficient way to weave baskets and he produces more new types.

Minoru begins to specialize and he produces one kind of basket.

Most islanders have a sufficient number of baskets.

Minoru begins to make baskets for everyone.

Minoru makes baskets for himself.

Fig. 4.   Diagram of productivity

In sequences of activities like these, the children are taught to analyze economic systems and subsystems. This particular systems approach is designed for upper elementary school children.

Geography: Man and His Spatial Systems

The geographer studies the interaction of man and his physical environment. As George Cressey expresses it:

> What geography seeks is no less than an over-all understanding of the personality of a place, a correlation of all those phenomena which make one location different from all others. It asks many questions: Why do the people live where they do? What are the potentials of this place or that? How much of what is where?[13]

The geographer types human reactions to environments such as deserts and tropical rain forests. He observes how economic institutions vary with environment, and how man alters his milieu and causes it to adapt to him. He looks at population distribution and related factors. He examines the use of land and other resources as well as the effects of culture on their use. Although many laymen have been conditioned to regional approaches to geography, today many geographers prefer to study environmental phenomena throughout the world.

The geographer has developed intricate systems of concepts that describe and organize the data with which he works. As in other social sciences, these concepts are of three types. Observed concepts form the basis of geography, the descriptive science *par excellence*. Even complex concepts like population distribution are actually observed concepts. Inferred concepts include prediction. The effect of damming up a desert river, for example, would be predicted on the basis of inferences about the relation between water supply and agricultural product. Ideal-type concepts are used by geographers in terms such as *tundras*, *rain forests*, and *nomadic herders*.

Teaching strategies should focus on the interaction of cultural forms and natural environment—the same interaction that the geographer studies.

The *social-cultural* point of view, which recognizes man as the active agent, the earth as passive subject, is now generally accepted. It has led some geographers to concentrate on the study of human groups, others to investigate the earth as modified by human action. Whether one argues that geography studies man as inhabitant of the earth, or the earth as the home of man, is mainly a difference of personal inclination. All geographers hold in common a curiosity about places, and "place" includes a piece of land as well as the human group that occupies it.[14]

The child should learn how to identify certain climates, vegetation types, and natural resources, as well as the processes whereby culture conditions man's adaptation to his environment and the cultural effects of various kinds of adaptation. To see how culture influences adaptation, he might study two examples of an environmental type (such as two deserts or two rain forests) at the same time. In chapter 2 we saw how children could compare Bedouins and Israeli, both desert peoples, and thereby determine the similarities and differences in their adaptation to the same environment.

The Geography Curriculum Project at the University of Georgia, Marion Rice, director, has used a systems approach like those used in political science and economics. The program systematically presents concepts, illustrating them profusely. Written words are used economically and efficiently: before each passage, an idea called an *advance organizer* is presented as an intellectual framework for the new material. A teacher using this strategy in a course or unit presents the most abstract ideas first, then the more specific ones, then specific facts to illustrate both kinds of ideas.

The Georgia geography unit on rural areas begins with an abstract systems-derived model for analyzing rural landscapes (fig. 5). The model is developed systematically throughout the unit. After the verbal presentation of the model, the "Earth Complex" is described in terms of its three major components: land, climate, and vegetation. These are explored, as are the other subcomponents or subsystems of the four major components of the rural landscape model. Gradually, the entire model is presented in detail and the children are led to apply it to analyze a variety of rural landscapes and patterns, such as farm trends in the United States and the Soviet Union.

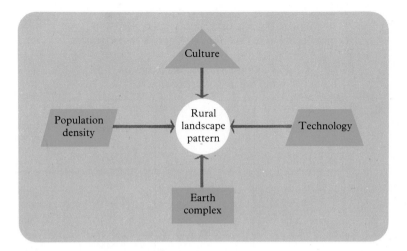

Fig. 5.   A rural landscape model

INQUIRIES

1. The following tables concern the social and economic status of blacks in the United States. Plan an approach in which children can use economic concepts to analyze these and related data.

MEDIAN FAMILY INCOME IN 1968, AND NEGRO FAMILY INCOME, 1965–1968, AS A PERCENT OF WHITE, BY REGION

	Median family income, 1968		Negro income as a percent of white			
	Negro	White	1965	1966	1967	1968
United States	$5,359	$8,936	54	58	59	60
Northeast	6,460	9,318	64	68	66	69
North Central	6,910	9,259	74	74	78	75
South	4,278	7,963	49	50	54	54
West	7,506	9,462	69	72	74	80

SOURCE: U.S. Department of Commerce, Bureau of the Census.

NOTE: Reprinted from *The Social and Economic Status of Negroes in the United States, 1969,* prepared by the Bureau of Labor Statistics and the Bureau of the Census.

Median Income of Families of Negro and Other Races as a Percent of White Family Income, 1950–1968
(Annual figures shown are based on the current population survey)

Year	Negro and other races	Negro
1950	54	(NA)
1951	53	(NA)
1952	57	(NA)
1953	56	(NA)
1954	56	(NA)
1955	55	(NA)
1956	53	(NA)
1957	54	(NA)
1958	51	(NA)
1959	52	(NA)
1960	55	(NA)
1961	53	(NA)
1962	53	(NA)
1963	53	(NA)
1964	56	54
1965	55	54
1966	60	58
1967	62	59
1968	63	60

NA Not available. The ratio of Negro to white median family income first became available from this survey in 1964.

SOURCE: U.S. Department of Commerce, Bureau of the Census.

NOTE: Reprinted from *The Social and Economic Status of Negroes in the United States, 1969,* prepared by the Bureau of Labor Statistics and the Bureau of the Census.

2. How would you help children study the school community in terms of political, economic, or geographic systems? Perhaps some class members can plan the study from one perspective and some from another and then compare their results.

3. Political, economic, and geographic systems are interrelated. Prepare an outline of concepts you would use to study a U.S. city so that the children inquire into two of these systems and their relationships.

NOTES

1. Evron M. Kirkpatrick and Jeane J. Kirkpatrick, "Political Science," in Erling M. Hunt and others, *High School Social Studies Perspectives* (Boston: Houghton Mifflin, 1962). In this essay will be found a brief summary of the approaches taken by political scientists and a fine introductory bibliography to political science.

2. Charles S. Hyneman, *The Study of Politics: The Present State of American Political Science* (Urbana: Univ. of Illinois Press, 1959), p. 105.

3. Kirkpatrick and Kirkpatrick, "Political Science," p. 111.

4. Maurice Duverger, *An Introduction to the Social Sciences with Special Reference to Their Methods* (New York: Praeger, 1964), p. 47.

5. Ibid.

6. John Patrick, "American Political Behavior: A New Approach to Civic Education in Secondary Schools," an unpublished paper from the High School Curriculum Center in Government, mimeographed (Bloomington: Indiana Univ., March 1971), pp. 5–6.

7. Howard D. Mehlinger and John Patrick, *American Political Behavior*, High School Curriculum Center in Government, bk. 2 (Bloomington: Indiana Univ., 1968), pp. 129, 131, 132.

8. David Easton, "A Systems Approach to Political Life," Social Science Education Consortium, publication no. 104 (970 Aurora, Boulder, Colo. 80302), p. 3.

9. Bruce W. Knight and Lawrence G. Hines, *Economics* (New York: Knopf, 1952), p. 6.

10. Lawrence Senesh, "The Organic Curriculum: A New Experiment in Economic Education," *The Councilor* 21 (Chicago: Illinois Council for the Social Studies, 1960), p. 3. Senesh's approach is being published as *Our Working World* by Science Research Associates, Chicago. Grade One, *Families at Work*, was published in 1964; Grade Two, *Neighbors at Work*, in 1965; and Grade Three, *Cities at Work*, in 1966.

11. Ibid., pp. 7–10.

12. *Economic Man*, Elementary Economics Project, William D. Rader, dir. (Chicago: Benefic Press, 1971), p. 40.

13. George B. Cressey, "Geography," in *High School Social Studies Perspectives*, p. 85.

14. Jan O. M. Broek, "Modern Viewpoints in Geography," in *Geography: Its Scope and Sequence*, Charles E. Merrill Social Science Seminar (Columbus, Ohio: Merrill, 1965), p. 27.

GENERAL
SOCIAL
SCIENCE
STRATEGIES

We have so far attempted to build a general framework for viewing the social sciences on the basis of the individual disciplines. It is possible, however, to build curricula from an analysis of elements common to them all. Three approaches will be considered. The first is built around the question "Who is man?" The second applies several of the social sciences to human interaction. The third emphasizes inductive teaching as the essence of the social sciences.

Man: A Course of Study—
A Philosophical Social Science Approach

In the last few years Education Development Center has begun to make available the long-awaited fifth-grade program, *Man: A Course of Study*. This program was heavily influenced by

129

Ways of integrating the social sciences

Jerome S. Bruner, the Harvard psychologist whose ideas on the structures of the disciplines have generated much discussion. This program leads children to use social science techniques in dealing with a series of global questions.

> The content of the course is man: his nature as a species, the forces
> that shaped and continue to shape his humanity. Three questions
> recur throughout:
>   What is human about human beings?
>   How did they get that way?
>   How can they be made more so?[1]

The children study several animals in a way that illuminates human characteristics. In studying salmon, for example, they become familiar with the concept of life cycles. Another study helps them distinguish between innate and learned behavior. The teacher's guide for the program presents this subject as follows:

> Any behavior that an animal performs automatically we call an innate
> behavior. The animal may be able to perform the behavior at birth
> (a herring gull chick automatically and immediately pecks at red
> spots), or the behavior might appear later in the animal's life (herring
> gulls automatically incubate eggs, but not until they are old enough to
> reproduce). A behavior that develops through experience is called a
> learned behavior (herring gulls learn the location of food).
>   However, the distinction between innate and learned behavior is not
> as clear as the examples imply.
>   We use the word innate rather than instinct. This is because
> children easily say, "Oh, that happens because of instinct," without
> thinking about what they mean. They do not consider the complexity
> of the behavior, its internal motivation, and the environmental clues
> necessary for the behavior to be performed. It is not incorrect to use
> the word instinct as long as the children think about the complexity of
> the causes of the behavior.[2]

The children's study of the baboon introduces the subject of social organization, which is dealt with also in their study of the Netsilik Eskimos. One of the purposes of the program is to encourage cultural awareness.

> In judging others, particularly those of different cultures, children
> must learn to know when their judgments, and the judgments of all
> men, are shaped by the culture in which they live.[3]

Each unit in the course features the depth study of one subject, about which much data is presented in the form of films, pamphlets, and pictures. The child is invited to raise questions such as a social scientist would ask and to share the social scientist's interpretation of the data. The general teaching strategy is illustrated by the following three topics taken from the unit on the herring gull.

A. Introduction to herring gulls (1 day)
   Using a method of observation and research, the children learn about the life of the herring gulls.
B. Examining the causes of gull behavior (1 day)
   After examining the motivation behind the interactions between gull parents and offspring, questions are raised about the behaviors of human parents and their offspring.
C. Innate and learned behavior (1 day)
   Children read the third booklet that develops ideas applicable throughout the animal kingdom. Here, behavior is discussed in terms of what the animal is able to do automatically and what it is able to learn.[4]

Unlike other projects so far described, *Man: A Course of Study* does not articulate and strive to teach a conceptual framework about the nature of one or more of the social sciences. Instead, it emphasizes philosophical issues. The student investigates a series of topics much as leading scholars have and thus becomes acquainted with the work of a few social scientists rather than with the conceptual structure of one or more of the disciplines. Although based on scientific activity, the course is not tightly instructional. The goals for each section are explicit but do not require a series of performances. Rather, the student is helped to ask questions about authentic data supplied in depth and reflect on the answers. Each student and class is expected to generate different thoughts about the same universal issue.

Bringing the Social Sciences to the Child's Study of Human Interaction

Curriculum plans in the social studies have usually been organized around topics or broad social objectives. In regard to topics, for example, it has been generally accepted that the child should become acquainted with the American Revolution as a critical part of his national heritage. Similarly, the Civil War, westward expansion, and the important international wars involving the United States have been assigned through the grades. Some world geography has also been considered essential to an understanding of international affairs. Most curriculum guides have listed topics that the teacher could select and with each topic have indicated generalizations that the child might learn as the product of his study. Selecting general topics, however, by no means ends the job of content identification. Deciding to plan an inquiry into westward expansion, for example, only narrows the possible content. How we treat such a topic determines which topic elements will finally be included.

To name the broadest objectives of the social studies also helps little in resolving the task of specific content selection. One authority has stated that the goals of social education are "to understand the concepts that describe and explain human society and to develop the insights and skills required by democratic citizenship."[5] This statement provides important criteria, but almost all concepts of social science relate in some way to human society or to democratic citizenship. Broad objectives for social education are not sufficient guidelines for selecting specific content. It is necessary to develop a strategy whereby the most promising elements of content can be selected.

The selection of content may affect not only the factual knowledge children acquire but also the thinking processes they develop. For example, if a child is directed to learn chiefly about the natural resources and agricultural products of a nation he studies, he may tend, when studying another nation, to ask questions about that country's natural and agricultural resources. In other words, the selection of content determines to some extent the way the student will be taught to think while he is in school.

In a recent research study conducted by the author, 60 third-grade and 180 fifth-grade children were asked to pose questions dealing with what they would like to know about a country or people they were to study. The number of questions dealing with the interaction of people and their values, customs, and habits declined from the third to the fifth grade. About 40 percent of the questions asked by both grades dealt with physical and economic geography. While about 42 percent of the third-graders asked questions about people or customs, only 29 percent of the fifth-graders asked questions in that category. Questions about history and government increased from about .5 percent to about 13 percent, reflecting the increased attention to those topics in the middle grades. Apparently when teachers repeatedly stress certain topics, children come to regard those topics as the important ones, the ones to be looked for in new areas of study.

Experience in mathematics may support this contention. For many years computation was the aspect of arithmetic content that was stressed. Students learned to think of arithmetic as computation. Now that mathematical understanding and problem solving are stressed by mathematics educators, both parents and teachers constantly ask: "But won't that interfere with teaching number facts?" "It sounds O.K., but isn't the important thing for kids to learn how to add and subtract?" Such questions indicate that the adult, taught to compute rather than to think about numbers, has come to regard computation as a more important aspect of content than the properties of number systems and the techniques for solving problems.

Can we make the assumption, therefore, that *content, when taught, gradually instills in the learner the same thinking processes that directed the teacher to that content*? If this assumption is valid, then the systems we use to analyze and select content become important not only because they edit the world that we formally present to the child but also because they shape his thinking. If our systems emphasize material products and neglect people, can we be surprised when the child comes to believe that we think products are more important than people? If our history courses neglect esthetic and cultural life, are we not helping the child to place a low value on that quality of life?

The methods a child uses to analyze topics are as important as the topics themselves. If a child is directed merely to memorize facts and conclusions, he will lack the necessary organizing knowledge to tie these facts together and make useful meaning out of what he has learned. Lacking understanding of the modes of inquiry of the social scientist, he will have difficulty managing and interpreting new sets of conditions in a rapidly changing world.

The curriculum of a subject should be determined by the most fundamental understanding that can be achieved of the underlying principles which give structure to that subject. Teaching specific

133

topics or skills without making clear their context in the broader fundamental structure of a field of knowledge is uneconomical. . . . Such teaching makes it exceedingly difficult for the student to generalize from what he has learned to what he will encounter later, and knowledge one has acquired without sufficient structure to tie it together is knowledge that is likely to be forgotten.[6]

These words may be taken as a challenge to teachers of social studies to lead children to discover fundamental ideas about human relations. What fundamental ideas can be explored in the study of the local community or of westward expansion? How can we help children to explore those ideas, to see them in as many combinations as possible? What guidelines can we set down when we analyze content so that what we select will not be trivial, or one-sided, or fragmented?

Several considerations determine the kind of strategy we need for selecting content. First, content for elementary social studies needs to be drawn from a number of academic disciplines without damaging the identity or integrity of any of them. Perhaps some-day, if only for teaching purposes, scholars may be able to syn-thesize the various social sciences into a single discipline called, say, behavioral science. At present, however, any strategy for selecting content needs to blend all the social sciences without our pretending that they have fused into a single study.

Second, content should be selected with a view toward pro-viding continuity in the curriculum and growth of ideas through the grades. The strategy for selecting content should be applicable to topics that can be studied by children of all ages. It should focus on fundamental concepts that can be approached by children of limited experience and explored in depth by more sophisticated learners.

Third, in elementary school the strategic emphasis should be on content that relates the child to his community: in dealing with such content, the child should be able to draw on his own experience and apply it to his experience. This aspect of our strategy accords with current theories of learning. Moreover, the ideas that the child uses to view his own life and community will help him understand the study of other communities and cultures.

Fourth, the strategy should allow for continual study of topics of immediate import—that is, topics dealing with daily happenings in the classroom and in the world. The child should observe the actual workings of democracy and of human relations. At the same time that he is learning new organizing concepts and new ways of viewing and analyzing life, he will have the opportunity to apply his concepts to current problems and see whether they are valid.

Human beings relate to one another largely in groups. "Dwelling together in groups is as characteristic of man as the shape of his teeth or his inclination to laugh."[7] All social sciences focus on groups. Recorded history is the history of national, religious, and ethnic groups. Biography usually presents a person in terms of what he has in common with others: Beethoven is thought of as a German, a musician, a deaf man; Alexander is a Macedonian, a Westerner, a conqueror, a general. Political science is the study of government of groups and the relations between groups. Within a political unit or group are other groups, such as parties, factions, the Loyal Opposition, the unfranchised. Sociology concentrates on the forms and functions of human groups. According to the concept of culture, men in a given area develop common attitudes, codes of behavior, and beliefs: they become a group and then act as a group on other human groups. Anthropology could not exist if men did not live in groups. Economics, dealing with the production, distribution, and consumption of wealth, implies that men are organized for these purposes; furthermore, men can be identified by their position in the production, distribution, and consumption systems of a society. Human geography is essentially the study of the distribution of human life in terms of environment; it views human groups in terms of their milieus and adaptations.

If we accept the thesis that groups are a common focus of study for the social sciences, we must still determine whether the concept of group can be used to identify specific content for the social studies. Perhaps we can make this determination by imagining that we are a teacher approaching a general topic listed in a curriculum guide. What questions must this teacher ask himself in order to identify the kinds of content that focus on the human group? The four questions that follow seem valuable for analyzing topics.

135

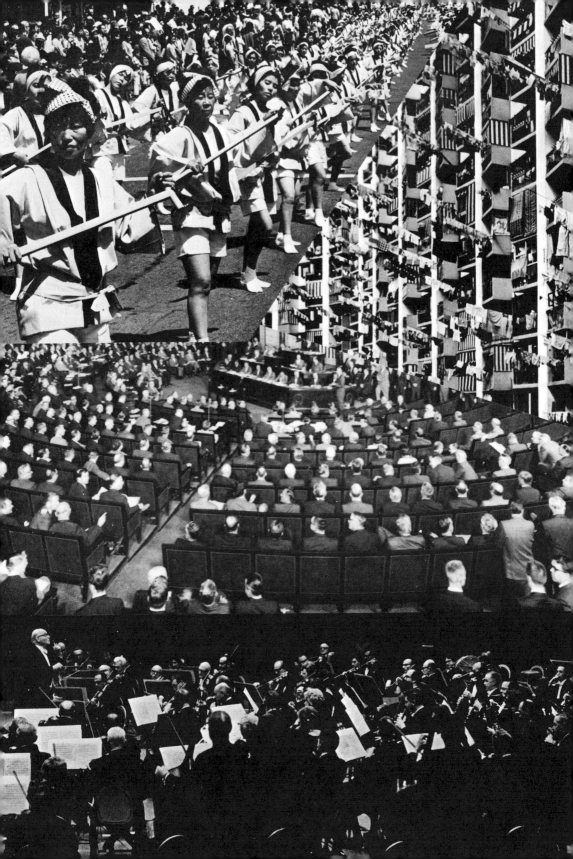

1. What human groups can be found in this society, in this region, in this era that we plan to study?

In the study of the local community, for example, one finds that there are different economic, racial, political, and religious groups. The study of a nation, a region, and a historical period reveals such groups. Frequently groups overlap. The racial groups in the Union of South Africa are also groups of economic interest. In the United States, political affiliation is somewhat related to economic interest. In the San Francisco Bay region, several ethnic groups have retained some of the culture and customs of their native land while adopting some of the customs of their new home.

This kind of analysis is useful for most topics now included in social studies curricula: "Our Home," "Our Family," and "The Community" as well as nation-states and cultures and past ages. The teacher can ask himself: What groups would an economist, an anthropologist, or a human geographer identify, were he to study this topic? This question forces him to look below the surface of a general topic. It keeps him from viewing events without considering the human groups involved.

2. What relations do these human groups bear to one another?

As groups are identified, it becomes obvious that they are related to one another. For example, the economic groups in a nation cannot be considered intelligently without considering the political organization of the country. Consider the American Revolution as a topic of study. Among the Continentals, Whig and Tory were related politically. Sailmaster and farmer bore economic relations to one another. Soldier and civilian were related, as were Hessian mercenaries, British grenadiers, and Virginia sergeants. Somewhere in the relations of these groups lies what is significant about the movements and pressures on individuals at that time.

3. How did these human relations come about?

This question requires us to think of causation as a part of content. It enables us to identify ideas that lead children to think of social events in terms of their causes. History, then, is viewed in terms of process. Contemporary society becomes a part of history.

In the study of English history, this question implies other questions: How did lords and ladies get their position? How did the government become representative? What in human relations made castles develop? Why did London become so large? When children answer these questions, they find that kings and queens, steel furnaces and fishing boats, beefeaters and Ulstermen are all part of human culture. From these questions can come the human stories on which lasting generalizations can be built.

4. What is the future of these group relations?

Consider the study of a local community by third-graders. The children have heard opinions about the need for land for recreation. They have learned that the city government can buy and maintain parks, that the American Association of University Women wants a park, and that the Chamber of Commerce opposes it. How will the issue be resolved? Will the businessmen come to see that the parks will benefit their children? Will the American Association of University Women come to believe that the land should be saved for industry? What will sway the voters?

When I was growing up, I learned that India was part of the British Empire. I did not realize until the break occurred in 1947 that India was seeking more independent status, even though I was in high school at the time and was actually studying about India. Egypt's quarrel with the British also came as a surprise to many of us, and it is my impression that the African and Asian nationalistic movements have come as a surprise to most U.S. citizens whose education has not been directed toward appraising the possible changes in the relations between peoples of the world.

Answering this fourth question helps keep the content we teach up to date with our world. Content comes to be viewed as the emergence of relations, and current happenings are seen as part of the historical process. As one author wrote, "If the social studies program is not based on a careful analysis of our changing society, the accusation that schools teach for the past half-century and not for the next half-century could be true."[8]

These four questions can be used by teachers to identify content that focuses on human relations. A study of the economic geography of Italy, for example, becomes an attempt to find people with a livelihood in common and compare them with other people who share another economic position. Social studies teachers in the elementary school can use these questions to develop continuity in their programs. The study of various regions, historical eras, current events, and the local community will have a common thread if the focus is on group relations. The organizing elements for this continuity will emerge in the children's search to find people with something in common and their attempt to compare or contrast these people with other people.

The logic of the four questions can be taught to children so that they will develop a useful framework for approaching social studies topics in class and on their own. As children progress through the grades, they can learn to ask the four questions and to structure their research around the questions. As they grow older, they can use the questions to include more types of groups and more complex relations between groups. Used in this way, the questions provide a means of introducing the basic ideas of the social sciences. As we teach students to identify political groups, for example, we have the opportunity to introduce them to major organizing concepts of political science.

There are limitations in using these questions, however. Imposed on topics without regard for the maturity of the learners involved, they could result in the identification of unteachable content. The fact that there are several races in a neighborhood, for example, does not mean that first-graders are capable of exploring theories about race relations objectively and maturely. Furthermore, the strategy provides a means of focusing the social studies but does not include all desirable content. Should a study of Paris omit the Eiffel Tower and the Louvre because the content analysis does not include touristic or artistic relations?

Although the strategy can be used to analyze the ideals and loyalties that people possess in common and to identify dynamic elements in democratic groups, it does not provide for the development of desirable attitudes in the students. It leaves the implications of values to be developed by the teacher. Another limitation of the strategy is that it does not ensure development of the basic concepts of the social sciences. An untutored person could use the four questions to identify political relations that the political scientist may not consider valid.

Although human relations are certainly based on group relations, the essential element in society is the individual. The test of understanding in the social studies is the ability to project oneself as a person whose characteristics, group memberships, environment, or desires differ from one's own. If the focus or groups became such that individuals were ignored or groups were perceived to be more important than individuals, then the social studies would be dehumanizing.

139

An Approach through Inductive Thinking

The late Hilda Taba was probably most responsible for the popularization of the term "teaching strategy." In her work with the Contra Costa County California Schools she provided an example of the development of a strategy for teaching inductive reasoning. Taba began with the assumption that thinking can be taught, but not in the sense of being given by a teacher or absorbed as the product of someone else's thoughts. According to Taba, thinking is an active transaction between the individual and data. The student can and should be taught to use available materials of instruction in order to organize facts into conceptual systems; relate points in data to each other and generalize about these relationships; make inferences and use known facts to hypothesize, predict, and explain unfamiliar phenomena. "The teacher can only *assist* the processes of internalization and conceptualization."[9]

Another of Taba's assumptions was that the thought processes evolve in lawful sequence. To master certain thinking skills, one has to master certain earlier ones: the sequence cannot be reversed. "This concept of lawful sequences requires teaching strategies that observe these sequences."[10] Specific teaching strategies must be designed for specific thinking skills, and these strategies must be applied sequentially. With her associates Taba developed a social studies curriculum that introduces elements of inductive thinking one by one. She identified cognitive tasks, such as concept formation, that make up the process of inductive thinking. To induce those tasks, she developed teaching strategies.

An illustration of the concept-formation strategy can be drawn from a second-grade unit of Taba's Contra Costa Social Studies Curriculum. The unit attempts to develop the idea that "the supermarket needs a place, equipment, goods and services."[11] It opens with the hypothetical situation: "Mr. Smith wants to open a supermarket. What will he need?" This question might also be phrased, "What do you see when you go to the supermarket?" "What do you see in this picture of the supermarket?" Depending on the wording of the question, children can be expected to identify food items, stock boys, cashiers, equipment, a building or place, deliveries of food. Their responses can be recorded and the listing continued until several categories are represented. When the enumeration is complete, the children are asked to group the items on the basis of similarity. "What belongs to-

gether?" Presumably, if the enumeration is rich enough, the children will identify "things the market sells" and "things done for the supermarket owner." These concepts can then be labeled "goods" and "services."

This example shows that, according to Taba, concept formation involves identifying and enumerating the items of data relevant to a problem, grouping those items on the basis of similarity, and developing categories and labels for the groups. It also shows that to cause students to engage in each of these activities, Taba used a form of question she called an "eliciting question." Concept formation elicited by such a teaching strategy is thought to reflect hidden mental operations, referred to by Taba as "covert." Figure 6 illustrates the relationship between the overt activity in the concept-formation teaching strategy, the mental operation that the students presumably perform during the activity, and the eliciting of questions appropriate to lead students through the concept formation activities.

Overt Activity	Covert Mental Operations	Eliciting Questions
1. Enumeration and listing.	Differentiation.	What did you see? hear? note?
2. Grouping.	Identifying common properties, abstracting.	What belongs together? On what criterion?
3. Labeling and categorizing.	Determining the hierarchical order of items. Super and sub-ordination.	How would you call these groups? What belongs to what?

Fig. 6. Concept formation

Similar strategies are developed to elicit the other mental operations that form the structure of the curriculum. The goals of such a curriculum are to teach inductive thinking rather than ideas or methods specific to any of the social sciences, although ideas and methods from specific disciplines can be used effectively to teach inductive thinking. Students are to expand their conceptual system by forming concepts they can use to handle new information.

INQUIRIES

1. Plan a lesson for children that includes what you believe to be significant social content and uses Taba's inductive strategy.

2. How would you use the four question strategy to help children manage the study of their own group?

3. The materials for *Man: A Course of Study* are among the most beautiful ever prepared for children. Examine them if you can, and deal with two controversies they have raised:

    Are they too realistic for children in their treatment of hunting, food preparation, life and death?

    Are subjects such as baboons inappropriate for children because some people compare racial minorities to animals like baboons?

NOTES

1. *Man: A Course of Study: Talks to Teachers*, Education Development Center (Cambridge, Mass., 1968), p. 4.

2. *Man: A Course of Study: Teachers Guide*, p. 7.

3. Ibid.

4. *Man: A Course of Study*, "Herring Gulls," p. 6.

5. Ralph C. Preston, "The Role of Social Studies in Elementary Education," in *Social Studies in the Elementary School*, 56th Yearbook of the National Society for the Study of Education (Chicago: Univ. of Chicago Press, 1957), p. 4.

6. Jerome S. Bruner, *The Process of Education* (Cambridge, Mass.: Harvard Univ. Press, 1960), p. 31.

7. Stuart Chase, *The Proper Study of Mankind* (New York: Harper, 1956), p. 65.

8. Stanley E. Diamond, "Current Social Trends and Their Implications for the Social Studies Program," in *Social Studies in the Elementary School*, 56th Yearbook of the National Society for the Study of Education (Chicago: Univ. of Chicago Press, 1957), p. 75.

9. Hilda Taba, *Teaching Strategies and Cognitive Functioning in Elementary School Children*, San Francisco State College Coop Research Project no. 2404 (San Francisco, 1966), p. 34.

10. Ibid., p. 35.

11. Hilda Taba, *Teachers Handbook for Elementary Social Studies* (Palo Alto: Addison-Wesley, 1967), p. 52.

SUMMARY INQUIRIES FOR CHAPTERS 2–5

On page 145 are pictures showing two different cultures: ancient Roman (Pompeii) and contemporary French (Paris). These pictures are the basis for several inquiries concerning geography, sociology, and anthropology.

1. Develop a plan for helping children use data such as these pictures to explore the use of space in these societies and in their own neighborhoods. The following chart may help them.

Land Use Patterns

Roman Empire	France	My Neighborhood

2. Pictures can give clues about the institutions within a society. Develop a plan to help children compare the institutions within these cultures and with those in their own community. Use the pictures to start the inquiry.

Institutions

Roman Empire	France	My Town

3. Anthropology can be brought to life for children through data that allow them to try on anthropological concepts. How can children use these pictures to try on such concepts?

Some anthropologists emphasize cultural universals, elements shared by most cultures. Use the pictures to help children begin an inquiry into some of these universals. Compare, for example, housing, transportation, and religion in the ancient Roman, contemporary French, and contemporary American societies.

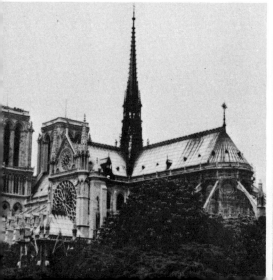

part 2

THE SOCIAL DIMENSION

GROUP
INVESTIGATION
AND THE
DEMOCRATIC PROCESS

It is the responsibility of the social studies to develop citizens who can comprehend human society and contribute effectively to it. As the intellectual dimension provides the conceptual strength of the social studies, the social dimension provides the interpersonal context and the moral imperatives of the curriculum.

The potential social emphases of social studies are so many and so complex that they cannot all be treated here. We will examine a few emphases and approaches that lead to competence and commitments in three areas of social life: the interpersonal, the intergroup (community), and the international (macrosocietal). These three levels of citizenship provide opportunities for contributing to social life. We can contribute to the primary groups we belong to. With somewhat greater difficulty we can contribute to the community and even to society if we work with others and know how to direct our activities for maximum effect.

Group Investigation: A Basic Teaching Strategy

In *Democracy and Education*, John Dewey recommended that the entire school be organized as a miniature democracy in which students participate in the development of the social system and, through this participation, gradually learn to apply the scientific method to the perfection of human society.[1] This, Dewey felt, would be the best preparation for citizenship in a democracy. John U. Michaelis has extracted from Dewey's work a formulation specifically for teaching the social studies at the elementary level.[2] Central to his method of teaching is the creation of a democratic group that defines and attacks problems of social significance.

In many respects Herbert Thelen's[3] Group Investigation strategy resembles the methods recommended by Dewey and Michaelis. Although its goal is not to teach the democratic process while indirectly instilling the scientific method, it does attempt to combine the form and dynamics of the democratic process and the procedures of academic inquiry. Thelen has formulated an experience-based teaching strategy in which democratic groups practice method and apply it to their own experience.

Thelen's conception of the democratic process and the basis of his teaching strategy come from a set of postulates regarding social man: "A man who builds with other men the rules and agreements that constitute social reality. . . ."[4] Social man cannot act without reference to his fellows. In contributing to the establishment and modification of social agreements, each individual helps to determine both prohibitions and freedom for action. These rules of conduct, both implicit and explicit, affect religious, political, economic, and scientific areas of life and constitute the culture of a society. For Thelen, this negotiation and renegotiation of the social order is the essence of the democratic process.

149

> Thus in groups and societies a cyclical process exists: individuals, interdependently seeking to meet their needs, must establish a social order (and in the process they develop groups and societies). The social order determines in varying degrees what ideas, values and actions are possible, valid and "appropriate"! Working within these "rules" and stimulated by the need for rules the culture develops. The individual studies his reactions to the rules and re-interprets them to discover their meaning for the way of life he seeks. Through this quest, he changes his own way of life, and this in turn influences the way of life of others. But as the way of life changes, the rules must be revised, and new controls and agreements have to be hammered out and incorporated into the social order.[5]

The classroom is analogous to the larger society. It has a social order and a classroom culture. The students care about the way of life, the standards, and the expectations that develop there.

Educational procedures should seek to harness the energy generated by concern for creating the social order. Through negotiation the students learn the academic domains of knowledge and ultimately learn to engage in social problem-solving. According to Thelen, knowledge in the disciplines, like the social order, is manufactured and revised by the process in other aspects of negotiation and renegotiation. One should not attempt to teach knowledge from any academic area without teaching the social process by which it was negotiated.

Thelen rejects the normal classroom order that develops around the basic values of comfort, politeness, and keeping the teacher happy. He replaces them with the normative structure, teacher roles, and student roles that support inquiry.

> The teacher's task is to participate in the activities of developing the social order in the classroom for the purpose of orienting it to inquiry, and the "house rules" to be developed are the methods and attitudes of the knowledge discipline to be taught. The teacher influences the emerging social order toward inquiring when he "brings out" and capitalizes on differences in the way students act and interpret the role of investigator—which is also the role of member in the classroom.[6]

The first element of inquiry is an event to which the individual can react, a problem to be solved. In the classroom the teacher can facilitate this by selecting content and casting it in terms of problem-situations. The provision of the problem will not in itself generate the necessary puzzlement. The student must add an awareness of self and desire for personal meaning, causing him to give attention to something and seek its reality. This requires the distinction between self and object. The student has to assume the dual roles of participant and observer characteristic of any experience-based learner situation. That is, the student simultaneously inquires into something and observes himself as an inquirer. He tries both to learn and to improve himself as a learner.

Inasmuch as inquiry is basically a social process, the student is aided in his self-observer role by the opportunity to interact with other people. In comparing his reactions with those of others, he is able to see himself. This process occurs throughout the course of inquiry and serves different purposes at different points. At first it illuminates the student's reaction, and the conflicting viewpoints stimulate his interest in the problem. Later the differing viewpoints serve as parameters for the problem-situations.

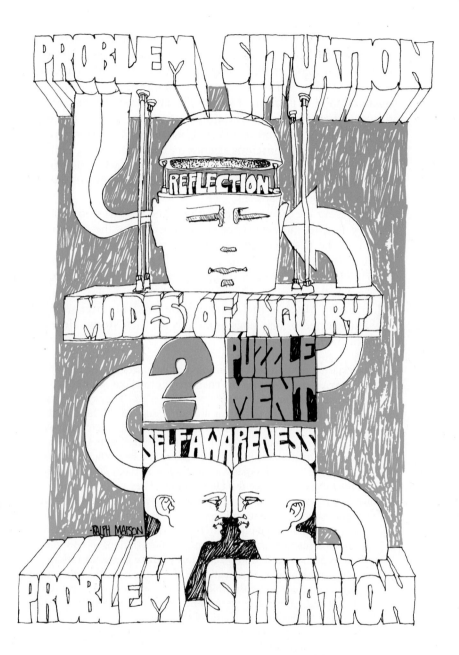

151

Elements of social science inquiry

Inquiry calls for firsthand activity in a real situation and ongoing experience that continually generates new data. The student must know how to collect data, associate and classify ideas recalling past experience, formulate and test hypotheses, study consequences, modify plans, and so on. The student must also develop the capacity for reflection, the ability to synthesize overt participative behavior with symbolic verbal behavior. Reflection requires the student to give conscious attention to his experience, explicitly formulate the conclusions, and integrate these with his existing ideas. In this way ideas are shaken up and reorganized into new and more powerful patterns.

Let's examine two examples that Thelen gives to illustrate inquiry and to indicate when an activity lacks the elements of inquiry. The first example is drawn from a second-grade social studies class dealing with the question "How do different people live?" The teacher proposed that the students select some group of people, find out how they live, and write a play using this information. Much to their surprise, the students after some discussion selected prairie dogs as a focus for their study. Here is an account of their inquiry.

> They started their study by naming the characters for the play they would write, and of course the characters turned out to be baby, chicken, mother, father, farmer's boy, snake, etc. They made lists of questions to be answered: What do prairie dogs eat? Where do they live? What do they do with their time? How big are their families? Who are their enemies? etc. Individuals sought answers to questions from science pamphlets, books, the science teacher, officials of the local zoo, and I have no doubt at least a few of them talked to their parents to be taken to see the Disney opus. They reported their findings in compositions during the writing lessons. The plot of the play gradually took shape and was endlessly modified with each new bit of information. The play centered around family life, and there was much discussion and spontaneous demonstrations of how various members of the family would act. Most of these characterizations actually represented a cross-section of the home lives of seven year old children, as perceived by the children. But each action was gravely discussed and soberly considered, and justified in terms of what they knew about the ecology of prairie dogs.
> They built a stage with sliding curtains and four painted backdrops—more reference work here to get the field and farm right. The play itself was given six times, with six different casts, and each child played at least two different parts. There was never any written script; only an agreement on the line of action and the part of

it to occur in each scene. And after each presentation the youngsters sat around and discussed what they had been trying to communicate, how it might be improved.[7]

Thelen contrasts this example with one drawn from a high school social studies class in which the students were to put on a series of television programs on the history of the community. As preparation the students looked up information and visited historical sites, taking pictures of important evidence.

Harry and Joe took pictures of an Indian mound, left there by original settlers. They took it from the south because the light was better that way; and they never discovered the northern slope where erosion had laid bare a burrow full of Indian relics. Mary and Sue spent two afternoons on a graph of corn production in the region; the graph was in a geography book the teacher gave them and the time was mostly spent in making a neat elaborately lettered document for the camera. The narrators were chosen for their handsome appearance, and much of the staging of the show (which used reports mostly) centered around deciding the most decorative way to seat the students. A lot of old firearms and household implements were borrowed from a local museum and displayed a sentence or two of comment for each.[8]

In this instance, Thelen acknowledges that the students may have learned something about the region, but he points out that most of the energy went into making the television program entertaining and informative. The roles in which the students inquired "were those of a reporter with a keen eye for human interest angles, rather than the sociologist's or historian's with a disciplined concern for the course of human events."[9]

These two examples illustrate the distinction between inquiry and activity. The actions of the second-grade class investigating prairie dogs contained the elements of inquiry: problem-situation, self-awareness, puzzlement, methodology, and reflection. But were there questions in the latter example? Who formulated them? Who sought their answers? How was this information obtained? Was the information applied? Were conclusions drawn and who drew them? Activities are potential channels for inquiry, but inquiry must emanate from the motivations and curiosity of the students. Activities cease to be inquiry when the teacher is the sole source of the problem identification and the formulation of plans or when the end product of inquiry takes precedence over the inquiry process.

153

An Example of Democratic Teaching

The general possibilities and limitations of democratic teaching are much easier to identify than the practical skills needed for democratic process teaching. The remainder of our discussion will be based on an actual account by a teacher[10] of a democratic, problem-solving unit that has many of the elements of group investigation. The inside column of the succeeding pages contains her account. The outside column gives the author's comments.

FOOD FOR INDIA: A DEMOCRATIC PROCESS PROJECT

Social studies experiences give children an opportunity to learn about the world, about people, and about themselves. The project I am about to describe, I feel, did all that and more. What it did in addition was to give me an opportunity to learn about children.

We were studying India. One textbook dealt with all of the orthodox content areas with which texts are obliged to deal—geographic location, population density, agriculture, industry, major cities, products, etc. A second gave brief descriptions of important historical developments, described four divisions of the caste system, and the beneficence of the British during their three hundred year rule. These topics sufficed for a starting point. But to achieve an understanding of the feeling and flavor of the Indian culture we had to go beyond the textbooks. Our study included such topics as the British East India Company, the maharajas and the untouchables, the meanings of Buddhism and Hinduism, literature and art, contributions to human knowledge, Gandhi and passive resistance, customs and beliefs, daily life, partition and independence, major problems, the historical, religious, political, and social forces that bear on those problems— in short, we sought to enter the lives of these people who belong to this distant and different culture.

Miss Greco assumes that the children will participate in planning. They (sixth graders) are expected to select goals and organize themselves. She has shared in the planning, however. The focus on people is important to her. She allows the selection of topics within the overall study of India to be made by the children, but she guides the focus toward the lives of the people.

155

We approached the study by outlining the areas of interest that would yield the distinctiveness of India. The focus was on the people in relation to the various topics of the outline. The class decided that they would select one topic at a time, work independently at gathering relevant information from sources in and out of school, then bring the information to class for discussion, raising and answering questions, seeking and analyzing implications, tracing causal relationships, etc.

However, the children brought in more than information. They also brought in their reactions to the things they were finding out about this vastly different culture. For example, Student A, whose emotional honesty prohibits him from squelching anything he feels, upon hearing of the sacrosanct position of the cow in Indian society expressed the opinion, "That's stupid! Why would people treat a cow that way?" As the severe hardships of life in India came to light, the attitude that it was stupidity on the part of the people which perpetuated their difficulties also emerged. The underlying reason for the impatience and derision that was expressed was due, of course, to the ethnocentric attitudes with which the children viewed the information they were gathering. In these beginning discussions, it was apparent that the class was having difficulty in understanding ways of life so different from their own. Their judgment of what was good, bad, or "stupid" in that society was based almost entirely on the degree to which Indian customs, beliefs, and values were similar or dissimilar to our own. The discussions provided an opportunity to place the various aspects of Indian life in a broader social, historical, religious, or political context— the context, that is, of the Indian culture, not the American culture. Gradually derision diminished and a rather sympathetic accepting attitude developed with the growing understanding of the forces that shaped the lives and dictated the customs of the people of India.

Miss Greco tolerates the students' inability, at first, to appreciate the culture of India. She understands their problem and, by opening up the discussions, provides a way of dealing with the difficulty.

All was going along smoothly. There were activities in the way of bulletin board displays, additional reports on the philosophy of the major religions, picture displays of famous places and art objects, and biographies of famous people.

Although none of these activities were particularly spectacular, they were sufficient evidence to me that the class was interested in the study and deriving meanings that were among my goals. In about three or four weeks we would be ready to move on to a new study and to some new goals I would have established. I had no way of knowing at that time of a force that was imminent which would set my goals aside like a feather in a storm, a force which came about by the confluence of world events and the aroused interest of twenty-nine sixth-grade children.

As part of social study activities, each child was required to read a newspaper article about a national or international event. Six to ten children reported on their selections each day. The reports were concluded by an invitation to the class for questions or comments. Frequently this resulted in discussion, informal debate, suggested topics for a formal debate, or simply a time of expressing opinions and reactions to current affairs. At the beginning of the school year, the reading of a news article each day was a purely mandatory assignment that often met with resistance. Gradually, for many children, it evolved into a genuine interest as the development of opinions and the expression of reactions deepened their involvement with the issues. I knew this had happened when, in planning the day's activities, news reports began to be selected as one of the first items on the agenda. Or when, on those days when we hadn't been able to get to everything on the agenda and news reporting had been omitted, there was an implied reprimand to me in the complaint, "We haven't done our news report today!" (The reprimand was justified, the apology offered was honest, the intent to do better in the future was sincere; but, somehow, the problem of not getting to all the things we wanted to do recurred.)

Her sensitivity to the children shows clearly here. She has created an atmosphere in which their desires are important. They know she will take their wishes seriously. Consequently, they speak their minds and she can easily tell what is most productive for them—in their view.

We had arrived at the topic of major problems of India, which was last on our outline. The children had long since ceased viewing the different cultural behaviors of the Indian people as "stupid." Considerable understanding had grown as to the overwhelming forces that created and perpetuated hardship in the lives of these people. Just about that time, several children had selected and reported on news articles about the drought in Kerala and the impending famine expected as a result. There was considerable discussion about this both as a historic problem and as a current emergency. The class was very moved by one report that 150 million people were expected to perish, 20 million of whom were children. Student B, who was very knowledgeable about such matters, reminded us that these figures represented total populations of some countries. As discussion proceeded, there was a mounting intensity of feeling coming from many of the children. At the time I thought the excitement was due to the fact that a bit of history was coming alive before them. Perhaps this did explain, in part, the events that followed.

As the discussion continued, the words "famine in India" dropped out. Instead the children were now speaking in terms of people being hungry and in danger of starvation. Although I was unaware of it at the time,

*Miss Greco's
sensitivity to this shift
in the level of discourse
prepares her for what
is to come. She hopes
that the cooperative
study will become an
exciting, humanizing
one. Somehow this has
occurred, and the
students begin a
different, more deeply
motivated level of
activity.*

*The cooperative
activity has prepared
the way for an
entirely different kind
of planning. The plan
that emerges is not a
simple one. Many
people have jobs and
the students recognize
that sending food to
India depends on
many factors they are
uncertain about.*

I think the shift in language represented a humanizing of the problem, a response, not in terms of a depersonalized state of being occurring at a particular geographic location, but a recognition of an intensely human tragedy happening to a people they had come to feel they knew. Unable to contain himself, Student C ignored the usual procedure of class discussion and shouted out, "Why don't we send food there?" The idea caught on immediately. Out of the excitement and exuberance a plan emerged. Student A added, "We could get all the other schools in town to collect food too." Students D and E thought we could submit information to a local Westchester radio station so that perhaps other communities could follow suit. It was even suggested that perhaps we could publicize our idea on a major TV network and get children all over the country to collect food for India.

We discussed the details. There was the question of how to contact the other schools and coordinate our efforts; there was the problem of where to store the canned and dried foods we collected; there was the problem of picking up the food we collected and delivering it to the ship. But what ship? At this point we realized that finding an agency that would ship the food free of charge was the starting point of our project. It was decided that I would not request official permission from the principal to carry out our plans until we secured information about shipping.

Students E, D, and A volunteered to call such agencies as CARE, the Indian Consulate, and UNICEF as a beginning. Plans were made to ask several store owners in the area if posters advertising the campaign might be placed in their windows. We were not certain at this point whether to make the posters in homeroom or whether to ask the art teacher if it could be done during her class. We made a note to ask her advice.

Student F's father owned a truck; Student D's father had a friend who owned a truck. They each would speak to their parents about helping us out with the trucking. Student G suggested that we make up a flier to be distributed to all parents and people in the neighborhood describing our food campaign and informing them as to when they could expect collectors. The date was not yet decided. Several parents could be asked to do the mimeo-graphing of fliers for us.

Within the space of about forty-five minutes the children had outlined the major aspects of their plan. Within that short period of time, history and world events had reached in and touched them and they had responded. The response was entirely their own.

After that first day's discussion of the project, I was not at all sure how far we could take the plans in view of the realistic problem of shipping. But there was an aspect to the undertaking which I thought was very important to these children. Most of them come from middle- to upper middle-class homes. In my experience with these children, I have found, in many instances, evidence of a kind of deprivation. What many of them are deprived of is the awareness of the needs of others and the sensitivity and compassion such awareness brings. It is my personal belief that the development of such awareness is as important to these children as anything else I have to teach them. Because social studies lends itself so naturally to the establishment of humane values and attitudes, it is an effective vehicle toward this end.

It was therefore very gratifying to me to witness the spontaneous display of active and sincere desire to "do something about it" by children whose environment all too often stresses self-interest as a major goal in life.

The volunteers who had agreed to call some agencies for information or leads regarding the shipping arrange-ments reported to the class within the next few days. The following information was submitted.

CARE could not ship for us. They would accept a donation of money and send their own food packages. This was definitely rejected by the class. They said they wanted to send food, not money. The children expressed some doubt as to whether, under such an arrangement, all of the money would be used for the purpose for which it was intended. There seemed to be some cynicism in regard to some charitable organizations. I made some little noises to the effect that perhaps this wasn't a fair attitude but I didn't pursue it further as the shipping problem seemed of more immediate concern. At any rate, it was firmly established that food was to be sent,

A new direction is emerging—a new study, really. The product of a cooperative depth inquiry has become involvement in the human problems of others. Miss Greco is wise enough to realize that the result will be a highly productive kind of learning, one that would be denied entirely if she felt a great desire to push on to the next unit.

159

For a teacher, this kind of decision required great restraint. The CARE solution was simple, neat, and probably an effective practical solution. It did not satisfy the children, however—and this

was a cooperative inquiry, a problem-solving process involving self-exploration. The classroom exists within the larger framework of the school and the climate of the school limits or extends what the class can do. The leader of cooperative study— the teacher—has to mediate with the larger system. Miss Greco has made a commitment to her students, and now she has to sell the project to others.

The children have managed to involve many knowledgeable people. They are learning about the side of cooperation that requires them to operate with respect to the needs of others. Democracy does not ensure that everyone

as that was the most direct expression of their concern.

UNICEF could be of no help either. They knew of no agency who could ship for us. We had asked them if they could contribute money containers as the children had decided to give people a choice of donating food or money. With money collected, we planned to shop for food. UNICEF had no containers for us so we would have to make our own.

Student E, with the help of her father, contacted someone at the Indian Consul General's office who said they would ship for us. We were all delighted. We could now begin to put our plans into operation. We were ready to ask the principal's permission to carry out the project. I had intended also to ask his advice as to how we could go about getting other schools in the community in on our plans. There was some uncertainty on my part as to how the project would be received in view of the fact that it would entail considerable disruption of routine. I was not unaware that this was a rather late date for that reality to have dawned. With as much confidence in the desirability and plausibility of our project as I could muster, I prepared to approach the principal.

The principal, upon hearing of our plan, informed me that we would have to get permission from the superintendent of schools for a project of this nature. A meeting with the superintendent was arranged. He thought the idea was good but suggested that carrying it out on a systemwide basis was perhaps too ambitious. He suggested that before starting on a citywide plan, we should try it first in our own school with several classes participating. If that worked out, he would assign us an administrator to help coordinate the efforts on a broader scale. Finally, he suggested that we find out the name of a school in the famine area to which the food would be sent along with letters to the children so that the project would be carried out on a very personal level between the children of both countries.

Although the class was very pleased with the suggestion that we send food to a particular school, they were extremely annoyed with the fact that we could not conduct the campaign on a citywide basis. They considered this unjust interference with our plans. I tried to placate them by reminding them that if we were successful, we would be given an administrator to assist us. Somehow they were not as impressed with that as I seemed to be.

The modification of plans revealed some attitudes that had to be dealt with. Of course I realized that I had contributed to the problem by not explaining more carefully to the class on that first day of the conception of the plan that our project must remain tentative until routine procedure of official permission was granted. If it had been made clear, the modification of plans would not have been so resented. It might also have been wiser not to proceed so far with the plans before permission had been secured. However, the feelings that initiated the plan were so spontaneous and so full of conviction that both the children and I were swept along with little thought to possible impediments.

Some of the attitudes I observed in addition to the resentment of the "interference" and the feeling of injustice was a pessimism on the part of more than a few children that they were sure our plans would not come to fruition since we could not act autonomously. It was apparent that many children could not manage their frustration in the situation. As a consequence, we had several class discussions in which the emphasis was on a need for us to remain flexible in our thinking in order to achieve our purpose. We even predicted the possibility of the need to modify our plans in other respects if necessary. We had to learn that modifying our plans did not mean failure as such, so long as our goals were achieved.

The class struggled for several weeks with the problems of raising money, buying food, and getting it sent. They met a veritable legion of bureaucratic obstacles and made their way through a real social maze before they discovered how to accomplish their purpose. They reacted strongly and variously to their experiences, and their own reactions as well as their chosen problem became the subject of their study.

The children wrote stories about some of their experiences with people as they went about collecting food. They met with criticism, hostility, derision, apathy,

will want to participate in every project—far from it. It includes the attempt to create a government that respects all the people on any question.

Miss Greco again tolerates her students' problem. She knows that an eager, problem-solving group will need to talk out their frustrations and she sees that they do.

161

admiration, generosity, and kindness. In some instances they were totally rebuffed with such comments as, "We have plenty of people in this country who need help. Let those people take care of themselves." In other instances they were badly lied to. Student F reported that one lady told him she had no food in the house when a shopping cart of newly purchased groceries was in full view! In still other instances, they not only received donations, but praise and milk and cookies as well.

The anger and resentment they felt on meeting with the negative answers after the first day's collecting indicated a need for discussion. We started the discussion by my reminding them of the negative feelings they had had when they first began the study of India. We speculated that perhaps the lack of concern which they occasionally encountered was not due to "meanness," but rather to ignorance of the problem. In recollecting their own initial reactions, it became apparent to them that ignorance can have a profound effect on people's behavior. They were then ready to think of other reasons why people might not receive their request graciously.

She is able to turn the despair and anger of the children into a deeper exploration of their feelings and the motivations of others.

At times the children received information which both chilled them and spurred them on. For example, one letter stated:

> . . . in our high school in Trivandrum we have over fifteen hundred children and of these approximately three hundred are poor and go without a mid-day meal. The local government is providing some cooked food which is just sufficient for about one hundred. If the rice and beans could be delivered to us we could arrange for cooked meals to be provided for the other two hundred children. This would last for fifteen weeks and possibly get us over a crucial period.

Finally, the project was completed as the money was sent to a world-wide relief organization. The children had managed to learn about the enormous difficulties involved in serving one's neighbors half a world away. They had explored their own emotions and the values of others. They knew more about India and their own culture and they were much more knowledgeable about social action.

Miss Greco's description speaks for itself. Her commitment to democratic teaching springs from her belief that total, cooperative war on the problems of humanity must begin when the child first becomes a member of a group. She believes that they must learn from their own responses to human needs, including their own needs, and that their childishness, their confusion, their inadequacy need not be squelched but, rather, recognized as common to us all.

This is no easy commitment. Helping children reflect on themselves, their group, on the nature of man, requires an unhurried approach to teaching and a judgment that knowledge of the world can be acquired as effectively through inquiry as through knowledge of subject matter. This is an era when many schools are trying to standardize their curriculum. Democratic process is more likely to diversify the world of the school just as it makes room for diversity in society generally.

INQUIRIES

1. Analyze Dolores Greco's experience with her children. Outline the principles she followed in developing this cooperative enterprise.

2. How much self-government should children experience in school? Will democratic experience affect their later political and social values? Debate the proposition: Children taught democratically by a liberal Democrat will become liberal Democrats, while children taught democratically by a conservative Republican will become conservative Republicans.

3. Develop a series of exercises that can be used to stimulate group investigation. For example, how might you stimulate young children to explore their community? Or older children to study international relations? What would be likely to stimulate a group to study interpersonal relations? Or to compare cultures?

NOTES

1. John Dewey, *Democracy and Education* (New York: Macmillan, 1916).

2. John U. Michaelis, *Social Studies for Children in a Democracy* (Englewood Cliffs, N.J.: Prentice-Hall, 1963).

3. Herbert A. Thelen, *Education and the Human Quest* (New York: Harper, 1960). Thelen is one of the founders of the National Training Laboratory.

4. Ibid., p. 80.

5. Ibid.

6. Ibid., p. 81.

7. Ibid., pp. 142–43.

8. Ibid., pp. 143–44.

9. Ibid., p. 144.

10. Miss Dolores Greco, a graduate student at Teachers College, Columbia University, was a teacher in the Mount Vernon (New York) schools when she engaged in the teaching here. This account is presented with her permission.

164

APPROACHES
TO INTERGROUP
RELATIONS

Although cooperative, democratic teaching helps improve most aspects of human relations, there are several aspects that require specific teaching. One of the most critical and difficult of these is intergroup relations—relations between definable groups in the nation and the world. Poor relations between ethnic groups (groups representing cultural variations), national groups, social and economic classes and castes, and races (groups with identifiably different physical features) have contributed much to world strife. Many approaches have been developed to help children inquire into intergroup relations and to teach attitudes and ways of working together that will reduce intergroup conflict.

Social Attitudes: Development and Flexibility

The child, soon after birth, begins to take on the values and attitudes of his social group. The social attitudes around him affect what he learns. If, for example, his social groups, including his family, wish a high degree of social distance between their members and the members of another racial or ethnic group, then between the ages of six and sixteen, he is likely to take on that desire.[1] Often, when a great deal of social distance is wanted, this desire is accompanied by a fear of the group in question and a feeling that its members have undesirable characteristics.[2]

Even very young children are aware of prejudice and are involved in it. Helen Trager and Marian Radke found in Philadelphia that kindergarten and first-grade children from homes prejudiced against a minority group already showed this prejudice in word and action.[3] In the Philadelphia studies it was noticed that friendly contacts in the classroom did not prevent the growth of prejudices. Prejudices were seemingly absorbed from the home and neighborhood even while the children were having friendly school experiences with the group in question. Furthermore, Trager and Radke contend that the teaching of general democratic principles does not reduce prejudice.[4] Hyman Meltzer has reported the same general finding: there seems to be little relation between the course of study and the rise of prejudice.[5] Reviewing the research on altering racial and ethnic attitudes, Arnold Rose concluded that only one kind of experience appeared to affect such attitudes: when the child is having friendly contact with members of the group toward which he holds a prejudice, he must be caused to evaluate his attitudes.[6] This evaluation, made in an objective manner, will help him free himself of unwitting prejudices.[7]

All this evidence seems to indicate the following:

Beginning in very early childhood, social attitudes are absorbed from social groups.

To some extent, attitudes arise independently of contact with the objects of the attitudes.

Favorable experience with the object of a negative attitude is not likely to change the attitude.

General teaching about attitudes is not likely to affect attitude formation.

Teaching that combines experience with the object of the attitude and an evaluation of the attitude has some chance of helping individuals free themselves from their prejudices.

A Program That Encourages Social Action

The Intergroup Relations Curriculum, developed for elementary school use by the Lincoln-Filene Center for Citizenship and Public Affairs at Tufts University under the directorship of John S. Gibson, is built around some of these principles. It is designed to help children explore intergroup relations. The primary materials created by a working party headed by Joseph C. Grannis are especially interesting because they lead very young children to explore intergroup problems in a complex way. The curriculum emphasizes inductive teaching methods and activities that involve the students. It focuses on personal feelings and experiences. Three of the objectives of the program are:

> To help the child to reduce stereotypic and prejudicial thinking and overt discrimination with respect to all kinds of groupings of human beings.
>
> To assist the child in realizing that there are many differences among people within groupings or categories of people based on sex, age, race, ethnic classification, national origin, profession or employment, region (e.g. "Southerner," "New Englander"), and level of education.
>
> To suggest ways by which all individuals may contribute toward bringing the realities of the democratic civic culture closer to its ideals.[8]

The curriculum tries to teach children a framework for conceptualizing the governing process. Six main components make up this conceptual scheme: the people or the governed, the governing officials, the political process, the structure of government, decision making, and policy. Each of these is roughly defined in Gibson's report. Decision making, for example, is defined as follows:

> Decision making within the polity is another subprocess within the scope of the larger governing process. Most official policy is *formulated* under leadership of the principal officials of the polity, those who comprise the polity's power elite. Usually, but not always, they are identifiable. In the legislature of a democracy, policy is *implemented* through a legislative process and, following endorsement by the leading executive official, is then *applied* within the polity and placed into motion with respect to relations with other polities,

although the machinery of application often does not function smoothly. The United States is one of the few nation-states in which the supreme judicial body has authority to interpret the constitutionality of much of official policy.

Policy making constantly involves decisions which must be made by authoritative officials, and these decisions are based on considerations both of the wisdom of the policy that is being considered and the political power relationships affecting the decision makers. It is of little benefit, therefore, for a student to commit to memory the "22 steps" (or whatever number) in the policy-making process in the American democracy without taking into account the bargaining and trading among decision makers, political demands and expectations intertwined in the structure and substance of policy, and the manifold pressures upon governing officials exerted by interest groups and others with considerable political influence.[9]

The curriculum (see fig. 7) uses so-called "methodological tools" to facilitate children's inquiry into various aspects of the framework. Each tool is a form of inquiry. For example, similarities and differences are explored as conceptual organizers that guide the student's study of the political process, decision-making, and other aspects of the conceptual framework. The students use these tools and this framework in dealing with content ranging from their neighborhood to world cultures.

Let us look at a unit on poverty in Appalachia to see how Gibson approaches it.

Objective: To explore poverty in Appalachia

This lesson can be related to individuals, groups, interactions, the governing process, and here and now.

Materials: *The Shame of a Nation* by Philip M. Stern and George de Vincent

1. Show the children Kentucky and Appalachia on a map.
2. Explain that the stories you are about to read to them (or have them read) are true stories about people who live there in communities where most of the men have lost their mining jobs because they have been replaced by machines.
3. Read the stories (or have the children read them)

Grades	Governing process	Similarities Universal	Similarities Group	Differences Groups	Differences Individuals	Interactions	Ideals, myths, realities	Here and now	Learning activities and units
K, 1 Home Family									
2 School Neighborhood									
3 Community									
4 Region									
5 United States									
6 Area Hemisphere									

Fig. 7. Organization of *The Intergroup Relations Curriculum*

about the Graves and Newton families in *Shame of a Nation* (pp. 19–23) and show them the pictures.

4. Looking at the pictures on pp. 20 and 21, ask questions such as the following to encourage the children to empathize with the people and understand what their lives are like. Pursue whatever line of questioning seems to evoke the best response from the class. What is a shack? What are the rooms like? How many people must sleep in one room in the Graves' shack? To encourage the children to understand the problems of crowded living even better, have them draw the house with each of the ten members of the family doing something in it. Or divide the children into "families" of ten and assign them to a one-room "house" (a section of the classroom) with only a few chairs and other appropriately sparse furniture. Each family could enact a different time of day or year—bedtime, suppertime, winter, summer. What happens when it gets cold?

The children may remember the reference to the newspapers which provide the only insulation. This is shown in the picture on page 21.

170

Do you think the Graves have a shower? How often do you think each person gets to clean himself? How much do soap and shampoo cost? How much soap and shampoo do you think the Graves family can buy?

Prompt with more specific questions, if necessary. Do they have warm clothes, blankets, as much heat as they want, etc.?

5. What happens to the shack when it rains? What happens to the street?

6. What do you think you would do in bad weather if you lived there?

7. Based on your experience from the last lesson, how long do you think $20 would last this family?

8. What do you think the Newtons did when they had no money for six weeks?

9. How would you survive if you were in their position?

10. What is the longest you have ever gone without eating?

THE SOCIAL DIMENSION

11. When the children have some ideas of what it is like to live in Appalachia, encourage them to think of reasons why these families can't improve their conditions. These questions are only a few of those which might be possible: What jobs do you think that the fathers of these families could do? Are there any jobs available where these people live?

Go back to the map of Appalachia. If the children do not notice it themselves, show them that there are no big cities.

If so, what do they pay?

The children may remember that Mr. Newton earned only $10 for a day's work, $20 a week at most. If necessary, refresh their perspective about this amount by questioning them about prices they learned in the preceding lesson.

Could these families move to a place with more jobs if they wanted to? What do you need to move?

171

Money to move the family and its furniture, a place to live, a means of support until a new job is obtained.

Where could they go? What could they do when they got there? What were these men trained to do? What other kinds of jobs could they do besides the ones they have been doing? How much schooling did these men have? Will their children be able to go to school as long as they want? As long as you can? Who pays for a community's schools?

If the children answer "the government," ask them where the government gets its money.

What do you think their schools are like? Do they have as many books as they need? Who might teach them?

For those who are interested, some statistics about teachers in

Perry County, Kentucky, are given on page 29 of Shame of a Nation.

Crowded home, they are hungry, etc. If the children don't volunteer these answers, help them to discover them themselves by asking questions like: How do you like the house to be when you do homework? Do you like to have your brothers and sisters around? How might you feel about doing your work if you hadn't any dinner that night? Could you do your best in school if you hadn't any breakfast?

Why might it be hard for the children to learn and to do well in school even if they were bright and wanted to?

The children should decide for themselves that these families should be helped, or else they will not be effectively convinced. If they feel that the Appalachian poor should help themselves, try to show the weaknesses in their arguments by asking "Why?" and "How?"

12. The third line of questioning in this lesson should explore the possibilities for outsiders to help. Do you think that other people should help these families?

Possible answers might include sending clothes, food, money.

What do these people need? What could we do by ourselves to help them?

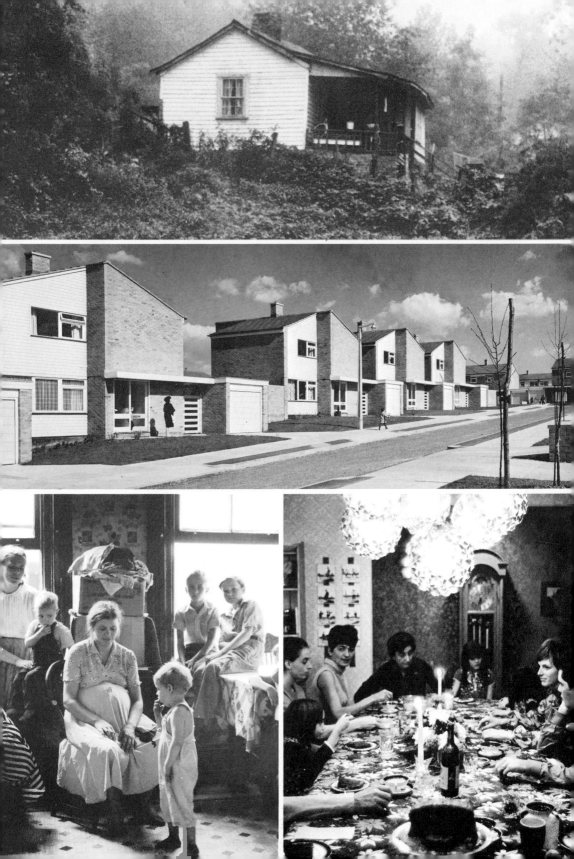

13. Explore those needs for which the remedies seem beyond the scope of a small group of individuals: better schooling for the children, jobs and job training, and so on. With which of these needs might we not be able to help the families by ourselves? Can you think of anyone who might be able to help them?

If the children are unable to come up with answers like "the government" or "large charitable institutions," ask questions like: What would be needed to help these people? Could it be done without lots of money or people? If so, how? If not, why not? What groups can you think of that are large enough and have enough money to do this? How could these groups help? Do you remember what suggestions the book made?

14. After the children have covered the unit on the governing process, try to help them to discover how they, as private citizens, could influence the government to carry out the policies they have just made up. If the children have only learned about the neighborhood or local government, discuss this as a local problem and then extend it by analogy to the federal government. Who makes the rules in the government concerning these policies? How could you help to affect these policies?

The children may not immediately come up with answers such as voting, writing to

Congressmen. If not,
prompt them with
questions such as: Why
do the people who
make the govern-
ment's policies have
the power to do this?
Who gave them this
power? Can we take
it away? How do we
know what policies our
Congressman is sup-
porting? If we do not
like these policies, how
can we let him know?
How can we make a
suggestion to him? If
he does not listen,
what else can we do?

15. The class as a whole could write to its Congressman and ask what the Congress is doing for Appalachia.[10]

The Intergroup Relations Curriculum combines social purpose with academic structure. The content, described in terms of topics, is not extraordinary (community, nation, internation, and so on). However, the content focus (intergroup relations) opens up humanistic issues and values. Further, the conceptual framework (governing process) and methodological tools (similarities, differences, and so on) sharpen inquiry so that the student learns to probe his intergroup relations and those of others in intellectual terms leading to social action.

The Lincoln-Filene approach to intergroup education has much in common with the Social Science Laboratory Units developed by the Michigan Social Science Project. The latter constitute an intellectual approach to the intergroup relations problem. By causing the children to apply social psychology inquiry techniques to problem areas such as friendly and unfriendly behavior, these units try to help children understand social attitudes and deal with them constructively.

Role-Playing for Social Values

Role-playing is the enactment of situations by individuals. The participants act out social situations designed to help them open up specific aspects of interpersonal relations and develop attitudes and skills conducive to better citizenship and personal adjustment. Innovators in education have for many years been using role-playing as a technique for exploring intergroup attitudes and values. The preeminent authorities in this area are Fannie and George Shaftel of Stanford University, who developed a large quantity of materials and approaches for classroom use.

> Role-playing, when properly and skillfully used, is uniquely suited to the exploration of group behavior and of the dilemmas of the individual child as he tries to find a place in the many and increasing groups in his life and at the same time struggles to establish personal identity and integrity. When properly used, role-playing permits the kind of "discovery" learning which occurs when individuals in groups face up to the ways they tend to solve their problems of interpersonal relations, and which occurs when, under skillful guidance, young people become conscious of their personal value systems. As a result, young people are helped to develop a sensitivity to the feelings and welfare of others and to clarify their own values in terms of ethical behavior.[11]

The participants should become deeply enough involved in role playing that their personal values manifest themselves in the way the participants approach decision-making.

> Through role-playing of typical conflict situations, children and young people can be helped to articulate the ways in which they tend to solve their problems. In the enactments, the consequences (social *and* personal) of the choices they make become more explicit. Analyses of these choices can lay bare the values underlying each line of action. Young people can thus learn that they act (make decisions) on the basis of the values they hold, which may be consciously, but most often are unconsciously, held. Once aware of their own valuing, they are in a position to modify their values.[12]

Role-playing can be used for many purposes, such as gaining practice in decision making. One series of stories, which the Shaftels recommend be played as a sequence, is built around the theme of self-acceptance.

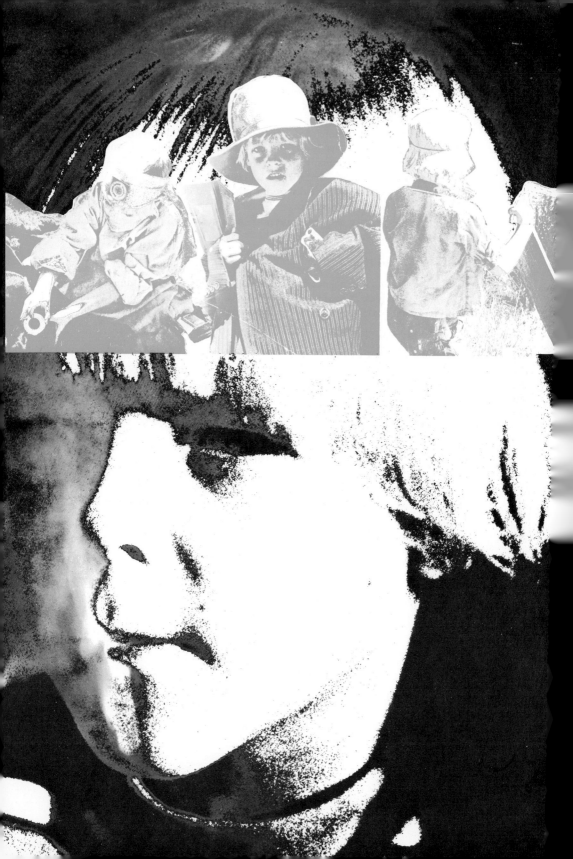

It is difficult to help young people to accept themselves, especially if they suffer some sort of serious disadvantage, real or fancied, inherent or imposed by the culture, such as having red hair or being crippled or cross-eyed or being of Indian or Negro or other racial background in an environment where the Caucasian is dominant, or belonging to a religion which seems exotic to the dominant culture. The approaches to this problem are many, of course, ranging in variety from in-service training for teachers that focuses on training the teacher to warmly "accept" pupils who are different to the varied cultural activities of "higher horizon" programs.

The sequence of stories presented here deals with just one approach to self-acceptance:

1. "The Big Comic"

   Tom has a chance to win acclaim in school by performing on a program, showing off a very special skill, but doing so will necessitate revealing that he has trouble in learning to read.

2. "Big Shot"

   Nora is a bright girl, eager to be prominent in school affairs. On the basis of an essay she has written, she is elected to editorship of the school paper, but she knows, in her heart, that she would not be as good in the job as the girl who is runner-up.

3. "Fast Ball"

   Eddie, who has a crippled foot due to polio, is a fine baseball pitcher. So good, in fact, that he enables his scrub team to beat a good Little League team. The Little League group invite him to join their team, to his great delight; but, although he can pitch very well, he can't run bases; all in all, he knows that he would be a handicap to a really good all-around team.

4. "Winner Take All"

   Lucia has a fine singing voice and has received excellent training from her father, who is a voice teacher. She enters a local beauty-talent contest, although she knows that she is plain. She discovers that the sponsors of the contest have decided in advance to award her the prize, because they believe that she needs the encouragement. Thinking about it, she is very upset: she is not pretty; she does not deserve to win a beauty contest; yet, she does have an outstanding talent.[13]

By acting out these situations, discussing the enactments, and analyzing the problems generated by the role-playing, the children will begin to see their own problems in self-acceptance and will become aware that everyone has to cope with the problem. Greater tolerance and understanding should emerge as well as greater sensitivity to one's own motives and those of others.

The Shaftels have provided a series of steps that can be used as a general guide to the conduct of role-playing:

1. 'Warming up' the group (problem confrontation)
2. Selecting the participants (role-players)
3. Preparing the audience to participate as observers
4. Setting the stage
5. Role-playing (enactment)
6. Discussing and evaluating
7. Further enactments (replaying revised roles, playing suggested next steps or exploring alternative possibilities)
8. Further discussion
9. Sharing experiences and generalizing[14]

In their very thorough book the Shaftels elaborate on these steps and illustrate them with examples. They supply materials for role-playing in many human relations situations.

Black Studies

In the last few years the study of black culture, especially African, has become very important. This study serves to acquaint both blacks and whites with the roles and contributions of blacks within human culture as a whole. In this respect black studies very much resemble the study of Asian, European, and Middle Eastern cultures. Black studies have also tried to develop black consciousness and racial pride. Much is taught about black culture so that blacks can come to see and appreciate their worth as individual members of a race.

Black militants have used black studies as a means of justifying and strengthening their demand for black separatism. They want blacks to develop separate enclaves, businesses, and cultural forms rather than create a black-white culture. The literature of separatism includes *The Autobiography of Malcolm X* and *The Wretched of the Earth: A Handbook for the Black Revolution*, and the separatist movement is very large.

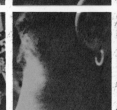

Intergroup relations programs and black studies approaches include the following:

Race and Culture: Intergroup Relations Curriculum (pp. 167–75).
Race, Caste, and Prejudice: Georgia Anthropology Curriculum Project (p. 183).
Role-playing for social values (pp. 176–79).
An approach to black culture through Swahili (p. 183).
Approaches through children's literature (p. 182).
Approaches through historical documentation.

These can be used from a historical perspective, a civil rights perspective, a black separatist perspective, or another. (Some people view race as a construction of the mind that will someday dissolve in decent brotherhood.) One of the great problems of nearly all teachers is getting to know the literature of the black experience in America. The following list is minimal, but provides a solid beginning.

Aptheker, Herbert. *A Documentary History of the Negro People in the United States.* 2 vols. New York: Citadel Press, 1951.
Baldwin, James. *Notes of a Native Son.* New York: Dial Press, 1964.
Bontemps, Arna. *American Negro Poetry.* New York: Hill and Wang, 1963.
Broderick, Francis, and Meier, August. *Negro Protest Thought in the Twentieth Century.* Indianapolis: Bobbs-Merrill, 1966.
Brown, Claude. *Manchild in the Promised Land.* New York: Macmillan, 1965.
Carmichael, Stokely, and Hamilton, Charles. *Black Power.* New York: Random House, 1967.
Cleaver, Eldridge. *Soul on Ice.* New York: Dell, 1968.
Coles, Robert. *Children of Crisis.* Boston: Little, Brown, 1967.
Ellison, Ralph. *Invisible Man.* New York: Random House, 1947.
Fanon, Frantz. *The Wretched of the Earth: A Handbook for the Black Revolution.* New York: Grove, 1968.
Franklin, John Hope. *From Slavery to Freedom.* New York: Knopf, 1965.

Hughes, Langston; Meltzer, Milton; and Lincoln, C. Eric. *A Pictorial History of the Negro in America*. New York: Crown, 1968.

Katz, William. *Eyewitness: The Negro in American History*. New York: Pitman, 1967.

Little, Malcolm. *The Autobiography of Malcolm X*. New York: Grove, 1964.

Parsons, Talcott, and Clark, Kenneth, eds. *The Negro American*. Boston: Houghton Mifflin, 1966.

Quarles, Benjamin. *The Negro in the Making of America*. New York: Macmillan, 1964.

Thomas Pettigrew's beautifully documented *A Profile of the Negro American* (Princeton, N.J.: Van Nostrand, 1964) is a must primer for the white teacher who is unclear about racial facts and the psychological, economic, and political situation of blacks in the United States.

Member of the Gang, by Barbara Rencoff and Harold James (New York: Crown, 1968) is a sensitively told story of a gang and the moral dilemmas that membership causes one of its members. It reveals the problems of growing up in an urban slum and delineates the choices possible in a life of city poverty. It could begin an inquiry into many urban problems and the dynamics of group pressures.

To Be a Slave, written by Julius Lester and illustrated by Tom Feelings (Dial, 1968) uses the words of black slaves to show the physical and emotional character of slavery. It is compelling, lucid, and devastating, and could make a strong beginning for an inquiry. Similarly authentic is *Young and Black in America* (Random House, 1970), compiled by Rae Pace Alexander. This book contains selections from the autobiographies of eight well-known black Americans, including Malcolm X and Jimmy Brown. The selections are mostly about the childhood or early adulthood of these men.

A valuable source of information about publications on black consciousness and teaching materials on the black experience is the *IRCD Bulletin*, edited by the Erie Information Retrieval Center on the Disadvantaged and published by the Horace Mann-Lincoln Institute, Teachers College, Columbia University. A recent issue, "Media for Teaching Afro-American Studies" (vol. 6, nos. 1 and 2) lists and evaluates films, tapes, filmstrips, and other nonprint media that might be used to help children explore the black experience. Among these materials are the filmstrips and records from Warren Schloat Productions, including *The Ghettoes of America* (1967), *Rush Toward Freedom* (1968), and *African Art and Culture*; the New York Times Company's filmstrips *Africa in Ferment*, which describe the new African nations that are struggling to be born and survive; Encyclopedia Britannica Educational Corporation's series of filmstrips about the black man in North America. Many of these materials can be criticized for their approach and point of view, but still can be used to stimulate inquiry.

A simulation entitled *Sunshine* (Lakeside, Calif.: Interact, 1968) and developed by David Yount and Pauk Dekock can also be used to help students explore race relations. In the simulation, crises erupt and important urban problems have to be dealt with; in these ways students face problems that cause them to learn what it means to be a member of a race other than their own. A variety of racial and ethnic attitudes are explored in terms of urban problems, and students become aware of their own racial attitudes.

The Anthropology Curriculum Project of the University of Georgia has prepared a series of units entitled "The American Minority Ethnic Series." The first unit provides a thorough introduction to race, caste, and prejudice and their effects. It poses the question, "What are we going to do about race, caste, and prejudice in the United States?" The section dealing with the tactics of racists, including pseudoscience, appeals to authority, and scapegoating, is unique in American social studies textbooks. The section on the problems of unconscious prejudice is also unique and an important area to open up to elementary school children. The series contains units also on the American Negro and Spanish-speaking Americans.

When black studies are centered around African cultures, a unique and potentially powerful approach is to study Swahili. The easy and comprehensive introduction developed by the Foreign Service and the Peace Corps provides material through which upper elementary school children or older can begin to study the language. The Bantu language, almost the *lingua franca* of Africa, provides a wonderful "feel" of African culture and a thorough introduction to the ideas and ways of thought of the black cultures of Africa. For the dedicated inquirers into black culture, the study of Swahili would be a preferable approach.

INQUIRIES

1. "Children should not study the less pleasant aspects of race relations because it will make them cynical." Debate this proposition.

2. Plan an experience to help children understand how their attitudes form. (You might want to use concepts from sociology and social psychology to provide intellectual structure.)

3. It is sometimes suggested that black studies promote racial separation. Discuss this issue, identifying as many aspects of it as possible. Where do you stand?

NOTES

1. Gordon W. Allport and Bernard M. Kramer, "Some Roots of Prejudice," *Journal of Psychology* 22 (July 1946), pp. 9–40.

2. Bernard M. Kramer, "Dimensions of Prejudice," *Journal of Psychology* 27 (April 1949), pp. 389–451.

3. Marian Radke and Helen G. Trager, "Early Childhood Airs Its Views," *Educational Leadership* 5 (1947), pp. 16–24.

4. Marian Radke, Helen G. Trager, and Hadassah Davis, "Social Perceptions and Attitudes of Children," *Genetic Psychology Monographs* 40 (1949).

5. Hyman Meltzer, "The Development of Children's Nationality Preferences, Concepts, and Attitudes," *Journal of Psychology* 40 (1941), pp. 343–58.

6. Arnold Rose, *Studies in the Reduction of Prejudice* (Chicago: American Council on Race Relations, 1948).

7. Robin M. Williams, Jr., *The Reduction of Intergroup Tensions* (New York: Social Science Research Council, 1947). A survey of the research bearing on the issues and problems involved in ethnic, racial, and religious attitudes. Though published in 1947, the survey is still instructive in dealing with issues of concern to educators, and every teacher should know the book and its implications for the classroom.

8. John S. Gibson, *The Intergroup Relations Curriculum: A Program for Elementary School Education*, vol. 2, Lincoln-Filene Center for Citizenship and Public Affairs, Tufts Univ. (Medford, Mass., 1969), pp. 2–3.

9. Ibid., p. 19.

10. Ibid., pp. 307–16.

11. Fannie and George Shaftel, *Role-Playing for Social Values: Decision Making in the Social Studies* (Englewood Cliffs, N.J.: Prentice-Hall, 1967), p. 9.

12. Ibid., p. 12.

13. Ibid., pp. 174–75.

14. Ibid., pp. 65–66.

INTERNATIONAL EDUCATION: LIFE ON SPACESHIP EARTH

There has never been consensus about the purposes of international education in the United States. Some people say that the social studies should vigorously promote world federalism; at the opposite extreme, some say that teaching about foreign nations and peoples, especially rivals such as the Soviet Union, is potentially subversive. To avoid such controversy, many schools have developed rather anemic international education programs. These programs tend to put America at the center of international relations, pay some attention to "our friendly neighbors to the north and south" and, in the study of Europe and Asia, emphasize the relatively safe ground of economic geography.

Such pussyfooting is by now easy to recognize as dangerously irresponsible. All the peoples of the world are the crew of our Spaceship Earth; and international citizenship, whether expressed personally or through national representation, is a moral necessity. The international aspect of citizenship must be learned, and learned well, by most people if the world is to survive, let alone become a joyous home for many societies.

chapter 8

Extensive analysis of international education recently resulted in a yearbook of the National Council for the Social Studies devoted to that subject and an exhaustive report by the Foreign Policy Association for the U.S. Office of Education. Each of these provides a thorough guide to rationales for approaching the area, curricula and teaching strategies, and the procurement of material. In addition, Leonard Kenworthy, one of the pioneers of international education in the elementary school, has for years scoured schools and publishers, identifying and annotating teaching strategies and materials. He is virtually a one-man clearing house for international education.

The essential intellectual goal of international education is to help the student attain a global perspective and see himself as a world citizen.

> Geographically it means that [the student] sees the network of world interdependence and influence. He learns that the exploitation and conservation of resources is not simply a local or regional affair, but a global affair as well. Economically he sees not only the processes of community and national economic interchange, but the networks of international interchange as well, and perhaps more critical, the moral and practical consequences of the actions of man everywhere on man everywhere else. . . . Anthropologically our young citizen begins to see interplay of the earth's cultures. He notes the processes of cultural conflict and interchange. He sees too the gradual formation of world culture. . . . Sociologically he sees the processes of assimilation and accommodation in the institutions and behavior patterns of the people around him, and he is able to identify the processes by which people are absorbed into the perspectives of their time and place and the processes by which this time of theirs socializes them to the global. Historically, our citizen sees the sweep of time as peoples all over the world have formed and reformed their heritages: mingled them, suppressed them, and found identity in them.[1]

To perceive the social, political, economic, and geographic systems of the world, however, is by no means sufficient. A person must also be committed to improving the world. Social studies teaching must help young people develop the perspectives of world citizenship so that they identify with people everywhere.

Lee Anderson, of Northwestern University, has made one of the most concise and incisive statements of the perspectives of international education. Drawing from the work of the political scientist Chadwick Alger, Anderson argues that the essential question is whether the world has a social system. If there is such a global system, then it must be taught as a part of the truth about human interaction. The student must come to see the global system and learn to look at his own life and his nation's life as part of that system. Anderson finds abundant evidence that a global society is in the making: a rapidly emerging worldwide system of human interaction, growing globalization of economic and military interdependence, an expanding network of cross-national organizations and groups, increasing similarity in mankind's social institutions, and an expanding homogeneity of cultures.[2]

> In short, we have become a single human community. Most of the energies of our society tend towards unity—the energy of science and technological change, the energy of curiosity and research, of self-interest and economics, the energy—in many ways the most violent of them all—the energy of potential aggression and destruction. We have become neighbors in terms of inescapable physical proximity and instant communication. We are neighbors in economic interest and technological direction. We are neighbors in facets of our industrialization and in the pattern of our urbanization. Above all, we are neighbors in the risk of total destruction.[3]

If Anderson, Alger, and Ward are correct, then international education requires teaching the cultural system that makes us interdependent and the ways of thinking and feeling that promote a sense of belonging to an international community and sharing an obligation to improve it. Such an educational program requires also helping children reach across cultures and understand people far removed from them. The following approaches to achieving these goals range from the systematic to the informal. At least one of them should be within reach of every teacher and school. They all, however, share the idea that international life must not just be taught about. Like democratic process, it has to be lived enthusiastically.

187

The World as a Social System: A Simulation of World Citizenship

The booklet *International Education for Spaceship Earth*, prepared for the Foreign Policy Association, vividly illustrates for children the problems of living in an overcrowded world with limited resources. A spaceship environment is simulated, using an audiotape and an overhead transparency of the inside of a spaceship.

As the spaceship travels through the atmosphere, problems are presented to the children: all aspects of an overcrowded situation, including the need for more air, food, and water. The children are encouraged to discuss these problems and suggest solutions that might benefit the group as a whole. At the same time they see how people react to deprivation, danger, and discomfort.

Discussion is kept open and moving; the making of judgments and conclusions is discouraged so that the children pursue their ideas as long as necessary in order to deal positively with the problem. One crisis the children discuss occurs when the captain has to ration the food and water to all people on the spaceship except certain crew members with critical job responsibilities.

> *Second:* I don't think it's fair that some of the crew should still be getting full rations. Just because they have to keep the ship running, it isn't fair.
> *Third:* But if they don't, then more things could go wrong on the ship and then everybody might die. . . .
> *Fourth:* Yes, but which jobs are the most important?
> *Fifth:* Maybe the passengers and the crew should talk about it together. Why should just the captain decide? Maybe he's got some favorite crew members and he just wants to treat them better.
> *Sixth:* No, he wouldn't do that.
> *Seventh:* But if you let everybody say what they want, you could end up with a big argument. That's why you have a captain, otherwise everybody is arguing and fighting.
> *Eighth:* Yes, they have to do what the captain says. He's supposed to know more about the ship and what to do. That's why he studied to be a captain.[4]

This part of the lesson was designed so that the children would identify what is essential for survival and begin to recognize the interdependence of people with each other and their environment. The lesson went on to describe the spaceship as a system with interdependent parts. Other interdependent systems were discussed: families, nations, mathematics, government, transportation, the telephone company. Earth was finally discussed and simulated as a giant system made up of many smaller ones, including water. Through experiments children saw how this system depended on lakes, rivers, and oceans and how pollution of the smallest part could affect the whole.

> *Teacher:* Let's consider those pollution experiments we did. What did you learn from them?
> *First:* Well, what you do on one side of the earth will go to the other side.
> *Second:* And what they do on the other side will come over here.
> *Third:* And if it's something bad, we don't want it to happen.
> *Fourth:* It's like on the spaceship. You have to take care of the system.[5]

This dramatic creation of an environment induces children to seek solutions to problems and to form generalizations about human social life. It avoids many preconceptions and prejudices by asking the children to generate their own answers. The world of the future will be built on our existing world, but we hope we will be able to deal with it from a fresh perspective. *Spaceship Earth* gives children a chance to look for new solutions to both persistent and fresh problems. It embodies the international perspective essential for world citizenship.

189

Cultural Interdependence: Reaching between Cultures

A teaching strategy for conveying international attitudes as well as content has been developed and applied by Barbara Powell, of Newark, Delaware. Her outline for the strategy appears in part below.[6] It deals with the liaison between the towns of Newark, Delaware, and La Garde-Freinet, France, which have proclaimed themselves "twin cities" and now exchange visitors and cultural products and even maintain a student exchange program for older children. The result has been that Newark abounds in experienced native informants on virtually every phase of life in La Garde-Freinet. With the help of film slides, visitors, artifacts, and whatever else can be obtained directly from the French town, the Newark children can study another culture in depth. They learn more about their own culture, too, for a foreign visitor often points out things that might be taken for granted by a native.

Mrs. Powell's teaching strategy drew from several of the social sciences. By entwining physical geography, economics, and government with questions designed to explore what these people hold important, she was able to include the study of attitudes and values. Basically, the strategy of the lessons was comparison. The sequence of the lessons called for cooperative planning, followed by data collection and data analysis.

Hands Across the Sea

A study of the twin towns of Newark, Delaware and La Garde-Freinet, Var, France

Explanatory Note: In the summer of 1959, through the efforts of a few people in Newark and of a former exchange student at the university, now a resident of La Garde-Freinet, "twinning" of these two towns was completed under the sponsorship of the United Towns Organization, an international agency with offices in Paris. In the fall of 1959 the mayor of La Garde-Freinet visited Newark, bringing many samples of products produced in his town, and was accorded a public reception by the officials of Newark. Much interest has developed, especially in the senior high school French classes. This outline is an attempt to make the twin cities a suitable and profitable study for the fourth grade.

I. Themes
  A. To develop understandings of a different culture
  B. To promote awareness of the essential similarities of peoples
  C. To encourage friendship through communication and through sharing with other peoples in the interest of world harmony

II. Objectives
  A. Development of attitudes of tolerance for differences between peoples
  B. Introduction to the history of these communities
  C. Knowledge of the physical and economic geography of the areas
  D. Comparison between daily lives of people in these communities

E. Appreciation of the culture of both populations

F. Acquisition of elementary map skills, including comprehension of distances and altitudes

G. Introduction to working and planning in groups

H. Knowledge of some elementary French words and expressions

III. Introductory activity to set purposes

    A. Teacher-collected display of products and artifacts, including cork objects, sachets, perfume, chestnut jam, mushrooms, honey flavored with lavender, dolls in Provençal costume, handwoven rugs, jars of olives

B. Questions to stimulate interest
   1. Where do the children think these things came from?
   2. How many children have been in a foreign country? What made it "foreign"?
   3. Would they like to take a trip to this one?
   4. If they were to take a trip to the town that produced these objects, what would they be interested in finding out?
   5. What questions would a typical boy and girl from this French town be likely to ask them about Newark?
C. Purposes set by children, guided by teacher, to cover planned content in a program flexible enough to incorporate other ideas and to eliminate those eliciting no interest

IV. Planning a trip to La Garde-Freinet
   A. Content
      1. Location on map—route to be taken—how far is it to Le Havre?
      2. Passports—what are they and how do we get them?
      3. Steamship—how much does ticket cost?—what is life like on a big ship?
      4. Train—from Le Havre to Marseilles—are French trains different?—what kind of terrain will our train take us over?
      5. Omnibus to La Garde-Freinet—roads, traffic, tourists
      6. What shall we wear?—will it be hot, cold, rainy, windy?
   B. Activities
      1. Tracing route to be taken on world map
      2. Collecting pictures of French steamship, train, bus, countryside, people
      3. Making passports, using some parent's passport as sample
      4. Reading travel folders
      5. Group research on climate; making maps of rainfall; gathering information on temperature and winds; using sand table for relief map of area
   C. Resources
      1. Travel circulars from French Line, New York; French Embassy, Washington, D.C.; Ministère des Travaux Publics, des Transports et du Tourisme, Paris IV

2. Pictures from magazines such as *Holiday* and from Sunday travel sections of newspapers
3. Information on passports, climate, relief map from encyclopedia

V. Information we will take to La Garde-Freinet about Newark
  A. Content
    1. The land
      a) Physical location, area, population, altitude, physical features
      b) Climate—effect on land use, occupations
      c) Natural resources—soil, streams
    2. The people and their work
      a) What do we do for a living?
      b) Do we all speak the same language?
      c) What are our houses like? Our schools? Our industries?
    3. How our town is governed
      a) Mayor and council
      b) Police and fire protection
      c) How our state helps—roads, sewers
      d) How we support our town
    4. Our means of recreation
      a) Sports and games—baseball and Little League; dancing, scouting, bowling, football, etc.
      b) Radio and television, movies
      c) Music—instruments, singing, records
      d) Festivals—Christmas, Easter, Mardi Gras and Halloween, July 4
    5. A day in the life of an American nine-year-old
      a) House and family—parents, sisters and brothers
      b) Food—where it comes from, how it is prepared, typical meals
      c) Clothing—for school, for dress-up, for festivals
      d) School day—classroom, teacher, books, how one travels to school
  B. Activities
    1. Preparing a map of Delaware, locating Newark
    2. Making relief map of papier-mâché showing canal, towns, etc.
    3. Individual research in sources such as *World Book* or other encylopedia to get overall picture of Delaware
    4. Locating school, home, public buildings on town map

193

5. Drawing typical house in development, farm, large old home
6. Field trip around Newark locating places found on map
7. Visit from town official on subject of Newark's growth and problems, specifically such problems as traffic, new houses to replace those beyond repair, swimming pool
8. Collecting postcards and snapshots of Newark for scrapbook

VI. Information we will want to bring back from La Garde-Freinet
A. Content
1. The land
   a) Location of town, area, population, physical features
   b) Climate and its effect on land use, architecture, occupations
   c) Natural resources
2. The people and how they live
   a) What are these people like? What do they hold to be important?
   b) How do they make their living?
   c) What industries do we find here?
   d) How do they travel?
   e) Their language
3. Their government and services
   a) Brief history of town, department, province
   b) Present government of town, officials, law enforcement
   c) Schools and education in general
4. Their pleasures
   a) Literature—legends, proverbs
   b) Music—songs, nursery rhymes, national anthem
   c) Sports and games—Tour de France (cycling), football, tennis, boules
   d) Fine arts—local arts and crafts; inspiration for Matisse, Cézanne, Van Gogh
   e) Festivals—14th July, Christmas, New Year, Easter, Mardi Gras
5. A day in the life of a French nine-year-old
   a) His house and family

b) Food—where it comes from, how it is prepared, typical meal

   c) His clothing—for school, holidays, festivals

   d) His means of recreation

   e) Typical school day

B. Activities

   1. Preparing map showing location of town

   2. Making relief map showing river valley, Mediterranean, mountains

   3. Using sand table to create typical village, with special attention to accuracy in depicting type of house and architecture

   4. Interview and discussion with people who have recently been there. (By the end of each summer, several Newark residents will have spent some time in this town.)

   5. Learning French songs, some already familiar, from records. (Cooperation with music teacher for best results!)

   6. Collecting scrapbook material by entire class, including also stamps, coins

   7. Research by small groups on different aspects of French life; reports to class illustrated by scrapbook material

   8. Flags—small group to work on producing French flag, La Garde flag, Delaware flag

   9. Gathering of collection of artifacts from this region—reproductions of paintings done by artists here, local crafts, costumes. (Teacher will have to arrange to borrow most of these from people who have toured the region. Class will help make labels explaining each item.)

   10. Murals to be made by group of children depicting day in life of French child and Delaware child

   11. Preparation of program for parents explaining work done and the exhibits, culminated by serving of refreshments prepared from French cookbook. (All foods to be given their French name. Cooperation of parents essential here.)

Not every teacher lives in a community that has "twinned" itself with a foreign community. However, there is much that teachers and schools can do to develop close relations and access to information in other lands.[7] It is not difficult, for example, to adopt a foreign school. Probably the most common method is to work through Americans who have lived abroad or people from other countries who have lived in the United States. Some teachers have made arrangements by writing directly to school districts abroad. Occasionally exchanges of letters by pen pals have developed into such a close relationship that the schools of these correspondents have made a formal liaison.

The teachers and children of the two schools can arrange to exchange experience records, creative writing, drawings, studies of their communities, lists of questions to be answered, and pictures and maps. If the languages differ, an interpreter will be needed—perhaps an elementary school language teacher, a secondary teacher, or a bilinguist from the local community or college. For linguistic and other reasons, countries with a culture similar to ours are probably the easiest to set up relations with; but, with determination, language does not remain a barrier for long, and contacts with different cultures can be exceedingly productive.

Adoption of foreign schools has several advantages for both parties. It facilitates the children's ability to collect honest, detailed information about the people of another country. To the children of a village in Normandy the children in a Pennsylvania town can address questions that would never be answered in a textbook or a commercial flier. The adoption of a faraway school can bring a realism to social studies that can come only from the consciousness that the respondent to one's question is actually on the spot. Whether the Pennsylvania sixth-grader asks, "Our trains run less often these days; do you have good train service?" or the French first-grader asks, "What did you have for dinner last night?" the answer that comes back has a ring of authenticity that no secondary source can inspire. There is also a freewheeling quality about a study that is not confined to the answers that can be found in the typical reference book. Adoption of foreign schools enables children to double-check the information and ideas in reference works and textbooks. "We read that French towns are dominated by cathedrals. Can you send us a picture of yours?" "Our textbook says that nearly 25 percent of the Italian people voted Communist in the last election. Is that true? What does it mean?" Some difficult questions can also come from the other direction: "Our book says that it is not legal to be a Communist in the United States. How can that be if you have free speech?"

Adoption also establishes a need to communicate information, together with an awareness of the problems and joys in human communication. A fifth-grader in Texas trying to describe local industries and products to children in Liverpool has a much more demanding job than if he were merely reporting to his classmates. Preparing a report takes on added dimensions when what one says becomes practically the whole source of ideas that someone else will possess. "Is this an honest description of our town?" "Are we saying what we really want to say?" These become crucial questions.

In the course of several years of association with the children of another nation, children gradually see the part that culture plays in behavior. Discovered through concrete evidence, the understanding can and should begin early ("They wear Lederhosen like we wear slacks"), continue toward more abstract issues ("These Irish kids don't like Englishmen, but they've never met any. I guess they learned that from their parents"), and eventually proceed toward self-understanding ("I like the English because Dad does. I've never met an Englishman either").

The exchange between children, carried on in their own words, is likely to remain within the level of their understanding. First-graders can exchange pictures, experience records that they dictate to their teachers, tape recordings of stories, songs, and plays, pictures they take and pictures they draw, and many other things. Through these devices, a first-grader in Denver can exchange ideas and compare communities with a first-grader in Tokyo. "They have policemen too." "They use a different kind of stove." "They have churches too." The eyes of the children in the adopted school become extensions of the eyes of the children of the adopted nation. The first-grader in Denver studies economic interdependence in his community and division of labor in his family at the same time he studies these concepts in relation to the community and families of his Tokyo friends.

Depth studies in the higher grades can also proceed on a comparative basis. "Please describe the political organization of your city. Here is our city charter. Do you have this kind of document? Can you send us a copy? We have included a tape recording of an interview with our mayor. He says the main issue in our city today is zoning to protect our recreation lands. What is the main issue in your town? Do you have good recreation facilities?" The possibilities from this kind of association are limitless. The adoption, in itself, ensures that through the grades the children will have the constant opportunity for a comparative depth study of the location situation and the society of the adopted school. Leonard Kenworthy has stated the urgency of this sort of contrast:

> It is no longer a question of whether we should prepare children
> to live in the world community; they will either live in a world
> community or not live at all.[8]

Many young people are studying in armed forces schools abroad or traveling with their parents or living in another country where their parents are on lengthy business. Occasionally a class will have access to such a young traveler and can count on him for information. The following letters are from a fifth-grade child who spent a year in the Republic of South Africa. His class continued to correspond with him, and conducted a depth study of South Africa, partly in order to take advantage of his presence and to prepare for his return. The following are excerpts from two of his letters.[9]

> I have just got back from Kruger Park. We had a lot of fun there
> except when we started seeing elephants and my six-year-old sister got
> scared. We saw only one lioness and no lions. It ran into the bush as
> soon as we saw it. We saw many impala and wildebeest, which looks
> like a bison. We saw a herd of about 400 water buffalo. We saw two
> crocodiles, one of which was far away, the other swimming about
> 15 feet away. We saw many elephants. The one that interested and
> scared me most was a male elephant with fairly large tusks, which
> trumpeted and came after us. There were some fairly large
> hippopotami which we always saw near the water.
> There is a bad drought here. It is the worst in 70 years. The
> Limpopo River has run dry. The worst drought-stricken places are:
> Brits, Petersburg, Harmbaths, Messina, and Ohrigstad.
>
> On November 5, 1963, and every other year, too, we will have a
> celebration called Guy Fawkes Day, where you shoot up fireworks.
> You can shoot as many fireworks as you want. (Guy Fawkes is a man
> who tried to blow up the houses of Parliament in London.) There is a
> field next to my cousin's house where we can set fireworks off.
> (Also it is the day after my birthday.)
> Some of you have asked how come I have to pay 10¢ and you 11¢.
> We actually pay more than you. One cent is 40% more than yours.

Some of you wanted to know if there were any black children in my class. People, they are so strict about that that they have special buses, train cars, benches, and places in post offices. Also, they probably couldn't afford a white person's school. So it would be impossible for a black to get into a white's school.

The flow of personal information, the ability to answer difficult questions about race relations simply and from direct observation, the ability to convey emotional atmosphere—all belong to our young observers.

Through Art and Literature

From many nations come literature, music, and art that can be used in depth study of a culture. Folk tales in particular have been translated, collected, and edited for children of all ages, and most nations and certainly every world region are represented. Literature can open up the study of a people's national values, their views of life, their reactions to plague and tyranny, and their ideas of pleasure or loyalty. Imagine children reading the following folk tale of India to find out what is important in the teller's message and what virtues are being extolled.

199

THE GOLDEN STAG   *by Isabel Wyatt*

An old hunter once saw a golden stag. He told no one till he lay on his deathbed. Then he told his son:

"It was up in the hills, far from the king's city. A rill ran over sands of silver. The golden stag led a herd of deer down to the rill, to drink."

The son was a hunter, too. He felt love for all things, and did not wish to kill. It was the wish of his heart to be a hermit and grow wise. But he was born a hunter, the son of a hunter; so a hunter he had to be.

One night, the queen of that land had a dream. In her dream, she saw a golden stag. The golden stag sat on a golden throne, to teach. The things he spoke of were so wise that as she awoke, she cried, "Catch that stag!"

Next day, the queen told her dream to the king.

"Did you ever hear of a golden stag in this land, Sire?" she asked.

"No," said the king. "But I will ask my hunters if they have."

Only one hunter had. "My father saw it, Sire," he said. "He told me of it on his deathbed. He saw it up in the hills, far from the city."

"Go and catch it," said the king, "and bring it to the queen."

The hunter went up into the hills, far from the city. He came to the spot his father had told him of, with a rill that ran over sands of silver.

Footprints of a herd of deer went down to the rill. So the hunter set a snare in the track and hid among the trees.

That night, he saw a herd of deer go down to the rill in the moonlight. The herd was led by a golden stag.

The golden stag set his foot in the snare. He cried the cry of capture. At that cry, the herd fled.

Then the hunter saw a thing he had never seen till now. Two of the herd came back to the golden stag. They tried to get his foot free. The thong cut his flesh to the bone, but he was still held fast.

"Go with the rest," cried the golden stag. "Go—you are still free."

"We will not go," said the two stags. "We will stay and die with you."

The hunter felt his flesh creep with pity. He came out from among the trees with his knife in his hand. He stooped down, cut the snare, and set the golden stag free.

"Why did you snare me, hunter?" asked the golden stag.

The hunter told him of the dream the queen had had.

"Then why do you set me free?" asked the golden stag.

"Out of love and pity," said the hunter.

"Hunter, you are no hunter at heart," said the golden stag. "What is the wish of your heart?"

And the hunter told him:

"To be a hermit, and grow wise."

"Brush my back with your hand," said the golden stag.

The hunter did so. Golden hairs from the back of the golden stag clung to the palm of his hand.

"Keep them," said the golden stag. "When a man feels love for all things, hairs from the back of a golden stag can make him wise. Now look into my eyes."

The hunter did so.

200

"What I know, you know," said the golden stag. "Go back now to the queen. What to say to her will come to you."

So the hunter went back to the city. He came to the king and queen and told them how he had met the golden stag and how he had set him free. He told them all that the golden stag had said to him. The new things came into his mind to say—wise things he did not know he knew.

When he came to an end, the queen cried, "But this is just how the golden stag spoke in my dream! Sire, give this man the wish of his heart. Let him be a hermit!"

"I will," said the king.

So the hunter got his wish and was a hunter no more, but a hermit. He grew so wise that even the king sat at his feet. And all his life he was able to help the king rule his land well, with the help of the golden hairs from the back of the stag.[10]

The children will quickly find the value that Indians place on love for all creatures and on charity and mercy. The place of wisdom in the story, a place which might have been taken by riches or security or the hand of the princess, will be detected. The belief in destiny—the "wish of the heart"—will be examined.

As the children examine other folk tales, they will find some with similar themes. They will, as in "The Golden Stag," find the theme of magic and the use of magic to redeem life from an otherwise cruel fate. Gradually, they will also isolate those themes that many nations seem to share. Both common values and special values will be identified. Perhaps the same unit, or perhaps a later study of India, will reveal to the children the tie between the wish to be a wise hermit and the tenets of the probable religion of the hunter. Much later, in senior high school or in college, the student will come upon these ideas again as he learns how Gandhi used the tales and religious ideas of the Indian people as he led them toward national independence.

Starting with a Book

Many publishers issue series of books about the countries and peoples of the world.[11] Most of these are written for the upper grades and contain, unfortunately, only a brief survey of each country. Some do provide considerable information about a limited topical area—economic geography, for example—but most spread their coverage rather evenly over several areas. The Lippincott series includes some history, leisure activities, art, architecture, and literature; the series comprises fairly short books and thus necessarily gives fairly brief coverage. Treating each nation very generally and providing very little data and illustration, such books present a compressed profile of a country but are not good information sources for an effective depth study. Nevertheless they do raise excellent questions and provide many general ideas that can be further investigated. The virtues and faults of these series become fairly evident when one reads the following passage from a book on Portugal:

> Elvas, on its steep hill overlooking the plain, is one of the largest, busiest, and most romantic of these old walled cities. Atop the hill is the castle. Below it are huddled the houses, glaring white, within the walls and moats that encircle the town. Inside the main gate one discovers a maze of narrow winding streets crowded with townfolk, peasants, and soldiers. From ramparts and towers there are splendid views across the plains which are brown, yellow, or green, depending on the season. In the churches is a wealth of sixteenth or seventeenth century tiles, paintings, and images. The aqueduct built near the end of the fifteenth century brings to the town its supply of water. From the orchards outside the walls come the sweet green plums for which Elvas is famous. Out of season they can be had preserved in liqueur and coated with icing. The town is equally famous for its dried fruits and olives.[12]

This passage is all that is given about Elvas. The concept load is enormous, and the child is asked to accept many conclusions for which the underlying reasoning is not given. Hence his previous knowledge must be substantial if he is to comprehend such description. Because of just these limitations, however, the passage could start an inquiry into the town's history, its economy, its architecture, and religion. The general ideas need to be made carefully explicit and then checked out, one by one. Highly motivated children with good reference books, a willing teacher, some writing paper, and the address of the Portuguese embassy could have a field day.

Some of the general discussions in the book on Portugal might be even better spurs to inquiry:

THE SOCIAL DIMENSION

When Portugal's Golden Age had come to an end there was a marked decrease in the production of books. Literary work had been financed or sponsored usually by grants from the King or the benevolence of wealthy members of the nobility. The slump in the nation's economy meant less financial aid to poets and prose writers. Books were very expensive. A large segment of the nation was illiterate. Despite these conditions, outstanding work was produced, but not in so great a volume as in previous decades.[13]

Children of some sophistication might take this passage and embark on a general study of the subsidization of the arts and its effect on literary production. Iron-curtain countries, Western Europe, medieval times, the United States might all be explored. Perhaps not many youngsters would seize this opportunity, but investigation of topics of like sophistication is not unknown by any means. A reminder, however: an effective depth study must deal with a limited facet of a topic. To approach a country from the point of view of politics or economics is probably all the children should be expected to handle at one time. Perhaps, the English version of the Macmillan "Lands and Peoples" Series could be used in a depth study: in some cases the point of view is different enough that an upper-grade class could compare the books with a series written by Americans.

In the last few years a very useful kind of trade book has appeared. It takes a small topic or even a small part of a small topic and develops it in detail. Books on limited aspects of many nations have begun to appear in increasing numbers. Such are the books by Sonia and Tim Gidal about villages in various, usually European, countries. *My Village in England* (Pantheon, 1963) is typical. Accompanied by black-and-white photographs, the text traces the life of a small boy in a village called Temple Grafton, a few miles from Stratford-on-Avon. The detail of daily activities helps the reader to get some idea of the orientation of the people, even the sociology of the family. The daily lives of the children, for example, can be compared with those of American children. References to historical events and figures bring out the people's sensitivity to their heritage. The forethought of the characters illustrates the thrifty, tidy culture of an English village. The material is especially suitable for sociological analysis because of the profuse description of people.

Focus on Asian Studies

Another way to work for international understanding is to emphasize those areas of the world about which Americans are generally ignorant. An example is to focus on Asian studies so intensively that the perspective of the Orient begins to fill the life of the student. John U. Michaelis has organized such an approach in a project to develop guides and materials on Asian countries for use in grades one to twelve.[14] Michaelis and his associates have developed a mass of materials on Asian studies, including two units for the primary grades and one for intermediate grades, as well as a secondary level course. The theme is simple, although the topic is complex and their approach is exhaustive: to teach children enough about the Asian perspective that they will be able to put themselves, at least partially, in the Oriental position and think about human life from that viewpoint.

INQUIRIES

1. Plan two studies of the United Nations, one for primary grade students and one for upper elementary grade students.
2. Show how anthropology as a discipline can help children study intergroup relations, democratic process, and international relations.
3. Describe how you would organize the social education of a racially mixed kindergarten class.

NOTES

1. Bruce R. Joyce, "Curriculum Reform Strategies in the World Affairs Domain," in *An Examination of Objectives, Needs, and Priorities in International Education in U.S. Secondary and Elementary Schools*, ed. James Becker, Final Report, Project no. 6-2908, Contract no. OEC 1-7-002908-2028 (Washington: U.S. Office of Education, Bureau of Research, July 1969), p. 33.

2. Lee F. Anderson, "Education and Social Science in the Context of a Global Society," in *International Dimensions in the Social Studies*, 38th Yearbook of the National Council for the Social Studies (Washington, 1968), pp. 82–85.

3. Barbara Ward, *Spaceship Earth* (New York: Columbia Univ. Press, 1966), p. 14.

4. "International Education for Spaceship Earth," New Dimensions Booklets on the Social Studies and World Affairs, no. 4 (New York: Foreign Policy Assn., 1970), p. 77.

5. Ibid., p. 83.

6. This outline is taken, with minor changes, from a paper submitted by Barbara Powell for a course taught by the author at the University of Delaware in the summer of 1960.

7. Much of the material in this section has been adapted or taken directly from Bruce R. Joyce, "The World-Widened Elementary School," *Elementary School Journal* 62 (April 1962), pp. 343–45.

8. Leonard S. Kenworthy, *Introducing Children to the World* (New York: Harper, 1955), p. x.

9. For these letters we are indebted to Mrs. Ruth Sutcliffe, teacher in Newark, Delaware.

10. Isabel Wyatt, "The Golden Stag," from *The Golden Stag and Other Folk Tales from India* (New York: McKay, 1962).

11. For more information about these books, see chapter 13, pp. 312–15.

12. Raymond Wohlrabe and Werner Krusch, *The Land and People of Portugal* (Philadelphia: Lippincott, 1960), p. 71.

13. Ibid., p. 92.

14. U.S. Department of Health, Education, and Welfare, Office of Education, Bureau of Research, *Preparation of Teaching Guides and Materials on Asian Countries for Use in Grades I–XII*, prepared by John U. Michaelis (Washington, 1968).

205

part 3

THE
PERSONAL
DIMENSION

MORAL DEVELOPMENT, CONCEPTUAL DEVELOPMENT, AND THE SOCIAL STUDIES

Teaching social studies involves teaching values, ideal types of behavior toward which people manifest positive emotion. Values are intangible. They exist in the minds of individuals, but their existence can be inferred from external behavior. Values provide the structure that give a person's life and a culture stability and direction.

In our culture there is a great diversity of values. Some people who claim to believe in freedom of expression feel that motion pictures should be censored in their portrayal of sexual activity; others who also claim to believe in freedom of expression feel that censorship of any kind is anathema. Although there are consistent patterns of behavior in our society or a common core of values and ways of thinking, ours is an exceedingly complex culture.

Only in primitive cultures is there uniformity of values. Members of such a culture absorb its values as they grow up. They do not need to be taught values formally, and the culture is static. In our culture, however, the teaching of values is critical because of their very diversity. One of our major social problems is developing frames of reference that anchor the culture but at the same time permit the range of values necessary for personal fulfillment and cultural growth.

The values issue has become an enormously sensitive one in the schools.[1] The public is quick to criticize a teacher who takes a position or permits a child to take a position that conflicts with the value positions of many people in the community. Even classroom discussion of various value possibilities, especially in regard to sexual behavior, is enough to alarm some people. Unfortunately, sometimes the best solution to this difficulty seems to be to keep the schools out of the important value domains. Even many secondary schools and colleges have avoided the critical value issues in our society and taken the position that schools should deal only in those areas of relative agreement. In a complex society, such a position has the effect of virtually prohibiting serious study of the culture by children. Nearly all our social institutions and social relations involve questions of unresolved values. If the children are to be prepared to live in this culture, then they need to deal in the value domains that are controversial.

209

Moral Development

Moral development entails developing an identity, an integrated, functioning self.

> The process of American identity formation seems to support an individual's ego identity as long as he can preserve a certain element of deliberate tentativeness of autonomous choice. The individual must be able to convince himself that the next step is up to him, and that no matter where he is staying or going, he always has the choice of leaving or turning in the opposite direction if he chooses to do so. . . .
> The functioning American, as the heir of a history of extreme contrasts and abrupt changes, bases his final ego identity on some tentative combination of dynamic polarities, such as migratory and sedentary, individualistic and standardized, competitive and cooperative, pious and free thinking, responsible and cynical, etc.[2]

Mass media, pressure groups, parents, teachers, politicians, advocates of all courses compete for the direction of a person's

life. He has to seek his identity in the midst of this powerful culture and cope with both its mainstream and alternatives to it. He wants to know he is free to choose the alternatives; but his struggle is lonely, for this fantastically complex society acts on him impersonally. The socialization process may be said to be successful to the extent that the values of the society become internalized and the individual develops an inner monitor or conscience. He is then able to think, feel, and act as the society requires, with a minimum of external controls.

At birth the human organism begins to absorb the values and patterns of action of people around him. "The self . . . is largely a private replica of the outer social world (or some part of it) of which the individual is a part; its social relations are mere continuations of those already existing within the group."[3]

Bernice Neugarten's study of fourth-grade youngsters dramatically illustrates the extent to which internalization of values affects a child's judgment.[4] Asked to judge their classmates according to cleanliness and leadership qualities, her group of children tended to rate both characteristics according to social-class origins. The higher the economic status of the parents, the "cleaner" was the rating of the child. Careful investigation revealed that there was in fact no relation between economic status and cleanliness. The children apparently had internalized the judgments of the adults about them, learned to judge economic background without having any idea what it was from a sociological point of view, and made their judgments of classmates on the basis of class-linked values.

Studies of prejudice support this conclusion. Prejudice is now regarded as an act of conformity to one's social group. It develops early, although it does not become fully differentiated according to race and ethnic background until the later elementary school years. Allport contends that prejudice arises in the school years of six to sixteen, which, incidentally, is the time of the most active formal social education.[5]

Kohlberg has analyzed moral conduct into three levels and six stages as follows:

LEVEL I—PREMORAL
Stage 1.—Obedience and punishment orientation. Egocentric deference to superior power or prestige, or a trouble-avoiding set. Objective responsibility.
Stage 2.—Naively egoistic orientation. Right action is that instrumentally satisfying the self's needs and occasionally other's.

Awareness of relativism of value to each actor's needs and perspective. Naive egalitarianism and orientation to exchange and reciprocity.

LEVEL II—CONVENTIONAL ROLE CONFORMITY

Stage 3.—Good-boy orientation. Orientation to approval and to pleasing and helping others. Conformity to stereotypical images of majority or natural role behavior and judgment of intentions.

Stage 4.—Authority and social-order-maintaining orientation. Orientation to "doing duty" and to showing respect for authority and maintaining the given social order for its own sake. Regard for earned expectations of others.

LEVEL III—SELF-ACCEPTED MORAL PRINCIPLES

Stage 5.—Contractual legalistic orientation. Recognition of an arbitrary element or starting point in rules or expectations for the sake of agreement. Duty defined in terms of contract, general avoidance of violation of the will or rights of others, and majority will and welfare.

Stage 6.—Conscience or principle orientation. Orientation not only to actually ordained social rules but to principles of choice involving appeal to logical universality and consistency. Orientation to conscience as a directing agent and to mutual respect and trust.[6]

First the child makes decisions in terms of personal want and avoidance of punishment. Then he seeks approval by conforming to rules and authority for their own sake. If he matures, he develops self-accepted principles and is concerned with the establishment of mutual respect and trust.

Kohlberg also identifies twenty-five aspects of moral growth that occur throughout the six stages. One of these aspects he refers to as "The Basis of Moral Worth of Human Life." This aspect develops as follows:

Stage 1.—The value of a human life is confused with the value of physical objects and is based on the social status or physical attributes of its possessor. Tommy, age ten: (Why should the druggist give the drug to the dying woman when her husband couldn't pay for it?) "If someone important is in a plane and is allergic to heights and the stewardess won't give him medicine because she's only got enough for one and she's got a sick one, a friend, in back, they'd probably put the stewardess in a lady's jail because she didn't help the important one."

(Is it better to save the life of one important person or a lot of unimportant people?) "All the people that aren't important because one man just has one house, maybe a lot of furniture, but a whole

bunch of people have an awful lot of furniture and some of these poor people might have a lot of money and it doesn't look it."

Stage 2.—The value of a human life is seen as instrumental to the satisfaction of the needs of its possessor or of other persons. Tommy, age thirteen: (Should the doctor "mercy kill" a fatally ill woman requesting death because of her pain?) "Maybe it would be good to put her out of her pain, she'd be better off that way. But the husband wouldn't want it; it's not like an animal. If a pet dies you can get along without it—it isn't something you really need. Well, you can get a new wife, but it's not really the same."

Stage 3.—The value of a human life is based on the empathy and affection of family members and others toward its possessor. Andy, age sixteen: (Should the doctor "mercy kill" a fatally ill woman requesting death because of her pain?) "No, he shouldn't. The husband loves her and wants to see her. He wouldn't want her to die sooner, he loves her too much."

Stage 4.—Life is conceived as sacred in terms of its place in a categorical moral or religious order of rights and duties. John, age sixteen: (Should the doctor "mercy kill" the woman?) "The doctor wouldn't have the right to take a life, no human has the right. He can't create life, he shouldn't destroy it."

Stage 5.—Life is valued both in terms of its relation to community welfare and in terms of life being a universal human right.

Stage 6.—Belief in the sacredness of human life as representing a universal human value of respect for the individual. Steve, age sixteen: (Should the husband steal the expensive drug to save his wife?) "By the law of society he was wrong but by the law of nature or of God the druggist was wrong and the husband was justified. Human life is above financial gain. Regardless of who was dying, if it was a total stranger, man has a duty to save him from dying."[7]

The child comes to appreciate the various positions from which any situation can be judged and, perhaps, ultimately develops ideals that embrace alternative positions and give a basis for action.

A child whose values do not develop in this way tends to adopt value positions as rigid, simplistic rule systems. He grows up believing that rules are for the best and cannot be changed. He thinks in dichotomous, black-and-white terms and is unable to build concepts that accommodate different stances or provide negotiation among them. He is unwilling to structure his own inquiry or to see himself as a transactor. He has yet to recognize the complexity of situations and the manmade nature of rules and categories.

Applying These Theories to Teaching

How can the social studies influence attitude formation? Unfortunately, nearly all the evidence on the effects of teaching values indicates that social studies education has failed in this respect. With few exceptions, civics education, political exploration, and cultural comparison have affected neither the values nor the visible behavior of the student. From Hartshorne and May's extremely thorough studies of civics education over forty years ago[8] to the recent analyses of the dynamics of "suburban deprivation"[9] and student rejection of the school as an institution[10] there is massive evidence that we have not learned how to teach values on a large scale. Perhaps, we have tended, however, to teach values only by reiterating rules and precepts. This need not be the only technique.

Kohlberg's analysis of moral development suggests that the teaching of values is a matter of helping children grow into increasingly advanced stages of personal organization, enabling them to mediate their needs and those of others. In Kohlberg's view, value education and personality development are inextricably related.

215

> The attractiveness of defining the goal of moral education as the stimulation of development rather than as teaching fixed virtues is that it means aiding the child to take the next step in a direction toward which he is already tending, rather than imposing an alien pattern upon him.[11]

Kohlberg's analysis can be used to diagnose moral development so that teaching can be matched to moral levels. To provide a "stage one" child with "stage five" tasks, for example, would be unproductive. Optimally, teaching should aim approximately one level above the student's level of functioning. Kohlberg's analysis also suggests that children should be exposed to conflict and thus introduced to new levels of reaction to it. For example, if a child argues in terms of his personal likes and dislikes, the teacher might try to help him find the general principles that underlie his preferences.

Another aspect of moral development concerns the ability to deal with complexity and to handle the many dimensions of social situations. To live successfully in a democracy one has to free oneself from dependence on authoritarian control and the desire to impose it on others. Teachers can help children in this process by helping them use abstract concepts to explore complex factors and issues. In this way the teaching of values becomes the teaching of complexity.

Moral development as a citizen requires also commitment to the improvement of society and participation in democratic process. Social action, both in and out of school, is probably the only reasonable way to change behavior. Viewed this way, the teaching of values means helping students become involved in the improvement of their community.

Strategies for studying and analyzing value problems can also be part of teaching values through social studies. Systems of concepts from the social sciences can be taught to students to use in analyzing social issues. Race, prejudice, politics, and religion are all subjects in which the social sciences offer procedures and data. The development of personal and social values is a rational as well as an emotional process to which knowing how to collect and interpret data and to analyze social issues objectively can contribute. In this respect, the teaching of values implies helping students apply the methods of the social sciences to social problems. Each aspect is dependent on the others. Growth in academic competence, for example, but not in commitment to social improvement would produce a person with insufficient impetus to act. It may be that the dimensions are causally related to each other, at least in part. That is, that a person cannot grow academically or democratically without also developing more complex views.

Moral development and increased complexity focus on personal growth. Democratic process and academic inquiry emphasize the specific knowledge and skills required to cope with the valuing problems of an open society. These two aspects merge to produce the person with both the disposition and the skill to develop values on a mature basis. To build the social studies around valuing requires bringing about growth in personality as well as developing specific skills, knowledge, and commitment.

Opposite page:
The aspects of teaching values complement each other.

An Example of Teaching Values

Let us look at a classroom where a team of five teachers are working with over a hundred children, ranging in age from seven to ten. The team depends on instructional specialists for help in several curriculum areas, but in the social studies they themselves organize and teach problem-solving units according to the children's needs and abilities. In the current unit the children study the government of the middle-sized eastern city in which they live. The unit emphasizes the processes of decision making, especially in regard to the city council, welfare, urban planning, and human relations. The teachers expose the students to the kinds of strategies social scientists use to analyze various phenomena: plotting voting patterns, identifying pressure groups and tracing their origins, preparing summaries about the implementation of laws, surveying attitudes, and organizing the findings. All this seems appropriate to the intellectual and social dimensions of the social studies, but there is in it also the personal dimension.

In one corner of the large all-purpose room, a group of ten-year-olds is discussing proposed laws. One of the children plays a tape of an interview he conducted with a member of the city council. The councilman's voice is heard:

"I don't know just how to say this to you kids, but I have been trying all year to get some kinds of laws passed that would deal with a couple of the problems of our city that I don't think anybody else, at least not anybody else on the city council, is paying much attention to. One of our problems is that each of the roads leading into our city is getting built up with a lot of small businesses. Do you know the kind? Gas stations, drive-in restaurants, drive-in movies, and small shopping centers are growing up all along our main highways. Because those are good places to attract business, there are a lot of people going in and out of those little businesses every day. And people travel our little highways to those places. The trouble is that because there are so many cars going to and from all the kinds of places that are built up around our city, it is getting very hard to go anywhere on our main roads. I would like to have some places kept for businesses and other places kept for houses and some of our roads kept free of either one of those things, so that we can quickly get into and out of the city. . . ."

At one point in this class session, Carolyn says, "I think it's awful that Councilman Wooten can't get these bills passed. He's trying to make the city better, and I don't see why these other people don't care."

One of the boys casually replies, "My father says that Councilman Wooten is a Communist." Both of them look up expectantly, as do the other children, at the teacher.

"Did he say why he thought so?"

"He says Mr. Wooten wants the government to own everything. They'd just tax everything people make and run everything."

Another girl adds, "My mother feels the same way. She says he doesn't care what happens to business in this town and he'd ruin us. He wants to give everything to poor people who are too lazy to work."

Carolyn, who seems upset, replies, "My father says Mr. Wooten is the only man who sees that when all the land is used up and there's no place to play or anything this will be an awful city!"

"I think" says the teacher, "we will have to spend some time getting some information about the controversies Mr. Wooten is involved in. Let's begin by deciding what kind of information we need."

They compile a long list: making a land-use map of the city; listing all bills about land use with voting records of councilmen, reactions of the local papers, and action by the executive branch, especially the city manager's office; developing devices for finding out how people feel about the issues and the individual councilmen.

The teacher here is not teaching the "right" views but guiding the children in their attempts to make judgments. If they believed that the teacher approved of Councilman Wooten's actions, they would probably agree with her. As it is, they tend to accept the views of their parents and to judge the actions of public officials in simplistic terms. Perhaps the teacher can introduce them to a more complex analysis by getting them to look at the general implications of their position. Already the children are to gather more information so that they understand the situation better. They are dealing with a complex issue in a complex but orderly way. They are concerned with the improvement of their community and becoming more involved in it. They are learning social science techniques by which to deal with social problems. These are all aspects of teaching values through the social studies.

219

Conceptual Development

Recent psychological research can help us get some idea of how a person develops concepts. In experiments conducted by Jerome Bruner, Jacqueline Goodnow, and George Austin, for example, several persons were studied in terms of the way in which they handled a concept-formation task. It was found that people, when given a problem, can be distinguished both by the modes they use to search for information and by the patterns they use to relate that information.[12] Some people grasp a few bits of information and immediately hazard a judgment. Others gather a good deal of information before venturing a hypothesis. In processing information, some people try out two ideas at once, while others are single-minded. Some become attached to the first idea they think of and resist letting it go, while others change their ideas easily as new evidence appears. A person's system for processing information and solving problems can be called his *conceptual style*.

A related line of inquiry, conducted by Milton Rokeach and his associates, has centered on the ways in which people organize their beliefs, especially with respect to whether their systems of belief are "open" or "closed."[13] Rokeach's studies indicate that belief systems can be described in terms of the extent to which a person automatically rejects beliefs contrary to his own ("People who oppose this idea must be Communists"), keeps his beliefs separated or compartmentalized, resulting in unrecognized inconsistencies ("I believe in equality for all men"; "Those immigrants should know their place and keep it"), distinguishes between ideas he regards as friendly or unfriendly to his system. These two belief systems are probably unrelated to specific beliefs. Two persons may have similar beliefs, but one may hold them concretely and rigidly and be unable to cope with conflicting evidence, while the other holds the beliefs flexibly and can weigh conflicting evidence without discomfort.

O. J. Harvey, David Hunt, and Harold Schroder have suggested that there are several stages of conceptual development through which a person passes, although his development may stop at any of the stages.[14] Unilateral dependence is the most rigid stage. The individual tends to use a few simple criteria received from authority figures or from his social milieu. He tends to submit to authority and carefully adhere to the norms of his groups.

Growth in complexity of concepts and in complexity of interpersonal
relations

Probably the infant needs to go through this stage of development, for he is dependent on the direction of his parents and their nourishment for his very existence. The individual who does not develop beyond this stage, however, becomes a good subject for a totalitarian regime. Research indicates that even in the United States many adults, including a surprising number of teachers, manifest the characteristics of this stage.[15]

The next stage, negative independence, can be described as a reaction against the conformity of the first stage. During negative independence the individual rejects external control and is less submissive, although he still tends to see things in blacks and whites; his concepts are still few and rigid. The rebellions of adolescence may be a necessary part of a person's struggle to free himself from the dependence of childhood. A person who does not develop beyond this stage would probably have considerable difficulty in dealing with other people.

A person who overcomes the hostility of the second stage and establishes relations with other people on an independent basis is likely to become preoccupied with interpersonal relations and to take other people's wishes and points of view into account. He tends to develop concepts that are more complex and more flexible. He can deal with confusing and stressful situations with greater ease. He can entertain alternative views of himself. ("Sometimes I do well in arithmetic, but I have trouble with word problems." "I can express myself clearly, but sometimes I offend people.") Whereas people in an earlier stage tend to resolve doubt by reference to formulas and easy solutions, this person is able to remain in doubt longer and to consider more alternatives. His awareness of others' intentions, however, can result in an other-directedness that renders him overly dependent on the approval of others. This stage may be called one of conditional dependence and mutuality.

In the most mature stage of conceptual development, a person possesses the most complex and flexible system of concepts, which enables him to adapt most easily to difficult and stressful situations. The interdependent person does not see conflicts of interest as necessary or long-lasting; he is less emotional about interpersonal difficulty; and he can understand the role of other persons and approach situations in a way satisfactory to both himself and others. When faced with a difficult problem, he tends to suspend judgment while seeking information that will make a decision more rational. When he is criticized or confused or when he is confronted by a conflicting belief, his reaction is to find

222

more information and to examine his beliefs to see if they need revision. Faced with a job, he tends to be task-oriented, although aware of others and their needs.

Harvey, Hunt, and Schroder's theory of development is by no means entirely tested. They present impressive evidence, however, that various training conditions or environments in which a child is raised or schooled powerfully influence conceptual development. Their thesis is that the way a child is treated at home and at school either helps him develop conceptually or tends to arrest his development at an immature stage. These training environments may be described in terms of the degree and kind of interaction between parent and child or teacher and student.

Unilateral training is characterized by the imposition of external rules and criteria of judgment. It may use threats to back up such rules. ("I will tell you the right way to get the answer. Your grade will depend on your using the right way as well as on the correctness of the answer.") Or it may imply that authority does not err and that criteria of rightness are found outside the immediate situation. ("The book is right. It was written by an authority and has to be right.")

Under unilateral conditions, knowledge is seen as rigid and definite. ("There are three causes of the American Revolution. They explain why we had to go to war against the British.") The student is rewarded chiefly when he arrives at answers that have been selected beforehand. ("Will you stand and recite the three causes of the American Revolution.") The object of training is relatively fixed and definite. ("Your job for the year is to read all the passages in this book so that you'll be ready for next year's book.") The child is valued for his achievement rather than for his efforts to search out ideas and information. ("You can't do any more reading until you've learned the week's spelling words. You seem to learn everything except what I want you to learn. Mary is a good girl. She does what I ask and then does something quiet.")

In an interdependent training environment the child is helped to understand himself and his relations with others as well as to inquire into his world through experiment. Search, rather than rote learning, is rewarded. ("You've done a good job of looking for information, but the answer still doesn't satisfy me. Let's write to the museum and see if they can help us there.") The emphasis is on hypothetical constructs. ("Do you think water put out the candle? I wonder how we could conduct the experi-

223

ment to see if you are correct.") Failure is treated as a source of information. ("Well, this time all the plants died again. Where shall we look for the cause?") The child shares in the development of standards of performance. ("What do you think of your progress? Are there places where we can improve this job?") Perhaps most important, the learner is valued for himself. His achievement and his personal worth are not equated. ("Well, you seem to have missed a lot of the questions this week. Can we work out a new way of studying? Charley has some trouble too. I wonder if you can work together.")

Several interesting experiments reinforce this theory about training environments. The famous studies by Kurt Lewin, Ronald Lippitt, and Ralph White more than a quarter of a century ago stressed "authoritarian" and "democratic" social climates. It was found that in these two social climates the interpersonal relations of children were quite different; children were more cooperative and treated one another with greater dignity after exposure to democratic conditions.[16] Harold Anderson and Helen Brewer studied young children who were exposed to "dominative" or "integrative" behavior by their teachers. Even five-year-olds who were being dominated by their teachers tended to dominate, or attempt to dominate, their peers, while children who were being treated with greater consideration and respect tended to be more integrative and respectful with their classmates.[17]

We need to consider carefully the theses that rigid environments produce rigid people and that interdependent conditions produce people with flexible conceptual systems and open minds. It seems likely that the predisposition to be open- or closed-minded is established in the very early years of life. Furthermore, the influence of the school may be dependent not only on the amount the child learns but also on the way he learns and the way he is treated by other people while he is learning.

Implications for Teaching

How does the foregoing influence our strategy of social education? What kind of social environment should be planned and what techniques of instruction have to be learned in order to carry out the plans? If we accept open-mindedness as one of our educational goals, then we have to consider the conditions that bring it about. What makes up the kind of training environment that helps children grow toward openness?

In the course of a unit of study the teacher handles much information and helps the children learn many concepts. He helps them locate reference books and develop skills for using them. He helps them find and interview people in the community who are good sources of information. He helps them evaluate information by assessing its authenticity and reliability and looking at it from many points of view. He helps them evaluate their thinking and decide whether conclusions are warranted and ideas need revision. Interdependence makes all ideas fair game and demands that supporting facts be examined, logic scrutinized, and better solutions sought. In an interdependent environment the teacher is guide, critic, and companion in search.

The teacher is also the child's most valuable source of information. Under unilateral conditions, however, information is presented as if law were being made. It is unequivocal, correct, and not to be challenged. In an interdependent environment the presentation of information is interspersed with opportunities to evaluate it. Some laymen think that the elementary school years are simply the ones when basic facts are poured into the child in preparation for the years when real thinking begins. If thinking does not begin in the early years, however, all we will have later is a closed mind.

In unilateral environments one of the teacher's main functions is to make conclusions and generalizations. Many beginning teachers have to learn to resist doing intellectual work for their students. To be sure, there are times when the teacher must offer generalizations, carefully buttressed by facts. But nearly always, in the interdependent climate, the child has the burden of making conclusions and defending them. When the teacher states them, he does so in such a way that challenge is encouraged and the reasoning he used is visible to the learner.

In a unilateral environment most of the questions are like "What year did the *Mayflower* land?": they have only one answer. The interdependent environment is characterized by questions such as "From the evidence we have, what might be the reasons for the Puritans coming to this country?": they require conclusions, reasons, and personal opinions. The former kind of question tends to deaden inquiry; the latter stimulates it.

225

There are many other ways in which a teacher can encourage or discourage search behavior and the acquisition of knowledge. To build an interdependent climate, the teacher continually has to reward search or problem-solving activity, even when it does not uncover anything particularly important. Most of us, however, have greater facility in rewarding the acquisition of knowledge. The tests we use are usually designed to determine whether certain facts have been learned. Knowledge is important, and its acquisition should be praised, but in balanced measure.

A teacher can also use rewards and punishments to establish order in the classroom. In a unilateral environment the teacher spends much time rewarding those who conform and punishing those who do not; rules take on much significance. In an interdependent environment the search for rules of behavior is as important as learning to live within rules. Each individual is learning to restrain his own behavior and to develop with others the regulation of group activity. Failure to conform becomes something to look into and study rather than simply to censure. The teacher needs to learn not only to reward conformity but also to encourage inquiry into the nature of rules and to stimulate the cooperative activity necessary to produce rules.

Similarly, the teacher should let the children help determine classroom procedures such as what questions will be explored and how committees will be organized. Unquestionably the teacher is the appointed leader; and, especially with young children, some procedures have to be thought out beforehand. As the child grows, however, he should take part in determining how his work is organized. The child needs to be encouraged to look to himself for leadership and responsibility. In the interdependent environment the teacher does not leave the children completely to their own devices, but he does counsel them continually to develop reasoned plans in an atmosphere of mutual agreement. The child is involved in the debate about ends and means, and shares in the allotment of authority.

The teacher must also see that there are standards by which growth can be judged. Students need some means of determining the adequacy of their performance. They need to know whether they are learning enough and are becoming more effective at inquiry. When the teacher imposes all the standards and assumes all responsibility for evaluation, the child comes to think of rules as ready-made and inflexible. At times the teacher may need to impose standards, but the interdependent climate depends in part on the children's ability to join in the search for means of judging progress.

Making a Training Environment

All the teaching behaviors described above are probably present in every normal classroom. How these behaviors are proportioned, however, determines the differences in the training environment of the child. The following diagram summarizes the behaviors typical of each kind of environment.

Interdependent Environment		Unilateral Environment
Teacher helps children find and evaluate	Information	Teacher gives conclusions
Directed at search	Rewards	Directed at following rules
Teacher helps children determine	Procedures	Teacher determines
Teacher helps children determine	Standards	Teacher determines

Theoretically at least, unilateral conditions are more likely to arrest conceptual development, and interdependent conditions are more likely to advance social development. But is any one set of conditions good for all at all times? It seems reasonable to suppose that different environments are good for students at different stages of development. For example, extremely rigid children, plunged into an open and interdependent environment, might simply be frightened and withdraw into ritualistic behavior. A considerably modulated interdependent environment might be best for them. Among the culturally deprived or those whose socialization has been erratic and partial, a moderately interdependent environment is probably advisable, at least until the children have internalized values enough to permit them to operate effectively in productive harmony.

The optimal procedure for inducing individuals to progress toward complexity and flexibility is to match their present stage of personality development to the training environment, tailored in such a way as to pull the individual toward the next stage of development. The following chart indicates how personality stages and training environments can be matched.

Characteristics of Stage	Optimal Training Environment
I. This stage is characterized by extremely fixed patterns of response. The individual tends to see things in terms of right and wrong. He tends to categorize the world into stereotypes. He prefers social relationships in which some people are on top and some on the bottom. He tends to reject or distort information that does not fit into his belief system.	To produce development from this stage, the training environment needs to be reasonably well-structured. At the same time, the environment has to delineate the personality in such a way that the individual begins to see himself as distinct from his beliefs and to recognize that different people have different viewpoints and that rights and wrongs can be negotiated. In summary, the optimal environment is supportive, structured, fairly controlling, but with a stress on self-delineation and negotiation.
II. In this stage the individual is breaking away from the rigid rules and beliefs that characterized his former stage. He tends to resist control from all sources, even nonauthoritative ones. He still tends to dichoto-	The individual needs to reestablish ties with others so that he can see their viewpoints and how they operate. Consequently, the training environment needs to emphasize negotiations in interpersonal relations

mize the environment. He has difficulty seeing others' viewpoints, and maintaining a balance between task orientation and interpersonal relations.

and divergence in the development of rules and concepts.

III. The individual is beginning to reestablish easy ties with other people and in his new-found relationships has some difficulty maintaining a task orientation. He is, however, beginning to balance alternatives and to build concepts that bridge different points of view and ideas.

The training environment should strengthen the reestablished interpersonal relations, but emphasis should be placed on tasks in which the individual, as a member of the group, has to proceed toward a goal. If the environment is too protective at this stage, growth could be arrested. While the individual might continue to develop skill in interpersonal relations, he would be unlikely to develop skill in conceptualization or to maintain himself in task-oriented situations.

IV. The individual is able to maintain a balanced perspective with respect to task orientation and the maintenance of interpersonal relations. He can build new constructs and beliefs, or belief systems, as these are needed to accommodate changing situations and new information. In addition, he is able to negotiate with others the rules or conventions that will govern behavior under certain situations, programs of action, conceptual systems for approaching abstract problems.

Although this individual is adaptable, he no doubt operates best in an interdependent, information-oriented, complex environment.

229

The very young child should be permitted first to internalize a few norms and rules and then to develop norms and rules in cooperation with others. By providing him early with some rules to follow, the teacher gives him some anchors for behavior.

But by gradually helping him to develop standards and procedures and evaluate information and conclusions, the teacher encourages his growing interdependence. Finally, when the child begins developing openness at a rapid rate, he should be given full responsibility for evaluating ideas, information, procedures, and standards.

Even when children of different levels of development are in the same classroom, as is most often the case, the teacher can find ways of varying his guidance methods. He can have the more open-minded children participate in inquiry-centered groups. The more rigid children can engage in structured, problem-solving activities. The immature and deprived children can join in socializing games. All these activities are possible in the same classroom. Many of them, particularly the socializing games, are appropriate for all. Nearly every unit activity provides many ways of fulfilling the conditions dealt with in this chapter.

The Personal Dimension as Anchor for the Social Studies

The pursuit of personal meaning is the central activity of human existence. It is also the chief goal of the personal dimension. The development of moral judgment and complexity, discussed earlier in this chapter, are aspects of personal meaning. A person's moral judgment indicates how he relates to his fellowman. The complexity of a person's beliefs reflects how much of reality he is aware of. The personal dimension can therefore be used to bring together the social studies, anchor the intellectual and social dimensions, and provide the impetus for a social studies curriculum.

Personal and social development are intertwined through the development of values and complexity. To participate in democratic process, for example, a person needs to be committed to it. To engage in international citizenship, a person needs to be oriented toward the international community of men. The social process can develop only among people who respect one another and recognize the need for all participants to negotiate policies. Similarly, democratic process requires that a person be able to develop policies and procedures that take into account the needs and capacities of many individuals—one aspect of complex thinking.

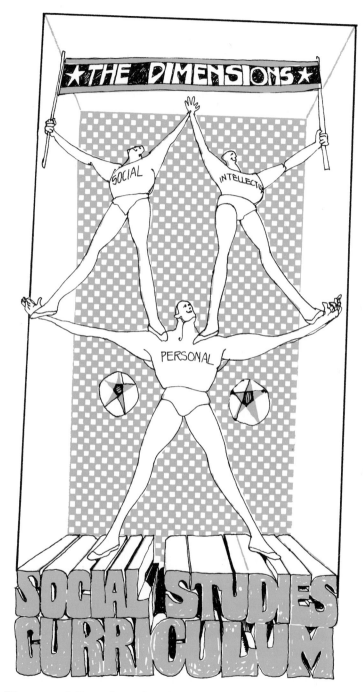

231

The personal dimension unites the social and intellectual dimensions.

Both the social and the intellectual dimensions supply content for personal growth. A person transforms social values into his own system of beliefs. Without social values as a basis, a person probably could not develop meaningful values and attitudes— values that commit him to social improvement, to participation as a citizen, to international peace and prosperity, to an appreciation of other people, and to the enhancement of the lives of others. These values form much of the sense of personal meaning.

The sharing of values is part of the social dimension as well as of personal meaning. Through shared efforts at analyzing and solving social and interpersonal problems, the individual comes to know that he is not alone, strengthens his values, and progresses in his search for knowledge and understanding. For the young child, value sharing is essential to the development of a meaningful framework for his life. The social milieu provides the values and support necessary for those values to be maintained. Furthermore, personal meaning necessitates social action, the living or acting out of values. Without activity, social values lose their authenticity and become mere verbal exercises. The social dimension includes the development of social skills needed for effective participation in society.

Similarly, a person cannot master a social science concept unless he is able to apply it to his own behavior and environment. A child who memorizes a concept about social caste systems but does not comprehend caste problems in his society or see himself as part of a caste system has not learned an operational version of the concept. To study economic behavior without perceiving one's own economic behavior is to fail to comprehend the concepts involved. The life of the student is the scene of meaningful social science education. Referents for social science concepts must be found in the world of the learner. If he can perceive social status in his own life, he can probably comprehend the concept of status.

As the social dimension provides tools for effective social action, so the intellectual dimension provides analytic tools with which the individual can sort out his world and make a reasonable search for meaning. The organizing concepts of the social sciences reduce the complexity of the world; through them the child can pick his way among social events with greater assurance. When he studies socialization, for example, he learns tools that will help him understand his family and school. When he studies social psychology, he learns tools that will help him understand how he is influenced by other people. The social science concepts he learns help him cope with problems.

The greatest difficulty for a teacher who tries to make the personal dimension the vital core of the social studies arises from the very uniqueness of personal development and its slow, uneven pace. The search for meaning is a personal one; and real personal meaning is a unique phenomenon, even though the values of others, affiliations with others, and social science concepts may be part of the individual's value structure. The social dimension can be taught directly: interpersonal skills, knowledge of the society, and strategies for working on social problems can be identified and teaching strategies developed to introduce them to children. The intellectual dimension can also be taught directly by identifying the structures of the social sciences and selecting strategies for teaching them. The personal dimension, however, can only be nurtured. Moral judgment, complexity, the internalization of social values, and the development of personal meaning and dignity cannot be imposed on individuals.

Much can be done, however, to further personal growth.

1. We can select content likely to increase students' opportunities to develop personally. (See pp. 279–83 for a description of a curriculum designed to emphasize personal development.)

2. We can give students the opportunity to explore their own emotions and values. During the study of intergroup relations, for example, students can look at their own feelings and consider why others feel differently.

3. We can help students use the social sciences to examine complex issues, sort out the facts, and think out value positions. When studying the city, for example, the student can begin to understand how urban life alienates and thus begin to develop intellectual defenses against alienation.

4. A strong, inquiring group can be developed and used as a platform for the development of inner strength.

5. Engaging in social action (see pp. 218–19) also provides a unifying group experience that will help the student develop social purpose and meaning.

6. The direct examination of values (see p. 216) can help the child explore crucial personal and social issues and the values surrounding them.

7. The teacher can attempt to increase moral judgment by pulling the students steadily toward a multidimensional level of discourse. (See p. 215.)

8. Continual attempts can be made to relate to students in ways that will help increase personal complexity (see pp. 215–16) and interdependence.

INQUIRIES

1. Discuss the relationship between the intellectual, social, and personal dimensions. Show how the intellectual and social dimensions support the personal.

2. Personal meaning depends on a person's developing a philosophy that gives direction and helps him improve society. Plan a teaching strategy that will promote the development of personal meaning. Suppose, for example, that your children become discouraged because of the slow pace of man's efforts to reduce environmental pollution. How can you help them develop values that allow them to continue to improve the environment but be realistic about the confusion and procrastination that accompany collaborative social effort?

234

NOTES

1. For more discussion of this problem, see Byron Massialas and others, *Structure and Process of Inquiry into Social Issues in Secondary Schools* (Ann Arbor: Univ. of Michigan, 1970).

2. Erik H. Erikson, *Childhood and Society* (New York: Norton, 1963), pp. 285–86.

3. W. Lloyd Warner, *American Life: Dream and Reality* (Chicago: Univ. of Chicago Press, 1943), p. 209.

4. Bernice Neugarten, "Social Class and Friendship among School Children," *American Journal of Sociology* 51 (1946).

5. Gordon W. Allport, *The Nature of Prejudice* (Reading, Mass.: Addison-Wesley, 1954).

6. Larry Kohlberg, "Moral Education," *School Review*, Univ. of Chicago Press Journals (Spring 1966), p. 7.

7. Ibid., pp. 8–9.

8. H. Hartshorne and M. A. May, "A Summary of the Work of the Character Education Inquiry," *Religious Education* 25 (1930), pp. 607–19, 745–62.

9. Alice Miel, *The Shortchanged Children of Suburbia*, Pamphlet Series no. 8 (New York: Institutes of Human Relations Press, American Jewish Committee, 1967).

10. William H. Orrick, Jr., "Shut It Down: A College in Crisis," Staff Report to the National Commission on the Causes and Prevention of Violence (Washington, June 1969).

11. Kohlberg, "Moral Education," p. 19.

12. Jerome S. Bruner, Jacqueline Goodnow, and George A. Austin, *A Study of Thinking* (New York: Wiley, 1956).

13. Milton Rokeach, *The Open and Closed Mind* (New York: Basic Books, 1960).

14. O. J. Harvey, David E. Hunt, and Harold M. Schroder, *Conceptual Systems and Personality Organization* (New York: Wiley, 1961), p. 3.

15. Bruce R. Joyce, Joan Sibol, and Howard Lamb, "Conceptual Development and Information Processing: A Study of Teachers," *Journal of Educational Research* (January 1966), pp. 219–22.

16. Kurt Lewin, Ronald Lippitt, and Ralph O. White, "Patterns of Aggressive Behavior in Experimentally Created Social Climates," *Journal of Social Psychology* 10 (1939), pp. 271–99.

17. Harold M. Anderson and Helen M. Brewer, "Domination and Social Integration in the Behavior of Kindergarten Children and Teachers," *Genetic Psychology Monographs* 21 (1939), pp. 287–385.

235

INQUIRIES FOR THE INTELLECTUAL, SOCIAL, AND PERSONAL DIMENSIONS BASED ON THE KENT STATE PHOTO ESSAY

I. THE INTELLECTUAL DIMENSION

For older children: Plan a teaching episode that will help the children explore the constructionist view of knowledge as a means of making judgments about a social event. The unit should consider first how a constructionist operates and then how a constructionist would investigate a social event such as the Kent State tragedy.

For younger children: Plan a teaching episode to help the children explore ways of handling conflict. As a basic strategy, have them role-play a series of conflict situations, discuss the conflicts, and act out ways of coping with or resolving them. As part of the unit, plan to help the children generate and test at least one hypothesis about why people react to conflict with aggression.

II. THE SOCIAL DIMENSION

For older children: Plan a teaching episode that will help the children inquire into alienation and its causes. Use the Kent State tragedy as a basis for helping them explore how alienation affects behavior. Perhaps they could role-play situations of civil conflict and explore how unalienated and alienated men might deal with conflict.

In addition, plan a study of the concept of war and of the major present views of war. How can a dialogue between these views, both inside and outside the government, be generated and maintained? Perhaps, the children could role-play a situation in which members of a local school administration are holding an emergency session because of a protest against war or against a school policy. As they receive information about the protest, they can explore the alternatives (should the National Guard be called in?) and the major views about those alternatives.

For younger children: Plan a study of playground behavior in which dealing with a bully is explored as well as relationships with authorities. Structure the unit and its activities around a series of problem situations.

III. THE PERSONAL DIMENSION

For older children: Plan a study that focuses on the problem of personal moral judgment with respect to the Kent State tragedy. Explore the levels of moral judgment used by your children, and plan how to help them develop more complex ideas and values. What can you do to help them develop meaning as they explore social issues and values?

For younger children: Plan a project to help the children make contact with some new people (perhaps a class next door) in such a way that new friendships are made. Help your group of children share stories, songs, and games with their new friends and learn how to reach out to others. Role-playing might be used in preparation for the meeting by helping the children explore ways of making contact and sharing.

237

Level	Topic	Approach
Intermediate	Analyzing group behavior	Introduction to social scien methodology
		Emphasizes ways of establishing facts, drawing inferences, making value judgments
	Our Social Heritage	Study of the evolution of democratic institutions and values
	Government in action	Study of contemporary social action

part 4

CURRICULUM ORGANIZATION AND PLANNING

TRADITION AND CHANGE IN SOCIAL STUDIES CURRICULA

240

One of the most difficult professional tasks is to develop a curriculum that has a cumulative effect on the child's intellectual and social growth. Each year's study should build on and amplify what went before. The planner must avoid unnecessary duplication from one grade to the next, but he must also allow a certain flexibility in order to encourage cooperative inquiry and exploit topics of interest not easily anticipated far in advance.

If the curriculum is underplanned, life in school becomes formless. If it is overorganized, the spontaneous flow of ideas is inhibited. If it lacks balance, instruction loses variety and perspective. The Project on the Instructional Program of the Public Schools, sponsored by the National Education Association, has provided a clear set of criteria that can be used by school faculties and other educators to improve curriculum planning.[1]

Criterion 1: A clear statement of objectives should guide the determination of learnings to be sought in the classroom. Each teacher should plan his lessons and units in relation to the overall

chapter 10

objectives of the curriculum. Because nearly all important social learnings take a long time to develop, the faculty needs to decide on the critical learnings to be emphasized as long-term goals.

> Unfortunately, school systems commonly lack a comprehensive and reasonably consistent set of objectives to guide them in making other curriculum decisions. More often than not, schools possess a rather vague statement of philosophy and of goals for each subject taught.[2]

Schools need to remedy this vagueness. A purposive statement should be clear enough for the teacher to use in planning lessons, broad enough to describe the kind of citizen and person the school hopes to foster, and selective enough that it can be easily remembered.

Criterion 2: The curriculum should be organized so that one experience builds on another with cumulative effect on the behavior of the child. The vertical organization of subject matter should take into account the logical structure of the subject and the difficulty of material in relation to the student's intellectual maturity.[3] (The relation of the social sciences to other disciplines such as language arts, arithmetic, and natural science is an important consideration also, but will be discussed under criterion 4, which deals with the integration of the various curriculum areas.)

The curriculum should be designed so that the organizing concepts of the various social sciences are gradually developed by the child in his study of human interaction. Studying the family in the first grade, for example, the child can begin to learn the ideas and questions the sociologist uses in analyzing roles. He can also begin to learn how the economist analyzes production in terms of division of labor. As the child studies his community a year or two later, he can extend the concept of role to municipal government and community decision-making and the concept of division of labor to factories and shops.

Comparative studies of human groups are also important through the grades. To establish the concepts used by the anthropologist, curriculum plans must provide for the pairing of culture groups—American and Japanese families in the first grade, for example, the Mexican and the French governments in an upper grade, and so on. The structure of geography also requires comparative study: the Sahara and the American desert might be compared, or the Congo and the Amazon basins.

The curriculum planner can use the organizing concepts of the social sciences to make sure that each social science is adequately introduced and explored. In economics, for example, emphasis on production one year might be followed by emphasis on exchange the next, distribution the next, and finally an analysis of all three. In sociology, an emphasis on norms might be followed by an emphasis on sanctions, then roles, values, and institutions; in an upper grade all these concepts could be seen operating together. A fourth-grade study of values and roles in a primitive society might be followed by a fifth-grade study of institutions in a nineteenth century frontier community and a sixth-grade analysis applying all these concepts to a study of the classroom group itself. Although the social studies curriculum needs to embrace the organizing concepts of every social science, the child should not be challenged with concepts from all the sciences simultaneously until he has learned them individually.

Today the sequential organization of most curricula is based on the assumption that young children learn most easily about things they have already experienced. Compared with the older child, the younger is disadvantaged in several ways. He has had less experience: he has seen less, thought less, heard less. He therefore has less ability to deal with abstract ideas and to provide illustrations out of his own experience. The young child is also less likely to apply ideas to experiences that are not immediately current. He is more egocentric and impulsive. He cannot reason as effectively from the viewpoint of another, and his attention wanders more frequently.

All these limitations do not mean that we are necessarily restricted to an expanding horizons approach. Vicarious experiences of the far away or long ago can be created for the young child in terms of everyday experiences. When the child reads about another land or time, his teacher can offer analogies from local conditions so that the child can associate the new idea with his own experience. The child can also be given many facts that illustrate each new idea or concept. Ideas such as "Whig," "Tory," and "Thanksgiving" need multiple illustrations, or they will be fuzzy and incomplete in the child's mind.

Oversimplification, a temptation to the elementary school teacher, should be avoided. It is better to emphasize a few honest but complex ideas than a host of distorted simple ones. The young child can learn realistic ideas. Because social life is complex, ideas about social life are complicated. Instead of accommodating the child's limitations by oversimplifying events, the teacher should explore a few topics deeply and honestly.

Criterion 3: The curriculum plan should identify a relatively few organizing centers around which activities can be built. These centers provide continuity. They are the important ideas, values, issues, and skills introduced to the child soon after his arrival in school and repeated in more mature form all through school.

> To help students achieve an increasingly mature organization of knowledge, the school program should provide for continuity and increasing breadth and depth of content from one school year to the next. The principles and generalizations selected for development should be sufficiently limited in number that the learners have many opportunities to reinforce understandings and apply them. The simpler principles to be developed with young children should be so formulated as to provide a basis for, be in harmony with, and lead naturally into the more highly differentiated and elaborated structures that can be developed by senior high school students. Learners, whatever their age, should be helped to relate facts and knowledge to concepts or organizing principles so that they continually expand their conceptual frames of reference for each field of study.[4]

243

The organizing concepts of the social sciences, continually and more maturely applied to the analysis of human behavior, can provide the organizing centers of instruction in the social studies. Just as the human group can be the focus of content, whatever the topic, so organizing concepts can be applied to the analysis of the human group, whatever the topic. In the early primary grades the child can learn immature but accurate forms of the questions that social scientists ask. Gradually he can sharpen his questions until by the end of the elementary school he is able to form inferred and ideal-type concepts from all the disciplines.

Many social scientists have felt that it is not possible to develop a unified approach to all social sciences and that the disciplines should be approached separately. Lawrence Senesh's economics project, described in chapter 4, uses the structure of a single discipline to approach the social studies. This kind of organization makes it easier to sort out important ideas and see that they are well developed. The frame of reference, however, of each discipline is relatively narrow. It is important that the child learn to apply to his analysis of human interaction not only the ideas of economics but those of other social sciences as well.

In chapter 5 we described a plan for focusing instruction on human groups and applying to the study of the human group the organizing concepts of the various social sciences, emphasizing one or two concepts at a time in the study of each topic and repeating year after year the emphasis on each concept until the concepts are fully developed. Another, somewhat different integrative plan has been developed by Paul Hanna and his associates at Stanford University (see also pp. 10–11). Hanna has identified several areas of basic human activity around which instruction can be built. Each area involves content from several of the social sciences, so that it integrates or fuses the disciplines. The following areas have been identified:

Organizing and governing
Providing recreation
Protecting and conserving human and natural resources
Expressing religious impulses
Expressing and satisfying esthetic impulses
Transporting people and goods
Producing, exchanging, distributing, and consuming food, clothing, shelter, and other consumer goods and services
Communicating ideas and feelings
Providing education
Creating tools, technics, and social arrangements[5]

In a series of research studies, Hanna and his co-workers have provided generalizations that can be used in building a curriculum around these areas. In such an arrangement continuity can be built both by revisiting the basic areas yearly and by selecting certain key issues or generalizations and emphasizing them throughout the years. Sequence can be accomplished by arranging the generalizations in order of difficulty or in order of logical development.

Criterion 4: The social studies and other curriculum areas should support one another. The division of knowledge among academic disciplines is arbitrary, and considerable overlap exists between them. Literature, for example, reveals the values of people, and thus can be considered a social study. In maps, graphs, and models, social data are represented by means of mathematics. Anthropologists use the methods of physicists to date artifacts, and the methods of biologists to study human beings. The well-planned curriculum uses the relationships between subject areas to reduce the number of topics that the student has to study, and to allow the practical application of knowledge.

Curriculum areas can be integrated through activities. Frequently an activity serving to achieve the objectives of one curriculum area can be used to achieve, simultaneously, the objectives of another curriculum area. For example, one reads and writes in the social studies. What could be more natural than to use social studies content as the vehicle for teaching reading and writing? Mapmaking provides many opportunities for teaching scale and even elementary geometry; in fact, some of the concepts of curved-line geometry are essential to an understanding of map projections and globes. A time line, so useful in history, is an application of a number line. The study of man's use of land or the distribution of plant life requires some understanding of biology. To study conservation of resources, the student applies knowledge learned in the natural sciences; he gains an understanding that the natural sciences alone could not provide.

At one time subject integration became a kind of goal of instruction in itself, and the teacher was admonished to look for opportunities to fuse the curriculum areas. Units on topics such as "The Postman" became embellished with poems, songs, dramatic play, and art production. Although subject integration should intelligently integrate the child's intellectual life and make learning activities in one area promote learnings in other areas, it is not necessary to invent poems celebrating community helpers in order to integrate, for example, the study of economic life with the study of literature. Subject integration does not need to be forced; the opportunity is present naturally.

Criterion 5: The various subject areas must be studied in proper balance. Time given to mathematics should not prevent the teaching of reading. Passion for poetry should not prevent attention to the social studies. No one social science should dominate social education to the point where the children do not learn others. In the past many curricula for the early grades have overemphasized the study of the community to the neglect of wider areas. In the later grades the study of economic geography, government, and American history has swelled to the point of forcing out the other social sciences.

245

A careful balance should be achieved among studies focusing on the class group, contemporary American society, world cultures, and historical periods. Any one of these four areas could serve to introduce social science concepts, but the child needs to understand all of these areas. He has to be able to think effectively about his own social groups. He has to know about other cultures. And he has to have some idea of the movement of events through time.

Patterns That Dominated until Recently

The pattern of social studies curricula has not varied from school to school as much as might be expected from the richness and variety of the social sciences. Both textbooks and curriculum guides have tended to use the expanding horizons approach. A recent social studies curriculum outline prepared for Montgomery County, Maryland, reflects this approach. The following concepts are among those identified in this outline as basic to a social studies program:

> Many individuals have contributed to world cultures.
> Environment influences man's way of living.
> Man seeks to utilize resources to satisfy his needs.
> Man has responsibilities and derives advantages from group living.
> All people are increasingly interdependent.
> New ideas and technology change societies.[6]

In keeping with the expanding horizons approach, topics were distributed by grade as follows:

K–1	Family and School
2	Immediate Community
3	Selected World Communities
4–5	American History and Geography Grade 4: Men and Movements in American History Grade 5: Patterns of Living in the United States Today
6	Cultures of the Past[7]

World geography is taught in grades 7 and 8; modern history and more advanced studies of the United States are offered in grades 9 and 10. Thus the material covered in the later years of the social studies program builds on that taught earlier.

The curriculum plan also identifies twelve behaviors that are to be expected of the twelfth-grade graduate. Among these goals, three describe general skills that may be acquired from any field of study; four concern values that may be instilled by other institutions besides the school; and five deal with behaviors that would most likely be derived from social studies education. These five are:

He understands and accepts the responsibilities, and appreciates the privileges, inherent in the American way of life.

He understands and evaluates the cultures and contributions of other peoples.

He attempts to understand the scientific truths of the universe and man's relationship to them.

He exhibits effective human relationships for democratic living as they apply to the individual in the family, in the school and community, in the country, and in the world.

He makes wise use of human, natural, and material resources.[8]

Each of these five goals is further refined so that it is appropriately expressed for each grade level. Responsibility for developing the sequence of behaviors by which these objectives can be achieved is left to the teachers, although illustrative texts and other materials are suggested. For example, the curriculum plan for teaching the second goal at the first two grade levels is as follows:

Level 1

K–1

Home and School

Identifies artifacts of his family
   Brandwein *et al. The Social Sciences: Concepts and Values*
   (Blue) (Text)
   People in Action (Pictures)
Observes and identifies the effects of some elements of the physical environment on his daily life
   Interaction of Man and His Environment (Picture Set)
   Brandwein *et al. The Social Sciences: Concepts and Values*
   (Red) (Text)

Learns that some of our customs are very old and came from different countries

    Interaction of Man and His Past (Picture Set)

    ERCSS. *Concepts and Inquiry: Children in Other Lands* (Text)

Investigates the different ways of doing things among people in his neighborhood

    Discussion Pictures for Beginning Social Studies (Picture Set)

    Hanna *et al. Investigating Man's World—Family Studies* (Text)

Becomes aware that families may celebrate holidays in different ways

    People in Action (Pictures)

    Schools, Families, Neighborhoods (Kit)

Begins to use books as sources of information

Level 2

2

Immediate Community

Identifies artifacts of the past

    Brandwein *et al. The Social Sciences: Concepts and Values* (Blue) (Text)

    People in Action (Pictures)

Relates the influence of some elements of the environment on community living

    Interaction of Man and His Environment (Picture Set)

    Our Working World—Neighbors at Work (Kit)

    MATCH—"The City" (Kit)

Investigates the origins of the customs common in his own community and hypothesizes about future customs

    Interaction of Man and His Past (Picture Set)

    ERCSS. *Concepts and Inquiry: Communities at Home and Abroad* (Text)

Identifies ways in which people of varying cultural backgrounds have contributed to the development of his community

    Discussion Pictures for Beginning Social Studies (Picture Set)

Identifies different cultural patterns within his immediate community

    Brandwein *et al. The Social Sciences: Concepts and Values* (Blue) (Text)

    People in Action (Pictures)

Discovers that contributions from different peoples add to his culture

    Our Working World—Neighbors at Work (Kit)[9]

The curriculum guide developed for the public schools of St. Paul, Minnesota, employs the expanding horizons approach but stresses four basic learnings:

People are interdependent and need to live in harmony.
Man's environment influences his way of living.
Living can be improved.
People of the past influenced our way of living.[10]

The curriculum guide indicates that these basic learnings function in several ways:

> Basic learnings help tie all elements of the social studies program together, giving it unity, purpose, and direction.
> Basic learnings should be used by the teacher to plan the recurrence of concepts from different approaches, and on increasingly mature levels.
> Basic learnings can and should be approached from many directions and through many varied experiences.
> Basic learnings will be developed and applied by children as they meet them in meaningful situations important to them.[11]

Significantly, the St. Paul guide merely suggests content topics that will contribute to the ends of the curriculum. The teacher is free to make the final decisions and to build the units with the children. Furthermore, the cooperative-planning approach implies that both the content units and the details to be learned will vary considerably from class to class. The children's interests help to determine the shape of the instruction; indeed, the children assume part of the obligation for planning. The curriculum makers have deliberately tried to provide continuity in the social climate of the school. The ways the children act and interact are part of the content they study. The philosophy of the St. Paul curriculum guide is evident in its description of the grades.

Kindergarten and Grade 1

Everyday Life—at Home and in School

The center of interest for the child is the home and family. School is the new, important change in his everyday living. Experience related to home and school will have the fullest meaning and produce the best results. Many of the activities initiated at the kindergarten level can be continued successfully on the first-grade level.

Grade 2

Living in Our Neighborhood

In this grade, the experiences with neighborhood activities create new interests. The environment broadens from the familiar and personal events of home and school to the wider scope of life in the neighborhood. Interest in the people and in the services of the nearby community become very important.

Grade 3

Basic Needs of Our Community

The child's interests and experiences at this grade level move to the larger community of a town or city. He becomes aware of the need for food, clothing, shelter, recreation, and companionship. He becomes particularly interested in how St. Paul endeavors to meet these needs for its people. The concept of interdependence becomes more meaningful.

Grade 4

Living in Our City and State

Study of the exploration and colonization of the United States by various groups leads to an understanding of the background for the settlement of Minnesota. The child begins to see the city and state as organized units of society. He learns how Indians, explorers, fur traders, and pioneers contributed to the origin and growth of St. Paul and Minnesota. He becomes aware of the resources and opportunities of representative communities in the United States and compares St. Paul with them.

Grade 5

Living in Our Nation and the Americas

From the background of their previous historical study of St. Paul and Minnesota, children begin the historical and geographical study of the United States. They learn how geography influences the industries and ways of life in various communities. Intensive study is devoted to this relationship as it applies to Minnesota.

Children learn to appreciate the foresight, courage, and endurance of our forefathers and begin to understand the dynamic nature of our society. Modern life in various regions of the United States, Canada, Latin and South America is compared with that of Minnesota.

Grade 6

Living in Our World

The experiences provided in earlier grades serve as a foundation for understanding other cultures. Children learn that human activities in any land are directed toward the satisfaction of basic needs, and that customs differ only as people adjust their environment to their needs.

250

They develop an understanding of interdependency of nations as they see how other peoples of the world have contributed to life in Minnesota and the United States. Some of the social processes and problems of modern societies are explored as they apply in our state, particularly education, churches, conservation of natural resources, and human resources. The government of Minnesota is studied as an outgrowth of Old World principles of democracy. Children begin to see the roles of the United States and other nations in world affairs.[12]

The St. Paul guide gives the teacher both direction and freedom. It identifies the important themes around which continuity can be built, but lets the teacher construct with his children the activities that will give those themes life and substance.

The Depth Study and the Unit Method

A curriculum can be planned in great detail, providing all the ideas, teaching materials, and teaching strategies necessary. Or a plan can suggest that the children study a certain aspect of their community and the teacher present relevant concepts. The first plan risks irrelevance to the student and the ongoing life of the society. It underplays the personal and social dimensions. The second plan slights the academic dimension. Unless the teacher is well equipped in the discipline, its systematic power will not come through.

To overcome these difficulties we need a planning strategy that capitalizes on all three dimensions. Curricula should provide guidelines but should not be so structured that they leave no opportunity for the children's needs and ideas or the topical to become part of the classwork. One way curricula can do this is by using depth studies.

To imitate the social scientist by adopting his methods, children must analyze substantial quantities of information about relatively limited topics. No child who is given only a sprinkling of facts or even a profusion of trivial information can build hypotheses or test and revise ideas. Most instruction should be organized into depth studies that help the child develop a fairly thorough understanding of a human group. The information that he examines should enable him to build well-founded ideas and to test organizing concepts used by the social scientist.

In some ways the depth study resembles the instructional "unit" that has been popular for many years.

A unit is a series of related learning experiences organized around a topic or problem. The unit method describes a process for systematically teaching a unit. . . . . It is flexible, allowing the individual teacher to develop fully his own teaching style. . . . It conforms to the psychology of childhood, permitting the teacher to work with the child, rather than engage in a kind of tug of war with him. . . . The unit method yields superior learning.[13]

The unit method was a child of the Progressive Era, especially the first forty years of the twentieth century. The earliest argument in its favor was that the unit method permits the practice of democratic behavior in the classroom. The teacher was to develop a miniature democracy by helping children formulate aims and methods and carry through problem-solving activities. To accomplish this, the teacher must himself have freedom of action and a voice in curricular decisions.

The democratic principle requires that every teacher should have some regular and organic way in which he can, directly or through representatives democratically chosen, participate in the formation of the controlling aims, methods, and materials of the school of which he is a part.[14]

The unit method seemed desirable also as a means of getting children involved in problem solving and away from memorization and recitation. The child was to acquire the tools of effective thinking as well as knowledge of subject matter. But in order to think effectively about a new idea and make generalizations, the child needed a wealth of new experiences related to that idea. By proceeding in unit fashion, being involved in many kinds of activity, the child gains these experiences and escapes ready-made, easily forgotten conclusions.

After or while acquiring experiences, the child must organize and evaluate them.

Finding the material for learning within experience is only the first step. The next step is the progressive development of what is already experienced into a fuller and richer and also more organized form, a form that gradually approximates that in which subject matter is presented to the skilled, mature person.[15]

In analyzing observations, the child should progressively learn to ask questions and use the organizing concepts of the scholar. Later these ideas are revised and extended as the child progresses to new units or higher grades. The child should never acquire a false sense of having exhausted a subject. He should perceive that what he learns from one study is a spur to new inquiries.

Inquiry that gradually reveals to the child the organizing concepts of the social sciences and stimulates further inquiry requires that unit studies explore limited topics in depth. Too often the unit study has deteriorated into a superficial study of very broad topics. The child must not be confused and overwhelmed with a spread of facts in a subject too comprehensive for close study. The very nature of concept formation demands that the child concentrate on a limited topic, searching among data for answers to questions, finding tentative answers, then searching for new data to supply clearer answers, and so on.

To do real thinking about real events, the child needs to pursue depth studies in which he can learn how the scholar assembles knowledge into ideas. The depth study is, in fact, a simulation of the conditions of scholarly inquiry. The teacher must guide the child into asking interesting, exploratory questions; help him gather quantities of relevant data; train him to build ideas out of the data; and encourage him to check his ideas against the ideas of other children and against the concepts of scholars.

Curricula can be built up of sets of depth studies that can be applied flexibly and interchangeably. Even the study of current affairs can be pursued in depth. Although the teacher should probably touch on all significant contemporary affairs, he should select a few headline events to be studied in greater detail. Such studies help to build the children's background and encourage them to apply the concepts learned in scheduled units.

History also benefits by a study in depth. Of all instructional methods, the depth study is perhaps the most successful in bringing the past to life. The class that "lives in ancient Rome" for a few months can become familiar with Roman art and architecture, Roman laws and commerce, the words of Roman senators, the map of Rome. A child learns enough to be able to compare his life with that of the Roman child and the political system of Rome with that in his community.

New teachers frequently wonder how large or how small a depth study should be. There is no one answer to that question. A unit should not wear on until it sickens. Nor should it be so

253

short that it hinders really significant hypotheses from being formulated and tested, for every unit should be planned to develop scientific facility. Some studies should be generated by the spontaneous interests of the children. The wise teacher plans the year so that part of the time is reserved for individual and small-group inquiry centered on special and personal intellectual interests. It is important that the children gradually develop the ability to select and carry on their own depth studies, making their own plans and judging their own progress. Their questions may extend what began as a short study.

The Capacity to Learn as It Affects Curriculum Planning

What do we know of the child's ability to think? Are there optimal ages for particular kinds of learning—learning concrete facts, for instance, as distinct from learning generalizations? We must have some guidelines for helping the child to grow intellectually. We must not try to impose on him learning for which he is not ready or delay important ideas past the time when he can best absorb them. Clear evidence and clear answers in these matters are very limited. Some of the available research and theories, however, have great implications for teaching strategies.

It has been found that the intelligence quotients of many children of lower-class parents tend to fall during the school years, while the intelligence quotients of upper-middle-class children rise somewhat. Apparently what we regard as intellectual capacity is affected by experience, at least through adolescence. The present view is that experience has its greatest effect on intellectual capacity during the first four or five years of life, its next-greatest effect during the next four or five years, and its least effect thereafter.

According to the noted Swiss psychologist Jean Piaget, intellectual growth depends on the development of intellectual structures or organizing schemata. Piaget describes these schemata in terms of advancing stages of sophistication; at certain ages the child's ability to organize concepts rises to new levels, and he develops more advanced types of thinking. For example, up to the age of eight, approximately, the child reasons only particular cases. He cannot carry on a generalized argument. He has trouble reasoning from the point of view of another person. And he feels no need for the logical examination of ideas.

Until about the age of eleven he is able to reason generally, but only in terms of concrete cases. That is, he can see that the population growth of two countries is related to the spread of railroads, but he cannot handle the idea as an abstract proposition (in grasslands where European culture was imported, population growth tended to follow the spread of railroads). About the age of eleven, according to Piaget, the child begins to be able to assume the viewpoint of others and to reason from another's beliefs. By the time he is eleven or twelve years old his schemata have become sufficiently developed to enable him to carry on formal abstract reasoning and to engage in real deductive activity. At about the age of twelve he is able to fully explain causal relationships.[16]

For the benefit of teachers, the British educator E. A. Peel has described and interpreted Piaget's stages of concrete thinking, with special attention to their implications for school instruction.[17] In the stage of concrete thinking, a child in social studies should be capable of discerning how the roles of a mother in Chicago compare with the roles of a mother in Samoa. However, he might have difficulty deriving generalizations from these specific examples. He may be incapable of formulating the general idea that maternal roles in primitive societies are in certain ways similar and in certain ways dissimilar to maternal roles in highly complex, technologically developed societies. In other words, the child can get the point of the specific examples, but he cannot fully develop the general idea that the examples represent.

Piaget's work has been attacked on the ground that the age limits for his stages are incorrect, for psychologists in countries other than Switzerland have reached somewhat different conclusions. Peel contends that the given ages are approximate and that if one recognizes that individuals reach various stages at different ages, Piaget's work has been substantially confirmed.

The British psychologist Victoria Hazlitt, with convincing evidence, has argued that the differences between adult thinking and child thinking result from experience rather than from capacity.[18] M. E. Oakes, too, has conducted research showing that the same kinds of errors Piaget found in the thinking of children can also be found in the thinking of adults.[19] Edna Heidbreder found that individuals vary widely in their ability to approach concepts, but that the processes or methods used to form concepts were similar in adults and children. She also discovered that concepts based on number are the last to be formed by children.[20] The implication is that concepts based on number are less obvious than concepts based on other kinds of clues. (Many social studies concepts, such as those concerning maps, charts, and graphs, are based on number ideas.)

Many research studies have shown that children are slow to understand the concepts of space and time in a form recognizable by geographers and historians.

> Although many time concepts are known by children in the intermediate grades, chronology and historical time cannot be grasped by most children until they are in junior or senior high school. Similarly, space concepts of sphericity of the earth, such as latitude and longitude, are not really learned by most children until they are in the upper grades or in junior high school.[21]

According to numerous status studies, children possess great quantities of surface information about social issues and about topics developed in the social studies and are alert to the transient vocabulary of newspaper headlines, but their information is of extremely mixed accuracy. They know the words, but they do not know consistently the meaning of the words. The accuracy or inaccuracy of understanding varies from child to child, and differences between children of the same age or grade level are often greater than the differences between children of different grade levels.

The evidence that young children have limited ability to generalize or think abstractly and conceptually and that they tend to use verbalized information inaccurately has had a fundamental effect on the design of curricula. The evidence has generally been interpreted to mean that the curriculum of the elementary school should emphasize the here and now and, especially in the primary grades, should center on the home and the family and on holidays and historical figures. In other words, the principle has been that the child can study only those things that are related to his immediate experience and do not require much understanding of spatial, temporal, or ideational relationships.

But can it be that this evidence has been overinterpreted to mean that he cannot effectively study anything lying outside his immediate life environment? As early as 1932, Joy M. Lacey, after researching the problem concluded not only that many children's concepts were confused and inaccurate but also that primary-grade curricula were so thin in content that they gave the child no chance to clarify his ideas.[22] Much later, in the 1950s, J. D. McAulay's interviews with primary grade children led him to much the same conclusion. He found that the home-and-neighborhood-centered study of the primary grades emphasized concepts which the children had acquired prior to school or prior to the grade in which those concepts were first emphasized. Consequently the curriculum did not extend the children's understanding.[23]

Ralph Preston has argued that the limits of children's thinking should not entirely restrict the range of content; rather the evidence indicates the necessity for treating fewer topics, but in depth, so that the child can acquire sufficient firsthand experience on which to build difficult ideas and have adequate time to clarify his concepts.

> While there are obvious limits to the school child's critical understanding, there is impressive evidence that children are quite capable of engaging in certain mature types of understanding. The full development of these capabilities and processes calls for the concentrated and unhurried application upon carefully selected bodies of content. A major condition is then present under which the child can learn to "drink deep."[24]

Arthur Jersild's observations point in the same direction—that the wise way to handle children so that they will acquire the experience and understanding necessary to build clear ideas is to have them engage in depth studies of a few topics rather than in a superficial study of a great many things. He calls the process the "seasoning" of ideas:

> In many areas it appears that in order to grasp certain meanings it is necessary for the child to have an accumulation of impressions and experiences distributed over a limited period of development as distinguished from lessons or impressions concentrated within a limited period of time. It has been found that impressions concentrated within a short period of time, even when quite dramatic and charged with emotion, are not likely to produce the same grasp of the subject as a child will obtain through a gradual accumulation of impressions and information over a longer period of time.[25]

A study by Melvin Arnoff demonstrated the feasibility of teaching concepts of government to children in grades 2 to 4. He reported that second-graders appeared to learn as rapidly as

257

older children. He concluded that traditional ideas of grade placement are outmoded.

> No longer tied to previous concepts of grade placement, the schools must bear the responsibility for developing social studies curricula which will prepare children to enter the world of their adult lives equipped to comprehend and harness the complex personal and global social forces which are no less important than the physical and chemical forces of our universe.[26]

If, as Piaget says, the pre-seven-year-old (approximately) cannot see abstract relations and the pre-twelve-year-old (again approximately) cannot express abstract relations, then perhaps elementary instruction should place emphasis on helping children to find relations in concrete data (How many of the colonies allowed religious freedom? Which didn't? Was there more religious strife in one kind or in the other?). Correspondingly, it might be fruitless to try to develop general propositions (on the whole, for the first hundred years, the United States successfully followed George Washington's advice to avoid foreign entanglements); conceivably only the most advanced elementary children would be capable of such abstract reasoning.

The social studies deal constantly with causation, whether seeking reasons for social legislation, explanations of business failures, the relation between climate and crops, or reasons why one nation has high production and another one low. Thus it is essential that the teacher carefully examine evidence not only about a child's ability to think but also about the means of accelerating and improving his thinking. The growing evidence is that training can improve thinking ability.

> Not many experimental inquiries have been carried out on this topic, but they tend to show that added experience, in the preoperational stage of manipulating, combining, dividing up, and matching up materials and objects leads to an acceleration of the onset of the concrete stage of thinking. . . . At the later stage of the transition from concrete to formal thought, added experience of the pupil in carrying out experiments combined with comments, suggestions, and criticisms by the experimenter or teacher can bring about the change to formal judgments.[27]

R. H. Ojemann carried on an experiment demonstrating that social studies teachers who emphasized causal thinking improved the causal thinking of their children.[28] Ethel Maw taught teachers to use twenty lessons so framed that they produced definite effects on children's scores in problem-solving tests.[29] J. I. Lacey and K. M. Dallenbach have concluded that proper training of the child can hasten the appearance of the successive stages of causal thinking.[30] More recently J. Richard Suchman developed some techniques for teaching children methods of inquiry. He assumed that exploration, manipulation, and the quest for mastery are intrinsically motivating, and he joined to this assumption the belief that children can be taught more effective ways of thinking by being led to analyze problems. He was able to train teachers to handle what he calls "inquiry training," and his results indicate that children develop more efficient and analytical problem-solving techniques as a consequence of the training.[31]

Assumptions about Instruction

Only a few issues have been treated in this review of the literature on the intellectual development of the child, but they have been selected because they have particular implications for the revision of social studies instruction. Some of these implications may be summarized in the form of assumptions to be considered when constructing a curriculum or a teaching strategy.

Assumption 1. The child's intellectual development depends in part on his experience. To introduce him to a new idea, we need to give him experiences to which that idea is relevant. The introduction of organizing concepts should be closely tied to concrete examples within the child's experience. It is easier to teach the child about things which he has already experienced, but the school must also lead him to new areas of reality.

Assumption 2. Proper instruction can improve the child's ability to handle abstract ideas and to use concepts more effectively in his inquiries. The elementary school child has difficulty reasoning from general propositions, but he can reason effectively when the facts are before him. Probably children should become accustomed to illustrating their concepts with concrete examples. When a child uses the word *colony*, he should be prepared to mention examples of colonies. New ideas should be put to work immediately so that they can be clarified and reinforced and their usefulness demonstrated.

Assumption 3. Time must be allowed for the development of thinking ability. Depth studies—or studying a few topics thoroughly—can ensure that the children will have enough time to acquire new experiences and to "season" new ideas and concepts.

Assumption 4. The study of other times and places should not emphasize space and time concepts. Apparently efforts have been wasted in attempting to teach these concepts for which the children need greater experience or maturity. However, depth studies can give children the vicarious experience of other times and places. There is no question that children can learn much about distant eras and peoples even without the chronological or spatial perspectives of the scholar. For example, first-graders in Texas, trading information about the family and the home with first-graders in Japan, can learn a great deal about Japanese life without having the geographer's ideas about where Japan is.

How Can Concepts Be Organized in Curricula?

In her analysis of the social sciences, Edith West suggests a number of definitions and propositions related to curriculum organization.[32] She distinguishes between *concepts* (categories or classifications), *generalizations* (relationships between concepts), and *theories* (explanations of relationships between phenomena). A field of study grows partly through emergent concepts, generalizations, and theories. West also developed six criteria for classifying concepts according to their difficulty.

1. Distance from the child's experience. The concepts easiest to form are those made from direct experience, then concepts made from vicarious experience and, last, concepts unrelated to either.
2. Distance from observed referents. Concepts are easiest if made from observed data, harder if made from idealized data, and most difficult if made from inferences.
3. Scope. Some concepts are made up of other concepts and show relationships between them. The narrower the scope of a concept the fewer the concepts subsumed under it. Thus scope, as it widens, increases the complexity and the difficulty of learning any concept.
4. Certainty of presence of attributes. The more certain the attributes (legislators are elected and make laws), the easier

Scale of Difficulty

Criteria of Difficulty	Easy	More Difficult	Very Difficult
Distance from child's experience	Within direct experience	Within vicarious experience	Unrelated to past direct or vicarious experience
Distance from observed referents	Referents are phenomena which can be perceived through senses. Physical objects / Relationships (Specified / Defined operationally) / Processes	Referents are idealized types which do not exist in actuality.	Referents are phenomena which must be inferred from observations of other phenomena. (constructs) Predispositions / Configurations / Processes
Scope of concepts	Narrow scope. Few concepts subsumed under it / Relates few concepts	Broader scope	Very broad scope. Many concepts subsumed under it / Relates many concepts
Certainty of presence of defining attributes	Always present		Tendency
Openendedness of concepts	Closed and so reliable	Not completely closed; somewhat unreliable	Openended; vague boundaries; unreliable
Way in which attributes of concept are related	Conjunctive (joint presence of several attributes)	Disjunctive (presence of one or another attribute)	Relational. Specified relationship (ratio, product, verbal) / Comparative / One attribute affects another / All attributes interact

Fig. 8. Criteria for determining the difficulty of concepts

the concept. The less certain the attributes (the role of decision-maker is often given to the person who exemplifies the direction of norms of the group), the more difficult the concept.

5. Openendedness. Some concepts are very reliable. Everyone agrees on their meaning and can tell you what they refer to. Others are used variously and have less reliable meanings. This makes them difficult to learn. (West uses "marriage" as an example of a reliable concept, and "democracy" as an example of an unreliable one.)

6. Way in which attributes are related. Here West uses Bruner's distinctions among conjunctive concepts (joint attributes are present as in the concept of agrarian society) and disjunctive concepts (may have one attribute or another: there is more than one way of being a "citizen") and relational concepts that indicate systematic relations among complex factors (economic status frequently affects political power in complex societies).

All together, these characteristics provide a system for predicting the hypothetical difficulty of concepts.

In the laboratory described earlier (pp. 42–54), Joyce and Joyce attempted to see whether children dealt with social science concepts in the ways that West predicted. They described social science concepts in terms of complexity, which is similar to West's definition of scope, and found that younger children had much more trouble with complex social science concepts than did older children. Their study suggests that children before about grade 5 cope adequately with simple social science concepts but not with the more complex ones. The study, in short, provides support for the idea that there are levels of difficulty of social concepts. It also reinforces the idea that social science concepts of considerable scope or complexity can be dealt with by upper elementary school children.

Another question in organizing curricula, besides the difficulty of concepts, is the significance of the ideas to be focused on. In figure 9 we can see West's system for determining the significance of concepts that might serve as organizing centers.

West's system unites several criteria to arrive at the scale of significance. The utility of her scale, of course, is in its potential for identifying the few powerful concepts around which a curriculum could be organized. The difficulty and importance of

Unimportant	Of More Importance	Of Great Importance
Limited Scope	Broad Scope	Very Broad Scope
Few generalizations using concept	A number of generalizations using concept	Many generalizations using concept
Generalizations using concept of little significance: (a) Nonexplanatory or predictive (b) Empirical	Generalizations using concept of some significance: (a) Explanatory and probabilistic (b) Theoretical	Generalizations using concept of great significance: (a) Explanatory and predictive (b) Part of a narrow or broad gauge theory

Fig. 9.   Scale of significance

concepts can serve as guides to curriculum organization. The more complex concepts are most important, but they must be built in the early years from less important ones.

263

INQUIRIES

1. Compare social studies curricula that emphasize the intellectual, social, or personal dimension. Which one would you feel most comfortable teaching? Why? How could you prepare yourself to teach the others? Could you use them together?

2. Most educational planners believe that curricula should be directed toward behavioral objectives. A minority of educators feel that the most important realities cannot be stated behaviorally. Debate each position after studying the alternatives to it.

3. Sequence in social studies curricula can be achieved through the organization of social science concepts or through the arrangement of social problems in order of their increasing complexity. What are the advantages of each of these methods?

NOTES

1. National Education Assn., Project on the Instructional Program of the Public Schools, *Schools for the Sixties* (New York: McGraw-Hill, 1963). The Project on Instruction (as the project is popularly called for purposes of abbreviation) originally consisted of a national committee which, under the direction of Ole Sand, identified critical decision areas for schools and the criteria for making the decisions. The project reports appeared in several volumes, of which *Schools for the Sixties*, published by McGraw-Hill, was one. The others, published by the National Education Association, are *Education in a Changing Society* (1963), *Deciding What to Teach* (1963), *Planning and Organizing for Teaching* (1963), *The Scholars Look at the Schools: A Report of the Disciplines Seminar* (1962), *The Principals Look at the Schools: A Status Study of Selected Instructional Practices* (1962), and *Current Curriculum Studies in Academic Subjects* (1962).

2. National Education Assn., Project on the Instructional Program of the Public Schools, *Planning and Organizing for Teaching* (Washington, 1963), p. 25.

3. National Education Assn., *Deciding What to Teach*, p. 44.

4. Ibid., pp. 44–45.

5. Paul R. Hanna and John R. Lee, "Generalizations from the Social Sciences," in *Social Studies in Elementary Schools*, 32d Yearbook of the National Council for the Social Studies (Washington: National Education Assn., 1962), p. 71.

6. *Elementary Social Studies Curriculum: Scope and Sequence* (Rockville, Md.: Montgomery County Public Schools, 1970).

7. Ibid.

8. Ibid.

9. Ibid.

10. Elementary Social Studies Curriculum Committee, *Social Studies for Elementary School Children* (St. Paul: St. Paul Public Schools, 1959), p. 2.

11. Ibid., p. 3.

12. Ibid., pp. 5–6.

13. Ralph C. Preston, *Teaching Social Studies in the Elementary School* (New York: Rinehart, 1958), p. 75.

14. John Dewey, *Intelligence in the Modern World* (New York: Modern Library, 1939), p. 716.

15. Ibid., p. 674.

16. See Jean Piaget, *Judgment and Reasoning in the Child* (New York: Humanities Press, 1947) and *Origins of Intelligence in Children*, trans. Margaret Cook (Washington: American Council on Education, 1956).

17. E. A. Peel, *The Pupil's Thinking* (London: Oldbourne, 1961).

18. Victoria Hazlitt, "Children's Thinking," *British Journal of Psychology* 20 (April 1930), pp. 354–61.

19. M. E. Oakes, *Children's Explanations of Natural Phenomena* (New York: Teachers College, Columbia Univ., 1947).

20. Edna Heidbreder, "The Attainment of Concepts," part III: "The Process," *Journal of Psychology* 24 (1947), pp. 93–138.

21. John U. Michaelis, *Social Studies for Children in a Democracy* (Englewood Cliffs, N.J.: Prentice-Hall, 1956), p. 74.

22. Joy M. Lacey, *Social Studies Concepts of Children in the First Three Grades* (New York: Teachers College, Columbia Univ., 1932).

23. J. D. McAulay, "Social Studies in the Primary Grades," *Social Education* 18 (December 1954), pp. 357–58.

24. Ralph C. Preston, "Teaching For Depth," *Childhood Education* 36 (January 1960), p. 213.

25. Arthur T. Jersild, *Child Psychology*, 4th ed. (Englewood Cliffs, N.J.: Prentice-Hall, 1954), p. 459.

26. Melvin Arnoff, "Adding Depth to Elementary School Social Studies," *Social Education* 28 (October 1964), p. 336.

27. Peel, *The Pupil's Thinking*, p. 181.

28. R. H. Ojemann and others, "The Effects of a 'Causal' Teacher-Training Program and Certain Curricular Changes on Grade-School Children," *Journal of Experimental Education* 24 (December 1955), pp. 95–114.

29. Ethel Maw, "An Experiment in Teaching Critical Thinking in the Intermediate Grades" (Ph.D. thesis, Univ. of Pennsylvania, 1959).

30. J. I. Lacey and K. M. Dallenbach, "Acquisition by Children of the Cause-Effect Relationship," *American Journal of Psychology* 52 (1939), pp. 103–10.

31. J. Richard Suchman, "Inquiry Training in the Elementary School," *Science Teacher* 27 (November 1960), pp. 42–47.

32. Edith West, "Concepts, Generalizations, and Theories," Background Paper no. 3, Minnesota Project Social Studies (Minneapolis: Univ. of Minnesota, n.d.).

265

CURRICULUM
PLANS
REFLECTING
ONE DIMENSION

There are a great many ways of constructing a social studies curriculum. The emphasis can be placed on a dimension, a social science, or a social problem. Let us look first at the mechanics of curriculum development and then at curriculum plans that emphasize each of the three dimensions.

Curriculum Essentials

A curriculum plan needs to contain the following elements:

1. *Objectives.* These should identify the chief behaviors desired in the student and the areas of life or content with which he should have experience. Here are some possible objectives for social studies curricula: describe the chief institutions of Western culture and how they developed; explain major issues in national and local elections; recognize the value of equalizing opportunity

for all men; show confidence in one's worth as a person. A curriculum can be thought of as aiming at the improvement of thinking, feeling, and doing. Hence, objectives can be divided into three general categories: cognitive, or intellectual; affective, or emotional; and skills.

2. Broad teaching strategies. There are many teaching strategies that are useful for different purposes, and the different components of the curriculum will probably require different approaches. One educator recommends a strategy whereby the student learns the social sciences by being taught to apply social science methods to social problems. Group dynamics skills can be improved by teaching students to analyze their group behavior and systems for improving it. Many skills can be taught through programed instruction.

3. Sequence. What will come before what? There are probably some ideas, skills, and ways of thinking that should be introduced early so that they can be built on or deepened later. Perhaps some learnings need to be repeated periodically. In the primary grades, one basis for sequence has been the "expanding horizons" approach, by which the child studies first those things that are physically (and presumably psychologically) close to him. Chronology is another possible basis for sequence, but certainly an event need not be studied first just because it happened first.

Curriculum plans can suggest possibilities but leave the choice to each group. For example, a guide might suggest that during one of the junior high years a class study one or two of the underdeveloped but rapidly developing nations and not specify which ones.

4. Continuity. This element can be supplied by the essential values, skills, and ideas that are studied and expanded year by year in different ways. For example, group dynamics skills might be begun in the first year of school and developed at first informally, and finally by formal study of methods for improving group processes. Certain methods from the social sciences might be introduced early and developed year by year. Or the study of democratic values might give continuity to the curriculum. One kindergarten through grade 7 project (the University of Georgia Anthropology Project) introduces "cultural universals" at the beginning and expands on them yearly so that the child's conception becomes more and more sophisticated and he applies the universals to the analysis of more and more situations.

267

5. *Evaluation and feedback.* The last element in a curriculum plan is a provision for determining what is being learned and communicating progress to the teacher and student. This is an exceedingly specialized problem. Ordinarily a school system requires the services of experts to help design and implement an evaluation system tailored to the local situation. A common and serious error is to develop an assessment system using devices that were not designed to do what a particular school system uses them to do. The indiscriminate buying of standardized tests is an example of this error. It is almost certain that an adequate system for assessment and feedback cannot be developed unless the school system employs a measurement expert or testing service to design one.

We will use these curriculum essentials to examine three curriculum plans, each of which emphasizes one of the three dimensions of the social studies. These plans include only a few objectives, teaching strategies, and plans for continuity and sequence, but they are complete enough to enable us to see what kinds of curriculum plans emerge when different dimensions are emphasized and how the curriculum essentials are used to make a curriculum plan.

A Social Science–Centered Curriculum

To achieve full scholarly control over a discipline, one needs to master its methodology, its frame of reference, and its organizing concepts. For the purposes of general education we have several choices. We can teach those parts of the social sciences that apply naturally as the students study social problems and prepare to be citizens and understand themselves. Or we can emphasize one discipline, teaching it well and letting it be an illustration. Or we can develop an integrated social science approach, teaching the general elements of methodology, the frames of reference of several disciplines, and some of the more important organizing ideas of each. Or we can teach the more general methods and concepts in the early years, and provide opportunity for depth exploration of some of the specific disciplines during the high school years. The following illustrates an integrated social science approach.

269

Social studies curricula can emphasize one dimension.

The student should be able to—

1. name the general elements of social science methodology
2. collect data, make inferences, and organize hypothecated experiments
3. recognize the general frame of reference of each social science
4. analyze small-group interaction using social science techniques and concepts
5. use social science knowledge to analyze social problems
6. describe the social movements that are changing the world
7. form personal values and develop a philosophy of personal and social life

These objectives emphasize the social sciences, but they also consider social life, citizenship, and the quest for personal meaning.

TEACHING STRATEGY

270

Several strategies are used according to their appropriateness to the different objectives. Depth studies emphasize the methods of the social sciences. For each depth study, materials are put together to facilitate cooperative inquiries using the social science methods. To introduce the frames of reference of the different social sciences, certain depth studies emphasize specific disciplines. Some of the depth studies each year focus on contemporary social problems, so that the methodologies and ideas learned are applied to contemporary problems. A group-dynamics laboratory method is used to teach students to analyze and improve their group process skills. Self-instructional units are developed to teach map skills and acquaint students with basic information from several of the social sciences. Independent study units facilitate depth inquiry by individuals into social problems.

Some of these strategies, such as group inquiry, are extremely inductive. Others, as the self-instructional units, are prepackaged for the students and use sets of readings or programed instructional techniques. In addition, "concept units" will be available. These are self-instructional units that can be used to review or catch up on work missed, or as preparation for group units. Each concept

unit is built around an important concept ("latitude," "power," "culture") and provides materials for self-teaching.

SEQUENCE

The pattern of units gradually develops the methodology and philosophy of social science and systematically introduces the frame of reference of each social science. This frame of reference is repeated several times in the twelve years. Two or three social science concepts are introduced early, repeated, and deepened. Group dynamic skills are also systematically developed.

CONTINUITY

The methodology of social sciences and the improvement of interpersonal understanding and skills are repeated throughout. At every opportunity, students are asked to examine assumptions, to build and test hypotheses, to weigh values. Frame of reference is stressed throughout. Alternatives are developed—alternative views of human interaction, alternative solutions to problems, alternative ways of seeing things.

The spread of topics results from the plans for sequence and continuity as they work together.

Level	Topic	Approach
Primary	What Is a Family? An Anthropological Approach	At length and at leisure, a superficial study of a primitive family (Trobriand Islanders), a Western family (French), and an African family (Bantu)
	What Is a Community? An Anthropological Approach	At length and at leisure, a superficial study of cultural universals in several communities (Trobriand, French, Bantu, Swedish, Thai)
	What Are Tools?	A beginning of the study of civilization; tools, technologies, ideas used by several peoples throughout the development of civilization

272

Level	Topic	Approach
	Our Group	A study of ways of having amicable and businesslike groups—study modulated to the character of the group
	Things to Believe In	A study of human interdependence; can relate to culture groups previously studied—family, community, and face-to-face group
	Basic Map and Chart Skills	An elementary self-instructional unit; teaches map and chart making and decoding
Inter-mediate	Our Political World	A study of decision making in families, communities, and nations
	Our Economic World	A study of economic processes in families and communities; follows "What Are Tools?"
	The Beliefs of Man	Follows "Things to Believe In"; studies values in primitive and modern communities
	The Political and Economic History of the United States	A self-instructional survey course; readings, films, programs
	Groups at Work	A depth study of group dynamics, including one's own groups
	The Social Sciences at Work	Observing methods of validating inferences; the concept of causation; fallacies in reasoning
	Frames of Reference	A study of perception experiments, showing how preconception affects perception
Junior High	What Is a Society?	A study of two small, well-defined societies: Israel and Ceylon
	A Study of Law	Freedom and authority in Greece (Athens and Sparta), Rome, and twelfth century England
	Urbanization in America	Economic and political factors

273

Level	Topic	Approach
	The Political and Economic History of Brazil	A self-instructional unit
	The Political and Economic History of Japan	A self-instructional unit
	My Community	Political, social, and economic aspects; an inductive study
	Group Dynamics and Perception	Laboratory techniques; advanced course
Senior High	International Relations	Using internation simulation— several units
	World Law	A study of international organizations—including NATO, SEATO, the UN—using original sources
	Demography	A study of population distribution and dynamics
	Political Belief Systems	Communism, democracy, etc.
	Macroeconomics	An emerging nation (as Nigeria); a small, well-developed one (as Sweden); a huge one (as India)
	Group Dynamics, Caste, and Class	A study of the relation between the internation system of a group and its external system or social matrix
	Collecting and Organizing Data	Self-instructional units

This curriculum plan leans so far toward the intellectual that extensive modification would be necessary to adapt it for use with fairly nonverbal or culturally disadvantaged children. However, most of these units can be adapted, because they deal with real events that are easy to see and feel. Also, the use of depth studies permits long periods of data collection so that the students will be less dependent on verbal learnings.

A Citizen-Centered Curriculum

The public expects the schools to prepare people to participate in and improve society. Sometimes this has been interpreted to mean that the school should indoctrinate the student with patriotic values and teach him the evils of communism, socialism, and other movements that challenge the existing social order. In other cases, it has been interpreted to mean the development of an aggressively revisionist citizen, aware of counter systems and prepared to revise and redevelop the present society. The curriculum illustrated here takes a moderate position. It neither avoids acquainting students with the movements that shape other societies nor expects a citizenry of active revisionists.

OBJECTIVES

The student should be able to—

1. take democratic action in groups large and small
2. diagnose and improve group performance
3. understand the development of democratic society
4. recognize the value of liberty, government by consent and representation, and responsibility for the welfare of all
5. analyze social forces
6. think productively about the improvement of the society

275

These objectives emphasize the societal processes. The intellectual is not neglected (nos. 2, 3, and 5), but it is subordinated to the social purposes of the curriculum.

TEACHING STRATEGY

Each class is organized into a group responsible for developing objectives and plans for attaining the objectives. Instruction begins with mutual interests. The processes of the inquiring groups are studied. Each class learns to analyze itself as a social system and develops skill in improving social dynamics. The social sciences are learned by practicing them. Hypotheses are developed and checked using social science methods; then results are checked against those of contemporary behavioral sciences.

Cooperative group inquiry requires teachers to be highly skilled in group process. They need to handle students deftly to see that significant issues are studied with vigor and efficiency. The strategy has to be modulated depending on the character of the group. Young children and socially immature students require more structure and stronger leadership. Units must help students develop greater group skills.

SEQUENCE

Like a person-centered curriculum, the citizenship-centered curriculum allows many topics to be selected by the teacher and learner, working together. However, many topics can be identified that will help the young child develop basic understandings and skills and lead the older student directly into preparation for citizenship.

Level	Topic	Approach
Primary	The Classroom and the School	The functional analysis of groups
	Families around the World	Interdependence and division of labor
	A Study of Games	Provides a gentle basis for the introduction to both conflict and cooperation
Intermediate	Analyzing Group Behavior	Introduction to social science methodology
		Emphasizes ways of establishing facts, drawing inferences, making value judgments
	Our Social Heritage	Study of the evolution of democratic institutions and values
	Government in Action	Study of contemporary social action
Junior High	Organizing a Group	Strategies for analyzing and improving group activity (More sophisticated versions can be introduced each year.)

277

Level	Topic	Approach
	The History of the United States Senate	A depth study of the practices and history of the Senate
	A Social Problem	Depth study of a contemporary social problem and what can be done about it
Senior High	Today's Isms	A study of communism, totalitarianism, socialism, authoritarianism, democracy
	Group Processes	An advanced inquiry into group dynamics
	Social Movements and World Government	Selected social movements and issues in world government
	Conflict and Cooperation in America	A study of public controversy

Group dynamic skills and social science concepts are introduced early so that they can be used later in studying democratic and other social institutions. Depth studies, in all curriculum plans, are preferable to the superficial coverage of broad topics.

CONTINUITY

Group inquiry and the constant analysis of group dynamics provide continuity in this program. Analysis of democratic institutions is also reiterated. The use of the analytic tools from social science is yet a third basis for continuity. The revisitation of values and controversial issues provides a sense of reality throughout.

EVALUATION AND FEEDBACK

Each person's acquisition of democratic skills and social science methodology can easily be evaluated. The group analysis of group process builds into this curriculum a constant evaluative device and puts much responsibility for the determination of progress on the group. Although the assessment of group dynamic skills is self-perpetuating, it does require special training for its inception.

A Person-Centered Curriculum

This curriculum plan was developed primarily to help each student find himself and prepare to live a coherent, meaningful life.

OBJECTIVES

The student should be able to—

1. understand himself, his purposes, and his relations with others
2. use knowledge of his heritage and his interdependence with others in his society
3. analyze his social relations and the structure of his society
4. examine his values and those of others
5. participate in the development of purposes in groups of which he is a part
6. participate in the development of human values

Each of these objectives gives prominence to the learner. His relations with others are approached from his frame of reference. The social sciences are not specifically mentioned but, as we will see, they are useful for achieving these objectives.

TEACHING STRATEGY

Any twelve- or thirteen-year-long curriculum needs a variety of teaching strategies. The primary goals of the curriculum and the beliefs of the faculty who design the curriculum, however, frequently result in the identification of one or two strategies that characterize the approach.

In this case the chief element in the teaching strategy is to handle instruction so that the student participates in the develop-

ment of objectives for each unit of work and has ample opportunity to explore personal interests. Because this kind of instruction demands that a teacher have a close and insightful relationship with the student, the school provides for "cycling" of social studies teachers. That is, each teacher has the same group of students for three years. Over twelve years, then, each student has four social studies teachers, one for each three-year cycle of the curriculum. This enables the teacher to use his knowledge of the student so that instruction is closely geared to the student's needs and problems. As adolescents begin to be disturbed by the alienating factors in modern society, they can examine and learn to cope with these factors. Similarly, if they begin to act in an alienated fashion, the teacher can make their behavior part of their study. The students can express their real feelings about values and controversial issues and endeavor to make their own quest for meaning a part of their study.

SEQUENCE

In such a curriculum, many topics cannot be predicted in advance. The important basis for sequence is that the student gradually examine his society and develop personal values. The older student can be led to study social movements and issues shaping the world in which he has to delineate himself and find a meaningful existence. The sequential plan can provide some topics and ideas, but permit many to be introduced by the teacher and his students. The following excerpt from a sequential plan illustrates this:

Level	Topic	Approach
Primary	Cultural Universals	Comparative study of families, communities, including the home scene
		Anthropological concepts emphasized to build base for later study
	Interdependence	Study of factories, communities, own groups; also basis for later study

Level	Topic	Approach
Inter-mediate	American Politics	Inductive study of the local political process
	American Values	Inductive study of beliefs, both from documents and from study of the local community
Junior High	What Is a Person?	Attempt to define what makes a human being and what makes an individual
	How Are We Different?	A study of the ways individuals and cultures develop particular frames of reference
Senior High	Ideas That Change the World	Historical studies of communism, democracy, religions, and other movements
	The World to Come	Study of movements that are shaping the future and their impact on individuals

The entire plan for sequential study would need to include many more topics. However, the above shows one characteristic approach and indicates how the sequence can include a progression of topics, ideas, and approaches to teaching.

CONTINUITY

Three sources of continuity might be used: personal quest, social context, or the social sciences. If the curriculum is shaped around personal quest, responsibility is continually thrust on the learner. Many individual projects are undertaken, and the issues and problems that concern the learner become the starting point for much of his education. If the curriculum highlights the student's social context, the student continually sees himself shaped by social influences and participating in the shaping of his society. If the curriculum focuses on the social sciences, critical social issues and methods for analyzing social influences are introduced to the student. Ideas such as "cultural universal" are repeated throughout the curriculum.

This curriculum creates many topics and approaches to teaching. In such cases, an overall testing program is probably not appropriate. Rather, each teacher has to identify the specific objectives for each unit of study and devise ways of determining whether they are accomplished. Specific performance levels for all students are probably not appropriate either.

Curriculum Designs

None of these three designs started with the assumption that there had to be world history courses or a problems of American democracy course or sequential courses in American history. In each case an attempt was made to develop a coherent plan that introduces fresh content and ideas each year and yet develops fundamental ideas, skills, and values.

To debate over whether to integrate the social sciences or treat them separately seems to be an empty one for a public school curriculum. The purpose of the K to 12 curriculum is not to prepare people for graduate work in one of the social sciences. Therefore, those parts of the social sciences that can be treated in common should be treated in common. Furthermore, the belief that the social studies should be confined to history and geography is not tenable today. There is important knowledge in all the social sciences, and they are all vigorous.

The above illustrative curriculum outlines, fragmentary as they are, were designed to show that there is no necessary incompatibility between the sources of the curriculum. The development of the person, the citizen, and the enlightened "socially scientific" individual are compatible goals.

283

INQUIRIES

1. Select a unit from each of the curricula discussed in this chapter. What differences would there be in the unit if it were to emphasize another of the dimensions than the one for which it was intended?

2. What are the chief differences between the three dimensions? Defend the position: The three dimensions depend on one another to such an extent that they cannot be separated.

3. Identify two techniques for achieving continuity and sequence in social studies curricula.

284

CURRICULUM PLANS INTEGRATING THE THREE DIMENSIONS

285

Let us look at three curriculum plans designed to give equal attention to the three dimensions. They take an integrated approach to the social sciences: they do not emphasize one or two of the social sciences but use them in conjunction with one another.

The Minnesota Curriculum Project

Edith West has organized an enormous curriculum effort to develop a curriculum framework and instructional materials for children from the earliest years of school through the secondary schools. After a thorough examination of the social sciences, West and her staff concluded that their project should not be organized around a single discipline: the social sciences need not be taught separately. This position derives partly from the fact that the social sciences all study social reality, although from

chapter 12

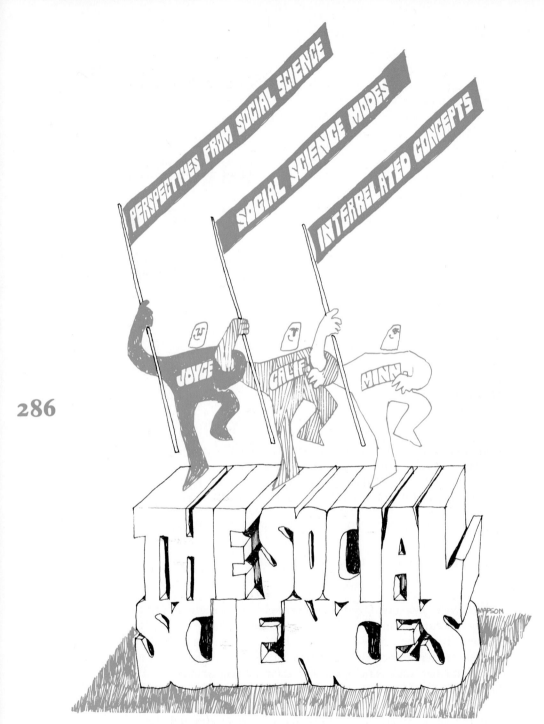

286

Integrated social science approaches

different perspectives. Therefore, the curriculum can be organized around important social topics and the appropriate social sciences brought to bear on them.

> It should be noted that problems within any society are not neatly separated into political, economic, and social problems. . . . The study of societal problems, therefore, requires interdisciplinary efforts.[1]

The Minnesota curriculum was constructed to lead students to apply social science methods to significant social content. The development of values is as important as the learning of any specific content or social science system. A statement from the "Teacher's Guide to the Sixth Grade Course on United States History" describes the relationship between values, content, and scientific skills.

> The sixth grade course was developed with a view to helping pupils develop many of the scholarly values identified by the Center's staff for the entire social studies program. It was designed also to develop a number of attitudes related to public values or the ground rules for the operation of a democratic society. It should be noted, moreover, that some of these attitudes are basic to an overall value which has not been stated for each of the units—the value of human dignity. Most pupils will come to the course with a fairly well-developed value for human dignity as a result of previous experiences at home, in school, in church, and in their many informal groups. Probably the more specific values of this course will develop as pupils see the need for certain things in order to protect this major value. However, the content used to teach these other values, such as those related to the protection of minority rights, evaluating events and institutions on the basis of their effects upon human beings, etc. may also help reinforce pupils' attitudes toward human dignity.
>   The sixth grade course is also designed to develop several attitudes which are likely to arise from the study of social science content. For example, several of the units try to help pupils develop a scepticism of single-factor causation in the social sciences and of panaceas for curing social problems.[2]

The Minnesota material has students learn the frame of reference of the various social sciences as they study human societies.

> It seems appropriate to have children begin their study of culture by focusing upon only one institution—an institution which is close to their lives. The two year sequence of "Families around the World" does introduce several other institutions in a simple way as children

focus upon the family. Children will notice differences in education and to some extent in religion. They will be introduced to simple economic concepts such as specialization and economic interdependence. However, they will wait to study other institutions in greater depth until grades three and four.

Grade three uses the theme of "Communities around the World" to introduce children in more detail to social and political institutions. Again some economic concepts are developed, but the major focus upon economic institutions does not come until grade four.

The fourth grade course uses the same theme of "Communities around the World" to introduce contrasting economic systems. Children will spend a large portion of their time finding out in simple terms how our own economic system operates. However, they will discover that in some societies the government plays a much greater role and that in some societies traditional reciprocal relationships among people are more important than a market system. They will see how the total way of life, including cultural values, affects economic systems.

In each of these grade levels, institutions are added to a study of other institutions which pupils have examined earlier. That is, as children look at the Manus or Paris community in grade three, they will also notice some things about the family life in these communities. As children look at economic life in the village of India in grade four, they will find out much about the family life and the social and political life in an Indian village. In this fashion, children study more institutions in each grade level until they are able to look at total cultures without too much confusion.

In grade five, children study in much more detail how different cultures or the same people over time use the same physical environment. The focus is upon the geography of the United States, Canada, and Latin America. The fifth grade course gives pupils some understanding of the physical environment of several places studied in the sixth grade. For example, pupils' study of the northeastern part of the United States provides useful background for the study of the Iroquois and the early English settlement in Plymouth. The study of the Midwest and of the South provides help when pupils look at expansion in those areas. The study of the South also provides background for the Civil War. Finally, the study of the Great Plains area, although not detailed, should provide useful background for the final unit in the sixth grade on expansion into the Great Plains area. Pupils can also draw upon what they have learned in the fifth grade to make comparisons between the Algonquins and the Iroquois and between the Sioux and other Plains Indians studied in the sixth grade course.

The sixth grade course differs from the fifth grade course by emphasizing culture contact and the movement of people with their culture to new places rather than the changing use of the same physical environment, even though that idea is reinforced in the course.[3]

The curriculum sequence is similar to the expanding horizons sequence in that family-size human units are studied first, then community life, and then the larger society; also, American geography and U.S. history are emphasized in the fifth and sixth grades. It differs from the expanding horizons sequence, however, in that many people and cultures are studied from the earliest years and social science concepts are emphasized systematically.

The Minnesota material teaches what is judged to be significant social content and brings the social sciences to bear as appropriate. It helps the student follow scientific practice and become aware of the frames of reference he is being taught. Although not using inquiry methods exclusively, the project gives considerable emphasis to social science inquiry so that the process of making knowledge becomes apparent to the student.

Perspectives from the Social Sciences: An Integrated Plan

289

The following curriculum plan uses the social sciences in such a way that the perspective of each is made clear with respect to important social concepts. The sequence is organized according to the levels of concepts described in chapter 3: observed concepts, inferred concepts, and ideal-type concepts.

Age of Child

5	Observed		
6	concepts		
7	through	Ideal-type	
8	the	concepts	
9	program	formed	Inferred
10		from	concepts
11		observed	(with
12			attention to
13			inference
14			making)

The sequence based on these three levels appears to satisfy Jean Piaget's contention concerning the thinking abilities of children at different ages.

This curriculum plan derives its sequence also from the comparative approach typical of anthropology and geography. The young child studies culture groups in pairs, using the home culture as one member of the pair. In this way, perhaps, the child avoids culture shock and learns not to stereotype things that seem strange.[4] Whether primitive cultures and Eastern cultures can be studied in the primary grades is a question that each curriculum planner must decide, as the evidence is inconclusive.

1. Our Home and the English Home
   Our School and the French School
   Music around the World

2. Our Town and a German Town
   Our Leisure Life and Mexican Leisure Life
   Folk Tales from Five Peoples

3. The Government of Our Town and of a Swiss Town
   Our State and Japan
   A New Mexico Pueblo and a Bantu Village

4. Religions and Their Origins
   The Oil Industry and the Middle East
   Biographies of Five Men from Five Nations
   Current Issues in the United Nations

5. The Modern Industrial State
   A Technologically Underdeveloped Nation
   The Art of the Southwest
   Worldwide Cultural Exchange

6. The History of the U.S. Government, 1776–1800
   The History of the United Nations, 1945–Present
   The History of Our Town, 1950–Present
   The Cold War

This plan of depth studies each year allows the teacher and children time to develop one or two depth studies out of their needs and interests or contemporary events. For example, an election year might provoke a study of town officials and voting procedures. A local newspaper campaign might result in a study of recreational facilities. "Mapping Our Town" might develop into a study of businesses or transportation or ways in which citizens depend on one another.

The first-grade child begins to study the human group. He is led to ask, in simple form, questions similar to those the economist, sociologist, anthropologist, or political scientist asks. What are the jobs different people do in English and American families? How do English (or American) mothers teach their children table manners? Who decides whether there should be a new French (or American) school? In this first year, observed concepts would be emphasized. Also, the relatively small units of the home and the school permit the younger child to explore in greater depth than would larger units such as cities or nations.

In the second year, human groups can be identified with the organizing concepts of the social sciences. Emphasis on economics and government could guide the study of the two towns. The study of leisure life might bring in the sociological concepts of values, roles, and sanctions. The folk tales are well suited to introduce certain facets of culture.

In the third year, the comparison between the local and Swiss governments might emphasize the organizing concepts of political science. The interrelations between political life and other facets of life should also be noted. Because the Pueblo and Bantu villages represent relatively small and simple societal units, their two cultures could be carefully examined in their totality. Japan and one's own state, however, are large and complex and thus demand lengthy, difficult analysis; it may be that their total cultures cannot be effectively studied by third-graders. On this first curricular venture into a macro study, perhaps only a few cultural elements should be studied from a circumscribed viewpoint. The concepts of economic geography could be useful, for they are chiefly observed concepts and are therefore easier to handle than inferred concepts.

The fourth-year study of religions involves inferred concepts (values) and would permit sufficient attention to be paid to the process of inference. The study of the oil industry might emphasize economic concepts, but not exclusively. The study of biography follows up the studies of music, folk tales, and leisure life by concentrating on an art form. The focus on individuals balances the focus on large societal units in the other depth studies. "Current Issues in the United Nations" introduces international government formally but stresses events in the news so that the study does not lapse into a description of the divisions and agencies of the organization.

291

In the fifth year, the study of one or two highly developed nations could introduce the study of macroeconomics and extend the concepts introduced in the oil study of the preceding year. A contrast would be provided by a study of one or two less developed nations. The children and teacher might find it productive to follow these two units with a look at the Alliance for Progress or another example of international cooperation. Similarly, the concept of cultural exchange can be introduced in a study of the art of the Southwest, which provides many examples of the mingling of Spanish, Indian, and Northern European cultures. After this unit, cultural exchange itself can be studied, with a look at the ways in which Oriental, European, African, and Latin-American cultural ideas and products are currently being diffused.

In the sixth year, concepts from every social science should be brought to bear on these studies. In the first two units, original documents should be used whenever possible. In the third unit, the techniques developed in the first two should be extended as the children explore local archives, newspaper files, resource persons, and actions of the town government. The study of the cold war provides a look at history in the making and permits the children to study the behavior of our government in confronting and interacting with other governments.

The virtue of this plan is that the frame of reference for each social science is brought to bear on the study of society. By concentrating on a very few topics, studied in depth, the student is permitted to collect and analyze enough data so that he can apprehend the modes of inquiry of the discipline and also achieve some independence of thought with respect to particular social issues.

Nowhere in the six years is a sweeping study of history suggested. The curriculum of the elementary school should prepare the children for later surveys of history. Most children do not have the mental maturity needed for chronological studies of history until the end of the elementary school years.

Any good curriculum plan should be developed with special reference to the local situation. The curriculum for a lower-class neighborhood should provide extra firsthand experiences as well as many extra topics concentrating on the local community or city. In addition, every opportunity to further language development should be exploited to the fullest. No large city should engage in the development of a prescriptive curriculum that would apply to all areas of the city.

A Proposed Plan for California Schools

The California Statewide Social Sciences Study Committee has developed a curriculum framework that applies social science thinking to a variety of social topics. The framework has been recommended to the State Curriculum Commission and to the California State Board of Education, but has yet to be adopted.

The program is structured around three elements: modes of social inquiry; concepts drawn from the social sciences; and particular times, places, people, issues, or problems. Each unit of the program helps the student develop modes of inquiry and concepts in respect to particular settings. Three modes of inquiry are used: the analytic mode, which is used in "systematic analyses of urban, economic, geographic, political, historical, or other cultural phenomena selected for study in depth"; the integrative mode, which is used in "studies designed to provide a relatively complete or holistic synthesis of the diverse factors involved in a particular time or place"; the policy mode, which is used in "making decisions or judgments related to urban, economic, political, and other issues or problems."[5]

The first diagram in the chart [fig. 10] is designed to indicate the nature of an analytic study of urban functions. Such urban functions as commerce, educational services, and government would be studied in several different cities in order to arrive at broadly applicable generalizations. Thus in the analytic mode selected phenomena (urban functions) are studied in depth. The second diagram illustrates a relatively complete and holistic study of a particular city in the integrative mode. Here the purpose is to study and synthesize the diverse features that are characteristic of the setting under study. Notice that urban functions, as identified through analytic studies, may be a part of the integrative study of a particular city along with other aspects that are needed to give a complete view. The third diagram illustrates the policy mode of inquiry in which the problem, "How to Improve Urban Life," is the focus of study. In this mode, the problem is defined, data are gathered, values are considered, solutions are proposed and assessed, and decisions are made.[6]

The designers of the California plan recognize that these three modes are very closely related both in theory and in reality. They believe, however, that these modes can and should be distinguished from each other and taught systematically in social studies.

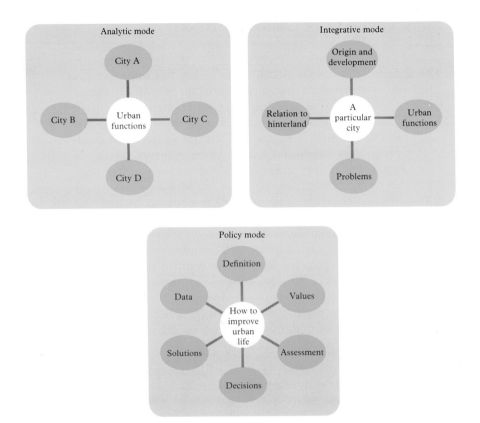

Fig. 10.   The three modes

Perhaps the distinctiveness of each mode can best be seen in the three different types of questions that they generate:

1. Why do these phenomena behave as they do? This question is central in the analytic mode as attention is given to such phenomena as roles of individuals, urban functions, division of labor, uses of power and authority, conflict and other processes of interaction, productive resources, and decision making in political systems.
2. Who am I, or who are we, or who are they? This question is basic in the integrative mode as studies are made of particular individuals, groups, or events such as the student's own family, his school, the history of California, life in colonial America, living in Mexico, the life of a significant individual, and the origin and growth of Los Angeles.

294

3. What should I, or we, or they do next? This question arises in the policy mode in a variety of studies ranging from the making and carrying out of rules, evaluating the actions of individuals and groups, and finding ways to improve urban life to the making of decisions on economic and political problems, assessing proposals for aiding newly developing countries, and considering alternatives to various international problems.[7]

In the overall design, topics, stated as questions, are arranged by blocks of grades (pp. 295–300) and explored in terms of modes of inquiry, illustrative concepts, and illustrative settings. The designers stress that teachers and schools should be flexible in choosing topics, settings, and sequences, so that the curriculum meets local needs. Many urban areas, for example, could be used as settings for topic 3 in grades 3–4.

GRADES K–2:   MANKIND: MAN'S DISTINCTIVE CHARACTERISTICS

Modes and Processes of Inquiry	Illustrative Concepts	Illustrative Settings
1. What is a man?		

Analytic
  Observation
  Classification
Integrative
  (Comparison)
	Human or man or mankind
	Reptiles, mammals, etc.
	(Infant dependency)
		Mammals, reptiles
		Members of the class
		A Pacific Island community

2. How do men and animals adapt to and change the land they live on?		

Analytic
  Classification
  Observation
  Communication
Integrative
  (Comparison)
	Landforms and water
	  bodies
	(Adaptation and ecology)
	Climate, weather
	(Topography)
		Landforms and water bodies
		The students and their
		  community
		Eskimos, other tribal groups
		Animals, including prehistoric

3. Why do things have names?		

Analytic
  As above
Integrative
  (Comparison)
Policy
  (Valuing)
	Name [symbol]
	Language, (written
	  language)
		Members of the class
		Plains Indians or
		  Japanese
		Animals

Modes and Processes of Inquiry	Illustrative Concepts	Illustrative Settings

4. Why are there rules for everyone?

Modes and Processes of Inquiry	Illustrative Concepts	Illustrative Settings
Analytic	Rules [roles]	Members of the class, their
As above	(Age and sex statuses)	families, community
Integrative	(Division of labor and	Animals
(Comparison)	of authority)	A dissimilar human group
Policy	Work, play	
(Valuing)	Needs, wants	

5. How are people alike and how are they different?

Modes and Processes of Inquiry	Illustrative Concepts	Illustrative Settings
Integrative	All previous concepts	Unfamiliar human groups,
Observation	(space, time)	over space and time
(Comparison)	Tools [technology]	Individuals, contributions
Policy	Individual differences,	
(Valuing)	individual contributions;	
	ethnic differences,	
	ethnic group contributions	

GRADES 3–4: MAN AND LAND: CULTURAL AND GEOGRAPHIC RELATIONSHIPS

Modes and Processes of Inquiry	Illustrative Concepts	Illustrative Settings

1. Why are particular animals found only in certain environments, while men live almost anywhere?

Modes and Processes of Inquiry	Illustrative Concepts	Illustrative Settings
Analytic	Biological adaptation	Selected animals
Classification	Cultural adaptation:	Indian groups in early
Definition (behavioral)	Technology	California
Contrastive analysis	Division of labor (social	Groups in different
Generalization	organization, role)	environments
Integrative	Scale, maps	
Comparison		

Modes and Processes of Inquiry	Illustrative Concepts	Illustrative Settings

2. Why do different groups of men develop different ways of living in the same or similar environments?

Analytic	Natural environment,	Early California Indians
Definition (behavioral)	resources	Mission and rancho in early
Contrastive analysis	Communities: tribal,	California
Generalization	peasant-urban,	Agricultural and mining
Integrative	rural-urban	communities in early
Holistic integration	Division of labor,	California
(cultural)	comparative advantage,	
Comparison	social organization	

3. How has urbanization altered man's relation to the natural environment?

Analytic	Factors of production	San Francisco in the 19th
Observation	Division of labor,	century
Classification	comparative advantage,	Los Angeles in the 20th
Definition (behavioral)	specialization	century
Contrastive analysis	Market, trade, middlemen	The local community
Generalization	Urban functions	
	Spatial distribution,	
	association, interaction	

4. How are problems of living being met in the modern urban environment?

Analytic	Cultural adaptation	Three urban centers in
As above	Urban form, functions	different parts of the
Integrative	Economic activities	world
Observation	Specialization	Local community
Classification	Comparative advantage	
Comparison	Intra-city patterns of	
Cultural integration	location, city-hinterland	
Policy	interaction	
Valuing	Decision making	

5. What is human about human beings?

Analytic	Adaptation: biological,	Selected animals
Observation	cultural	Indians in early California
Classification	Life cycle	Other groups (different
Definition (behavioral)	Culture: use of tools,	cultures)
Contrastive analysis	social organization,	
Generalization	communication, urge	
Communication	to explain	

Modes and Processes of Inquiry	Illustrative Concepts	Illustrative Settings

1. What happens when different groups of men come in contact?

Analytic
  Definition (behavioral)
  Contrastive analysis
  Generalization
Integrative
  Holistic integration
  (cultural)
Policy
  Valuing
	Interaction: cooperation,
	  conflict, domination
	Stratification, class
	Values
	Value conflicts
	Geographic setting
		Spanish-Indian interaction,
		  16th century Mexico
		English-Indian-African
		  interaction, 17th
		  century Virginia

2. How have ethnic minority groups and individuals affected American development?

Analytic
  As above
Integrative
  Holistic integration
  (historical, cultural)
	Migration, immigration
	Segregation, discrimination
	Cultural pluralism
	Ethnocentrism, racism
		The Irish in Boston
		The Chinese in
		  San Francisco
		Negroes and Mexican-
		  Americans in cities

3. How do different groups interact in the contemporary United States?

Analytic
  As above
Integrative
  Comparison
  Holistic integration
  (cultural, historical)
	Spatial distribution,
	  association, interaction
	Decision making and law
		Selected cases of group
		  interaction
		The student's community

4. How do groups interact in different cultures?

Analytic
  Observation
  Classification
  Behavioral definition
  Contrastive analysis
  Generalization
Policy
  Valuing
	Race: biological, social
	Culture, cultural diversity
	Class, caste
	Racism, ethnocentrism, and
	  related psychological
	  processes
		Brazil
		India
		Other societies

Modes and Processes of Inquiry	Illustrative Concepts	Illustrative Settings

5. How is any man like no other man?

Modes and Processes of Inquiry	Illustrative Concepts	Illustrative Settings
Integrative	Individuality, individualism	Periclean Athens
Observation	World view: myth, religion,	An African culture
Classification	ideology	Late medieval western
Definition (refined)	Creative expression	Europe
Holistic integration	Media of expression	Confucian China
(cultural, historical)	Expression of values	Mexico

GRADES 7–9: SYSTEMS: ECONOMIC AND POLITICAL; URBAN ENVIRONMENT

Modes and Processes of Inquiry	Illustrative Concepts	Illustrative Settings

1. How do societies decide what is to be done and who is to do it?

Modes and Processes of Inquiry	Illustrative Concepts	Illustrative Settings
Analytic	Political system	A tribal society
Definition:	Political culture:	Social groups to which
behavioral	authority, legitimacy,	students belong: family,
Others as in preceding	political, specialization	peer group, class, school
blocks	Constitution	
Policy	Decision making	
Valuing		

2. How do societies decide who gets what?

Modes and Processes of Inquiry	Illustrative Concepts	Illustrative Settings
Analytic	Economic system:	Ancient Egypt, England
Contrastive analysis	Needs	Comparative reference to
Others	Production	settings of topic 1
	Distribution	
	Decision making: tradition	

Modes and Processes of Inquiry	Illustrative Concepts	Illustrative Settings

3. How do market economies develop and function?

Modes and Processes of Inquiry	Illustrative Concepts	Illustrative Settings

Analytic
   Generalization
Integrative
   Holistic integration
	Economic system: market
	   Decision making: market
	   private enterprise,
	   profit motive, price
	   competition
	Economic growth: "takeoff,"
	   gross national product
		Woolens trade, England
		   and Low Countries,
		   14–16th centuries
		Anglo-American trade, 18th
		   century
		English industrial revolution
		American market revolution

4. How do democratic political systems develop and function?

Modes and Processes of Inquiry	Illustrative Concepts	Illustrative Settings

Analytic
   Generalization
Integrative
   Holistic integration
	Political system
	   Political culture:
	   political values
	Constitution: civil
	   rights and liberties,
	   federalism, separation
	   of powers, checks and
	   balances
	Social stratification and
	   mobility
		The English Glorious
		   Revolution
		Massachusetts, 17th Century
		Boston and the Continental
		   Congress, 1763–1776
		Pennsylvania in 1776
		Movement for the Federal
		   Constitution and Bill of
		   Rights, 1785–1791

300

5. How are decisions made in the command political economy of the Soviet Union?

Modes and Processes of Inquiry	Illustrative Concepts	Illustrative Settings

Analytic
   Contrastive analysis
Integrative
   Comparison
   Holistic integration
	Political system
	   Constitution: Commu-
	   nism, party bureaucracy
	Economic system: command
	   Production: socialism
	   Decision making: central
	   governmental planning
		The Soviet Union, selected
		   case studies

Reprinted, by permission, from *Social Sciences Education Framework for California Public Schools* (Sacramento, 1968), pp. 150–53.

INQUIRIES

1. Compare and contrast the three integrated approaches to curriculum in the social studies. Can you generate other curriculum approaches?

2. Develop an outline for an approach that integrates the social sciences in regard to either content or processes from the social dimension.

3. Develop an outline for an approach that integrates the social sciences in regard to the personal dimension.

NOTES

1. Edith West, "The Social Science Disciplines," Background Paper no. 2, Social Studies Curriculum Center (Minneapolis: Univ. of Minnesota, n.d.), pp. 14–15.

2. *Teacher's Guide to the Sixth Grade Course on United States History: From Community to Society*, Project Social Studies Curriculum Center (Minneapolis: Univ. of Minnesota, 1968), p. 1.

3. Ibid., pp. 8–9.

4. Leonard S. Kenworthy, *Introducing Children to the World* (New York: Harper, 1955).

5. Statewide Social Sciences Study Committee, State Board of Education, and the State Curriculum Commission of California, *Social Sciences Education Framework for California Public Schools* (Sacramento, 1968), p. 5.

6. Ibid.

7. Ibid., pp. 9–10.

301

part 5

SPECIAL CONSIDERATIONS

TEACHING
MATERIALS
AND RESOURCES

To introduce children to ideas and information about the social studies, a teacher needs many kinds of materials and resources. Direct experience can provide children with only a small portion of the data they need to comprehend the social world. Furthermore, the classroom can easily become removed from the world outside it—the commercial life of the city, the impact of changing technologies on society, political and social life around the world.

Instructional materials should provide authentic data about the most significant aspects of a subject of inquiry. When children are studying their own neighborhood, the crucial question about instructional materials is: What is the best way of revealing to the children the real neighborhood? For example, the children might best collect their own data from sources such as a local store or a local government official. When they are studying certain aspects of the American Revolution, the question becomes: How can the children obtain a realistic picture of those aspects? People who are far away or events that happened long ago have to be studied with secondhand information such as books, pictures, recordings, and films.

chapter 13

In addition to providing children with data, instructional materials must help them draw meaning from the data. Materials can do this by focusing on the subject areas and the questions that social scientists emphasize. In this respect the arrangement of instructional materials is crucial. A teacher may present the children with a Japanese folk tale and then an Irish folk tale, thus using contrast to encourage the building of useful concepts. The children might visit local stores and factories before reading about economic life; the data obtained from the local trips will make the readings more meaningful and the readings will help tie together the information gained from the trip.

Meaning can be conveyed not only by the arrangement of instructional materials but also by the conceptual content of the materials themselves. For example, a map might be constructed so that the relation between certain factors, such as the location of railroads, highways, and factories, can easily be seen. Some books are organized around an idea that dictates the order in which facts are presented. Such a book might describe the lives of New World explorers and then inquire into the motives that sent them on their adventures and conquests.

Instructional materials can offer children information and ideas, but only the teaching strategy can ensure that the children will interpret the data meaningfully, understand the concepts fully, and develop an ability to use the social scientist's modes of inquiry. There is no simple, fixed strategy for teaching the social studies. Every teacher needs to develop a wide repertoire of approaches to be used according to the children's individual needs. While learning to communicate with each other about important problems, children must also maintain their interests and aspirations as individuals. Thus instructional materials must be chosen with regard to both the approach to learning and the varying needs of individual learners.

Throughout this book we have identified instructional materials that provide data to which the child can relate the facts of his own life: the curriculum projects based on one or more of the social sciences; the Minnesota project, which contains data sources and instructional materials on dozens of nations, communities, and historical events or eras; *Man: A Course of Study*, which provides beautiful instructional films; the Tufts Intergroup Education project; and Shaftel's approach to role-playing.

Today there are so many sources of interesting books, pamphlets, films, and other data that every approach to the social studies described in this book can be carried out without textbooks or the products of curriculum projects, which in many cases have produced textbooklike material. The purpose of this chapter is to help teachers and schools identify enough sources of material so that they can assemble what they need for the approach they choose. First, however, let us look at criticisms of the textbook and its recent history.

Textbooks

Social studies textbooks have come to symbolize sterile teaching and misleading content. Critics usually charge primary social studies materials and curricula with being other-directed, unrealistic, racially and ethnically biased, inappropriate, superficial, and anti-intellectual. According to Riesman, the progressive school has been corrupted by its attempt to teach children to adapt to group life.[1] Textbooks introduce children to the happy milkman, the cheerful principal, and the happy factory workers; the child is supposed to learn from these the virtues of cooperation and interdependence. The school is pictured as a place where everyone cooperates and no one fails, the neighborhood as clean and safe, the factory as unaffected by strikes or worker discontent. The unreality of this picture appears also in the conspicuous absence of certain races, despite the implication that all races work harmoniously together. On the one hand, lower-class and rural children are likely to think that these books are fairy tales, and on the other, these texts probably will not disturb the cloistered world of the middle-class child.

"Home and Family" units have long been used to instill in the children concepts and skills basic to interdependence and cooperation, but J. D. McAulay has demonstrated that in many cases the children have already mastered these fundamentals.[2] Ralph Preston has made a similar charge—the elementary social studies have skimmed the surface of many topics with indifferent results.[3] One disadvantage of the expanding horizons approach is that topics are likely to repeat rather than deepen the child's experience. Similarly, intellectual inquiry in the social studies is considered by many elementary school administrators to be out of keeping with the teaching of reading, writing, and arithmetic.

307

In evaluating textbooks, a teacher may want to use several criteria such as these formulated by Cox and Massialas.

1. Does the text have a conceptual framework that gives it direction and purpose? Does it present and adhere to a consistent theory about social phenomena? Are the basic assumptions identified?

2. Is the content based on stated or clearly implied principles and generalizations? Does the author offer only relevant information and relate it clearly to these major ideas? Does the text provide hypotheses that can be tested by student inquiry?

3. Is the student encouraged to question various observations and related interpretations of reported social phenomena?

4. Is the text "inductively" oriented in order to promote the creative discovery of relationships by pupils? Does it provide "creative encounters" in the form of cases, episodes, or dilemmas?

5. Has the author used a defensible scheme for the selection of his material? Does the author make a continuous effort to apply the scientific method to his work? Does he show how his conclusions are supported? Does the book identify the existing gaps in human knowledge?

6. Does the book focus on or identify broad problems of social import that can serve as "springboards" for student inquiry?

7. Is the author consistent in his meanings or ideas? Is he careful to avoid ambiguities and vague terms? Does he make his meanings clear?

8. Does the author present information appropriately and freely from other cultures to support broad generalizations and ideas? Does he guard against an ethnocentric, Western bias?

9. Does the book reflect the most recent developments in scholarly research? Does it employ data from all the social sciences, and are these data reliable? Does it show the interrelatedness of all social knowledge?

10. Does the book attempt to interpret the methods of research in the social sciences as they apply to the statements of fact and relationships reported?

11. Does the author identify value issues? Does he differentiate between value judgments and descriptive propositions? Does he pose a systematic and defensible means for dealing with value issues?

12. Does the text deal freely with controversial social issues? Does the text identify all points of view where feasible? If it takes a point of view, does the text make clear on what grounds the conclusion was reached?

13. Are definitive, detailed, and annotated bibliographies provided? Are paperbacks included? Are statistical data sources identified? Are primary and secondary sources presented?

308

14. Does the author tailor his discussion to the age level of his student readers?
15. Do the end-of-chapter questions and exercises promote reflective thinking? Are they inquiry oriented?
16. Does the publisher provide a manual for the teacher that states the objectives and criteria of the textbook? Is the teacher provided with an additional, scholarly, annotated bibliography? Do the tests provided measure higher cognitive processes? Are suggestions given for the creative use of the text? Is further inquiry encouraged?[4]

In a series of informal studies applying these criteria to recent textbooks, very few books were found to meet the criteria. This can be accounted for largely by the fact that the production of instructional materials for U.S. public schools has been left almost entirely to commercial firms. It is reasonable that a publisher will not take on the expense of developing and publishing a textbook series unless he expects to sell his product at a profit. In order to produce textbooks that will fit into most school curricula, he examines curriculum guides published by school districts, consults educational theorists, and examines recommendations by national organizations of educators.

When several curricular and instructional patterns are used in schools or recommended by theorists, there is likely to be variety in textbook content and approach: some publishers cater to one pattern, and others another pattern. When a single curricular pattern or approach dominates a curriculum area, all textbooks are likely to follow that pattern. Such was the case for nearly forty years in the primary social studies. The expanding horizons approach dictated that the child study subjects physically and psychologically close to him and then gradually study his "expanding world."

This approach was rationalized by psychology: We learn best those things with which we have experience. Educational psychologists emphasized the difference between rote learning of symbols and slogans and building meaningful concepts from the child's own experience. Across the country curriculum guides tried to do the latter. In the experimental schools of the 1920s units on toys and ships led children from their personal interests and lives into vigorous analysis of the world.[5] Desire for integration of subjects resulted in the unification of social studies with art, music, and the home or bakery.

The expanding horizons approach affected not only the organization of content, but also the objectives of teaching. While exploring his milieu and social relations, the child was to develop the social knowledge and skills necessary for cooperative, democratic life. In studying fundamental ideas such as the interdependence of all men, he was to prepare to meet his fellow citizens and world neighbors. Through the study of national holidays and heroes, he was to develop an appreciation of his heritage. In these ways the expanding horizons approach lent itself to the cooperative-unit method typical of the Progressive Era. Working together, children and teachers could study their homes, schools, and neighborhoods and learn democratic behavior.

Leading educational publishers geared their textbooks to the expanding horizons approach.[6] These textbooks were carefully coordinated with the curriculum guides. The manual for one series even states that 150 state and city courses of study were consulted and that questionnaires were sent to curriculum directors asking their advice.

To facilitate the integration of curriculum areas, social studies texts became more and more like reading books, offering poems, dramatizations, and suggestions for projects. The texts are, in fact, closely coordinated with reading books. The manual for one first-grade social studies book reports that it "can appropriately be introduced when most of the children are prepared to begin the reading of Book One of their basic reading program."[7] Many of the manuals state that the books were written to be in tune with current trends in the social studies. They exhort teachers to use the cooperative-unit method; to provide rich experiences through field trips, motion pictures, and dramatization; to define objectives carefully; and to lead the children to discover significant issues, values, and concepts.

The titles of the six books in the Scott, Foresman & Company Basic Social Studies Program, edited by Paul R. Hanna, illustrate the expanding horizons approach. The first four titles are for the primary grades. These titles and annotations are taken from promotional materials for the 1963 edition of this series.

At Home (Primer) and At School
The Family and School Communities

In the Neighborhood
The Neighborhood Community

In City, Town, and Country
The Local, Metropolitan Area, and County Communities

In All Our States
The State Community and Regions of States

In the Americas
The National and Inter-American Communities

Beyond the Americas
Nations and Regions of Nations Across the Atlantic and
Across the Pacific

Nearly all social studies textbook series in the last forty years have had a similar pattern of titles. One exception is the Allyn and Bacon series. Its third-grade book, *Learning about Our Country*, includes the following chapter titles:

The United States of America
New York—Our Largest City
Boston—One of Our Oldest Cities
Miami—The Sunshine City
Pittsburgh—City of Steel
The Mississippi—Our Largest River
Texas—The Lone Star State
Montana—The Treasure State
Tacoma—Where Tall Trees Grow
California—The Golden State
Washington, D.C.—Capital of Our Country
Your Part in Our Country[8]

As might be suspected from the titles, this series includes material from regional economic geography earlier and in greater detail than do other social studies textbook series. The examination of specific cities is also unusual. It implies that there are advantages to treating a few cities in some depth rather than skimming over a region.

What may presage a new trend in textbooks, however, is W. A. Sadlier Company's *Urban America: Problems and Promises*. The text, teacher's guide, and "Research and Discovery" book are each divided into two sections. The first concentrates on what a city is and how it is governed. The material is realistic and clear. The second section breaks with tradition by dealing equally realistically and clearly with social and ecological problems. It seeks ways of solving these problems rather than simply cataloging them.

Trade Books: Juveniles

Trade books—all the commercial fiction and nonfiction designed for the general public and not specifically for schools—are being published in increasing numbers. Juveniles have shared in this startling growth. The teacher has the difficult task of sorting out those books most suitable for her use. Fortunately, there are a number of excellent bibliographical guides to help her.

Children's Books to Enrich the Social Studies, distributed by the National Council for Social Studies. Washington: National Education Assn., 1961. Includes annotated lists of 618 books, for all grades, dealing with common social studies topics. The annotations give detailed descriptions of content, treatment of content, and reading level.

Children's Catalog, 10th ed. New York: Wilson, 1961; annual supplements, 1962– . Contains thumbnail annotations of approximately 2500 children's books. Found in the children's room of virtually any public library and in almost every school library, this catalog is indexed by subject, author, and title, so that in a few minutes one can locate the recommended titles on any nation or topic.

Arbuthnot, May. *Children and Books*. 3rd ed. Chicago: Scott, Foresman, 1964. Its sections on social education include discussions and lists of both fiction and nonfiction and offer several valuable teaching suggestions.

Huck, Charlotte, and Young, Doris. *Children's Literature in the Elementary School*. New York: Holt, Rinehart & Winston, 1961. Gives considerable attention to the social studies.

Tooze, Ruth, and Krone, Beatrice. *Literature and Music as Resources for the Social Studies*. Englewood Cliffs, N.J.: Prentice-Hall, 1955. Book reviews in *Horn Book Magazine*. An important guide to children's books on all topics.

For a number of years Leonard Kenworthy has provided references for materials (films, slides, and recordings as well as books) dealing with culture groups. The appendix of his *Introducing Children to the World* (New York: Harper, 1955) lists children's books for both upper and lower grades under headings such as "Fun around the World" and "Pets around the World." His regional World Affairs Guides, published by Teachers College of Columbia University, provide comprehensive references to everything from book titles to sources for contacting pen pals.[9] Kenworthy has also written resource units (lists of learning aids pertaining to a specified topic) on individual nations, and many of these are available from the World Affairs Center at Brooklyn College. Kenworthy's *Social Studies for the Seventies* (Blaisdell-Ginn, 1969) surveys new developments in social studies education while emphasizing the cross-cultural approach. His bibliographic references are arranged according to topic and include both fiction and nonfiction. There are also lists of books for furthering the education of the teacher and his understanding of children. *Social Studies for the Seventies* can be a useful reference book for the classroom teacher as well as for library personnel in charge of ordering books.

The teacher should also become acquainted with the resource units found in curriculum guides published by many states and communities. One of the best guides to the books and other materials describing a particular city is frequently the curriculum guide written by the teachers of that city.

Despite the overall increase in the number of juvenile titles, there continues to be a serious lack in many subject areas. Communist China, for example, is represented by almost no useful book for children. Except possibly Japan, no Asian nation is represented by enough titles to make a depth study relatively easy. It takes nearly everything written for children about Africa to support even a superficial unit—and then only when the books are supplemented heavily with materials that the teacher has rewritten from adult sources. Asian and Latin American history have seldom been drawn on by children's authors, and many areas of European history are almost closed to children. Except for fictionalized biography, or histories that lean heavily on biography rather than on events and trends, even American history is neglected in many areas. In short, there are many subject areas for which the teacher must himself write materials or help his children to adapt suitable materials.

For the selection of informational books, Huck and Young have suggested several criteria that we paraphrase as follows:

1. *Authenticity and accuracy.* The poor informational book overgeneralizes because its author believes that children

314

cannot deal with the truth. The good books are not afraid of "sometimes," "usually," "apparently," and other words of qualification. The good informational book is also authentic. The author has done careful research on the topic and has checked his findings.

2. *Content and style.* The content should be presented without sugar coating, in a vivid style that does not stint detail. The book should relate to the child's everyday world so that he can easily sense the new information. Realistic fiction should also meet this criterion.

3. *Illustrations.* Pictures, maps, and other illustrations "should blend with the text. They should be accurate, large enough to show detail, and spaced so that the reader does not feel confused, and they should seem to flow with the text. Diagrams should be clearly explained. Photographs should illustrate one or two points instead of being general pictures."[10]

4. *Organization.* Paragraph and section headings, tables of contents, and indexes are all necessary as guides to inquiry; they are particularly necessary if children are to be properly taught reference skills.

In *Children and Books* Arbuthnot devotes over one hundred pages to an analysis of available books, many of which make ideal bases for units of study.

315

These social-studies books begin for the youngest as his books begin in every field—with pictures. Big picture books of trains, planes, and farmyards are as beautiful to look at and informative as the four and five year old can comprehend. Then come such forthright narratives as *The Little Auto* and *Pelle's New Suit*, informational stories of unusual charm. When we use such books, we don't say to a child who is entranced with the sequential pictures of *Pelle*, "Now, this is a story about the evolution of wool cloth." We don't have to, because the child who lives with *Pelle* over the years and loves Pelle's blue suit as much as if it were his own will know that evolution by heart. Nor will the child who has pondered over *The Little House* ever see a small dilapidated dwelling in a crowded city street without wondering if it, too, was not once a little house in the country with apple trees by its side and a clear view of the stars. Has this young reader of *The Little House* learned about the evolution of the cities? Of course he has. He knows it well in terms of one small house made memorable in beautiful pictures and a significant text.[11]

On selecting informational books, May Arbuthnot offers this cautionary advice:

Good informational stories of the caliber of *Pelle* and *The Little House* are not plentiful. But mediocre or poor informational stories are coming from the presses in staggering numbers. Most of them are written to fit a school unit or activity: food supplies in the city, safety, neighborhood stories. Too often these books are very dull reading. They have no sparkle, no element of surprise, no fun about them. Pedantically bent on informing and improving the young, they are examples of the didacticism of our day, and are almost as boring as their moralist predecessors. It is the age-old idea of sugar-coating with a story the informative pill a particular age or period believes in. Just now many writers apparently regard social studies as the pill which has to be overly sweet in order to be accepted by children, but the sugar coating results in just as arid reading as it did in the days when Morton and Sanford were paired in order to exhibit virtue and folly for the benefit of the young mind. To be convincing, children's stories in any field need a theme of sufficient strength to generate a good plot in which things happen and a climax is achieved. When both theme and plot are weak, neither beautiful pictures nor a utilitarian relationship to a unit in social studies can save a book from triviality.[12]

Books selected for the social studies influence a child's literary taste just as strongly as books selected primarily for teaching literature and language. Every social studies teacher must develop a sharp eye for literary quality.

The Fideler Company of Grand Rapids, Michigan, has published a series of books that blend the characteristics of the trade book with those of the textbook on human geography. Each book normally concentrates on a single nation and devotes an unusual amount of space to this limited subject. For example, Vincent H. and Ruth M. Malmstrom's *Norway* (1955) contains about 150 pages of text and vivid pictures, in contrast to a typical social studies textbook that describes Norway in about ten pages. The coverage of economic geography is thorough—sufficient for a depth study on that aspect. The pictures and a portion of the text concern other aspects as well, so that some political and sociological exploration would be possible if supplementary materials were made available.

The American Heritage Publishing Company is issuing a series of American history books carefully researched by scholars and packed with information, illustrations, and excerpts from original sources. For example, Edouard Stackpole, curator of the Mystic Seaport Maritime Historical Association, was consultant in the preparation of *The Story of Yankee Whaling*. This book describes the technical aspects of sailing and whaling and also gives realistic details about the recruitment of whalers, their lives and the lives of their wives (the book does not shrink from informing the young reader that few whaling men shipped out more than once), shipwrecks, and mutinies. The richness of anecdote and the specificity of sources make these books well suited to serious research by the young scholar. Children come to trust books when they find that there has been no censoring. Some other titles in the series are *The California Gold Rush; Lexington, Concord, and Bunker Hill; Pirates; Men of Science; Steamboats on the Mississippi; Trappers and Mountain Men; Texas and the War with Mexico*. Six new titles are scheduled every year.

The American Heritage books can be read by upper-grade children or recited to younger and less able readers with the help of the excellent illustrations. On a similar reading level are the *Life* magazine series dealing with various countries, religions, and the earth's environment. These books are beautifully illustrated; the cameras have caught many interesting facets of life and art. But even more important, these books provide excellent data for the building of organizing concepts in sociology and anthropology. Among the titles in the series are *The Arab World, Southeast Asia, Tropical Africa, Israel, Scandinavia*, and *Spain*. (What is still badly needed, however, are books of this sort written specifically for the younger child.)

Scholarly works that deal historically with arts and crafts and with the values they express are becoming more plentiful. Christine Price's little gem, *Made in the Middle Ages*, includes passages like the following, which help the child become aware of scholarly sources:

> Clothes do not last as well as armor. Linens, woolens, and silks worn in the Middle Ages have come down to us as fragments, and we have to look at Medieval pictures and statues to see how the people dressed and how fashions changed.[13]

In many little corners of her book lie opportunities for helping children examine human motives. Consider the following:

Embroideries in threads of silk, gold, and silver were made richer still by the addition of jewels—rubies, sapphires, and pearls. Such clothes were ruinously expensive, and a nobleman might wear half his fortune on his back. Jewelry was an important item for the well-dressed person. Medieval people liked the sparkle of gems, but they valued jewelry for other reasons, as we shall see.[14]

Following through on this last sentence, Price gives the child the opportunity to examine the medieval European's conception of the world:

Rings set with precious stones were supposed to have strong magic powers. This . . . was expected to cure eye diseases and protect its owner against poisoning. An opal, when wrapped up in a bay leaf was supposed to make a man invisible. . . . This ring . . . has a secret charm engraved inside it which would not only cure toothache but also calm storms and tempests.[15]

Here in these quoted passages are found the essential chracteristics of the truly useful informational book. Price does not simply report that rings were believed to have magical powers. She presents particulars from which the general principle can easily be induced.

With her companion book, *Made in the Renaissance*, the Middle Ages and the Renaissance can be compared in terms of clothing, arms, and decorative objects—all interpreted in the light of human values. A child who believed, for example, that the supernaturalism of the Middle Ages was fully supplanted by the rationalism of the Renaissance might be enlightened by the following information:

Rings [in the Renaissance] were the most popular jewelry of all, and the hands of the rich were loaded with rings, almost to the fingertips. People still held to the old belief in the magic power of gems. The turquoise ring on page 30 was supposed to protect its wearer against a fall from his horse, while the rare toadstone, set in this curious ring of horn and silver, was highly valued for its power to guard its owner.[16]

Publishers of juvenile books are definitely trying to put out books that contain precise information on topics important today. There are, for example, several new children's books about migrant workers. Sandra Weiner's *Small Hands, Big Hands*

318

(Pantheon, 1970) is a photographic essay that lets the migrants tell their own story. *Mighty Hard Road: The Story of Cesar Chavez* (Doubleday, 1970), by James P. Terzian and Kathryn Cramer, tells of Chavez's early years in Arizona. Carli Laklan's *Migrant Girl* (McGraw-Hill, 1970) shows the realities of migrant life through a story about a teenage girl. Books such as these can be found for various levels of students and used to create depth studies of national problems.

The trend toward realism and authenticity can also be seen in some recently published history books. *Red Hawk's Account of Custer's Last Battle* (Pantheon, 1970), by Paul and Dorothy Goble, attempts to recreate an event as seen by someone who lived through it. *Two if by Sea* (Random House, 1970), by Leonard Everett Fisher, tells about Paul Revere's ride but pays more attention to facts and details than have other renditions. E. Brooks Smith and Robert Meredith have adapted a number of historic accounts for children. Among these are *Riding with Coronado* (Little, Brown, 1964), adapted from an account by one of Coronado's companions, and *The Quest of Columbus* (Little, Brown, 1966), adapted from accounts by Columbus's son.

Books very obviously continue to be an important aid to learning. And, as we have seen, quality books are available and can be found through excellent bibliographical guides. Nevertheless, more and better books are needed, especially well-written informational books for the younger child and for the slower, poorer reader.

319

Data Banks

We are beginning to develop new technologies that promise access to more information than any single book is likely to provide. Earlier in this book (pp. 42–54) a primitive data bank was described. Let us look at the development of such a bank and consider its potential.

For several years a research and development team headed by the author has been working at Teachers College, Columbia University, to develop and test prototype information systems for elementary school children. One of our purposes has been to create a setting in which we could carry on research into the inquiry of children who have access to enormous quantities of information on world cultures. The second has been to develop a set of operating principles to support the creation of information systems for young children.

Information is always edited: some things are put in and others are left out. It is also structured—that is, it is organized in ways that reflect the author's frames of reference. In the creation of information systems for students, both editing and structuring should be minimized or controlled in ways that can be made known to the student. It is important that the student understand how the information has been edited and structured.

We began the developmental work for data banks on certain communities by defining principles by which to edit and structure information.

Principle One: Use a very broad and well-defined category system for searching for data.

To reduce the editorial effect of the search for information, we selected a very broad category system. Such a system necessitated studying many aspects of each community. The more aspects of a community studied, the smaller one's bias becomes. The more defined the category system, the easier it is to specify the framework of the system so that the student knows how the information has been edited. The defined system also provides a basis for comparing and studying alternative systems.

Principle Two: Use original sources.

As many categories as possible were to be filled with information from firsthand sources.

Principle Three: Store the information in such a way that the students have maximum random access to it.

Rather than structure the information in a narrative, we attempted to store the information in modules that could be retrieved by the student in answer to questions he asked. A broad, intricate system helps the learner obtain exactly what he wants and reduces the amount of unwanted information that is retrieved in response to a request. Such a system may, however, most benefit the user who comprehends it.

Principle Four: Store the information in modes that can be defined and manipulated systematically.

Our initial strategy for accomplishing this was to include both pictorial and written material wherever possible and to make tape recordings of all written material. The student could extract data from pictures, written material, and tapes and, in many cases, from charts, maps, and graphs as well. These modes could be varied to explore the effects of each.

Principle Five: Organize the information systems in such a way that the structure of the conditions under which the students use the system is known.

Conditions under which students use the sources were manipulated precisely so that optimal use conditions could be identified, and alternative teaching strategies investigated.

Our next task was to select an exceedingly broad category system. At the suggestion of David E. Hunt, professor of psychology, Ontario Institute for Studies in Education, we began with the Index to the Human Relations File. This index contains more than seven hundred categories covering most aspects of a culture. The index system is organized into 79 major categories and 629 subcategories. The first three general categories deal with introductory and methodological materials. The 76 remaining general categories are listed below:

Machines	Clothing
Tools and Appliances	Adornment
Property	Exploitative Activities
Geography	Processing of Basic Materials
Human Biology	Building and Construction
Behavior Processes and	Structures
Personality	Equipment and Maintenance
Demography	of Buildings
History and Cultural Change	Settlements
Total Culture	Energy and Power
Language	Chemical Industries
Communications	Capital Goods Industries
Records	War
Food Quest	Social Problems
Animal Husbandry	Health and Welfare
Agriculture	Sickness
Food Processing	Death
Food Consumption	Religious Beliefs
Drink, Drugs, and	Religious Practices
Indulgence	Ecclesiastical Organization
Leather, Textiles, and	Numbers and Measures
Fabrics	Exchange

Marketing
Finance
Labor
Business and Industrial
  Organization
Travel and Transportation
Land Transport
Water and Air Transport
Living Standards and
  Routines
Recreation
Fine Arts
Entertainment
Individualism and Mobility
Social Stratification
Interpersonal Relations
Marriage
Family
Kinship
Kin Groups

Community
Territorial Organization
State
Government Activities
Political Behavior
Law
Offenses and Sanctions
Justice
Armed Forces
Military Technology
Exact Knowledge
Ideas about Nature and Man
Sex
Reproduction
Infancy and Childhood
Socialization
Adolescence, Adulthood, and
  Old Age
Education

322

These categories and their subcategories became our preliminary classification system.

We selected a pueblo community as content for the first data bank. A great deal of information is available on it, and it is relatively easy to get to. Unlike typical American communities, it shows the influence of Indian, Spanish, and Northern European cultures. The atypical nature of the community was desirable because so few children in the eastern United States have more than superficial knowledge of pueblo life. Therefore learning experiments could be designed to determine what the children had learned about the culture as a result of experience with the data bank.

Having selected the pueblo, we proceeded to identify sources of data about it. Charles Lange, of the Anthropological Department at Southern Illinois University, has written a comprehensive analysis (Lange, 1955) of the pueblo, based largely on his own research; he led us to many other sources and let us use many of the pictures taken during his years of field work. A recent economic analysis of the pueblo, prepared by a management consultant firm, led us to current sources on nearly all aspects of contemporary economic and political life. The Heye Foundation's Museum of the American Indian was an excellent source of information about artifacts, pictures, and manuscript material. The Smithsonian Institution has manuscripts from nineteenth century anthropologists and a large collection of pictures taken by nineteenth century anthropologists and other observers. The pictures proved to be especially valuable because they included many aspects of pueblo life before American culture impinged on it.

Spanish records and books on the Spanish occupation are numerous, but information was abundant in some cultural areas and meager in others. Frijoles Canyon in Bandolier National Park is a good source of archeological evidence about life in pre-Columbian times. In addition, hundreds of monographs, books, and pamphlets were consulted; and numerous personnel from Mexican and government agencies and the Pueblos themselves provided documentary sources. We visited the Pueblos and made numerous pictures and observations of their life.

Although we had many sources, vastly different quantities of material were available for various historical periods. Between the periods that were best documented, documents were scant for many important areas and plentiful for others. We decided to provide documents for the area file categories in four periods of the pueblo's life: the prehistoric period; the nineteenth-century period (1865–1895) after the Spanish influence but before much contact with English America; the early twentieth century, when contact with English America was increasing; and the contemporary period. We hoped that this grouping would enable the children to explore processes of cultural interchange and contemporary problems, but keep the data bank from becoming too complex. We attempted to fill all the subcategories of the area file with information from each of these periods. Since the system has been continuously revised, the number of categories for which documents were available has varied. At peak, over seventy percent of the categories contained at least one document.

These documents could be either pictures, written material, graphs, charts, or maps. In the animal husbandry category, for example, the material is built around several pictures accompanied by written material.

323

2202	The village of La Stella is in this land. There isn't very much rainfall here. The horses and cattle of the people who live in the villages have to go a long way to find grass to eat.
2054	The Indians of the village of La Stella have fences in their fields for their animals. The fencing in this picture is wire. When a field is fenced in, it is called a corral.
2247	Here are some horses in a corral. They are grazing—eating the grass.
2083	The children of La Stella love to ride on their ponies. Here is a little boy riding bareback at a ceremony near the village.
2266	The horses of the village of La Stella are used many times for celebrations. Here a horse is being led onto the field. It will be a part of the show the people of the village are putting on.
2360	Horses from the village are used for many other things. In this picture the horses are pulling the wagon to bring the hay back to the village.

All the material was photographed and reduced to 35 mm slides. Written material was also taped so that children who could not read it effectively could listen to it. The slides were placed in storage trays, and the tapes were numbered consecutively and placed nearby. Large maps of the pueblo, displays of pictures and artifacts, and posters were prepared. Carrels were built to hold tape recorders, slide projectors, a small projection screen, a small map, and a writing area.

To get information a student asked a question. The question was translated by an adult attendant into an area file category. The student took the number of the category to the storage center, located and retrieved slides and tapes, and carried them to his carrel. In the carrel, he showed himself the slides and listened to the tapes, seeking an answer to his question. When finished,

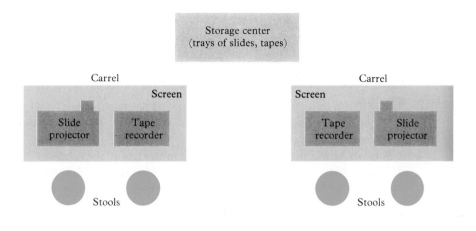

Layout of materials in the laboratory for the data bank

he returned the material and asked another question, beginning the cycle again.

Each student asked questions for several hours (one hour at a time) and then made a tape recording describing the pueblo. He was also interviewed to obtain impressions about what he had learned, difficulties he had in working with the system, his understanding of the task and other procedures.

The following means were used to control structure in the environment:

A. Tasks presented to students were varied in terms of content, complexity, and the restrictions they placed on students. For example, the "free inquiry" task simply asked the student to "learn about the culture until you feel ready to teach another child about it." The student could select his own content, level of complexity, and restrictions. A task asking the student to explore a certain social science concept with respect to the culture ("Find out if this is a matriarchal or patriarchal society") determined the content focus and intellectual complexity and placed restrictions on the search behavior of the student.

B. Control over the selection of information categories was varied. For example, the student might be free to select his own information or he might be presented with it or with the option of selecting more.

C. Input to students was varied. A task might be preceded by instruction in social science, by an advance organizer, or by other tasks or instructional programs.

D. Association with other students was varied. A student might work alone or in groups, and leadership patterns might be specified.

Manipulating these variables enabled us to use and study a large number of teaching strategies.

Schools working to make banks of information available to children need not engage in procedures as elaborate as the ones we followed. Using a fairly simple category system, they can collect and organize data on communities, nations, and other topics children might explore. The result could be a substantial support system for a curriculum.

Government Publications

The U.S. government, most foreign governments and their embassies and consulates, and many state and local governments provide publications that make good learning materials. The magazine *USSR* is available from the Russian embassy (the United States has the reciprocal privilege of distributing *Amerika* in the Soviet Union). Our federal government produces documents, books, and pamphlets on an amazing range of topics, from driving a nail to congressional hearings. The *Biweekly List of Selected United States Government Publications* is distributed free by the Superintendent of Documents. Bibliographies and price lists concerning particular government bureaus and topics can also be obtained. A full and current listing of government books and pamphlets, of course, is always available in the issues of the *Monthly Catalog, United States Government Publications*, to be found in virtually every school and public library. Much of the material so listed is simply written and can be easily adapted for the middle grades. The *Monthly Checklist of State Publications*, similarly useful, records documents and publications issued by the states and received by the Library of Congress.

Through the Government Printing Office, the Department of Defense distributes a series of more than fifty pocket guides to various nations. These are written in very simple language and give interesting information of the type often found in travel guides. They provide as much information as do many children's books. They also contain a few phrases in the appropriate language and suggest further readings.

An excellent source for the upper elementary grades and above is the series of over fifty U.S. Army handbooks, prepared by the Foreign Areas Studies Division to provide background material on many African, Latin-American, Asian, and even European countries. Each book was prepared by a group of scholars, and extensive bibliographies are included. The handbooks, each of which runs several hundred pages long, cover topics like the following, taken from the handbook on Senegal.

General Character of the Society
Historical Setting
Geography and Population
Ethnic Groups and Languages
Social Structure
Family
Health and Welfare
Education
Artistic and Intellectual Expression
Religion
Social Values[17]

All these topics are dealt with in the section on social background. Sections are also included on political background, economic background, and national security. Such thorough coverage of the major aspects of a society fits the model for cultural analysis presented as the core of the author's choice curriculum (pp. 411–14). The entire set of handbooks is available at an average cost of about four dollars.

The *Statistical Abstract* of the United States and the *Annuaire Statistique* of the United Nations, as well as many of the summaries of census data, provide enormous amounts of statistical data that can be used for a wide variety of purposes. Children with access to these data can compare nations on the basis of categories such as literacy, output, natural resources, and birth rate.

Thorough documents of racial status, opportunities, problems, and history are also available. A fascinating report, *Voting in Mississippi*, developed by the U.S. Commission on Civil Rights, tells the story of attempts to register blacks in Mississippi. It is a

327

contemporary historical document of great significance. Figure 11, for example, might be used to begin a group investigation. Other sources might be consulted, such as *The Social and Economic Status of Negroes in the United States, 1969* (Bureau of Labor Statistics and Bureau of the Census).

The self-instructional course in Swahili developed for use by Foreign Service personnel would give interested students a good look at Swahili and also stimulate inquiry into the development of the language and into other aspects of black culture. The course is simple enough to be used by any upper-grade student who is a fairly good reader.

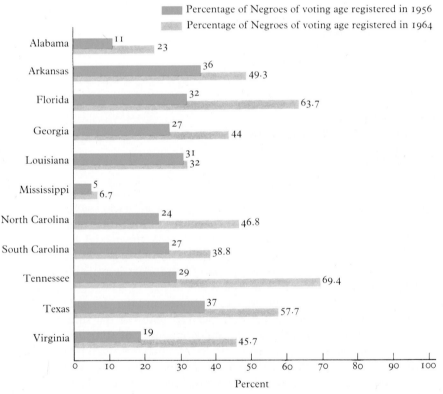

SOURCES: 1956 percentages: Price, *The Negro and The Ballot in the South* 9 (Southern Regional Council, 1959). 1964 percentages: Testimony of Wiley A. Branton, Director, Voter Education Project, Southern Regional Council, T 177-81.

Fig. 11. Estimated Negro voter registration in eleven southern states in 1956 and 1964

Both the teacher and the students should study primary sources of information whenever possible—that is, documents, diaries, tracts, and other firsthand accounts of events and policies. Various State Department pamphlets and bulletins are particularly interesting in their explanation and defense of current U.S. foreign policies: the pamphlet *U.S. Policy Toward Cuba* (May 1964) describes the assumptions on which U.S. actions in the Caribbean are based; *The United States and Africa* (July 1964) explains our problems in dealing with both the new African nations and the older regimes. Such pamphlets on current affairs help children to analyze causes and effects in politics and economics.

The obvious disadvantage of governmental material is its bias, but some interesting studies may arise because of the very differences in point of view. Much of the material available from the French embassy can be used in the study of world affairs to provide comparisons with U.S. positions on international issues. Fourth-graders might view a filmstrip from a South African information agency, "South Africa, the Other U.S.A.," which describes industrial products, occupations, native welfare programs, and living conditions in the large cities. Then the class might view a filmstrip produced by *Life* magazine, which documents the policy of apartheid, again in terms of industrial conditions, occupations, government treatment of natives, and living conditions in the large cities. Soon the discussion is not about South Africa at all, but about the use of emphasis and language and photographic style to create an impression.

Various instructional or do-it-yourself manuals published by the federal government are useful in model building and other kinds of classroom construction. Farmers' Bulletin no. 1720 of the U.S. Department of Agriculture, for example, offers detailed authentic directions on how to make adobe bricks and how to use the bricks in the construction of pueblo apartments, mission churches, and farm buildings. Authenticity in constructing objects, of course, is extremely important; playthings from a make-believe world merely "give the student concrete ideas of the way things are *not* and discourage any effort to discover the truth."[18] In making dolls, buildings, masks, clothing, furniture, utensils, or any other objects simulating real life, the children should be led to use authentic construction materials and to follow accurate instructions and procedures.

329

Other Kinds of Publications

Teachers who want to use the depth study approach to history whereby children learn about people and events from source documents have at last an exciting collection of such documents. Developed in England and Canada and distributed by Grossman Publishers in New York, the Jackdaws are kits containing packets of materials (facsimile charts, posters, letters, ship logs, and so on), a teacher-student guide, and some general descriptors (broadsheets). They are available in a series that concentrates on English history (the battle of Trafalgar, Joan of Arc, the South Sea Bubble, for example) but includes also subjects such as the Russian Revolution and the Spanish Inquisition. Two other series are also available—on science (Newton and gravitation, for example) and on Canadian subjects (such as Selkirk and the RCMP).

The selection of topics very much reflects a British point of view, but the U.S. student will probably profit from and be delighted by a different perspective. For example, the Jackdaw on the American Revolution contains a point of view that is different enough from the one usually contained in American texts that it is likely to encourage objectivity on the subject.

The Jackdaws characteristically deal with topics in a matter-of-fact way. For example, the Jackdaw entitled "Shaftesbury and the Working Children" is described as follows:

> In 1875 George Brewster, aged fourteen, was sent up a chimney to sweep it; he swallowed too much soot and died. The custom of sending little children up chimneys had been attacked by Jonas Hanway as early as 1773, and an Act of Parliament of 1823 improved working conditions for the children employed in factories and mines. It laid down that thirteen to eighteen year-olds should work *only* sixty-nine hours a week, nine to thirteen year-olds forty-eight hours a week, and children under nine should not be employed at all. But it was another half-century before George Brewster's death finally roused public opinion and enabled Lord Shaftesbury to get a bill passed by Parliament to prevent the use of climbing boys.
>
> Lord Shaftesbury was the great emancipator of factory children and was tireless in advocating a few hours compulsory education for them. This Jackdaw embraces the whole struggle against child slavery in the 19th century, using contemporary engravings, newspaper cuttings and speeches to present the full horror of the situation.[19]

A social studies series called *A Social Studies Picture Program* (Grand Rapids, Mich.: Fideler Co., 1970) could operate much the same way as a data bank. It breaks away from the textbook format by providing materials for independent study: forty-five kits, each of which is made up of large pictures, a text containing information about the pictures, and a teacher's guide to help teachers involve their students in inquiry and discussion. The kits deal with U.S. history as well as with major countries of the world. The difficulty in obtaining good source material on some subjects is evident here: Asia and Africa are treated in one kit each.

Another series with an international perspective has been derived from the work of the Oxford Committee for Famine Relief (Oxfam). This committee was founded in 1942 to help feed European victims of the war, and after the war it extended its activities around the world. As part of their work this British group has published a number of pamphlets describing cases of need in the world's developing nations. These pamphlets provide a solid introduction to the human problems of developing countries. Each one focuses on a person, a school, a town, and a disaster —that is, a specific situation of human struggle to improve life.

The pamphlets contain pictures, dramatic narratives, documents, and suggested activities. They are now published in the United States by Houghton Mifflin Company as *Case Studies of Developing Nations* (1967). The following titles provide some idea of the topics dealt with.

Ecuador: Learning by radio
Nigeria: A boy and leprosy
Tibet: Refugees from the roof of the world
Botswana (Bechuanaland): "This is a hungry year"
East Pakistan: In the wake of the cyclone
Korea: The aftermath of war

At the Ontario Institute for Studies in Education in Toronto, a group of educators have developed a collection of materials that may become the prototype for future inquiry kits. Designed to help children explore the social life of the 1930s, the kit contains films, newspaper clippings, the text of speeches by prominent people (Franklin Roosevelt, for example), and other memorabilia that the student can use to create a picture of life in that decade. Further information about "Ten Years in a Box" can be obtained by writing the Ontario Institute.

331

One example of the simulations available for teaching various concepts or parts of the social sciences themselves is an approach to teaching archeological methods. The simulation is called DIG (Lakeside, Calif.: Interact, 1969) and was developed by Jerry Lipetzky. In the simulation, teams of students bury artifacts representing cultures they have created. Other teams of students excavate the materials and reconstruct the cultures. The excavations are conducted in such a way that they teach ways of identifying artifacts, detecting patterns among the artifacts, and making inferences from the patterns.

The Coca-Cola Company has, with the help of the Institute of Ecology at the University of Georgia, produced a teaching aid called "Make Your Own World." It is designed to help children become aware of the ecological balance in their environment. The children are divided into eleven teams representing various community interests, such as farmers and developers, and interests within the environment, such as wildlife, water, air. New projects are proposed for the community, and the various interests vote on them. Since all the interests are intertwined and involved in the future of the community, there are no winners or losers— only, one hopes, a better world for all.

There are available some materials that concentrate on the personal dimension of the social studies. One of these, *First Things* (1970), is published by Guidance Associates and was developed by their staff, Virginia Schone, and Joseph C. Grannis. *First Things*, a series of filmstrips and cassettes or records, begins with a picture story about a child attempting to establish his identity; it goes on to portray how group activities and conflicts reinforce his identity. The focus is on the individual and his learning to respect others by first learning self-respect.

Paulist Press has published several series of books in a similar vein, but directed toward teenagers. A variety of views are presented on many current problems, and students are encouraged to form opinions consistent with their own moral judgments. In the *Discovery Series* (1969), for example, students analyze various elements in the communications network, looking for the forces behind it and its impact on the reader or viewer. Although written for Catholic young people, this program offers much to all young people who are trying to cope intelligently with today's problems.

Another program that could become an important part of the personal dimension of the social studies utilizes research by David

C. McClelland and Richard C. Atkinson concerning achievement motivation. Albert Alschuler, Diane Tabor, and James McIntyre have published a thorough description of the approach in *Teaching Achievement Motivation* (Middletown, Conn.: Education Ventures, 1970). The approach uses games, discussions, and problem-solving activities to help people explore their motivations, understand their attitudes toward achievement, and want to achieve more. The developers cite substantial research evidence about the success of achievement motivation training and provide a number of devices and exercises for implementing it.

Recently there have been attempts to use a multi-media approach to teach children about the city. One filmstrip series, put out by Hudson Photographic Industries, seeks to offset the impression a child is likely to have of the city as a huge, frightening place.

> This series of filmstrips is designed to explore the beauty and joy of city life from the point of view of the small child. Through these filmstrips, the four seasons in the city are recreated. Important holidays are explored, as well as the simple day-to-day activities that relate to the lives of children. The overriding concepts, however, are that city life can be enjoyed, that children have an important place in city life, and that the daily events in the lives of people have a logic, an order, a structure. Similarly, there is an order and structure to nature revealed by the pattern of the changing seasons.[20]

333

Although the developers were especially concerned with reaching the deprived child or the child with a reading or language disability, these filmstrips can be used in any classroom. The commentary is short, and students need read only signs. The photographs have been imaginatively used as the basis of the material.

Warren Schloat Productions have also used audio-visual materials to deal with a current problem—race relations. Their titles include *What is Prejudice?*, *The Ghettoes of America*, and *Minorities Have Made America Great*. Most of this material is directed toward the high school student, but *The Black and White Statue* could be used with younger children. It tells about a man who puts a small statue of a black boy on his lawn and one morning finds that the statue has been painted white. These materials seek to help children solve some of their problems with regard to race by examining them openly.

Resource Persons

In every community, no matter how small, there are people who know something or do something about which children should know. Examine accounts of the teaching units conducted at the Lincoln School of Teachers College, Columbia University, during the late 1920s and the 1930s. One of the distinguishing marks of these cooperatively planned, problem-solving units was the thorough and appropriate use of resource persons. For example, in the unit on ships and navigation one group of fifth-graders visited the liner *St. Louis* and interviewed the purser.

> The purser explained each important step in the mechanical operation of driving his ship through the water. The boys and girls inspected the motors while their guide explained how they were operated. He showed them where the oil flowed into the cylinders, and told them how compressed air ignited the oil, and how hot gas from this fire drove the piston. He also showed them the two great propeller shafts which are turned by the motors. Then the children followed these shafts aft through the bulkhead doors and saw where they emerged at the stern of the ship to connect with the propeller. They already knew, of course, where the propellers were and that they pushed the ship through the water, so the story of the way that the *St. Louis* gets its power was complete, and the details sufficiently clear to satisfy them and meet their needs at this grade level.[21]

Somewhat later on in the tour of the ship there arose another question:

> The children asked the purser to tell them how lifeboats were lowered. They grouped themselves along the taffrail while he explained that a place was reserved on one of the lifeboats for each person on the ship, how they would enter the boats in case of need, and how the davits would operate to swing the boats free of the ship and lower them into the water.[22]

This account illustrates first-rate use of a resource person. It adheres to the following criteria for such interviews:

1. The children are well prepared beforehand with information from books and experiments.
2. They are prepared to ask questions and to integrate the answers with other information. They are not dependent on the rehearsed tour or lecture.

334

3. The contact is planned so that there is room for spontaneous questions and ideas.
4. The inquiry is conducted so that the resource person has access to concrete examples of every point or idea he offers. By no means must children always be taken to the scene of the physical material (for example, to a ship). An antique dealer, for example, either can be visited in his shop or can come to school, bringing along samples or pictures. But in any case, without illustrative materials very few adults can effectively lecture to children or answer their questions.
5. The use of the resource person (for example, the purser) is a natural outgrowth of the study. The children need him as a source of information.
6. The resource person has control of his subject. He can speak from experience, and he can efficiently guide the children on a tour and make sure they see the important things.

The same unit of study that dealt with the ship's purser led to a study of India. The children had found that ships go somewhere, and they became interested in some of the destinations. Another resource person appeared at the school.

When Ben's mother, Mrs. Z, learned of the group's interest in Indian hand products she came to school, bearing a collection of these articles. The children examined each article with interest, and asked Ben's mother how it was made, what it was made of, and how it was used or worn. The boys and girls tried on the shawls and scarves, and Mrs. Z adjusted them in the native manner. . . .

In a picture of a temple which Ben's mother displayed, the children saw with amazement that a cow "stood on the church steps!" Mrs. Z told them that the Hindus considered the cow a sacred animal, and gave them an idea of the various religions prevalent in India.[23]

Not long after the visit by Mrs. Z, still another visitor made an appearance:

A day or two later, Ben's father appeared in the classroom bringing with him a model of a houseboat that is typical of those used on the rivers in the hill country of India, and also a sort of sedan chair which he called a "dandy." With the models and through the children's questions and his answers the class gained an idea of these and other means of transportation in India. Mr. Z then placed a fez-like cap on Herbert's head and skillfully wound around it a silk cloth in the true Indian turban fashion.[24]

The potential use of resource persons is almost infinite. Industrial workers and executives can bring special knowledge to the children. As part of their public relations departments, business firms such as telephone companies provide experienced resource personnel. Local storekeepers, policemen, political officials, members of chambers of commerce, recreation workers—all have special knowledge about a local situation. In fact, it is inconceivable that a study could effectively concentrate on a local community without the involvement of resource persons. The teacher cannot have the varied information and insights necessary to do an adequate job of instruction, and there are too few reading materials on community affairs written at the elementary school level.

The willingness of local citizens may become an American legend. A few years ago, for example, one class in a Midwestern city undertook to build a combined playhouse and storage facility for younger children, a little house to stand on the playground. A local architect helped the children draw up plans and went into the intricacies of architectural planning and drawing. Local vendors of building materials discussed timberwork and carpentry and helped select the most suitable material. A local cement firm poured the foundation and explained its industrial operations in general. A PTA committee helped with the financing. The social world around the school had become the chief instructional resource for the unit.[25]

Realia

The unit discussed above involved first-rate use of Hindu and Indian realia, those things (such as costumes, tools, dwellings, and religious objects) that relate to the daily living of people. In general, children are better able to picture a culture or society if they see real things, real activities. Watching a train being moved by switchmen at a railroad yard leaves a far more lasting impression than any picture. Better than any story, a visit to the local airport supplies the reality of human interaction.

Realia should be more than merely a pretty display. They should be accompanied by ideas from books, movies, pictures, and resource people. Consider, for example, the kinds of ideas that could be inspired by the realia donated by Mr. and Mrs. Z:

These are a pair of vases that came from India. They are handmade. First, they cut the design out of brass with a knife. The person that makes these gets only twelve or thirteen cents for his work.

In India men wear shawls, too. This is a Kashmiri shawl of Pashmina wool. Notice the design. It is supposed to look like the Jhelem River which winds around the city of Arnagar.

This is a Buddhist prayer wheel. Inside is a roll of papers. When it is turned around one way a prayer has been said. When it is turned around the other way, a curse has been said.

This is a beggar's bowl. They attach a string in such a way that they can carry it over the shoulder. Many people spend most of their lives begging. It is part of their religion. Some beggars don't wear many clothes at all, some cover themselves with ashes.[26]

Used this way, realia can help in the formation of ideas and concepts. They can inspire further inquiry.

The field trip is the time-honored device for taking children to realia and resource people, but the sites visited should be chosen with discrimination. Often a site that may not at first seem most appropriate for a certain study will prove to be more suitable than a more obvious choice. For instance, a visit to a real farm is not necessarily the best way of studying agriculture or even life on the farm. A zoo farm or a local green nursery may staff experts better qualified to discuss plant growth or food production with young children. Moreover, in studying farm production, a group of children may take special interest in or need more enlightenment on some particular phase of the food industry—processing, storage, or productivity. In such cases, a visit to a mill, grain elevator, or fertilizer plant may be preferable. Probably the choice of the site for a field trip should not be made until the study is fairly well advanced, when interests and needs have become evident—unless, of course, the trip is to be used as a stimulus to questioning.

The field trip imparts a sense of realism and fixes information in the child's mind better than other media of study except possibly television and motion pictures. The field trip enables children to see spontaneous human interaction in the adult world. For example, to see a legislative body function is to see the interaction of its members. Only when congressional hearings or political conventions are televised does one see anything like it in the political sphere. One can read about a legislature, examine the laws it passes, look at the voting records of its members, follow issues in the newspapers, correspond with its members, and obtain a great deal of information and ideas about it. However, the essence of a legislature is the interaction of its members.

The interaction of workers in a factory, the excitement when a plane comes in at an airport, and the confusion in the city room of a newspaper are difficult to get from any source but direct experience. Of course, a sense of excitement should not be all that the child derives from seeing a legislature or newsroom in action. He should be carefully coached beforehand to look for certain subtle operations; he should, if possible, be accompanied by informed guides; his chaperons from school should be briefed sufficiently so that they can help him sort out the important information from the apparent confusion. If the child and those who aid him are not well prepared, he might assume, upon seeing the vote on a bill, that he is seeing the whole story of lawmaking; the caucus, the hearing, and the trading of votes will not become known to him. The field trip, while it can be an exciting stimulus to learning, can be really successful only if supported by many other learning activities. The function of the field trip should be to sharpen the child's perception of human interaction.

Many museums in large cities maintain educational staffs that conduct lessons, distribute bibliographies, and provide other instructional services—all of which can stimulate or further unusual inquiry. [27] For example, the Philadelphia Museum of Art provides combined lessons and tours, including one dealing with "The Woman in Art Through the Ages," conducted for third- or fourth-graders. The tour, which illustrates changing styles of art, might be used by a teacher to introduce a historical study of the relation of art to other areas of life.

The University Museum of the University of Pennsylvania provides, in addition to the museum exhibits, pamphlets that show children how to construct some unusually effective models and handicrafts. For example, their list of crafts for the unit "The History of Records" includes directions for making the buffalo-skin records of the Plains Indians, wampum belts, an Inca quipu, a Babylonian clay tablet, a wax tablet, a scroll, and papyrus paper (by the ancient method). In addition the museum sells, or provides without charge, directions for making a number of useful models. Included with a model of an Egyptian nobleman's house excavated at Tell el 'Amarna is a description of the estate so detailed that the daily life of the times might easily be dramatized or discussed by the children. Several other models of houses are available; thus, with the help of other sources, children could compare the

338

home life of several peoples living in critical eras of Western civilization.

Many other museums offer tours, loans, and printed materials. The Commercial Museum in Philadelphia periodically devotes one floor or another to exhibits of a single nation or culture and provides a complete program of lessons, tours, and classroom exhibits. The Museum of Science and Industry in Chicago includes exhibits of modern industrial society, as do the Henry Ford Museum and Greenfield Village in Dearborn, Michigan, the Smithsonian Institution in Washington, the California Museum of Science and Industry in Los Angeles, and several other museums nationwide. Many smaller museums are also exceptionally rewarding. For example, from the Henry Frances Dupont Winterthur Museum in Greenville, Delaware, the author has borrowed sets of slides on the American decorative arts, which have been used by his pupils to illustrate their study of life in colonial America.

A surprising number of small towns have historical societies that maintain small depositories of materials illustrating local history. Frequently one finds copies of the local newspaper going back a hundred years or more. Poems, letters, and other writings of early-day citizens will often be collected. Maps, the stories of early industries, the decisions of the town government, records of good times and bad—all these are available. In large cities the library or historical society frequently maintains a department on local history. In small towns, the material is often tended by one or two interested volunteers.

339

NOTES

1. David Riesman, *The Lonely Crowd* (Garden City, N.Y.: Doubleday, 1953).

2. J. D. McAulay, "Social Studies in the Primary Grades," *Social Education* 18 (December 1954), pp. 357–58.

3. Ralph C. Preston, "Teaching for Depth," *Childhood Education* 36 (January 1960).

4. As in the social studies units carried out at the Horace Mann–Lincoln Institute at Teachers College, Columbia University. See, for example, Tompsie Baxter and Bess M. Young, *Ships and Navigation* (New York: Teachers College, 1933).

5. C. Benjamin Cox and Byron G. Massialas, *Social Studies in the United States: A Critical Appraisal* (New York: Harcourt, Brace & World, 1967), pp. 8–9.

6. Scott, Foresman; Silver Burdett; Ginn; American Book; Rand McNally; Follett; Heath; Holt, Rinehart & Winston; Allyn and Bacon; and Macmillan. To some extent Allyn and Bacon and Macmillan have introduced the wider world a little earlier than have the others.

7. Paul R. Hanna and Genevieve Anderson Hoyt, *Guidebook to Accompany* At School (Chicago: Scott, Foresman, 1963).

8. Kenneth D. Wann, *Living in Our Times Series* (Boston: Allyn & Bacon, 1962–).

9. The World Affairs Guides published by Teachers College, Columbia University, Bureau of Publications, include *Studying Africa in Elementary and Secondary Schools* (1962), *Studying South America in Elementary and Secondary Schools* (1962), and *Studying the Middle East in Elementary and Secondary Schools* (1962), and *Studying the World: Selected Resources* (1962). Two other Kenworthy books containing resources are *Telling the UN Story: New Approaches to Teaching about the UN and Its Related Agencies* (Dobbs Ferry, N.Y.: Oceana, 1963) and *Free and Inexpensive Materials on World Affairs* (New York: Teachers College, Columbia Univ., 1963).

10. Charlotte Huck and Doris Young, *Children's Literature in the Elementary School* (New York: Holt, Rinehart & Winston, 1961), p. 132.

11. May Arbuthnot, *Children and Books* (Chicago: Scott, Foresman, 1957), p. 559.

12. Ibid.

13. Christine Price, *Made in the Middle Ages* (New York: Dutton, 1961), p. 30.

14. Ibid., p. 36.

15. Ibid., p. 39.

16. Christine Price, *Made in the Renaissance* (New York: Dutton, 1963), p. 33.

17. Foreign Areas Studies Division, *U. S. Army Area Handbook for Senegal* (Washington: American Univ., 1963).

18. Ernest Horn, *Methods of Instruction in the Social Studies*, part 15: *Report of the Commission on the Social Studies*, American Historical Assn. (New York: Scribner, 1937), p. 421.

19. John Langdon-Davies, "Shaftesbury and the Working Children," Jackdaw Publications no. 7 (London, n.d.).

20. *Teachers Guide to H.P.I. Filmstrips* (Irvington-on-Hudson, N.Y.: Hudson Photographic Industries, 1969), p. 1.

21. Tompsie Baxter and Bess M. Young, *Ships and Navigation* (New York: Teachers College, Columbia Univ., 1933), p. 26.

22. Ibid., p. 27.

23. Ibid., pp. 35–36.

340

24. Ibid., p. 38.

25. This construction project was observed in the schools of Ferndale, Michigan. The exchange program between Newark, Delaware, and La Garde-Freinet, France, described in chapter 8, is another excellent example of the use of resource persons.

26. Baxter and Young, *Ships and Navigation*, p. 38.

27. For a general description of museum collections and services, consult Erwin O. Christensen, ed., *Museums Directory of the United States and Canada* (Washington: American Assn. of Museums, 1961).

341

STRATEGIES FOR TEACHING THE ELEMENTS OF INQUIRY

It may seem that the least controversial part of the social studies curriculum deals with study skills. But what are the basic study skills in the social studies? There are some simple ones, like learning to use an alphabetical index; but the important skills are complex and require a long time to learn.

Study skills in the social studies are more than psychomotor skills. They are made up of ideas and mental operations: they are the skills of thinking. What, for example, must we do in order to read a map? We must learn the special system and language of cartographers, how they use small amounts of space to represent large amounts of space and symbols to represent things and actions. Similarly, using a reference work requires that we learn a system for retrieving information. Studying requires thinking in the sense of asking critical questions, gathering appropriate information, and handling it wisely.

The skills of the social studies approximate those scientists use in studying society. The skills that should result from the social studies curriculum are those needed to carry out objective and thoughtful studies of social phenomena. Why is this? Because our most important education is for the self-education of the future. Our students must become lifelong learners. They must be able to obtain information and ideas and to handle many different values and concepts. We are unsure what facts our students will need to know. We can, however, teach them how to find information and build ideas.

Four kinds of scientific activity form the basis of most social studies skills: making observations (or using the data of others); making categories that note similarities and differences in data (or using the categories of others); making inferences about relationships or causation (or using the inferences of others); making judgments about the goodness or desirability of events (or examining the judgments of others). After examining these general study skills, we will consider methods of creating a self-instructional skills laboratory, methods of developing a sequential curriculum in the geographic skills, and specific approaches to skills learning.

Making Observations

Social life—human life in groups—is the subject matter of the social studies. The study of social life rests on the collection of information about human interaction. There are three general sources of such information: direct observation of social life, records of past events, and relics from which human interaction may be inferred. To develop independence in the study of social life, the student needs to learn how to collect samples of human behavior and how to handle records and relics of the past. Because social life is all around him, the student can be taught to collect samples of political behavior, economic behavior, small- and large-group behavior, and so on.

Even the younger child can make observations about his culture. He can observe parent-child relationships, the mass media, the legislative process—mechanisms by which culture is transmitted. He sees older brother playing baseball with younger brother, father fishing with sons, mother cooking with daughter. His awareness of these relationships and processes can help him in the study of anthropology, the creation and transmission of culture.

From the earliest years the student can observe and record words, glances, and patterns of interaction. He can learn to use observational schedules and attitude inventories, and to make

diagrams of interaction. In other words, the techniques of social psychology appropriate for studying small-group behavior should be introduced to him. In the primary grades he can observe family patterns; by high school he can be observing nonverbal communication, groups making decisions, and other large-group behaviors.

Large groups are more difficult to observe directly, since the mass of behavior is so much greater and involves sampling. Sampling theory can be introduced, however, in the upper elementary grades. Interview and questionnaire techniques can also be learned by students at that level. Imagine junior and senior high school students studying how the fame of popular singing groups spreads, making observations about when and how people encounter their records and films, what they and their parents say about them, and so on. By the high school years, students should be prepared to make observations about interracial behavior, class behavior, and other large-group interactions. They can observe advertisements (the use of sports and entertainment figures, and so on) in preparation for the study of attempts to influence large-group behavior.

Since the past is not as easily observed as the present, students investigating the past have had to work mostly from the observa-

tions of others. Recently, however, there has been a resurgence
in the use of original documents that provide the student with
the same kind of data the historian uses to make his observations.
The Educational Services Incorporated project is developing
elementary school resource units on colonial America including
records from town meetings, newspapers, letters, and other
materials from that period. Museums like Colonial Williamsburg
provide artifacts and activities that can be directly observed or
brought to the student through still and moving pictures. A book
by Byron Massialas and Benjamin Cox provides many ideas for
using original documents at the secondary school level,[1] as does
Edwin Fenton's discussion of inquiry in secondary schools.[2] The
social studies magazine *Social Education* has run a series that
supplies packets of materials about important court decisions,
including judges' opinions and facts about the cases.

I cannot stress too strongly the necessity for providing observational data in history. History will probably continue to be a
large part of the social studies curriculum, and it is necessary to
free the student from complete dependence on the observations
of others. Probably this cannot be done effectively if the course of
study attempts to cover too much ground. If, for example, a
single course tries to deal with the whole of the ancient world, or
the period from the exploration of North America through the
colonies, then there will be little time for the student to gather
information from original documents and build ideas from the
information.

Teaching students to make observations is at times as simple
as "getting the facts about population growth in our town" and
at times so complex that special collections of documents have to
be prepared. The skills program should progress from gross observation of the familiar in the primary grades to the development
and administration of observation schedules and examination of
documents by high school students.

Using the Observations of Others

If all we studied were what we can experience directly, our education would be sadly confined. We have to use sources prepared by
others. The student tries to gather information from other people
directly, such as from resource visitors, or indirectly, such as from

reference books, resource books, films, or filmstrips. What skills are required for this task?

Probably the skill most difficult to learn but most fundamental in using other people as sources involves figuring out the basis they used for selecting what they did and did not include. Every source edits the data somewhat. An author, an interviewee, a film maker uses some process of selection. Encyclopedias cannot tell about every facet of a nation; they tell a few things in a compressed language. A person who has visited another country can tell us only what he saw and remembered. The more "scientific" the source, the more we can hope the slant or basis for editing is made clear. Pressure groups, of course, deliberately select facts that will persuade us to their point of view.

The child's introduction to identifying the basis of editing should be gentle and natural. The teacher can point out some of his biases. "When I tell you about the Pueblo Indians, notice that I let my interest in art take over. I brought many baskets and rugs and pottery and drums to show you. Our visitor next week is interested in dances—he will emphasize those. Each of us omits many things that impress other people."

In every unit of study there is the opportunity to have the children compare facts from different sources. Middle graders, for instance, will find that the magazine *USSR*, distributed by the Soviet embassy in Washington, includes many facts about Russia that are not included in American social studies texts. From the middle grades through high school, studies of speeches, advertising, propaganda, and even the most standard sources will reveal how the frame of reference affects the facts selected.

By the end of high school, students should have a set of mental checklists that they can use to authenticate sources and determine how balanced they are. For example, a student should be able to say to himself: "Whenever there is conflict or controversy, there is likely to be distortion by most observers. So I have to look at the versions produced by several observers who may represent several points of view."

Obtaining the data of others involves learning to use libraries, standard references, and interviews.[3] Some traditional ways of teaching these mechanics are still very effective.

1. See that the students have many problems to solve and then help them learn how to use the references that contain the the information they need.

2. Through the years, see that they call on resources (government summaries, business reports, newspaper files) that get them closer and closer to on-the-spot reporting.

3. Junior and senior high school students should compare different sources, such as the claims of advertisers with information from consumer magazines, a newspaper editorial with one expressing a different view, or a pamphlet with one published by an opposing group. The student should learn not only how bias slants data, but how to find the good data hidden under the slant.

Exercises like the following help the student practice deciding which items in a passage are opinion and which are factual. The student should learn to sort out the factual from the opinionated not only in the writing of others, but also in his own writing.

Number your paper from 1 to 3. Skip five lines under each number. Under each number below is a report. Read it carefully. Then decide whether the report gives opinions that do not belong in it. If the report gives no opinions, write "An objective report" after its number on your answer paper. If there are opinions in the report that do not belong there, write "Not an objective report" after its number. Then copy on your answer paper the sentences that show the opinions of the reporter.

Remember that the information in a report should be fact. The report should be objective. Opinions that are not supported by facts are not objective. They do not belong in an objective report.

1. A Chinese Secret

Hundreds of years ago the Chinese discovered a way of making paper from scraps of silk and other cloth. I don't think there is anything that the Chinese did not invent. As they did with so many of their discoveries, they tried to keep this one a secret. The secret remained with them for many years.

A war caused the Chinese to lose their previous secret. After a hundred years of fighting, Arab warriors had conquered land stretching from Spain to India and China. What great warriors they must have been! In 704 they captured some Chinese papermakers and forced them to tell their secret. I don't think that was fair. At last the secret was out.

The art of papermaking spread quickly to all parts of the Arab world, to Europe, and finally to the Americas. A paper mill was set up in Bagdad in 793. There is a record of a paper mill operating in Egypt by the year 900. By 1100 there was one in Morocco, and by 1150, one in Spain. From Spain the secret of papermaking passed to the rest of Europe. The Europeans were happy to learn the secret. When the earliest settlers came to America from Europe, they brought the craft of papermaking with them. American paper is probably the best in the world.

2. Land Purchases of the United States

From a small colony in Jamestown, Virginia, the United States has grown to a nation of fifty states that stretch from the Atlantic to the Pacific coast and beyond. This land did not always belong to the United States. Some of it was given by other countries. Certain sections were added as a result of wars. Many large pieces of land were added to the United States through purchase.

The first of these land purchases was called the Louisiana Purchase. In 1803, the United States government bought 825,000 square miles of land from France for $15 million. This vast area stretched from the Mississippi River to the Rocky Mountains, and from Canada to the Gulf of Mexico. This one purchase more than doubled the size of the United States. A smaller purchase in 1819 added Florida to the growing country. Another famous purchase is known as the Gadsden Purchase. The United States paid the government of Mexico $10 million for 45,535 square miles of land between the Gila River and the present border of Mexico. The most recent purchase was completed in 1867. In that year the United States paid Russia about $7 million for Alaska.

In 260 years, from Jamestown to Alaska, the United States has multiplied its size many times through these great purchases. For a small amount of money the United States acquired land for its rapidly expanding population. The rich soil and great natural resources of these lands have already more than paid for themselves.

3. Alaska, the Last Frontier

Throughout the history of the United States, several places have marked the last frontier, or the edge of settled country. I suppose even New York City was once the last frontier. At different times the Appalachian Mountains, the Mississippi River, and the Rocky Mountains were each called the last frontier. Each at one time marked the border of an area that was wild and had few settlers, an area with great natural resources yet to be developed. Now that all the country from Maine to California has been settled and developed, the new state of Alaska represents America's only frontier.

The development of this new frontier into a rich, strong state is only a matter of time. Alaska's long cold winters have slowed its progress. In winter, transportation comes to a standstill, but more and better airplanes are helping to solve that problem. Industry has had to stop during the winter. Mighty machines and newer methods are being developed to solve this problem. I think it will take less than fifty years for Alaska to become a productive member of the United States.

The new state of Alaska has a great supply of natural resources. Industry is helping to develop these resources, but there are still many things that stand in the way of Alaska's industrial growth. When the problems of industry are solved, Alaska will become a stronger member of the family of states. Someday Alaska will be the richest state in America.[4]

The student should have many experiences such as those provided by the above exercise. The exercises do not have to be pre-packaged, but can come in the natural course of the student's inquiry into the world about him.

Learning to Build Categories

Were we to do no more than observe social interaction, we would have simply a mass of data. We would increase our contact with the world, but would not be able to think about it more effectively. To handle information meaningfully, we need to build categories that organize it. From nursery school through high school, the building of categories should be worked on. It begins with noting likenesses and differences in data, grouping the information, and naming the resulting categories.

In the first years of school, the children can classify activities in the community, finding activities that get them from one place to another, activities that make things, activities that grow things, and so on. Gradually, they can build categories that distinguish economic, political, religious, and other activities. The students learn to handle categories that are more precise and more general at the same time as they make finer distinctions and deal with larger slices of reality.

In analyzing face-to-face interaction, the student becomes able to identify clique behavior; in dealing with macroeconomics, he becomes able to form concepts such as the concept of an under-developed nation. In the study of original documents ("What kinds of events did Governor Bradford and Captain John Smith both mention [avoid] in their diaries?") and current political events ("What were the likenesses and differences of voters supporting Republican and Democratic candidates?"), the student should form, test, and revise categories. When he has observed that certain products and climates are associated in one place, he should see if they are associated in another and, if not, be helped to revise his categories.

A relatively simple teaching strategy can be used in helping children to build and revise categories.

1. Determine when, in the course of a project, the students have collected enough data (as data about UNESCO) that likenesses and differences can be well documented.
2. Ask the students to classify the information they have collected on whatever basis they choose, working as small groups or individuals (classifying, for example, kinds of UNESCO activities, participation by member nations, kinds of controversial issues that have arisen).
3. Have them compare the categories they use and the ways in which these categories reveal different things in the data (as the difference between technological exchange, educational projects, and cultural projects).
4. Help them debate the usefulness of the different category systems they have developed (as describing activities on the basis of money required versus type of assistance or exchange given).

350

Using the Categories of Others

While we should encourage students to build and use their own categories, we should also help them test their categories against those used by professional scholars. Two methods can be used to do this.

1. The student compares categories he has built with the ones social scientists use.
2. We systematically introduce the student to the categories social scientists use.

As the student studies the economics of his community, nation, or other nations, he can learn the categories of economists (market, exchange, scarcity, work, supply). As he studies cultures, he can learn the categories of anthropology (mores, folkways, taboos, the cultural universals). A sequential plan can be developed easily

transportation

to ensure that the student meets the major categories he will need and sees them often enough to refine and deepen his understanding of them. By the secondary school, most students should understand that the operational definition of a category gives the criteria by which one decides whether an item belongs in the category. (*Roles* are "those behaviors that accrue to individual members of a group"; hence, if an individual always does some things that the others do not, he plays an exclusive role.)

Imagine, for example, that the curriculum is organized around a series of depth studies that occur each year. During each depth study the learner meets new categories from relevant disciplines. The following outline shows how the categories can be introduced at various levels.

Grade	Depth Study	Categories
I	Economic study of bakery	Work, wages, division of labor, money, supply, demand, competition
	Anthropological study of Burmese, Italian, American family life	Cultural universals, family roles, division of labor, decision making
5	Historical study of the movement west in the United States	Frontier, communication, law and government, free enterprise, public domain
	Political study of the Supreme Court decision in the _____ case	Legal system, judge, precedent, social policy, appeal, constitution, unconstitutional
10	Comparative study of economic systems	Socialism, free enterprise, welfare state, nationalism, private property, public enterprise, incentive, collectivity
	Studies of the ideas that unify men	Nationalism, religion, world government, law, government, beliefs

Through the years the categories are revisited and deepened as the student's capacity for making and testing categories grows.

Students can also be introduced to social science categories through the use of maps, graphs, charts, and reports—devices that store information in categories and symbols. A physical map of one's state, for example, represents information that is organized using the concepts of physical geography. Maps showing climatic information use concepts from physical and human geography. Maps showing population distributions use concepts from sociology, and maps showing land use and economic development use concepts from economics. The same is true of charts and graphs.

The table in figure 12 shows the relationship between agricultural and livestock production for five years in one New Mexico pueblo. Such a table might be consulted or constructed by a group of students who wanted to know whether the two kinds of production varied together or a decline in one was offset by a rise in the other. Use of the table requires learning the concepts by which information is stored in it. These are concepts of quantity (the dollar yield) and kind (the economic distinction between the two kinds of products).

Year	Agriculture	Livestock
1941	3.3	19.1
1946	17.4	18.3
1948	16.7	35.4
1949	17.8	32.1
1951	26.0	44.1

Fig. 12.   Comparison of agricultural and livestock production for one New Mexico pueblo (in thousands of dollars per annum)

Similarly, making a report requires the use of concepts from the social sciences. If one decides to report on the economic growth of a nation, he uses concepts from economics (what concepts do economists use as indicators of economic growth?); in his report he explains those concepts and supplies data from the particular country on which he is reporting. A good report also makes clear whether observations, inferences, or value judgments are being reported. The following exercise from a program for building skills shows how students can identify the logical justification of the ideas in a written passage.

On this page is a story called "The Family." Read it so that you know what it is about. Then read it again and make an outline of the story. Your outline should give the main and supporting ideas in each paragraph. Write your outline on the next page. When you have finished, check to be sure your outline is complete.

Remember these things when you make your outline:

1. The main ideas of each paragraph should be marked with a Roman numeral. Use as many Roman numerals as there are paragraphs in the story.
2. Make a note for each supporting idea in a paragraph. Make only one note for each idea even if it is given in more than one sentence.
3. Indent each supporting-idea note of the paragraph. Mark supporting-idea notes with capital letters.
4. Keep the Roman numerals and the capital letters in straight lines.

The Family

The family is different now from what it used to be. Long ago, man lived in a joint family. In this family a child, his parents, and all his relatives lived and worked together. Today a family usually is made up of a father, a mother, and their children. Relatives live in their own families.

The joint family made it easier for man to feed and protect himself. Hunting wild animals and gathering plants for food was hard work. Many people working together in a joint family made this work easier. The many men in a joint family protected the family from dangers. Wild animals and other men sometimes attacked the family. The men in a joint family could drive them away.

People live differently today from the way they did many years ago. The family no longer hunts animals and plants for food. Instead it buys food from farmers or stores. Wild animals no longer are a great danger. They do not roam freely where most people live. Men who break the law are still a danger to the family. But today soldiers and policemen protect people from lawbreakers.

Joint families are not needed today, but the family as we know it is needed. The family brings children into the world. The human race would die out if no new children were born. The family cares for its members. Fathers and mothers feed and clothe their children and give them a home. Parents care for children when they are sick. The family is important as a teacher. It helps children learn to talk and to love and to get along with others. In all these ways the family is important.[5]

After students have practiced identifying the logical justification of ideas in passages written by others (like the one above), they can apply the same technique to their own writing and that of their peers. In one junior high social studies class the students practiced writing essays in which they deliberately varied the logical and factual justification of the main ideas. Then they studied the degree of justification in each essay, and each student explained the techniques he had used to strengthen and weaken his arguments. The product was a booklet entitled "How to Play Fair and Unfair in Writing."

The most likely setting in which to teach students to organize and handle information effectively is during an inquiry they are carrying on. The more social science categories the student knows, the better able he is to guide his inquiry so that he touches on the information that social scientists consider important. He need not become lost in a mass of magazine articles.

Suppose, for example, that a student is attempting to understand the causes of the Watts riots in Los Angeles during the summer of 1965. He might first collect information on the demographic factors. For this he needs concepts from economics, and he collects information on the jobs and years of schooling that characterize the Watts population. He then might find information on the political behavior of the people, first looking at voting patterns and then the political leaders and what they stand for. He might then look at percentages of home and store ownership in Watts by race. Finally, he might look at newspaper accounts and magazine analyses of the causes of the riots. By collecting and organizing data using the categories of the social sciences before looking at newspapers and magazines, he is able to read them against a background of information and to check the accuracy of the stories, in some areas at least. When he is ready to make his report, he can divide it into sections, such as political and economic background of Watts, racial composition of Watts, facts agreed on about the riots, facts differed on about the riots, interpretations of the causes, where the interpretations agree and disagree, my opinion about the causes of the riots.

Whenever students study social phenomena, the teacher can extend their ability to use the categories of social science. When they study the people of some part of the world, the teacher can see that they learn how to study and report the physical geography of the area, the economic development, political composition, and that they use the categories of anthropology to describe the culture and its transmission. Learning to make charts, graphs, tables, maps, and reports flows naturally from attempts to use these concepts.

355

Similarly, learning to extract information from charts, graphs, maps, and the reports of other people is a natural part of every study. From the middle grades of the elementary school up through high school, each child should have a statistical abstract or fact book on the United States and the world, atlases showing political, religious, and cultural as well as physical information, and reports on economic conditions. Games like the *Inter-Nation Simulation Kit* require continual use of such references as the student learns about "his" nation and seeks information to help him to deal with the problems before him. There are many ways in which mechanical skills can be taught, as they should be, in relation to the concepts that the skills depend on.

Learning to Infer Relationships

Social studies should not stop with the gathering of data or the building of categories. We study society in order to increase our understanding of it. To do this, we must make inferences about causes. We have to try to identify the factors that cause change. From the middle grades through high school, much attention should be given to the making of inferences about causation and relationships.

Making inferences depends largely on establishing relationships and then making educated guesses about causation. For example, a student who is studying Mexico and the United States finds that in Mexico there are few navigable rivers and there are many in the United States. He finds that there is much more industry in the United States. Are the two factors related in such a way that we can assign cause? Perhaps the student should look at another large country. He examines these factors in Brazil, and finds that there are many navigable rivers, but not a great deal of industry per capita. If he continues to add to his sample of nations, he will find that the factors are not related in such a way that a steady increase in the number of navigable rivers results in a steady increase in per capita industrial output. However, if he looks at industrial cities throughout the world and makes a classification of them on the basis of whether they are located on or near a navigable river or ocean, he will find that the majority are near such waters. Can he infer that the presence of rivers causes the

	MEXICO	US
Navigable rivers	75	41,26?
Industry	3.5	6,71 7

rise of industrialization? Of course not. However, he can postulate that it may be one of the causative or facilitating factors.

The above example represents a problem in which multiple factors are involved, as is almost always the case in the social studies. Only rarely do we find a situation in which there is a single causative factor. It often turns out that a factor, considered alone, has no effect on a situation, but when combined with another factor or other factors contributes substantially to the turn of events. Consequently, one of the major tasks in teaching students to make inferences in the social studies involves helping them to plot several factors at once and to see how these are related. It is probably a mistake even in the elementary grades to introduce students to the making of inferences by examples where only one cause operates, for it leads the children to expect that there will be single causes or factors that explain events. It takes time and patience to help the younger students ferret out multiple causes, but it is more realistic and in the long run will benefit the students.

Suppose that a junior high class is trying to predict the outcome of an election. They poll one hundred people chosen as a sample of their community, and they assume that their community is a good sample of the state. Their task is to predict how various parts of the state will vote from what they find out about their community. First, they find out how the one hundred people say they voted in the last election: 60 percent Tory and 40 percent Whig. Then they break this down by sex.

Men: 62 % Tory   38 % Whig
Women: 59 % Tory   41 % Whig

They conclude that sex of voter was not a major factor in the last election and that it will not significantly affect the next election. Then they look at the industrial affiliation of the men to see whether agricultural, commercial, or industrial employment are associated with voting patterns.

Agricultural	90 % Tory	10 % Whig
Industrial	20 % Tory	80 % Whig
Commercial	60 % Tory	40 % Whig

Some of the students are tempted to conclude that they have found the chief factor. However, they continue their study and look at religious affiliation.

| Religion A | 75 % Tory | 25 % Whig |
| Religion B | 40 % Tory | 60 % Whig |

From this they infer that there are multiple factors operating—assuming, of course, that they are getting valid information from their questionnaires. As the study proceeds, they assemble a more nearly complete picture of the factors that may be operating. When the election comes and they are able to compare their predictions with the actual results, they revise their picture of multiple factors.

This teaching procedure can be used in any unit of study, even those that are not quantitative. The process of making inferences from documents and other nonquantitative sources is much the same. Suppose, for example, that the students are trying to picture the process whereby the Pilgrims set up the Massachusetts Bay Colony. They have minutes of meetings, letters from the governor, newsletter accounts of the political machinery, and an outline of the form of government that replaced the original one. Their task is to fill in the missing links by making inferences about what went on. They cull the documents for evidence of who advocated what procedure and what he did to plead his cause and how people reacted to various proposals. Very early the students should learn the law of parsimonious yield in research. For example, they may read in the governor's diary that he proposed something and that it was well received. In the paper they may find support for him. Then, in a letter from one citizen to another, they find sharp dissent that the letter writer claims is general. The students may have to conclude that they are unable to arrive at a conclusion about the facts, let alone about the causative factors.

Permitting students to make inferences when the data is insufficient or conflicting is a dangerous practice. The teacher has to encourage the intuitive jumps that lead to interesting inferences and innovative solutions to problems, but he also has to see that the resulting discussions are rigorous and that hypotheses are tested as fully as possible. Sometimes these two requirements seem contradictory, but it is the quality of thinking that must receive the greatest attention and be rewarded most by the teacher.

The younger the children, the more tangible should be the experiences from which they build inferences. Quite young children are able to handle data about economic factors in their town, because the data are visible and easily verified. They can also compare cultures on the basis of concrete objects (homes, clothing, and the like). They will have difficulty inferring beliefs, however, or dealing with large quantities of data or with objects or events far removed from their experience.

359

Using the Inferences of Others

Although a much larger percentage of instructional time should be spent helping students make and check inferences of their own than should be devoted to using the inferences of others, there are at least three good reasons for teaching students how to use causative inferences that others have developed. First, nearly everything written on social issues contains inferences. The student should learn to identify and test the inferences he reads. Lawrence Metcalf has suggested that a student be taught to identify the logical propositions that underlie important statements. For example, a student who reads that the Pilgrims came to America as a result of religious persecution should examine the general propositions implied by that statement, such as "When people are subject to religious persecution, they will tend to migrate," and see if such propositions hold for other groups or for groups generally.

Second, in learning how to use the inferences of others, students become acquainted with the major theories of the social sciences. Suppose that our students of the Massachusetts Bay Colony conclude their inquiry by examining how historians have pieced together the events. In my own teaching I feel that students, even those in the primary grades, have a more exciting time when their inquiry is fresh and they have not already been presented with conclusions of others. It is hard for a young student, once he has been introduced to the authoritative version, not to be dominated by it in his thinking.

Third, the inferences of others can guide the inquiry of the student. The most elaborate version of this strategy has been developed by Oliver and Shaver.[6] They believe that high school social studies should center on the controversial areas of societal interaction, because it is in those areas that the society is growing and changing. They argue, however, that the student needs a framework for analyzing public issues. They derive this framework from their analysis of American society and its government: in our society we tolerate differences among people but find it difficult to decide public issues on the basis of human dignity alone. Oliver and Shaver discuss many other aspects of the American value system as the framework within which students can analyze public issues. Hence they are suggesting that their system of inferences direct the inquiry of the student, although the student is expected to develop a framework of his own.

In the senior high school curriculum there probably should be a course or extensive unit on the history of a discipline. The course might be organized around groups of students studying various disciplines. The purpose of such a course would be to unfold the development, past and present, of an academic area, its categories and major theories. My own preference would be to pick anthropology or social psychology and to use case studies of the development and revision of theories in these fields; but if the materials were present it would probably be more effective for groups of students to study disciplines of their own choosing. The study of the social sciences should gradually reveal to the students the ways in which social sciences arrive at and justify inferences. The students will find that not all disciplines have a standard language and clearly identify inferences.

Making Value Judgments

We do not teach children social studies so that they will analytic- ally watch the events of society without making judgments about what they see. We do not want our children to observe prejudice without judging it or to examine war without wondering about its morality. Yet, developing skill in observing, building cate- gories, and making inferences are simple compared with learning to make value judgments.

The elementary school child lacks the experience necessary to make value judgments. He simply has not seen enough to be able to arrive at independent assessments of what life is about. Of necessity, the younger child is dependent on the values of his parents. The society quickly transmits its values to the child, making him its prisoner long before he reaches the age when he can independently reason. Unless social values are transmitted in such a way that they serve as flexible means of making judg- ments, it is very difficult to help the student do more than parrot them. While there are many conflicts in cultural values that are useful focuses for instruction, the most controversial areas are the most difficult to discuss rationally. Despite these problems, however, the school must face the problem of helping its students analyze the value issues in its culture and develop and examine their positions on these issues.

There really are no skills for making value judgments. Rather there are some things we can do to help make values and issues clear so that when students make value judgments they are aware of what they are doing. One such thing we can do is to see that the skills for observing, building categories, and making inferences are employed wherever controversy exists. For example, if students are studying our involvement in Vietnam, we can see that they find out the sequence of events according to various observers such as the State Department, the World Affairs Council, pacifist groups, and many nations of the world. After collecting information from several sources, the students should organize this information using economic, political, religious, and cultural categories so that they can see the areas in which the various sources agree and disagree. Next, the students can see what inferences are made about causative factors, which ones seem to be supported by data, and which ones seem to be unsupported. Now they are ready to see what value judgments are being made by the various sides and to challenge or agree with those positions.

Although discussion of value issues should be preceded by the application of observational, categorical, and inferential methodologies of the social sciences, these can only clarify the facts and issues. The scientific method is a systematic attempt to eschew value judgments in favor of analysis. The social studies, however, have to lead the students directly into the valuing process. The curriculum should be organized so that the student faces many of the serious value issues of our society and of the world community: race, public morality, alienation, collectivism, the conflict between internationalism and nationalism, the frayed edges of foreign policy, the problems of class and caste.

Gradually we are developing methods that can help students handle values effectively. The Oliver-Shaver formula for teaching a framework by which secondary students can identify and analyze public issues is a promising one. Cox and Massialas have written a thorough book describing ways of leading students to inquire into important issues.[7] Clements, Fielder, and Tabachnick have presented many ways of helping elementary school children deal with issues.[8] Perhaps the familiar charge that social studies teachers avoid the important issues will soon disappear as social studies classrooms become filled with active debate about important questions.

Examining the Value Judgments of Others

Long before the end of elementary school every child beginning to read a book or newspaper should have learned to ask himself: What is the frame of reference of the author? What basis did he use for including and excluding information? What categories does he use? How do his values affect what he is writing? What are his values? He should also begin to ask questions about his own written and verbal statements: What are my values? What are the assumptions of my parents, my community, and my society? By junior high the student should practice analyzing editorials and other opinionated material. The senior high student should find values different from those he has inherited or more sophisticated expressions of them. The more academically talented can begin to examine the Federalist Papers and the writings of political philosophers. The less able may have to use secondary or heavily edited original sources.

Probably the critical thing is to develop within the secondary school a climate in which the debate of values is a normative activity. A great part of the social substances of secondary education should be the engagement of the students in what one educator has referred to as the great dialogue that began with Socrates. The history of social philosophy, both Eastern and Western, should become a part of the continuing debate of the school. In such a climate the student can naturally learn the skills of debate and apply what he has learned about the analysis of issues.

Building a Study Skills Curriculum

The skills for making observations and building categories and using the categories of others need to be introduced in the elementary school years and continued through high school. Making inferences and using the inferences of others appear to be most appropriately introduced in the later elementary and junior high school years and continued through high school. Helping students make and use value judgments should be a primary business of the secondary schools. The use of maps, charts, graphs, reference works, and original sources and the writing of reports should start in the early school years. Such a sequence would be like the one below. (Skills new to each level are italicized.)

Primary	Making observations Organizing observations and making categories Using observations by resource visitors Learning basic social science categories Making simple maps, charts, tables
Intermediate	Making observations Building categories and making and using maps, charts, graphs *Using standard references* *Using original sources* *Making inferences (introduction)*
Junior High	Using standard references Making inferences Using multiple original sources *Charting multiple factors* *Making inferences about multiple causation* *Making reports using social science concepts* Extending map, chart, and graph skills
Senior High	Making inferences about multiple causation *Examining theories from social science* *Analyzing controversial public issues* *Making value judgments* *Seeking sources of value judgments* *Learning frameworks for social analysis*

There are, of course, enormous individual differences in the learning of these skills. Hence the making of observations is repeated throughout. Every study involves the collection of data and so some students can relearn basic skills while others sharpen and deepen them.

Building a Program for Reference Skills

The skills involved in using maps, charts, graphs, tables, and reference works and in writing reports are also acquired at vastly different rates. They cannot be assigned to certain grades. The concepts of latitude and longitude, for example, may be taught in the fifth grade, but a sixth-grade teacher will probably have to teach them again. Some children may already have certain concepts well in mind before the grade in which those concepts are customarily taught, some may be ready to assimilate them at that time, and others may need further instruction.

To meet these different needs, we can provide units of self-instructional material on certain skills for learners of many ages and abilities. A self-instructional skills laboratory could be used to advantage in any elementary, junior high, or senior high school. It should be operated in such a way that students have free access to it. They can work through the appropriate units, testing themselves and adjusting their program as indicated.

Through commercial outlets schools can obtain a great many films, programed materials, and books whereby children can teach themselves—provided they are given help setting goals and selecting the material they need for their goal. A comprehensive book by Hanna and his associates[9] contains a bibliography of such materials, including three courses in physical geography for the middle grades; several programs on map reading and the concepts necessary for handling maps and globes; about two hundred motion pictures and filmstrips, many of which are appropriate for self-instruction; many books on maps, map history, map symbols, and world regions.

With these materials self-instructional units can be built that are more precise and cover more skills and concepts than was before possible. Whereas self-instructional materials have been used largely for students needing remedial work on skills, the self-instructional laboratory can have several functions. For students who have developed their ability to work independently, self-instructional units can serve as the major formal introduction to concepts and skills. In the Valley Winds School near St. Louis, for example, students identify learning goals ("to understand the different kinds of map projections and their advantages and disadvantages") and then in the laboratory attempt to reach their goals by reading, working through skill programs, and viewing films. Self-instructional units can be used by students who, in the course of a project, find they need to learn a certain skill. A student who needs to know how to use an atlas can find in the laboratory a book or program or film to help him.

A Geographic Skills Sequence

According to Hanna and his associates, a sequence of geographic skills should be identified with the levels (primary, intermediate, junior high, and high school) where students need them. As unit activities are conducted, these skills should be introduced and practiced. The authors have provided an excellent overview of the geographic skills and the concepts these skills depend on. Their book should be read by any faculty planning a sequential geography curriculum or a skills laboratory. Let us examine some of the goals identified in this book, beginning with three major geographic goals of the K–12 program.

1. The ability to observe, collect, and reorganize data gained from firsthand and vicarious experiences and to represent them on maps with appropriate symbols.
2. The ability to read and comprehend data recorded on maps and globes and to differentiate, classify, and translate these symbolic data into conceptual patterns of landscape.
3. The ability to analyze and interpret the locations and distributions that are portrayed on maps and globes and to reason about things geographic.[10]

These objectives, like the approach we have taken to all study skills, depend on the ability to observe, categorize, and make inferences. This is true also for the specific skills to be developed throughout the program:

1. The ability to observe systematically and to identify and note the location and distribution and density of features of the landscape.

2. The ability to orient self and to note directions in space and on maps and globes.
3. The ability to locate places, distributions, and densities on maps and globes.
4. The ability to use scale and to judge or measure distance in space and on maps and globes.
5. The ability to use and understand symbols and to visualize the realities for which they stand.
6. The ability to use cartographic principles of map composition and graphic expression.
7. The ability to recognize and express relative location.
8. The ability to use and understand basic map projections.
9. The ability to understand and relate areal distributions.
10. The ability to use and understand the globe as a model of the earth.[11]

These are the skills necessary to achieve the three broad objectives of the entire geographic skills program. Each is quite complex. A number of self-instructional units could be built around any of these. Most students would probably develop the full skills and understandings only after several years of study.

To illustrate the complexity of each of the ten skills, let us examine a few of the observations that make up the concept of scale. Hanna and his collaborators suggest that these understandings can be developed by the end of the middle elementary grades.

Scale is the relation of distance on the map to the distance it represents on the ground.
The scale of a map is large or small in relation to the object it represents.
The use of a large scale for a map enables the mapper to show many details about a small area.
The use of a small scale for a map enables the mapper to show a large area but fewer details.
Scale on the globe may be used to measure the distance between any two points on the earth's surface.
The scale on one part of a map may be different from the scale on another part (an inset map, for instance).[12]

It is important to note that even this collection of understandings does not by any means encompass the entire idea of scale. Not until the student can understand advanced mathematics can he achieve competence. However, the above ideas serve most purposes.

Specific Approaches to Skills Teaching

The opportunity to teach skills occurs constantly in any social studies program. This plethora of opportunities can become a problem unless the teacher approaches each unit systematically. Like any other element of the social studies, skills should not be taught in isolation. They should be related to ends other than the mastery of the skills themselves. The child can use these skills as tools to help him gather information about human groups or assimilate social science concepts. Even in making a map, the child can engage in some depth study, and the map he makes can be used to objectify certain ideas or data in his study.

Sometimes classroom instruction may need to focus on a particular skill. "Projection" in cartography, for example, is a geometric concept that may need to be studied independently before students can begin to acquire the skills of map reading. In general, however, skills can be learned in the course of social science inquiries. The whole range of diagrammatic materials can be found and used throughout the social sciences.

Because maps use many geometric and geographic terms and concepts, children must gradually develop the language of maps. Almost every general map requires the user to comprehend such spatial concepts as latitude, longitude, scale, compass direction, elevation, and sea level. Also necessary is the vocabulary of land forms, such as archipelago, peninsula, alluvial fan, inlet, gulf, plateau, and strait. For his own information and for instructional techniques, a teacher might consult these two reference works on cartography: Ruby M. Harris, *Handbook of Map and Globe Usage* (Chicago: Rand McNally, 1959); Ervin Raisz, *General Cartography*, 2d ed. (New York: McGraw-Hill, 1948). The first contains suggested activities for the classroom. In the second work, the section on the history of cartography could provide the teacher with background for an interesting classroom study.

The school faculty must identify the essential concepts and skills to be learned and then arrange them in the curriculum in some reasonable order. (On pages 368–75 are printed two skill-development charts—one adapted from the *Curriculum Guide for the Social Studies for Kindergarten, Grades 1, 2,* published by the Board of Education of the City of Chicago, 1964; the other published by the Denoyer-Geppert Company.) Next, diagnostic tests must be prepared so that each teacher can easily identify the vocabulary, skills, and concepts that the class members have and have not learned. Each teacher should plan instruction on the basis of the test and keep progress records, which are passed on to the teacher in the next grade level.

Obviously learning rates differ so greatly from child to child that the determination of the grade levels at which specific skills should be introduced cannot be exact and inflexible. A sequential chart, however, will permit a teacher to measure the relative progress of his class and to differentiate instruction for individual children. To concentrate on a very few concepts, words, or skills at any one time is the wisest course—particularly in dealing with the slow learner, the very person we are tempted to rush so that he will come up to the class average. The slow learner, however, achieves more and feels more confident when he is not overwhelmed with learning tasks.

Mapmaking. Perhaps no means of acquiring an understanding of maps is quite so effective as the actual making of maps. From the child's first year in school—when he learns to map the room, the school, and the neighborhood—to the day when he can make a series of map overlays showing how various factors affect, say, agricultural production in Italy, the child learns through mapmaking to represent reality in a compact and symbolic form. He learns scale, legend, orientation, and the other cartographic principles as they serve his needs to handle data and ideas.

For children aged eight to twelve, Harold Tannenbaum and Nathan Stillman have developed a mapmaking kit that includes a compass, a transit, a protractor, and other measuring devices.[13] Of particular interest is the accompanying instructional booklet that teaches the child to make picture maps and landmark maps, to orient a map according to compass directions, to draw maps to scale using measuring cords, to interpret scales on various maps, to use graph paper in mapmaking, to employ protractor and transit, to use triangulation to measure hills, and to translate these measurements into contour maps. All these self-instructive guidelines involve simple and pleasant activities that can be adapted to personal and classroom needs. Geographic and geometric knowledge—such as knowledge of direction, projections, and triangulation—is instilled in the child as he progresses through the experiments. In short, the cartographic method is employed to teach the child geographic concepts; the child actually learns scientific mapmaking. With a minimum of help, even the child aged six or seven can do many of the lessons; the

369

older child can use the material with considerable independence. The teacher, incidentally, would do well to examine the arrangement of activities in the book, for the sequential programing builds one idea on another.

SUGGESTED SEQUENCE CHART FOR MAP AND GLOBE SKILLS
BOARD OF EDUCATION, CITY OF CHICAGO

The grade placement of the map and globe skills suggested in the following table is flexible. With each group of pupils, the teacher will find it necessary to make adjustments according to individual abilities, previous learnings, and topics of interest. Any selection should be based on the specific need for this skill and the immediate, practical use which can be made in understanding the problem or topic under study. The skills should begin with simple concepts and understandings, and the experiences should progress successively to include more complex understandings and broader generalizations at each grade level.

	K	1	2	3	4	5	6	7	8
ABILITY TO EXPRESS SELF ON MAPS		▷——————————————————							
MAKING AND CONSTRUCTING MAPS									
Reading and making maps		▷——————————————————							
ABILITY TO ORIENT AND NOTE DIRECTIONS USING MAPS									
Using maps and globes to learn directions and map orientations									
Left and right		▷——————————————————							
Up and down		· · · ▷—————————————							
North and south		· · · ▷—————————————							
East and west			· · · · · ▷————————						
The 4 main in-between directions			▷——————————————						
ABILITY TO LOCATE PLACES AND TO EXPRESS RELATIVE LOCATION ON MAPS AND GLOBES									
Using maps and globes to locate key places									
Continent		· · · ▷—————————————							
Country			· · · ▷—————————						

· · · · · · · · Readiness
▷ Formal introduction
———→ Simple to more complex understandings

370

SPECIAL CONSIDERATIONS

	K	1	2	3	4	5	6	7	8

State · · · · · · · · · · · ·▷——————————→

Province · · · · · · · ·▷——————————→

City · · · · · · · · · · · ·▷——————————→

Capital · · · · · · · ·▷——————————→

Historical places · · · · · · · ·▷——————————→

Points of interest · · · · · · · ·▷——————————→

*Understanding the use of map grids
for specific location*

North Pole and South Pole · · · · ·▷————————————→

Equator · · · · · · · · · · · ·▷——————————→

Tropics of Cancer and Capricorn · · · · · · · · · · · · ·▷————————→

Arctic Circle and Antarctic Circle · · · · · · · · · · · ·▷————————→

Great circle routes · · · · · · · ·▷————————————→

Latitude and longitude–degree · · · · · · · · · · · · ·▷————————→

Low, middle, and high latitudes · · · · · · · · · · · ·▷————————→

*Understanding the relationship
between surface features and
man's ways of living*

Elevation · · · · · · · · · · · · · ·▷————————→

Relief · · · · · · · · · · · · · ·▷————————→

Slope · · · · · · · · · · · · · ·▷————————→

Mountain · · · · · · · · · · · ·▷————————→

Hill · · · · · · · · · ·▷——————————→

Plateau · · · · · · · · · · · ·▷————————→

Plain · · · · · · · · · ·▷——————————→

Valley · · · · · · · · · ·▷——————————→

Moraine · · · · · · · · · ·▷——————————→

Canyon · · · · · · · · · · · ·▷————————→

*Using globes to understand man's
exploration into space* · · · · · · · · · · · · · ·▷————————→

ABILITY TO READ MAPS AND NOTE
DISTRIBUTIONS

*Using map symbols and reading the
map legend*

Color and pattern · · · · ·▷————————————————→

Relief symbols · · · · · · ·▷————————————————→

Pictorial symbols · · · · · · · · · ·▷——————————→

Semipictorial symbols · · · · · · · · · ·▷——————————→

Abstract symbols · · · · · · · · · · · · · ·▷————————→

37I

	K	1	2	3	4	5	6	7	8

Identifying land forms

Continent
Island
Coastline
Harbor
Delta
Peninsula
Isthmus
Cape

Identifying water forms

Ocean
Sea
River and lake
Canal
Bay
Gulf
Strait

ABILITY TO RECOGNIZE SCALE AND
COMPUTE DISTANCES

Determining scale of miles

Determining area visualization

372

ABILITY TO CORRELATE AND COMPARE
MAPS TO MAKE INFERENCES

*Interpreting and drawing inferences
from special-purpose maps and
globes*

Products
Mineral resources
Precipitation (rainfall)
Vegetation
Waterway
Railway
Highway
Time belt

*Becoming acquainted with various
projections—their advantages
and limitations*

Globe (the most accurate map)
Mercator
Polar-centered

SPECIAL CONSIDERATIONS

	K	1	2	3	4	5	6	7	8
Equal-area							·········▷——————►		
Conic							·······▷———————►		
Relief						·················▷——————►			
Using the globe to learn the causes of day and night and the differences in seasons				·····▷————————————————►					
Identifying man-made forms									
Cultural form						▷——————————————►			
Natural boundary						·····▷—————————►			
Economic grouping						·····▷—————————►			
Social grouping					············▷—————————►				

Adapted from "Suggested Sequence Chart for Map and Globe Skills" in *Curriculum Guide for the Social Studies for Kindergarten, Grades 1, 2.* Copyright 1964, Board of Education of the City of Chicago. Adapted by permission.

Service Publication #M44   *Denoyer-Geppert Company, Chicago, Illinois 60640*

SUGGESTED SEQUENCE FOR GLOBE AND MAP SKILLS
GRADES 1–6, JAN. 1958, P.S. 116, QUEENS, NEW YORK CITY

Directions and Distances	Locating Places	Reading and Interpreting Symbols on Maps	Developing Concepts	Geographical Terms on Grade Levels
		GRADE 1		
Developing sense of direction, e.g., left, right.	Placing objects in proper relationships when building with blocks.	Representing objects by blocks, e.g., automobiles, boats.	Observing pictures and drawing conclusions.	bridge water river
Use of *further*, *nearer*, etc. Number of blocks to a specific store.	Observing surface features on neighborhood trips.	Representing hill on sandbox. Large floor map with aid of teacher.	Understanding that information can be summarized on charts.	

Directions and Distances	Locating Places	Reading and Interpreting Symbols on Maps	Developing Concepts	Geographical Terms on Grade Levels
		GRADE 2		
Near enough to walk. Number of blocks to different stores.	Neighborhood walks. Map of school block.	Large floor map with aid of teacher, using pictures as symbols.	Studying and interpreting pictures to determine significant relationships between man and his environment.	ocean mountain lake shore north east south west
North, East, South, West.		Dramatizing bridges, rivers, etc.		
Position of sun during day.			Understanding that pictures or symbols may represent objects.	

Review of Previous Grade Work

Directions and Distances	Locating Places	Reading and Interpreting Symbols on Maps	Developing Concepts	Geographical Terms on Grade Levels
		GRADE 3		
Blocks to a mile. Time needed to travel distance. Using directions (N,E,S,W) in games in reference to schoolroom.	Map of community with special reference to places of interest. Floor map of classroom and/or school.	Picture symbols on maps, developed by class. Land and water masses on globe.	Earth is round like a ball. Understanding that a large area may be shown on a small map.	sea island forest waterfall globe earth
Cardinal directions in relation to rising sun.	Table maps of clay, etc. Maps of class trips.		Understanding there is a greater water area than land area. Understanding sun may be used to determine direction.	

Review of Previous Grade Work

SPECIAL CONSIDERATIONS

Directions and Distances	Locating Places	Reading and Interpreting Symbols on Maps	Developing Concepts	Geographical Terms on Grade Levels
		GRADE 4		
North and south lines on globe and map. East and west lines on globe and map.	On globe to show where child lives, places read about, places studied. Use of outline maps to label places of interest in N.Y. City. More detailed school community maps, using symbols. Position of Jamaica with respect to Queens, of Queens with respect to N.Y.C., of N.Y.C. with respect to N.Y. State.	Globe points north. Simple globe and map language, e.g., ocean, country, river, lake. Using maps to plan trips.	Understanding similarity between globe and earth. Understanding map hung on wall does not change directions of north and south. Understanding earth spins in space (like globe). Earth's rotation causes day and night. Understanding map is really a diagram.	country bay continent desert oasis harbor valley volcano reservoir dam glacier iceberg city state borough

Review of Previous Grade Work

Directions and Distances	Locating Places	Reading and Interpreting Symbols on Maps	Developing Concepts	Geographical Terms on Grade Levels
		GRADE 5		
Directions of north and south toward poles. Directions, e.g., NE, SE, etc.	Use of grid system to locate places. Source and mouth of rivers.	Reading and interpreting legend on map, e.g., colors on maps.	Rivers flow downhill and land may slope toward north; therefore rivers	mesa peninsula canal slope mountain range strait

STRATEGIES FOR TEACHING THE ELEMENTS OF INQUIRY

Directions and Distances	Locating Places	Reading and Interpreting Symbols on Maps	Developing Concepts	Geographical Terms on Grade Levels
Directions from equator.	Position of N.Y. State with respect to U.S. Locating land and water masses on globe and map. Locating the four hemispheres. Locating North and South Poles. Making maps in connection with class trips. Zones on maps and globe. Use of outline maps. Locating places studied. Position of U.S. in relation to other countries affecting our historical development.	Recognizing different types of symbols on map. Knowing some symbols represent real places, e.g., oceans; others represent imaginary places, e.g., equator.	may flow to north on maps. Map represents part of globe. All land and water areas are not alike. It's hottest near the equator. Climate becomes colder as we go toward the poles. A hemisphere is half of our earth.	cape prairie upland lowland rapids swamps plateau plains gulf hemisphere rotation equator North Pole South Pole Arctic Circle Antarctic Circle Tropic of Capricorn prevailing winds

376

Review of Previous Grade Work

GRADE 6

Understanding and expressing distance in	Use of outline maps to note historical and	Reading and interpreting symbols and	Flat map distorts (flatten orange peel to	isthmus water shed reef

Directions and Distances	Locating Places	Reading and Interpreting Symbols on Maps	Developing Concepts	Geographical Terms on Grade Levels
terms of time as well as by miles. Measuring distance by scale. Prime meridian relationship of longitude to time; of latitude to miles. Great circle routes as shortest distances between two points on globe.	geographical information. Position of U.S. in relation to other countries studied and to bodies of water. Earth is slanted on its axis. Earth revolves around sun. Meridians and latitudes. Using them to locate places studied. The continents.	keys on different kinds of maps, e.g., rainfall, population, political, etc. Color and shadings on map, e.g., surface features. Use of maps for reports. Use of world map to show relationships. Use of relief maps.	prove). There are different kinds of maps for special purposes. Man's natural environment will influence his activities, e.g., kind of houses lived in. Longitude is related to time. Latitude is related to temperature. Oceans influence weather on continents. Mountains influence rainfall. A city to be large must be accessible. Revolution of earth causes change of seasons.	irrigation altitude meridian latitude tributary axis revolution continent longitude

377

Review of Previous Grade Work

NOTE: Experience with globe and floor and table maps should precede experience with wall maps.

This chart is neither prescriptive nor exhaustive. The teacher may introduce geographical terms and map skills as the need arises regardless of grade level. This chart is suggested as a guide. The teacher may add to it as she sees fit.

© by Denoyer-Geppert Company, Chicago, Illinois 60640 (Used by permission)

STRATEGIES FOR TEACHING THE ELEMENTS OF INQUIRY

Among other aids to mapmaking are the elementary atlases that explain map concepts simply enough to guide the young cartographer. "Conservation trays" are also helpful teaching aids. Modeled into hills and valleys and other natural features, the soil in these waterproof trays is subjected—by means of water pumps—to simulated rain and streams in order to show the effects of erosion, patterns of drainage, and techniques of soil conservation. Because the experimenter himself must mold the soil into topographic features, every child learns skills and devices similar to those used in making a relief map.

A globe gives the only true representation of the surface of our planet. That a flat map must in some way distort this curved surface can be demonstrated to children by attempting to flatten a slit tennis ball—an impossible feat without stretching or tearing the rubber. Only a globe can show simultaneously the correct shape of surfaces, all areas in true proportion, accurate distances, and true direction. The various projections used in flat maps can accurately represent one or two of these properties, but only at the expense of severely distorting the others. A globe should be used in every classroom as a basic reference to assure the development of accurate concepts of physical geography, especially such concepts as the equator and the poles, latitude and longitude, the great circle routes, the change of seasons and of night and day, and the directions of the compass. The construction of globes, is important because it compels children to put geographic concepts to practical use; the concepts become working tools, visually conceived.

The principle in using all these materials is that learning how to interpret maps and learning how to construct maps (that is, how to translate data into graphic symbols) should proceed concurrently. For example, a group of first-graders may first use a published map to locate churches, stores, and railroads in their community, but they must immediately begin construction of their own map, using some kind of symbolic representation of churches, stores, and railroads. Or the sequence may be reversed. After measuring a local hill by means of triangulation, a group of fourth-graders may symbolize that hill on their own relief map; then they may study a contour or relief map of the United States to learn how elevations are represented by the professional cartographer. The possible teaching strategies are limitless. The map kits available from many airlines offer excellent descriptions of cartographic projections, air routes, and climatology; these kits could be studied by children who wish to draw polar projections showing water surfaces, ice formations, or climate.

Floor Maps and Modeled Relief Maps. For children in the early primary grades, realistic three-dimensional maps are perhaps the most easily understood of all types of graphic representations. Using blocks, boxes, and cardboard, children can make a simple floor layout of box houses, paper trees, and wooden automobiles, all simulating a map of their neighborhoods. Similarly, they can lay out a farm with farmhouse, barn, silo, fences, trees, and animals. Airports, harbors, railroad yards, zoos—almost any identifiable locale can be represented in a floor map. Sand-table maps decorated with miniature cutout buildings are realistic and have the added advantage of topographical representation—indented lines for roads, mounds for hills and mountains, depressions for bodies of water.

The making of modeled relief maps and globes, constructed from materials like papier-mâché or burlap and patching plaster, comes closer to true cartography. In such maps the elevation or vertical scale is almost always highly exaggerated relative to the horizontal scale. Aside from this inevitable distortion, authenticity can be achieved if the children's attention is directed to it. In the process of construction many map and globe skills can be learned.

Outline Maps. Outline maps for children to complete in detail should always be on hand in quantity. The primary teacher should have maps of the school, the community, the neighborhood, and perhaps the state. In studying school, first-graders can paste on outline maps various pictures—of desks, of people walking, of the teacher, of the nurse, and so forth. Exit routes for fire drills or any routes between classrooms and offices can be the subject of maps. The upper-grade teacher should have state maps, regional maps, maps of continents, nations, and hemispheres in various cartographic projections. These maps can be the basis for illustrating any of the wide variety of data customarily shown on standard maps.

Political maps—boundaries, cities, states, countries

Physical relief maps—land elevations, bodies of water

Climatic maps—climatic regions, temperature, rainfall, winds, ocean currents, vegetation

Population maps—density, racial distribution, resources, environment

Economic maps—natural resources, agriculture, industry, occupations

Transportation maps—highways, streets, waterways, airways, railroads

Historical maps—territorial or boundary changes, migrations, military campaigns, explorations

Ideational or cultural maps—distribution of religions; locales of works of literature, music, and art; locales of native sports

Sightseeing maps—historic sites, scenic places

Using the opaque projector, the children can trace the information from individual outline maps to one large mural map, thus combining political, topographical, climatic, cultural, and other data. Analyses of the relations between the data can then be made. Or individual maps can be retraced on separate sheets of cellophane or polyethylene to create overlay maps, which can also be used for analyzing relations among data.

Comparing Maps in the Search for Information. A map showing waterways on the Atlantic seaboard and a map showing the distribution of population in the American colonies might be compared to determine the importance of water transportation to people living in a wilderness before the advent of modern technology. In an interpretation of this kind we are using maps not necessarily for the specific purpose that the cartographer had in mind, but for our own purpose.

This use of materials is characteristic of any imaginative, scholarly inquiry. For example, by comparing the map in figure 13 with the map in figure 14 and adding information gathered from documents and other sources, one can learn a good deal about the history and sociology of Indian migrations in the United States. The one map shows the location of Indian tribes prior to the voyage of Columbus; the other shows the location of Indian tribes today. A comparison of the maps shows, for instance, that eastern tribes tended to move westward but few western tribes moved eastward. Why? Other questions may arise: Did a prolonged migration tend to reduce a tribe's population? Did those tribes that adopted the white man's culture tend to remain where they were or did they also migrate?

Maps and the Study of History.[14] The study of history relies heavily on the use of maps. Chronology, which young children often find hard to comprehend, can sometimes be pictured by a series of maps. The growth of American railroads, for example, can be illustrated by maps showing the total rail mileage in 1840, 1850, 1860, and so on into the present century. Advancing settlements or territorial expansion can also be mapped serially by time units. In addition to chronology, maps can be used to indicate geographic conditions affecting the history of a nation or a people, an important consideration even if one rejects pure environmentalism. No study of military campaigns should neglect ridges, hills, open country, or naturally protected flanks. No study of migrations or advancing settlements should overlook geographic obstacles or natural avenues of easy movement. The American frontier for example, might initially be studied in terms of the successive obstacles to westward migration—the Fall Line, the Appalachians, the vast forests of the Ohio-Mississippi basin, the semiarid plains, the Rockies, the Sierra Nevada.

There are less obvious but no less important uses of maps in historical study. A map like that in figure 15, showing the ground plan of a California mission village, can be used to develop concepts about social and economic uses of land, which could be

381

382

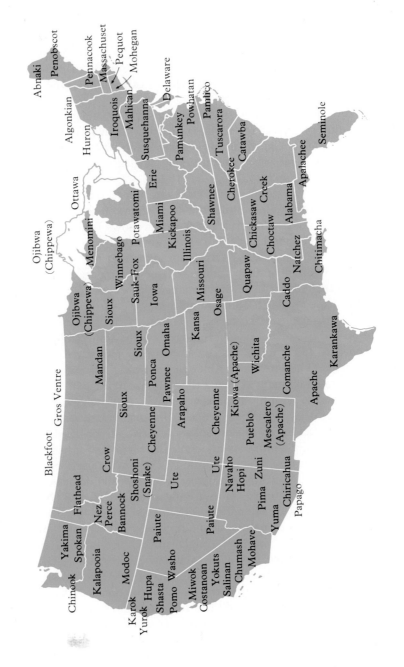

Fig. 13. Probable location of native Indian peoples before Columbus discovered the New World.

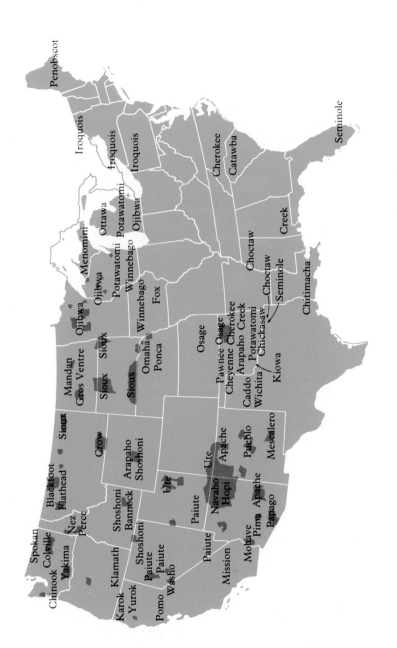

383

Fig. 14. American Indians today: major concentrations of Indians in the general population and the location of the larger federal Indian reservations.

applied to present-day land uses. Or perhaps land use in this Spanish settlement could be compared with land use in nearby Indian villages or in the pueblos near other Spanish missions in the Southwest. An additional map of Franciscan missions along the California coast would be helpful in determining the extent to which Spanish and Indian cultures intermingled.

Reproductions of antique maps can have more than curiosity value. Pre-Columbian conceptions of the world or seventeenth century notions of a Northwest Passage reveal a great deal about our predecessors' attitudes, values, and aspirations. Even old geographical terms still in use, such as West Indies, Near East, and Far East, are handy indicators of European ethnocentrism. Maps of medieval towns, ancient Rome, the Acropolis, Revolutionary Boston, colonial Williamsburg, and the like can also help the child visualize past events.

Graphs, Charts, and Tables. Learning to decode material in charts, graphs, and tables should proceed concurrently with learning how to encode data in such forms for the same reasons that map reading and mapmaking should go together. Because elementary arithmetic now tends to emphasize mathematical concepts and reasoning such as ratios and proportions, equational unknowns, sets of numbers, and sets of points, the child should be able to cope with graphs and other diagrams. The social studies and the study of arithmetic can be integrated to the extent that the social sciences use such concepts as the number line (in line graphs), volume (in bar graphs and many pictographs), and percentages (in many statistical tables).

In almost all reference works there are graphs and tables that can stimulate inquiry. Even the data on sporting events recorded in almanacs can motivate young boys to learn how to decode tables. Children can be spurred into an inquiry whenever a graph or table they have been reading together seems to indicate an odd or unexplained trend. For example, reading a line graph showing the growth of union membership in the United States, children may ask about the reasons for the decline in membership in the 1920s and the extraordinarily sharp rise in the late 1930s; the teacher can thereupon encourage search into the business practices of the twenties and the New Deal policies of the thirties. A somewhat less complex study—a study of fire control, for example—could be stimulated by a table such as the one in figure 16, which shows the incidence of destructive fires in New Mexico between 1950 and 1957. The table lists those forest fires caused

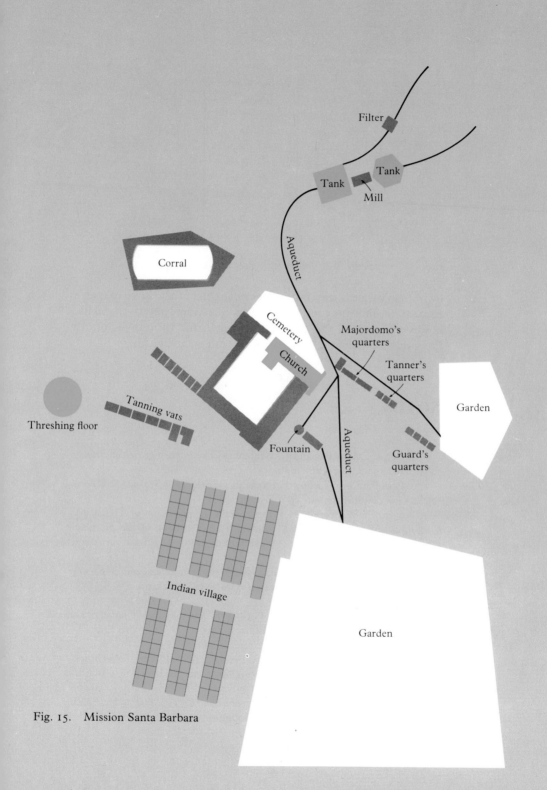

Fig. 15. Mission Santa Barbara

Filter

Tank

Tank

Mill

Aqueduct

Corral

Cemetery

Church

Majordomo's
quarters

Tanner's
quarters

Garden

Threshing floor

Tanning vats

Fountain

Aqueduct

Guard's
quarters

Indian village

Garden

Year	Man-Caused Forest Fires	Percentage of All Fires
1956	164	13.7
1955	89	23.3
1954	106	14.2
1953	86	12.9
1952	53	11.6
1951	107	17.2
1950	161	24.4

Fig. 16.   Destructive fires in New Mexico, 1950–57

by human carelessness, but it does not explain the degree of man's success in fire prevention. Asking questions about the data, however, can lead the children to search for various factors in fire control—climatic, technological, and sociological.

NOTES

1. Byron G. Massialas and C. Benjamin Cox, *Inquiry in Social Studies* (New York: McGraw-Hill, 1966).

2. Edwin Fenton, *Teaching the New Social Studies in Secondary Schools* (New York: Holt, Rinehart & Winston, 1966).

3. An excellent overview of these skills is provided in Helen M. Carpenter, ed., *Skills in Social Studies*, 33rd Yearbook of the National Council for the Social Studies (Washington: National Education Assn., 1963).

4. Robert A. Naslund and Richard E. Servey, *Organizing and Reporting Skills Kit* (Chicago: Science Research Associates, 1962), pp. DR 8.

5. Ibid., Pupil Booklet, p. 35.

6. Donald W. Oliver and James P. Shaver, *Teaching Public Issues in the High School* (Boston: Houghton Mifflin, 1966).

7. Massialas and Cox, *Inquiry in Social Studies.*

8. H. Millard Clements, William R. Fielder, and B. Robert Tabachnick, *Social Study: Inquiring in Elementary Classrooms* (Indianapolis: Bobbs-Merrill, 1966).

9. Paul R. Hanna and others, *Geography in the Teaching of the Social Studies: Concepts and Skills* (Boston: Houghton Mifflin, 1966).

10. Ibid., pp. 8–9.

11. Ibid., p. 12.

12. Ibid., p. 25.

13. *Science Book-Lab: Map-Making* (New York: Science Materials Center, 1963).

14. To obtain inexpensive maps on various historical subjects, the teacher may write the National Geographic Society and the U.S. Geological Survey. The latter distributes aerial maps of the United States, which make good outline maps for filling in historical information.

387

TEACHING AS A CONTINUOUS EXPERIMENT

A school should be characterized by continuous inquiry into who the learner is, what he feels, what motivates him. It should constantly attempt to understand him and to use that understanding to generate instruction relevant to him and suited to his abilities. A school should be a center of inquiry into the teaching-learning process.[1]

Important though achievement of academic learning is, it is not the only goal of the social studies and should not be the only kind of growth evaluated. Furthermore, individualizing instruction demands more than different activities for high and low achievers. Personality, creativity, and open-mindedness, among other factors, demand their own adjustments. There are many points of view from which we can study our students. In this chapter we will examine several such viewpoints that correlate with the dimensions already discussed: achievement of knowledge and skills, growth of creative thinking, development of concepts and open belief systems.

Evaluation has important implications both for the present and for the future. Some measures discussed here can be applied immediately. Some may suggest ways in which schools should be reorganized. If, for example, a teacher is to study his students adequately and create educational programs for them, then his class load should probably be greatly reduced. Studying students and individualizing instruction require time both for study and for the acquisition of new skills.

The Intellectual Dimension

The following list contains the names and addresses of sixteen test publishers. Catalogs with descriptions of their tests are available from them. Some of these firms provide consulting service to schools and districts developing testing programs. Many of them study curricula to determine what content to include in their tests. Harcourt's *Metropolitan Achievement Tests,* for example, cover skills and information commonly taught in the upper elementary and junior high grades.

Acorn Publishing Company, Rockville Centre, Long Island, N.Y. 11570

Bureau of Educational Measurements, Kansas State Teachers College, Emporia, Kan. 66801

Bureau of Educational Research and Service, State University of Iowa, Iowa City, Iowa 52240

Bureau of Publications, Teachers College, Columbia University Press, 525 W. 120th Street, New York, N.Y. 10027

Cooperative Test Division, Educational Testing Service, Princeton, N.J. 08540

CTB/McGraw-Hill, Del Monte Research Park, Monterey, Calif. 93940

Educational Test Bureau, 720 Washington Avenue, S.E., Minneapolis, Minn.

Educational Testing Service, Princeton, N.J. 08540

Harcourt, Brace & World, Inc., Tarrytown, N.Y. 10591

Houghton Mifflin Company, 2 Park Street, Boston, Mass. 02107

Ohio Scholarship Tests, State Department of Education, 751 Northwest Boulevard, Columbus, Ohio 43215

Psychometric Affiliates, Box 1625, Chicago, Ill. 60690

Public School Publishing Company, Test Division of Bobbs-Merrill Co., Inc., 1720 E. 38th Street, Indianapolis, Ind. 46206

Scholastic Testing Service, 3774 W. Devon Avenue, Chicago, Ill. 60645

Science Research Associates, Inc., 259 E. Erie Street, Chicago, Ill. 60611

Western Psychological Services, Box 775, Beverly Hills, Calif. 90210

Standardized tests cannot reveal the nuances of achievement in a given situation, nor can they measure the achievement of uncommon objectives. The following are useful references for the teacher who creates his own tests. They contain information on the availability of tests, test construction, and general testing theory.

Buros, Oscar K. (ed.). *Tests in Print.* Highland Park, N.J.: Gryphon, 1961. Good for judging what available tests can and cannot do.

Green, John A. *Teacher-Made Tests.* New York: Harper, 1963. Provides practical advice on test construction.

Making the Classroom Test. Princeton, N.J.: Educational Testing Service, 1959. Provides practical advice on test construction.

Masia, Bertram B. "Evaluating Behavioral Outcomes by Means of Formal Social Science Instruments," *Teachers for the Disadvantaged,* ed. Michael Usdan and Frederick Bertolaet, pp. 187–218. Chicago: Follett, 1966. A good overview of most testing techniques.

Ordinarily the object of evaluation is either to diagnose what needs to be learned or to determine what behaviors have changed during a period of instruction. In order to measure change, at least two measurements are necessary. If a teacher measures behavior only at the completion of a unit of study, he will not know whether the behaviors tested have been acquired before or during the unit.

One problem in testing a child twice is that his second performance is likely to improve simply because of the practice provided by the first attempt; the second time he may sense the nature, formula, or direction of the questions. Hence it is frequently wise to make two distinct versions of the test or of the testing situation. Sometimes two questions may approach the same problem or behavior from two different angles, and one of these questions may be put into each test. This is a good testing policy, but its accomplishment is admittedly difficult.

Every measurement of group behavior is described in terms of two characteristics: the *central tendency* of the scores, or their tendency to group around the average or median score (that point in the distribution of scores that is exactly in the middle—half the scores being higher and half lower); and the *variability* of the scores, or the extent of their dispersion around the average or median. Hence, when we describe how children scored on a test, we describe the average or middle score and the range or spread of the scores on either side of the average.

Because different children respond differently to content, teaching methods, and materials and because they vary widely in interest and adaptability, one of the results of instruction is to increase the variability or the spread of behavioral adequacy. A rise in the median scores and in scores in general on a particular test indicates overall gains in knowledge and skills. An increase also in variability is normal, since not all students will make the same gains. If the variability does decrease—if *all* the scores improve and draw closer together—then either many students did not learn as much as they might have or the test did not measure all the behaviors the students were to have learned.

HIGHER-ORDER ACHIEVEMENT

Nearly all commercially available achievement tests and most teacher-made tests tap recall of facts and performance of simple skills much more than the ability to apply, analyze, synthesize, and evaluate information. We need to experiment with ways of studying the student's achievement so that his ability to use information and think about it receive as much attention as his ability to remember it.

One system for classifying various abilities divides them into cognitive-memory (the ability to remember), convergent thinking (the ability to put facts in logical or sequential order), divergent thinking (the ability to consider many possibilities), and evaluative thinking (the ability to make judgments).[2] A group of first-graders who have completed a comparison of Navaho and Eskimo family life might be tested with questions like these:

Cognitive-memory: What weapons and tools were used for hunting in the two families? What did the women in each family do as their daily chores?

Convergent thinking: Why do you suppose their clothing was so different? Why was wood scarce in both places?

Divergent thinking: Suppose you went to live with these families. In what ways would your life be different from what it is now?

Evaluative thinking: How would you like spending some time in these families? What are some of the things you would particularly like? What are some of the things that bother you about the idea?

Another useful guideline for measuring higher-order types of academic growth is the *Taxonomy of Educational Objectives*,[3] which classifies educational objectives in the cognitive domain according to the following levels: knowledge of terms, specific facts, conventions for organizing and judging facts, classification and category schemes, concepts in academic fields, and theories and structures of fields; the ability to use knowledge, translation to new symbolic modes, interpretation, extrapolation, application; analysis; synthesis; and evaluation in terms of internal and external criteria.

Even the best achievement tests for the college population contain only about ten percent of level two items and none at levels three to five. This is partly because it is extremely difficult to test a student's ability to analyze and synthesize facts and theories unless the test maker is sure that the student knows the information and theories that are tested. A school faculty is in a much better position to develop tests of thinking ability than is a test publisher, although this may change as computer-assisted simulations become more common and standard tests of higher-order thinking are built using simulations.

FACTORS RELATED TO ACHIEVEMENT

Too seldom has the study of academic achievement been accompanied by the study of factors related to that achievement. Intelligence, social status, motivation, and achievement are positively correlated with each other. Therefore, a student's achievement is likely to mean little except in the light of these other factors. A high score on an achievement test, for example, means something quite different for a low-status student than for a high-status student.

Among the factors we need to consider in studying achievement is intelligence, the ability to solve problems. In a school where both intelligence tests and standard tests of achievement in social studies were administered, scores on these tests were positively correlated (table 1). Suppose that one of the students at this school has a score of 4.2. If he is in the top group in intelligence, then he is near the bottom of that group in social studies achievement. However, if he is in the bottom group in intelligence, he is near the top of that group in social studies achievement.

TABLE 1

FOURTH-GRADE ACHIEVEMENT IN SOCIAL STUDIES
RELATED TO INTELLIGENCE

Student IQs (Otis Quick Scoring)	Metropolitan Achievement Tests Social Studies Scores in Grade Level	
	Average	Range
Over 120	6.2	4.1–9.4
Between 90 and 110	4.3	3.0–6.2
Below 80	2.9	1.4–4.6

There is a similar relationship between growth over a period of time and intelligence test scores. The lower the intelligence the lower the expected rate of growth. Table 2 expresses this relationship.

TABLE 2

GROWTH IN SOCIAL STUDIES ACHIEVEMENT RELATED TO INTELLIGENCE

Intelligence Level	Expected Growth in Years of Achievement	
	Average	Range
High Intelligence (IQ 120+)	1.5	1.0–3.5
Middle Intelligence (IQ 90–110)	1.0	.6–2.4
Low Intelligence (IQ below 80)	.7	.1–1.8

The greater the intelligence, the greater the expected achievement. What is average for one level of intelligence is not average for another level. Many teachers of less able classes think that their children learn too little whereas those children may be learning as much as they are able to. This does not mean that intelligence is fixed. Psychologists believe that it is possible to increase intelligence, especially during a child's early years. However, as measured at any one time, intelligence is a strong indicator of achievement potential.

It is well recognized that growing up in poverty-stricken homes results in severe educational and cultural disadvantage. I recently conducted a survey of social studies achievement in a large city, the results of which indicate the effects of social status on achievement. For example, four-fifths of the fifth-grade students from a middle-class neighborhood could tell what NATO represents and how it operates, whereas only 10 percent of the twelfth-grade students from a lower-class high school could do so. Knowledge of NATO by itself is not critical, of course, but the example is typical. Probably more serious, the lower-class senior high students were so verbally disadvantaged that they had great difficulty responding to essay questions, while the middle-class elementary school children were largely able to respond.

Intelligence and language development show the same kind of correlation. In a middle-class school in the same large city, the median IQ is 115, with a range of 90 to 150, while a lower-class school shows an average of 88 with a range of 60 to 140. The range is as interesting as the average, because it indicates that some lower-class children have very high academic aptitude. It has long been contended that intelligence test scores are not fair to lower-class children. However, attempts to develop culture-free tests have not been notably successful. If anything is not fair, it is the social status system itself, rather than the tests that pick up the effects of the system.

A third variable that affects achievement is motivation. David McClelland and Richard Atkinson have developed questionnaires that measure the motivation to achieve and instruments that enable us to study the degree to which students are motivated to learn.[4] The more highly motivated students tend to learn more. Although this factor by itself is not as powerful as intelligence or social status, its effects are substantial. Students of the same ability and social status who differ in achievement motivation are likely to show very different patterns of achievement.

A teacher of a social studies class in a rural high school combined intelligence, status, and motivation in studying achievement. His class represented all economic levels, and so he divided

394

them into "high" and "low" income groups. He drew intelligence test scores from the school records. He administered and scored one of the measures of achievement motivation. Before and after teaching a unit on the American Constitution, he administered a test that he had developed himself. Table 3 gives the results.

TABLE 3
GAINS IN ACHIEVEMENT FOR ALL STUDENTS

Pretest		Posttest		Gain (Loss)	
Mean	Range	Mean	Range	Mean	Range
46	18–63	77	51–93	33	6–61

The students appear to have increased their scores as a result of the unit, although some of the gain may have been due to practice on the test, as the same test was used. Table 4 shows the intelligence test scores, economic status, and achievement motivation of the ten students who gained 38 points or more during the unit. The students who gained least had characteristics that were almost the reverse of the ones belonging to the high achievers. The lowest gainer of all, however, was high in economic status but low in intelligence and achievement motivation.

TABLE 4
CHARACTERISTICS OF HIGH SCORES

Characteristics	High	Low
Economic Status	8	2
Intelligence	7	3
Achievement Motivation	7	3

By continuing this type of study throughout the school year, this teacher was able to learn which units resulted in the greatest gains for which students. Units that required library research resulted in very high gains for students who were of high intelligence and achievement motivation and very low gains for some of the others. Another unit dealt with urban renewal and resulted in no difference in gain between high- and low-status students; this was the only unit in which the two groups were equal. Interestingly enough, achievement motivation made less difference in that unit than usual.

An inner city elementary school faculty has found that achievement motivation is so strong a factor in achievement among their students that they have developed a special program to increase motivation. At another inner city elementary school students below a certain IQ rarely achieved in the normal curriculum. A new social studies and science program was designed specifically for those students. Infinite possibilities for growth and change are discovered in schools that study teaching and learning.

TESTING FOR ORGANIZING CONCEPTS

Effective analysis of problems involves understanding and using organizing concepts. A student's ability to understand and use such concepts can be tested in situations concerning certain identifiable concepts. As an example, let us give a class that has studied factors in agricultural production the following testing problem:

> Create a map of an island in the Pacific Ocean that is likely to have a climate suitable for the production of cacao, rubber, and tropical fruits. Indicate latitude and longitude, elevations, and other data related to these products. Show what parts of the island would be best for each of the three kinds of plants.

With such a problem, we soon determine whether the children have learned the pertinent general concepts and can apply them. This type of problem is often most revealing when solved by a group that is allowed to debate the reasons for its choices and conclusions. Also, in a group discussion the teacher can give specific information if the children have forgotten or cannot locate the information easily.

Another problem question could begin with a map such as the one in figure 17 and with a set of related statements and questions.

> This map shows an island in the middle of a lake. The island is connected to the shore by a causeway made from stones piled on the bottom of the lake until the pile reached the surface.

Fig. 17.   An island connected to the shore by a causeway

Then smoothed stones were laid down to make a road. The lake is surrounded by mountains, and the only flat land is near the lake. The island is covered with buildings whose walls are still standing although the roofs are now gone. It is completely uninhabited. What do you think happened to the people who lived there? What caused the place to become empty of human beings? Relate your reasons to the conditions for human life and the kind of life you believe was being lived there.

The teacher stands by and is prepared, when asked, to provide information about such things as climatic conditions, possible evidence of a war or other struggle, and the existence of lake fish suitable for food. By observing how the children's queries are phrased, the teacher can fairly well measure their ability to apply the concepts they have learned. How they seek information about soil fertility and the fish population, for example, could indicate to what degree they have mastered economic concepts. What they ask about certain natural phenomena like earthquakes or climatic changes could reveal their ability to apply geographical concepts or related concepts from the natural sciences. And if they ask whether the large central building had been a temple or whether the government had been theocratic, they could be revealing their understanding of political concepts.

The hypotheses raised by the children show where they have learned to look for information and how they go about looking for it: "Their houses covered the whole island and there wasn't much land around the lake that they could grow things on. I think they just ran out of food and had to leave." "Maybe there was an earthquake and the priests thought it was a sign; so they left." "I think another tribe guarded the causeway so that they ran out of food and had to surrender. Then they burned the town —that's why the roof is gone—and took them away."

In my own teaching, I use a sand table to provide a setting for problem-solving activity. In studying colonial times, the children use the sand table to create colonial settings, such as a Southern plantation and a Northern harbor. The problem is to re-create the Southern setting without cotton and tobacco, or the Northern setting without the China and Indies trade, and so on. I can observe whether they are able to apply the information and economic ideas I have been teaching.

The social studies try to teach the general methods of the social sciences—the processes of observing, classifying and naming, and inferring cause and effect at increasing levels of generality. Testing these skills is most directly accomplished by asking the students to apply them to problems. If a high school teacher has been teaching students to use historical documents, the most unambiguous way to tell how well the skills have been learned is to provide the students with documents about a particular fact, event, or trend and see how they solve a given problem. Or, if a group of second-graders have been learning to identify economic factors in their community, information about another community can be used to see what they can do with it.

The Social Dimension

Social growth is complex and very slow. Therefore evaluating it is extremely difficult. Changes in social behavior may take months to manifest themselves. Yet we must learn about social growth and evaluate it as carefully as academic growth has been evaluated in the past.

The measurement of social growth advanced considerably when Hilda Taba and her associates developed a large array of informal devices that teachers can use to find out how children feel about themselves and others and how involved they are with social issues.[5] Taba's book should be consulted for information on these devices and on their use in learning whether children's social behavior is being affected by social study.

Game-type simulations (pp. 183, 332) provide a good setting for testing whether students can apply knowledge, principles, and theories to real-life, social situations. For example, Guetzkow's *Inter-Nation Simulation Kit* (Science Research Associates, 1966) requires making decisions about international interaction. Coleman's Legislative Game functions similarly for the study of domestic politics and can be used from the upper elementary grades through high school. The Spaceship Earth game (pp. 187–89) and role-playing offer other possibilities. These can be used in themselves or as models for making other materials.

Another useful device is to pose questions that give students a chance to apply information, principles, or theories and to think about the practical effects of certain actions or conditions. In the early grades, the study of the community can be followed by asking, "How would our town [neighborhood] be different if . . . ?" Completion of the question depends on the objectives of the previous study. If the study had focused on transportation, the question might end with ". . . we had no gas or electric motors?"

The study of contemporary affairs lends itself to many problem-solving situations. "What will the UN do if . . . ?" Such a question makes it possible to test the student's understanding of blocs, coalitions, and values. "What kind of structure should a world nuclear cooperative have?" This question requires the student to synthesize information and principles and at the same time encourages him to think about world problems. Following the study of comparative political and economic systems one can ask, "For [name of country] what are the advantages and disadvantages of each of the common types of economic and political organization?" This question requires the student to develop criteria for judging the adequacy of the systems he has been learning about.

Sometimes it is useful to devise specific tests to measure certain skills. The following item for upper elementary grade children tests ability to infer cause and effect in a social situation.

Causes are things that make other things happen. *Effects* are things that are caused by other things. In the following story, some events are causes (make things happen), while others are effects (are made to happen). Read the story and then list on the paper provided the causes and effects.

To the teacher: If your students are in the seventh grade or less read the story aloud while they follow along.

The Green Helmet

Charles Wilson was a happy soldier. Although he was afraid sometimes, he liked to be in combat. It excited him to match his wits against the enemy. When he lay behind a tree in the jungle, listening for any sound that indicated the enemy was coming, he forgot that he was afraid and just kept at his job.

In the jungle, the thing he hated most was crossing swift-flowing rivers, because he could not swim. However, he was given a medal for wading down a river and saving one of the other men.

One morning Charles Wilson and some other soldiers were watching a field in which some of the enemy were supposed to be. Each soldier had picked a place which was high enough that he could see easily, but which had some cover so the enemy could not easily see him.

As the sun rose higher and higher, each man became more worried. If night came before the enemy was found, then he might creep away. The enemy might, under cover of darkness, even attack Wilson and his friends. Yet each man kept silent. No one wanted to give his position away.

After noon the air became very still. Each soldier looked very hard at the field of grass, for when there was no breeze, anything that moved might be an enemy.

Suddenly, all the soldiers froze. In the center of the field they saw a green helmet rise from the grass. Higher and higher it rose. As it did, Charles Wilson and the other soldiers raised their guns ready to fire. But none did shoot, for they could soon see that the helmet was on a stick.

Then, they heard a faint voice. It said, "Save us. Please save us. We are hungry and sick. Please save us."

No one moved. No one replied, because a reply would have let an enemy know where our soldiers were.

"Please help us. Don't shoot!" The voice was very sad.

Charles Wilson decided he had to speak. If it were the enemy he knew he was risking his life. But, he thought, it might be a child, or someone from one of the native villages. So he spoke.

"Stand up," he said. "Stand up and walk to the big tree at the edge of the woods."

There was silence. Minutes ticked by.

"Stand up," he said again, "or we'll shoot."

This time the green helmet slowly withdrew. A human figure began to stand. As it did ten fingers tightened on the triggers of ten guns.

Slowly, very slowly, the figure, wearing a straw hat, made its way through the tall grass. As it moved, the soldiers could see that it was a woman—a woman who seemed to be dragging something through the grass. As the woman drew near the big tree, Charles Wilson said, "Put your hands up." The figure did put her hands up, but she still seemed to be dragging something.

Then, suddenly, she came out of the grass and stood next to the tree. As she did, the thing she had seemed to be dragging came out of the grass after her. It was not a thing, but a lot of things: children, in fact, who gathered around her and held on to her skirt!

As Charles Wilson came near, she looked at him in fear. But seeing his face, she tried to smile, but cried instead.

"Thank you, thank you, thank you," was all she said.

For this story please list on the left side of this paper the causes, or the things that caused other things. On the right side, list the effects that were made to happen by each cause. For example, a cause was that Charles Wilson liked to match wits with the enemy. An effect was that he forgot to be afraid. You have fifteen minutes to list all the causes and effects you can.

CAUSES	EFFECTS

Items like the above provide the student with information and then ask him to analyze it. This kind of item can be used at almost all levels. First-graders, for example, who have been learning to observe the economic concept of division of labor might be presented with a description of people at work and asked to plot the division of labor (or lack of it). High school students learning to make inferences about urbanization and industrialization can be presented with a case study and asked to analyze it. Such items might also be worked on by groups of students. This situation could help the teacher evaluate the students' ability to work together.

We get another perspective on our students when we study their ability to sense problems or gaps in information and create solutions and original ideas in response. This definition of creativity is a useful one for educators. As Torrance pointed out,[6] this kind of creativity is appropriate to the daily activity of normal people —sensing incompleteness or a problem and fooling around with the environment, trying to solve the problem. We can not only study it in our students, but also do something about it. We can handle ourselves as teachers in such a way that we help our students grow in creativity for solving social problems.

Torrance and his associates have developed several tests for studying creativity. Their basic test is called the Test of Imagination. It presents to students a number of tasks requiring them to use their imaginations. Individual tests are called the Product Improvement task, the Product Utilization task, the Unusual Uses of Tin Cans task, and the Circles task. Each of these is scored in terms like fluency, flexibility, and originality of ideas. This battery of tests permits the study of creativity from kindergarten through college. In the appendix of his book, *Rewarding Creative*

402

Behavior, Torrance describes another set of tests useful in studying creativity and also in judging creativity in writing and other behavior.

Creativity can be observed directly when students are given an opportunity to create something such as a story or solutions to problems or explanations of difficult phenomena. In the social studies, students can be asked to think up new forms of world government or new ways of developing and enforcing international law. They can try to create ways of handling lawbreakers besides the ones we have. They can try to develop new and fair means of taxation, new schemes for urban transit and for control of urban sprawl.

There are many social problems that require imaginative solutions, some of which can challenge the younger student as well as the high school student. Fifth- and sixth-graders can approach ideas like ways the Civil War might have been avoided, ways of creating recreation areas for their town, ways of eliminating air and water pollution. Even the youngest children can have contests on subjects like new ways of making friends. They use creativity in their approach to the study of families, communities, and songs and dances.

There is growing evidence that the social climate of the classroom has a considerable effect on creative behavior. Where the classroom climate is more controlling and the "right thing" is rewarded, then we can expect to see a decline in creative behavior in children. Where the classroom climate is open and encourages the unusual and the creative, then that kind of behavior is likely to flourish. Creativity—at least on a verbal level—is usually regarded as a desirable goal in school. If we are going to develop it, we are going to have to learn how to study it and how to measure progress in it, and perhaps most critical, to adjust our instruction to the learner.

The Personal Dimension

There are many ways of looking at personality development.[7] One of the most interesting is the view developed by Harvey, Hunt, and Schroder,[8] described at length on pp. 220–23. They look at personality in terms of the way the individual proves or handles new information and relates to other people. Suppose a student believes that the United States is the foremost military power in the world. When someone suggests that several other nations have as much military might in certain areas as does the United States, does the student reject the new information? Does he accept it? Does he suspend judgment while he seeks new information? Is he able to develop new concepts that admit truth to both positions if the facts warrant such a concept?

The child, they suggest, begins with a few simple ways of dealing with his world and relating to people. As he grows, he may develop more complex ways of dealing with the world. His conceptual systems enable him to react more flexibly to situations. The following list summarizes the development of conceptual systems under optimal conditions.

From:	To:
Simple rules, seen as fixed	Complex rules, seen as changeable
Simple relationships	Complex, subtle relationships
Few concepts	Many, flexible concepts
Rigid reactions to problems	Flexible, creative reaction to problems

How can personality development, viewed as the development of conceptual systems, be measured? The appendix of Schroder, Driver, and Streufert's *Information Processing in Humans,*[9] contains three instruments that are reliable indicators of conceptual development. Directions for scoring are also included. In addition, one may write to David E. Hunt, Ontario Institute for Studies in Education, for copies of instrument and scoring manuals specifically designed for use with younger children. All these instruments are projective and relatively difficult to score. They consist of sentences to be completed and problems to be solved by integrating information and tolerating ambiguity. They give the student an opportunity to demonstrate flexibility or rigidity in his thinking.

Perhaps a better way to begin to measure a student's conceptual level is to observe him in situations that permit his personality to manifest itself. *Inter-Nation Simulation Kit* might provide such a situation. Schroder and his associates at Princeton have found

404

that persons of low conceptual development explore fewer alternative solutions to the problems posed in the inter-nation game and have greater difficulty shifting strategy when the solutions tried bring them into difficulty. A teacher observing conceptual development might ask the following: Which students explore more possibilities? Which ones seek more information when faced with a decision-making situation? Which ones welcome having their solutions examined and criticized?

Another indication of conceptual level is behavior in political situations. Low conceptual level people want to have rigid rules, strictly applied. They tend to want someone to be boss and tell people what to do. They tend to see issues in black and white and to feel negatively toward people who take sides opposed to theirs.

Yet another way to observe conceptual level is to examine students' reactions to situations requiring them to compare and contrast objects of inquiry. For example, after students have observed differences between Japanese and American culture, they can be asked to indicate ways in which these two cultures are similar. This requires breaking set and noting likenesses in things previously described as dissimilar. The more rigid personality will have difficulty with tasks that entail adoption of a new task orientation or set.

Taking the position of another person, a task used by debaters in training, provides another way of observing personality. Students can discuss issues like permitting U.S. citizens to travel in Cuba, first arguing that they should be permitted unlimited travel, then taking the State Department position. This task requires great flexibility, especially when one has strong feelings on an issue.

Another way of looking at personality development concerns a person's belief systems, the network of ideas and attitudes that he accepts and rejects.[10] Rokeach and his associates use several concepts to describe the openness and closedness of belief systems. Among these are:

1. To what extent does a person hold contradictory beliefs? For example, does a person believe that all men have dignity but treat waiters, taxi drivers, and other service industry personnel with scorn? Openness in belief systems tends to reduce contradictions, because the inconsistencies become apparent and can be dealt with. In closed belief systems contradictions tend to persist.

2. To what extent does a person accentuate differences between beliefs he holds and beliefs he rejects? Some people find it necessary to stress how unlike their beliefs are from others. A closed system tends to be accompanied by this accentuation of differences; the closed-minded person builds defenses around his beliefs.

3. How much does a person distinguish between information he receives about the world and information he receives about the source of the information? Every time a person is communicated with, he picks up information about the communicator. The more open a person's belief system, the more he is able to distinguish between information about something and information about the source of information.

All people have two needs that greatly affect their belief systems: to comprehend the world and to ward off or prevent threat from the outside world. People with a powerful drive to know and to understand the world are likely to develop open belief systems; open systems can be modified as more information comes in and as one weighs his beliefs against those of others. The greater one feels the need to ward off threat, the more likely he is to develop closed belief systems.

Rokeach and his associates have included in their book a number of ways of testing or measuring open-mindedness and closed-mindedness. A scale called the Dogmatism Scale can be used with high school and college students. It has about the same reliability as achievement tests do. If a school faculty wishes to study the open- and closed-mindedness of its students, it probably should begin with direct observation of the students in situations where their open- and closed-mindedness will show. The faculty needs to see how the students react to information that does and does not fit in with their patterns of belief. Or the students can be observed as they discuss issues with people who have different stands on those issues.

Social studies is a particularly good area in which to do this. Suppose a teacher has discovered that his students are developing the attitude "you can't fight city hall." Suppose further that these students are presented with information about instances in which officials are responsive to the needs of citizens. The open-minded student will tend to look at the information and evaluate it. He will tend to wonder whether the information comes from a source with something to gain by presenting the information that way. The more closed-minded student, holding the same belief, would tend simply to reject the information as untrue or absorb it without changing his belief. Similarly, political platforms, diaries, and speeches can be used to observe how students distinguish the quality of information from its source. Thoreau's "Essay on Civil Disobedience," for example, will tell an open-minded student as much about Thoreau as about politics and the obligations of social life.

An elementary teacher can tell much about the belief systems of his students by seeing how well they can empathize. For example, after reading or dramatizing a play about the Civil War from a Northern point of view, one can ask the students to reconstruct the play from the Confederate point of view. Or, if the leading character was a Northern general, the students can rewrite the play as if the leading character were a Southern general. They can try to tell the story of Pocahontas and John Smith from the points of view of Pocahontas, John Smith, John Rolfe, Powhatan, and other observers. They might speculate on how different people would have reacted to Lincoln's "Gettysburg Address" or to other critical documents. Even in the earliest grades, some children can see another viewpoint, although that viewpoint may differ from the generally accepted one.

Individual differences in open- and closed-mindedness are as important as individual differences in achievement and intelligence. A highly intelligent but closed-minded student is no more like a highly intelligent open-minded student than he is like a much less intelligent person. As we study our students from more and more vantage points, we have to seek more effective ways of differentiating instruction so that it is tailored to the students.

NOTES

1. Robert Schaefer, *The School as a Center of Inquiry* (New York: Harper & Row, 1967). In this book Schaefer analyzes factors that have prevented the school from developing into a center of inquiry and makes some interesting suggestions on what to do about the situation.

2. James J. Gallagher, "Research on Enhancing Productive Thinking," in *Nurturing Individual Potential* (Washington: Assn. for Supervision and Curriculum Development, National Education Assn., 1964), pp. 52–53.

3. Benjamin S. Bloom, ed., *Taxonomy of Educational Objectives: Cognitive Domain* (New York: McKay, 1965).

4. David McClelland and Richard Atkinson, *The Achievement Motivation* (New York: Appleton, 1953).

5. Hilda Taba and others, *Diagnosing Human Relations Needs* (Washington: American Council on Education, 1955).

6. E. Paul Torrance, *Rewarding Creative Behavior: Experiments in Classroom Creativity* (Englewood Cliffs, N.J.: Prentice-Hall, 1965).

7. For a description of several of the more familiar systems for studying personality formation, see Alfred L. Baldwin, *Theories of Child Development* (New York: Wiley, 1967).

8. O. J. Harvey, David E. Hunt, and Harold M. Schroder, *Conceptual Systems and Personality Organization* (New York: Wiley, 1961).

9. Harold M. Schroder, Robert Driver, and Siegfried Streufert, *Information Processing in Humans* (New York: Holt, Rinehart & Winston, 1967).

10. Milton Rokeach, *The Open and Closed Mind* (New York: Basic Books, 1960).

408

part 6

AUTHOR'S CHOICE

"IF I
WERE
LEADER..."

The purpose of this book has been to make clear what options there are in teaching social studies and how these options can be realized. Every effort has been made to lay out the alternatives and to give fair attention to some that I would not choose. In this chapter, however, I describe a curriculum structure that is my own. It can be tailored to a wide variety of children and local conditions. It draws on the work with data banks described earlier (pp. 42–54 and 319–26) and uses many of the units and techniques discussed in the chapters on the dimensions. My purpose in presenting it is to stimulate teachers, curriculum planners, and makers of social studies materials to formulate curricula that can be adapted to local conditions and that help students understand and recreate society.

I believe that children must begin, from their earliest days in school, to explore important social and personal problems and to join the effort to recreate and rejuvenate our society. There can be no personal meaning outside a social context, and those who merely watch the battle for societal reform will feel empty and alienated in the decades to come. The social sciences are essential tools for social inquiry, closely related to the problems of living together on this planet.

chapter 16

I also believe that only in the liveliness of the classroom can any program or curriculum come alive. No matter how well prepared, a curriculum is useless unless exciting teachers and excited, involved children make it come alive. The search for personal meaning, above all, cannot be planned. We can only develop curricula that help make it happen.

In light of these considerations, I suggest a program that teaches students to use models, or systems of concepts, to analyze and improve social life at three levels: the macrosocietal, the community-urban, and the interpersonal. Models—verbal, mathematical, or constructed—are frequently used in both the natural sciences and the social sciences to describe entities (such as atoms or money) or processes (such as the mixing of fresh and salt water in an estuary or the growth of nationalism) that cannot be observed directly. A model helps students to see and understand such phenomena. It also helps them to explore an actual phenomenon. My curriculum plan uses two models, one for analyzing culture and one for analyzing interpersonal relations. Students can use both these models to study problems of social life and to learn ways of improving it. Children should learn not only *what* the problems are, but also *how* to approach solutions to them.

In this program the three dimensions are closely interrelated and thus reflect my belief that personal meaning depends on social purpose and comprehension of social events. The intellectual dimension is represented by the two models. The social dimension is represented by a recurrent emphasis on international, national, community-urban, and interpersonal problems; the students analyze these three levels of social life in many cultural settings, continuously trying out the models and generating proposals for improving social life. The intellectual and the social dimensions are meshed with the personal dimension in that the student is helped to find personal meaning through coming to understand social life and becoming committed to the improvement of human conditions.

413

A Model for Analyzing Culture

A culture is essentially the behaviors that a people or several peoples rely on to adapt to the physical and social worlds. It is a body of ready-made solutions to problems. For example, when the Romans colonized Europe, they carried systems of justice, systems for ensuring adequate water supply and for building roads, and ways of entertainment. In their new environment they solved problems of justice, water, transport, and leisure out of this storehouse of solutions.

An extremely stable culture will apply the same solutions generation after generation. Frequently, the rate of change varies from one aspect of a culture to another, and problems of dislocation arise when changes in one area are not accompanied by changes in others. The mechanisms of cultural change and stabilization are of enormous importance in understanding a culture and developing solutions to societal problems. Education, for instance, can serve either to stabilize or to promote rapid adaptation and change.

Culture permits consensus among members of a society. It enables them to predict one another's behavior and to act in concert, even though they are not in direct communication. Without consensus on many aspects of life, a large society could not function; with consensus, a society can support a diversity of ethnic, racial, religious, and social groups.

To *know* a culture is to be able to predict behavior in the societies that share that culture. If we know the ready-made solutions to the problems of living that a culture contains, we can predict how the societies that characteristically use those solutions will solve problems. We also know the critical areas of consensus among the people of those societies.

What facets of a culture should be examined by young children? Which should receive the greatest attention, and how should they be approached? The countless possibilities make a decision difficult. For example, a culture can be analyzed using categories that describe major aspects of it—political behavior, economics, interpersonal relations, and so on. Such categories can describe features common to all cultures, such as the family. Or they can describe entry points for studying cultures. An approach that is less systematic but more dynamic than using such categories is to study cultural problems (alienation, stability, poverty, and so on) and the solutions the cultures apply to them.

Yet a third way of approaching a culture is to examine cultural problems in light of several basic orientations. This approach combines the first two. The model that emerges shows a culture as a set of problem-solutions. Our particular model consists of five orientations and twenty-two subcategories.

Man and Space: Man's relation to the physical environment (its geology, climate, vegetation and animal life, air and water) and also to the space that he creates (his use of land, his architecture, the ways in which he plans communities and exploits or conserves his environment).

Man and Commerce: Man's tools, technology, and economic system, and the devices he uses to arrange transport, communication, industry, and the exploitation of agricultural and mineral possibilities. Whereas the first orientation considers the distribution of man's efforts in his environment and the ways he plans to utilize space, this orientation emphasizes his tools, both technological and economic.

Man and Socialization: The broad configurations of a culture and the variations among human cultures. The emphasis is on the nature of culture and the ways in which it is transmitted to the young, especially through the family and through formal education.

Man and his Affective Relations: An analysis of values, personality, interpersonal behavior in a cultural context, and esthetics, including art, music, and formal and informal religious behavior.

Man and Community: Man's social organization in communities, political life, family, and status relationships. Much attention is given to political and economic decision-making, both formal and informal. This orientation is very closely linked to human relations analysis.

Orienta-tions	Man and Space	Man and Commerce	Man and Socialization	Man and his Affective Relations	Man and Community
Categories	1. Geology 2. Climate 3. Vegetation 4. Animal life 5. Architecture 6. Land use and planning	7. Agriculture-pastorage 8. Industry 9. Exploration 10. Transport 11. Communication 12. Commerce and monetary system	13. Ethos and cultural variation 14. Education 15. Socialization	16. Religion 17. Values 18. Interpersonal behavior 19. Visual and performing arts	20. Status 21. Politics 22. Unity and nation-building

Fig. 18.   Orientations and categories for cultural analysis

This culture model (fig. 18) is taught in such a way that the children learn to use it in studying several representative cultures, especially that of the United States and Canada, and cultural problems. (The culture of the United States and Canada is emphasized because it is the immediate environment within which the students live and the most readily available for study; the United States and Canada together make up what might be called North American culture or, more loosely, American culture.) Each year certain aspects of the model receive special emphasis, and those aspects dealt with earlier are revisited and deepened. Gradually, the students' competence is extended to the entire model.

The Structure of the Program

Each year's course consists of four phases. The first is called the instructional unit. It introduces students to one of the five basic orientations in the culture model and emphasizes one or more of the twenty-two categories within the basic orientations. Furthermore, it prepares students to apply these ideas during the next three phases, which are called inquiry, or application, units.

A series of data banks (about ten are needed) can be used to provide a large amount of information about the major world cultures as represented by nations such as Kenya, Nigeria, Brazil, Mexico, India, Japan, Russia, Israel, Canada, and the United States. There can also be subbanks on cities or areas within these nations. Any of these banks can be chosen as content for a year's work and shaped to suit the needs and interests of particular groups of children. For example, if a teacher desires to carry on more inquiry phases at the community-urban level, then information on cities can be substituted for the macrosocietal level. Similarly, a year's work can focus on Asia, Africa, Europe, Latin America, or on a single nation simply by including more material from the appropriate data bank. Moreover, other units, such as the *Social Science Laboratory Units* or the Chicago Economics Project, can be added to this plan.

The content and sequence can be organized so that each of the ten nations is studied frequently. By the end of the program, the students will have a fairly intimate knowledge of these ten nations,

Orientation by year		Inquiry Phase		
		One (Macrosocietal)	Two (Community-urban)	Three (Interpersonal)
Early Childhood Years	One (Space: architecture)			
	Two (Commerce: transport)			
	Three (Affect: interpersonal behavior)			
Primary Years	One (Commerce: industry)			
	Two (Socialization: education)			
	Three (Community: status)			
Middle School Years	One (Socialization: ethos and cultural variation)			
	Two (Community: politics)			
	Three (Commerce: exploration)			
	Four (Community: unity and nation-building)			

Fig. 19. Worksheet for selecting content (orientations filled in)

417

a large city within each of these nations, and a smaller community within each of these cities. The United States and Canada should be studied in each year's work, with emphasis on a different orientation for analyzing the culture, so that by the end of the program the culture of the United States and Canada has been very thoroughly explored. Enough units should be included on historical aspects of these cultures so that students gain a reasonable acquaintance with the heritage of the United States and Canada.

The program can be designed to cover the early childhood years (nursery, kindergarten, first grade), the primary years (grades two through four), and the middle school years (grades five through eight). Content from the data banks can be filled in on the worksheet in figure 19 so that the children are led to inquire into their own community and lives. Figure 20 shows content filled in for the primary years. European, Asian, Latin American, and African societies are compared with the United States and Canada.

Orientations by year		Inquiry Phase		
		One (Macrosocietal)	Two (Community-urban)	Three (Interpersonal)
Primary Years	One (Commerce: industry)	Kenya	Brazil (São Paolo) Montreal New York	
	Two (Socialization: education)	France	Russia (Kiev) Toronto Chicago	
	Three (Community: status)	England	Japan (Tokyo) Vancouver San Francisco	

Fig. 20.   Content for the primary years

A Closer Look at the Interpersonal Level

In this program, interpersonal relations are studied in the fourth phase of every course. Through intellectual analysis and interpersonal training activities this phase attempts to teach students ways of analyzing and improving interpersonal relations. Both the model and the activities are taught systematically, so that by the end of the program, the students will be able to apply the model to the analysis of interpersonal behavior and use the training activities to help themselves and others increase their interpersonal capacity.

The model for analyzing interpersonal relations was derived from the work of sociologist George Homans.[1] The source of the training activities is the work of William Schutz and his associates, who have developed a program of awareness training.[2] The work of Homans and that of Schutz are compatible, in that one provides an intellectual system for analyzing interpersonal relations and the other provides a system for skill training in interpersonal relations.

George Homans uses three basic concepts for analyzing the human group: sentiment, activities, and interaction. By sentiment, he means the feelings that the members of a group have toward each other and their activities as they interact. By activities, he refers to the kinds of things that are done by the group and its members when they are together and when they are apart but are still acting in relation to each other. By interaction, he means the patterns of interpersonal behavior by which decisions are made, activities are initiated, affection is expressed, and so on.

Homans looks at sentiment, activities, and interaction as the internal system of a group. He describes this system as it relates to the external system, the social matrix of a group. For example, in a large commercial firm there may be a department or a section of a department that operates as a tightly knit group. It has distinctive patterns of sentiment, activities, and interaction. But this group also operates within a larger social context made up of the firm itself, the community, the culture, the families to which the group members belong, the economic system, and many other things. All the members of the group come, of course, from the external system, and the group is in fact an extension of it. However, it also develops its own system and reacts to the external system.

In the interpersonal phase of the program this system of thinking is taught much as Homans presents it. That is, a concept is presented and then analyzed with regard to pertinent research. Or this procedure may be reversed. Each unit is built around one or more of Homans' concepts, beginning with those that can be built from direct observations, and proceeding gradually to inter-action patterns and finally to the entire set of concepts about internal and external systems. One of the most valuable aspects of Homans' work is that he includes many references to patterns of interaction in societies other than the United States and northern Europe.

The other element of the interpersonal level of our program deals with sets of activities designed to help students cope with three aspects of interpersonal relations: affection, control, and inclusiveness. Schutz suggests that the interpersonal relations of all individuals can be described in terms of these three concepts. All people are conscious of affection and their need for it. They have a position with respect to control: they either initiate activities, or others initiate activities for them. They are conscious of this and need to cope with it. They are conscious of exclusion or inclusion and need to develop feelings of inclusiveness and to cope with the feeling of being excluded.

Schutz and his associates have designed tasks through which people can become aware of and cope with these aspects of their interpersonal relations. In one of the exercises concerning making contact with others, two individuals sit across from each other, eyes closed and just their fingers touching. Each attempts to describe how the other person feels toward him, judging from the contact of the fingertips. They discuss their reactions to these descriptions and, still working only through their fingertips, try to make a deeper, more controlled kind of contact with each other. This activity is designed to help students become aware of their own situation and learn techniques for projecting themselves. It might be followed with an activity such as role-playing the first stages of one's presentation of self to another. A student might be given the task of standing before others and introducing himself in such a way as to make it clear that he wants to be honest and open. Another follow-up is for students to practice playing a role in which they accept the positive interpretation of an ambiguous statement rather than the negative one.

In Summary

The total design combines the intellectual, social, and the personal dimensions of the social studies in the search for a more meaningful, harmonious, and comprehensible experience of life. The intellectual models are applied to social topics through cooperative inquiry. The individual meets and analyzes values, including his own, at all three levels. The three levels of social analysis are continued and deepened throughout the program.

A century ago the schools conceived of their main task as teaching the culture and its tools. Increasing numbers of people were to be educated to participate more fully in the best of the culture. Now our task is to help the society recreate itself. Our culture is in serious difficulty. Some of its troubles can be patched readily. Many of our institutions and patterns of behavior, however, require vigorous and creative action to change or replace them. That task is part of the work of the social studies.

NOTES

1. George C. Homans, *The Human Group* (New York: Harcourt, Brace & World, 1950).
2. See, for example, William Schutz, *Joy* (New York: Grove, 1968).

THE INTELLECTUAL DIMENSION

American Council of Learned Societies and the National Council for the Social Studies. *The Social Studies and the Social Sciences.* New York: Harcourt, Brace & World, 1962.

Association for Supervision and Curriculum Development. *Using Curriculum Developments.* Washington: National Education Assn., 1963.

Banton, Michael, ed. *The Social Anthropology of Complex Societies.* London: Tavistock Publications, 1966.

Beard, Charles A. *A Charter for the Social Sciences.* New York: Scribner, 1932.

Beard, Charles A. *The Nature of the Social Sciences.* New York: Scribner, 1934.

Berelson, Bernard, and Steiner, Gary. *The Behavioral Sciences Today.* New York: Basic Books, 1963.

Center for the Study of Instruction. *Principles and Practices in the Teaching of the Social Sciences: Concepts and Values.* New York: Harcourt, Brace & World, 1970.

Commager, Henry Steele. *The Nature and the Study of History.* Columbus, Ohio: Merrill, 1965.

Duverger, Maurice. *An Introduction to the Social Sciences with Special Reference to Their Methods.* New York: Praeger, 1964.

Ebenstein, William. *Today's Isms: Communism, Fascism, Capitalism, Socialism.* Englewood Cliffs, N.J.: Prentice-Hall, 1964.

Ebenstein, William. *Totalitarianism: New Perspectives.* New York: Holt, Rinehart & Winston, 1962.

Easton, David. *A Systems Approach to Political Life.* Chicago: Social Science Education Consortium, 1966.

Hanna, Paul R.; Sabaroff, Rose; Davies, Gordon; and Farrar, Charles. *Geography in the Teaching of Social Studies Concepts and Skills.* Boston: Houghton Mifflin, 1966.

Hyneman, Charles S. *The Study of Politics.* Urbana: Univ. of Illinois Press, 1959.

Krug, Mark M. *History and the Social Sciences.* Toronto: Blaisdell, 1967.

Ortega y Gasset, José. *The Mission of the University.* Princeton, N.J.: Princeton Univ. Press, 1944.

Pelto, Pertti J. *The Nature and Study of Anthropology.* Columbus, Ohio: Merrill, 1965.

Phenix, Philip H. *Realms of Meaning.* New York: McGraw-Hill, 1964.

Schwab, Joseph J. *The Teaching of Science.* Cambridge, Mass.: Harvard Univ. Press, 1962.

Sorauf, Francis J. *Political Science: An Informal Overview.* Columbus, Ohio: Merrill, 1965.

THE SOCIAL DIMENSION

Banfield, Edward C. *The Moral Basis of a Backward Society.* New York: Free Press, 1958.

Becker, James, and Mehlinger, Howard D., eds. *International Dimensions in the Social Studies.* 38th Yearbook of the National Council for the Social Studies. Washington: National Education Assn., 1968.

Blau, Peter M. *Bureaucracy in Modern Society.* New York: Random House, 1956.

Conant, James B. *Slums and Suburbs.* New York: McGraw-Hill, 1961.

Dewey, John. *Democracy and Education.* New York: Macmillan, 1916.

Elkin, Frederick. *The Child and Society: The Process of Socialization.* New York: Random House, 1960.

Frankenburg, Ronald. *Communities in Britain: Social Life in Town and Country.* Harmondsworth, Middlesex (England): Penguin Books, 1966.

Gibson, John S. *Race and Culture in American Life.* Medford, Mass.: Tufts Univ., 1967.

Gilbert, Harold G. *Children Study American Industry.* Dubuque, Iowa: Wm. C. Brown, 1966.

Hollingshead, August DeB. *Elmtown's Youth.* New York: Wiley, 1949.

Homans, George C. *The Human Group.* New York: Harcourt, Brace, 1950.

Honigmann, John J. *The World of Man.* New York: Harper, 1959.

Hoover, Edgar M., and Vernon, Raymond. *Anatomy of a Metropolis: The Changing Distribution of People and Jobs within the New York Metropolitan Region.* Garden City, N.Y.: Doubleday, 1962.

Kenworthy, Leonard S. *The International Dimension of Education.* Washington: Assn. for Supervision and Curriculum Development, National Education Assn., 1970.

Massialas, Byron G.; Sprague, Nancy F.; and Sweeney, Jo Anne Cutler. *Structure and Process of Inquiry into Social Issues in Secondary Schools.* Ann Arbor: Univ. of Michigan Press, 1970.

National Education Assn., Project on the Instructional Program of the Public Schools. *Deciding What to Teach.* Washington: National Education Assn., 1963.

National Education Assn., Project on the Instructional Program of the Public Schools. *Planning and Organizing for Teaching.* Washington: National Education Assn., 1963.

National Education Assn., Project on the Instructional Program of the Public Schools. *Schools for the Sixties.* New York: McGraw-Hill, 1963.

Nesbitt, William. *Simulation Games for the Social Studies Classroom.* New Dimensions Series, no. 1. New York: Foreign Policy Assn., 1968.

Orwell, George. *Animal Farm.* New York: New American Library, 1946.

Passow, A. Harry, ed. *Education in Depressed Areas.* New York: Teachers College, Columbia Univ., 1963.

Schermerhorn, Richard A. *Society and Power.* New York: Random House, 1964.

Taba, Hilda. *Diagnosing Human Relations Needs.* Washington: American Council on Education, 1955.

Thelen, Herbert A. *Education and the Human Quest.* New York: Harper, 1960.

Tyler, Ralph W. *Basic Principles of Curriculum and Instruction.* Chicago: Univ. of Chicago Press, 1950.

U.S. Commission on Civil Rights. *Mobility in the Negro Community: Guidelines for Research on Social and Economic Progress.* Prepared by Eli Ginzberg and Dale L. Hiestand. Clearinghouse Publication no. 11. 1968. (Available from the Superintendent of Documents, U.S. Government Printing Office.)

THE PERSONAL DIMENSION

Adorno, Theodore; Frenkel-Brunswick, Else; Levenson, Daniel; and Sanford, R. Nevitt. *The Authoritarian Personality.* New York: Harper, 1950.

Allport, Gordon W. *The Nature of Prejudice.* Reading, Mass.: Addison-Wesley, 1954.

Bloom, Benjamin S. *Stability and Change in Human Characteristics.* New York: Wiley, 1964.

Bruner, Jerome S.; Goodnow, Jacqueline; and Austin, George A. *A Study of Thinking.* New York: Wiley, 1956.

Chase, Stuart. *The Proper Study of Mankind.* New York: Harper, 1956.

Coles, Robert. *Children of Crisis.* Boston: Little, Brown, 1964.

Dalton, Robert H. *Personality and Social Interaction.* Boston: Heath, 1961.

Durkheim, Emile. *Moral Education: A Study in the Theory and Application of the Sociology of Education.* New York: Free Press, 1961.

Estvan, Frank J., and Elizabeth W. *The Child's World: His Social Perception.* New York: Putnam, 1959.

Festinger, Leon. *A Theory of Cognitive Dissonance.* Evanston, Ill.: Row, Peterson, 1957.

Friedenberg, Edgar Z. *Coming of Age in America: Growth and Acquiescence.* New York: Random House, 1965.

Fromm, Erich. *Man for Himself: An Inquiry into the Psychology of Ethics.* Greenwich, Conn.: Fawcett Publications, 1967.

Gagne, Robert M. *The Conditions of Learning.* New York: Holt, Rinehart & Winston, 1965.

Hunt, J. McVey. *Intelligence and Experience.* New York: Ronald Press, 1961.

CURRICULA AND SKILLS

Buros, Oscar K., ed. *The Fifth Mental Measurements Yearbook.* Highland Park, N.J.: Gryphon Press, 1959.

Carpenter, Helen McCracken, ed. *Skill Development in Social Studies.* 33d Yearbook of the National Council for the Social Studies. Washington: National Education Assn., 1963.

Dewey, John. *The Child and the Curriculum.* Chicago: Univ. of Chicago Press, 1959.

Dewey, John. *The Child and the Curriculum: The School and Society.* Chicago: Phoenix Books, 1956.

Dunfee, Maxine, and Sagl, Helen. *Social Studies through Problem Solving.* New York: Holt, Rinehart & Winston, 1966.

Education Development Center. *Man: A Course of Study—A Guide to the Course.* Cambridge, Mass.: Education Development Center, 1969.

Fantini, Mario D., and Weinstein, Gerald. *Toward a Contact Curriculum.* New York: Anti-Defamation League of B'nai B'rith, 1968.

Gibson, John S. *A Program for Elementary School Education,* vols. 1 and 2: *The Intergroup Relations Curriculum.* Lincoln-Filene Center for Citizenship and Public Affairs. Medford, Mass.: Tufts Univ., 1969.

Goodland, John I. *The Changing School Curriculum.* New York: Fund for the Advancement of Education, 1966.

Goodland, John I. *School, Curriculum, and the Individual.* Toronto: Blaisdell, 1966.

Grambs, Jean Dresden. *Intergroup Education: Methods and Materials.* Anti-Defamation League of B'nai B'rith. Englewood Cliffs, N.J.: Prentice-Hall, 1968.

Harris, Ruby M. *Handbook of Map and Globe Usage*. Chicago: Rand McNally, 1959.

King, Arthur R., Jr., and Brownell, John A. *The Curriculum and the Disciplines of Knowledge*. New York: Wiley, 1966.

Kohl, Herbert. *36 Children*. New York: America Library, 1967.

Neill, A. S. *Summerhill*. New York: Hart, 1960.

Rogers, Carl R. *Client-Centered Therapy*. Boston: Houghton Mifflin, 1965.

Rogers, Carl R. *Freedom to Learn*. Columbus, Ohio: Merrill, 1969.

Rokeach, Milton. *The Open and Closed Mind*. New York: Basic Books, 1960.

Torrance, E. Paul. *Rewarding Creative Behavior*. Englewood Cliffs, N.J.: Prentice-Hall, 1965.

Wallace, Anthony F. C. *Culture and Personality*. New York: Random House, 1961.

INSTRUCTION AND TEACHING

American Educational Research Assn. of the National Education Assn. *Handbook of Research on Teaching*. Edited by N. L. Gage. Chicago: Rand McNally, 1963.

Anderson, Robert H. *Teaching in a World of Change*. New York: Harcourt, Brace & World, 1966.

Arbuthnot, May Hill. *Children and Books*. 3d ed. Chicago: Scott, Foresman, 1964.

Ashton-Warner, Sylvia. *Teacher*. New York: Simon & Schuster, 1963.

Assn. for Supervision and Curriculum Development, and Center for the Study of Instruction of the National Education Assn. *Report of the Seminar on Teaching: The Way Teaching Is*. Washington: National Education Assn., 1966.

Ausubel, David P. *Learning Theory and Classroom Practice*, Bulletin no. 1. Ontario: Ontario Institute of Education, 1967.

Black, Hillel. *The American Schoolbook*. New York: Morrow, 1967.

Bloom, Benjamin; Davis, Allison; and Hess, Robert. *Compensatory Education for Cultural Deprivation*. New York: Holt, Rinehart & Winston, 1965.

Bruner, Jerome S. *The Process of Education*. Cambridge: Harvard Univ. Press, 1960.

Children's Catalog. 10th ed. New York: Wilson, 1961. Annual supplements, 1962–.

Combs, Arthur W. *The Professional Education of Teachers*. Boston: Allyn & Bacon, 1965.

Coombs, Philip H. *The World Educational Crisis*. New York: Oxford Univ. Press, 1968.

Cox, C. Benjamin, and Massialas, Byron G., eds. *Social Studies in the United States*. New York: Harcourt, Brace & World, 1967.

Cremin, Lawrence A. *The Genius of American Education*. New York: Vintage Books, 1966.

Douglass, Malcolm P. *Social Studies: From Theory to Practice in Elementary Education*. Philadelphia: Lippincott, 1967.

Fantini, Mario, and Weinstein, Gerald. *Making Urban Schools Work*. New York: Holt, Rinehart & Winston, 1968.

Fenton, Edwin. *The New Social Studies*. New York: Holt, Rinehart & Winston, 1967.

Fox, Robert; Luszki, Margaret Barron; and Schumuck, Richard. *Diagnosing Classroom Learning Environments*. Chicago: Science Research Associates, 1966.

Guetzkow, Harold. *Simulation in International Relations: Developments for Research and Teaching*. Englewood Cliffs, N.J.: Prentice-Hall, 1963.

Henderson, George, and Bilbens, Robert F. *Teachers Should Care: Social Perspectives of Teaching*. New York: Harper & Row, 1970.

Huck, Charlotte S., and Young, Doris A. *Children's Literature in the Elementary School*. New York: Holt, Rinehart & Winston, 1961.

Kenworthy, Leonard S. *Social Studies for the Seventies*. Toronto: Blaisdell, 1969.

McLendon, Jonathon C., ed. *Readings on Social Studies in Secondary Education*. New York: Macmillan, 1966.

Miel, Alice, and Brogan, Peggy. *More than Social Studies*. Englewood Cliffs, N.J.: Prentice-Hall, 1957.

National Council for the Social Studies. *Children's Books to Enrich the Social Studies*. Washington: National Education Assn., 1961.

Oliver, Donald, and Shaver, James B. *Teaching Public Issues in the High School*. Boston: Houghton Mifflin, 1966.

Ragan, William B., and McAulay, John D. *Social Studies for Today's Children*. New York: Appleton-Century-Crofts, 1964.

Selakovich, Daniel. *Problems in Secondary Social Studies*. Englewood Cliffs, N.J.: Prentice-Hall, 1965.

Selakovich, Daniel. *Social Studies for the Disadvantaged*. New York: Holt, Rinehart & Winston, 1970.

Smith, Louis M., and Geoffry, William. *The Complexities of an Urban Classroom: An Analysis toward a General Theory of Teaching*. New York: Holt, Rinehart & Winston, 1968.

428

INDEX

431

432

About the Author

Bruce R. Joyce grew up in the East and has also lived and worked in other parts of the country. He earned a bachelor's degree in philosophy at Brown University and a doctor's degree in education at Wayne State University, where he studied under Ole Sand and Ruth Ellsworth. After serving in the Korean War, he taught school in Delaware and at the University of Delaware and the University of Chicago. He is now Professor of Curriculum at Teachers College, Columbia University.

He and his wife live on a Pennsylvania farm with their four children and various domestic animals. The Joyces have done research together on using data banks to teach social studies. To develop these, some of which are described in this book, they have travelled extensively with their children in the United States, Canada, and Europe. Their report *Data Banks for Children* is based on this work.

In addition to this book and its predecessor *Strategies for Elementary Social Science Education,* Dr. Joyce's *The Structure of Teaching* has been published by SRA as a basic text for introductory education courses and for general courses on curriculum and instruction. His other books include *Alternative Models for Elementary Education, Models for Teaching, Renaissance in Teacher Education*—the latter two co-authored by Marsha Weil—and the *Teacher-Innovator,* a plan for a performance-based teacher education program.

This book
was set in 10-point *Plantin* Monophoto,
with display lines
in *Avant-Garde Medium*,
composed by Holmes Typography, San Jose,
and printed by
Stecher-Traung-Schmidt Corporation,
San Francisco.
The *Plantin* typeface,
named after the Antwerp printer,
Christophe Plantin,
was designed in 1913
by F. H. Pierpont for The Monotype Corporation
from a sixteenth century Roman typeface
cut by Robert Granjon.
The cover was silkscreened on Holliston sailcloth
by Auto Screen Lehigh, Pennsauken, New Jersey.

434

Project Editor	Gretchen W. Hargis
Designer	Barbara Ravizza
Photo Editor	Joy Locke
Sponsoring Editor	Karl Schmidt

345/98765432